THE STATE OF
LATIN AMERICA

BOOKS BY

GERMÁN ARCINIEGAS

Caribbean: Sea of the New World (1946)

A VIVID, DRAMATIC, SOUND HISTORY OF THE CAR-
IBBEAN FROM EARLY TIMES TO THE PRESENT.

The Green Continent (1944)

*A Comprehensive View of Latin America by Its
Leading Writers*

AN ANTHOLOGY OF THE FINEST WRITINGS ABOUT
LATIN AMERICA BY ITS OWN WRITERS, REVEALING
THE TRUE NATURE OF THAT REGION.

THE State OF Latin America

Germán Arciniegas

TRANSLATED FROM THE SPANISH BY
HARRIET DE ONÍS

1952 ALFRED A. KNOPF *NEW YORK*

L. C. *catalog card number: 51-13220*

⚜) ⠀⠀⠀⠀THIS IS A BORZOI BOOK, ⚜
⠀⠀⠀PUBLISHED BY ALFRED A. KNOPF, INC.

FIRST EDITION

To Gabriela,
MY COMPANION OF TWENTY-FIVE YEARS,
WITH LOVE

To Jorge Soto del Corral

To the anonymous peasants of Colombia,
PERSECUTED WITHOUT CHRISTIAN PIETY BECAUSE THEY
LOVE A GOOD THING: LIBERTY

ACKNOWLEDGMENTS

To MANY FRIENDS in the twenty republics I owe thanks for the assistance they have given me, now collecting data for the separate chapters, now suggesting alterations and reading the final draft. For obvious reasons, I do not think it discreet to name them.

As far as possible, I have tried to allow the actors in the Latin American drama to speak their own lines. In this connection I ought to thank some of the dictators for the frankness with which they have expressed themselves, as well as all those who have left the marks of their ideologies in official documents.

What I omit is much more voluminous than what I publish. My task has been the selection of data. But there are chapters in which the reader must see that materials for a whole book have had to be compressed into a few pages. In order to excuse omissions, it is essential to understand the space-limitations of this work.

With respect to this English version, I have had constant stimulus and aid from my publishers and my translator. Alfred A. Knopf and Blanche W. Knopf, my friends of long standing who make this book available to English-speaking readers, have on this occasion been literally irreplaceable. Herbert Weinstock has given me excellent counsel after reading both the original chapters and the translation. Finally, Harriet de Onís (whom I ought to name first) has extended her work of translation to a line-by-line collaboration that lives in every page, and for which I want to express the most special thanks.

GERMÁN ARCINIEGAS

CONTENTS

CONTENTS

INTRODUCTION

The Reason for This Book

I WROTE THIS BOOK at the invitation of my publishers. They thought that the moment had come for a Latin American liberal to tell the truth as he sees it about what is happening in Latin America today. During the last few years my time has been devoted to my university duties and to a study of certain aspects of the Renaissance. I had no desire to take one minute from those activities. But for me, a Latin American, not to have undertaken the writing of this book would have been a breach of my loyalty to those who have fought—and are fighting—for freedom and democracy.

A vast conspiracy against democracy, liberty, and respect for human rights has been set in motion in Latin America. This movement is in direct opposition to the history of a huge region that, like the United States, was conceived in freedom. What takes place in Latin America is, or should be, as much the concern of the rest of the world as of the Latin Americans. With its vast material and human resources, which have scarcely begun to be utilized, this is one of the regions of the future. Given education, well-being, and opportunity—three things they have been denied—the people of Latin America could play a major role in the world of tomorrow.

The outside world knows next to nothing of what is happening in Latin America. Brazil or Mexico receives very little attention in the daily news, Ecuador or Uruguay none at all. The case of Argentina has been publicized widely, but Argentina, seen in proper perspective, is only one part of farflung

Latin America. Brazil is larger, Mexico has more people, Colombia is governed worse. From a purely material point of view, what Argentina represents in meat and grain, Bolivia represents in tin, Chile in copper, Venezuela in oil, and Brazil in tropical products. Colombia is the sentinel of the Panama Canal, Mexico the great Indo-Spanish region of North America.

The twenty Latin American nations form the largest group among the sixty members of the United Nations. One hundred and fifty-three million Latin Americans constitute a huge human reserve, and the rate of population growth among them is very high. Little attention has been paid to the fact that four of the seven largest cities of the Western hemisphere are south of the Rio Grande. After New York and Chicago, according to recent statistics, come Mexico City, Buenos Aires, Rio de Janeiro, São Paulo, and Los Angeles. This is the world, growing so fast and acquiring so much international importance, with which the Devil is trying to make off. At this very moment it is the scene of a life-and-death struggle between the forces of totalitarianism and those opposing it, but the details of this struggle remain, for the most part, unknown. The routine cant of official pronouncements about the democracy of Latin America is the accepted medium of diplomatic negotiations. The outside world proceeds on the assumption that Latin America's political development is so rudimentary, its spirit of anarchy so widespread, that strong-man rule is its only possible form of government. It is also assumed by some people that these nations are, and will continue to be, subservient to the will of the United States. A reading of this book will prove that these are unwarranted, hasty conclusions.

To divine the direction in which China, India, or Western Europe is moving would be as easy as to know which way Latin America is going. We know, or think we know, the direction of Russia or the United States. But neither outsiders nor the Latin Americans themselves can predict Latin America's future orientation. There would be no problem if Perón in

Argentina, Gómez in Colombia, Odría in Peru, the military *junta* in Venezuela, Somoza in Nicaragua, Chaves in Paraguay, or Trujillo in the Dominican Republic really represented the public opinion of their countries, and thus, in a sense, that of Latin America. In that case there could be no doubt that Latin America is blindly heading for totalitarianism with all its consequences.

But to what degree do the dictatorships represent public opinion? To what degree can the dictators' empires be considered secure? United States capitalists who blithely invest money in countries where their new friends fling the doors wide to welcome them—on what sort of rock are they building their fortunes? When arms are given or lent to the dictators, against whom are they going to be used? The many changes of regime that have occurred in Latin America within this century merely point up the confusion. White republics have turned black in six months, in one week, between night and morning. At one stroke the black republics could turn red. Ever since party flags began to be replaced by shirts, every change of shirt is like a portent of disaster.

The precarious balance in Latin America is recognized most clearly by those who maintain order by force. The very people who invite foreign investments deposit their own fortunes in the banks of New York or Switzerland. The meaning of this two-way street seems to us Latin Americans like that of the roadside warning: PROCEED AT YOUR OWN RISK!

A huge number of the more than one hundred and fifty million Latin Americans is governed by strong men who have abolished the free expression of opinion within their territories. Argentina, a nation with a tradition of liberty, was caught off guard in an evil hour of confusion and set to marching with fixed bayonets against liberty. This is only one example. No less than fifty million Latin Americans are moving backward today, and the figure increases each year. In Argentina the Perón regime has made it impossible for the Radicals and the

Socialists to exercise their political rights; in Colombia, Venezuela, and Peru the majority parties have been practically outlawed. But anyone who has been in touch with the people of those countries knows that the Radicals in Argentina, the Liberals in Colombia, the members of Acción Democrática in Venezuela, and the *apristas* in Peru are still majorities. The spirit of resistance has had to go underground, but the members of these parties are more firmly united now than when they were able to demonstrate their strength in free elections.

Congresses have been closed by force. Universities have been brought under government domination, and any member of the faculty opposed to the regime or considered politically undesirable has been dismissed from his post or forced to resign. The judiciary has been packed. Political leaders have been reduced to silence—sometimes the silence of the grave. Why? If the regime in power represents the people's will, why these repressive measures? How many heads of state would be left in power if Latin America were to say: armaments are for international war or for maintaining order, and soldiers will leave their barracks for no other reason? The irony of this situation is the fact that the dictators first received machine guns from the United States to safeguard the liberties represented by Roosevelt and menaced by Hitler, and received more machine guns later to reinforce the United Nations system based on respect for human rights. But a survey of the present chiefs of state of many Latin American nations reveals that those who now hold the machine guns were at one time Hitler's most fervent admirers. The enemy they pursue today is not the Communists, but anyone who stands up for freedom. They have hit upon an opportunistic formula: their political adversaries, the democratic majorities whose rights they wish to deny, are "Communists."

How long can an order thus imposed endure? A government maintained by terror is seated on a powder-keg.

There are two Latin Americas, one visible and official, the other invisible and unofficial. In those countries in which the representative system of government has been done away with, the visible reflects a temporary situation resting on violence and favored by fortuitous circumstances. Invisible Latin America is the liberal spirit that lives on in the suppressed majorities. Visible Latin America, with the United States, has one of the largest international organizations in the world, born out of the noblest sentiments and consecrated in an almost perfect charter of rights. This is the Organization of American States. But seated around its table in the Pan American Union are many delegates who represent nothing but the dictators they serve. Invisible America includes the multitudes who cannot express themselves freely—political leaders, workers, journalists, teachers, all those who cherish in their hearts the word that made independent nations of former colonies: freedom. Out of invisible America must come the Pan American Union of Free Opinion.

What I have put down in this book is what Latin Americans concerned with the destiny of their lands think to themselves every day. I have tried to be as objective as I could. The whole drama of this half of America could be reduced to two actors: the Dictator and the People. At times the People speaks, at others the Dictator; the People says its lines, the Dictator his. But this dangerous dialogue admits of only two outcomes. One is strong personal governments that will develop the national economies under military discipline, turning the people into communities of workers with a minimum of liberty and just enough material advantages to anesthetize all sense of individual rights and personal responsibility. The alternate is representative, democratic governments that, while developing their countries' economic potentialities, will raise the level of the workers to that of human beings worthy of a better life and entitled to the full enjoyment of the rights guaranteed by law.

INTRODUCTION

Outside the dictatorships, public opinion is still free to decide in favor of one outcome or the other. If the solution dictated by justice is not chosen, the Devil will call the tune.

GERMÁN ARCINIEGAS

Montclair
January 1952

THE STATE OF
LATIN AMERICA

I

WHICH WAY LATIN AMERICA?

Liberty, Sancho, is one of the most precious gifts Heaven has given to man: neither the treasures the earth holds nor those the sea encompasses can be compared to it. For liberty, as for honor, one may and should hazard life.

CERVANTES

TUCKED AWAY in the April 23, 1951, issue of *Time* is this paragraph: "For the first time in history the population of Latin America exceeds that of the United States. According to preliminary results of the first coordinated Latin American census, the population of the 20 Latin republics is now 152,800,000, compared with the official 1950 U.S. count of 150,698,361."

What is the political destiny of 152,800,000 Latin Americans? Are they gravitating to the left or to the right? Is the doctrine of Justicialism, proclaimed by General Perón, going to spread throughout the continent? Will there be a return to the barbarous *caudillos* who held sway in the nineteenth century and maintained each republic isolated from its neighbors? How long will the dispirited masses remain submissive to an order imposed by harsh masters? Are there unforeseen surprises in store? What are the leaders thinking? What are the masses thinking?

Statistics can be misleading. Only fifty years ago, at the turn of the century, the population of Latin America was computed in terms not of inhabitants, but of souls. Each nation or city was said to number so many souls, important in the other life, not here. Some would go to Heaven, some to

Hell. This extraterrestrial balance-sheet was of slight concern to the heads of state, of even less to foreign observers. Nor is this surprising: the same thing was true of other parts of the world. China's 460,000,000 "souls" lived within the Great Wall for centuries. It was only yesterday that their affairs became a matter of serious import to the rest of the world. Who can say just what is taking place within China's ancient borders today?

For Latin Americans the figure 152,800,000 is charged with dramatic significance. The souls of the nineteenth century have become men and women with worldly aspirations, who seek to earn more, to eat and dress better, to achieve a measure of security, at least in this world, and to organize freely to gain these objectives.

There is one error, however, in the *Time* report. It says that this is the first time in history that such a disproportion in population has been noted between the two parts of the Western hemisphere. But the fact is that in 1825 the population of Latin America exceeded 18,500,000 whereas that of the United States had barely reached 13,000,000 five years later. During the nineteenth century the United States underwent a miraculous expansion. The winning of the West, the industrial revolution, and the flood of immigrants who entered the country were factors of paramount importance in giving it the position it enjoys today. An analogous development is taking place now in Latin America. The changes there bring to mind the awakening of California with the Gold Rush, the growth of the Middle West, and the rise of New York City. A glance at the population figures in the Latin American capitals will bear this out. Mexico City is a good example: in 1518, 60,000 dwellings were listed there. Four centuries later, in 1900, the census registered 368,000 souls. In 1940 there were 1,464,000 inhabitants. Today its population is approximately 3,000,000 men, women, and children of flesh and blood.

4

The world population increases an average of one per cent annually. The rate of increase in Latin America is twice the world average. This is what experts of the United Nations, as quoted in *The New York Times* of March 28, 1951, have to say: "Latin America appears to be the fastest growing part of the world. In this region relatively high birth rates and the reduction of mortality due to improved living conditions have combined to produce an average rate of increase of about two per cent annually. In other parts of the world high birth rates in combination with equally high death rates, or low birth and death rates have resulted in a rate of growth of between .08 and 1.5 per cent a year."

It often escapes attention that today Buenos Aires is larger than Paris, Rio de Janeiro than Madrid, and Mexico City than Rome. In the nineteenth century when wealthy Latin Americans went to Paris everything dazzled and impressed them. Today, when the ladies of Lima, Caracas, or Bogotá go to Europe they complain of the inconveniences in hotels and homes that lack the comforts and improvements to which they are accustomed in their own countries. When a Latin American finds someone who lives exceptionally well in the United States he says: "So-and-so lives like a prince. He has a house almost as good as those in Caracas." In all this there is no exaggeration. The new Buenos Aires follows a French pattern and is adorned with sculptures by Rodin and Bourdelle. Rio de Janeiro is considered one of the most beautiful cities in the world. Many of the smartly dressed women one sees in Paris are Argentines. This is a far cry from fifty years ago, when the French lumped the Latin American republics together under the phrase *"les pays sauvages de l'Amérique du Sud."*

The changes in Latin America have not been mere surface transformations. As the cities have grown and education has become more general, its people have begun to acquire a greater awareness of the world about them. The dormant "souls" become ambitious as they awake. Even those who can neither read nor write have sources of information. The most ignorant know that there is a war in Korea, and they have even formed their own opinions on that war. *Reader's Digest*, with its circulation of one million copies in Latin America, has popularized a multitude of easily grasped facts and ideas in the cities and villages.

The question is not how well-founded the opinions of the masses are. Many of them may stem from errors of judgment or lack of common sense. But the signal fact is that the lower classes form their own opinions. The people of Latin America attribute a perhaps exaggerated importance to the benefits of formal education. Other media contribute to the revolution of ideas in a manner at times difficult to gauge. The movies, for example, bring to the Latin American spectator an incredible picture of how the workingman lives in the United States. In Russia, American films showing workers wearing good shoes or wrist watches or listening to their own radios are considered subversive. The effect on audiences at village theaters in Brazil or Colombia, or in the poorer sections of the large cities, of movies that show farmers or workers who have refrigerators in their kitchens and ride to work in their own automobiles is little short of breath-taking. In the eyes of the Latin American worker a modest Ford or Chevrolet is on a par with a Rolls-Royce. These pictures of life in the United States have a much greater effect than all the writings of Marx, who, to the majority, is at best a man with a bushy beard.

The thing that radically differentiates the 152,800,000 Latin Americans from the 150,000,000 North Americans is that the latter are reasonably satisfied, the former dissatisfied. All that has contributed to bettering the condition of the Latin American falls dismally short of the dreams conjured up by his lively imagination.

By and large, the Latin American is a frustrated person.

The demagogues have promised him democracy and a good standard of living. He has followed them blindly. But once the spellbinders have won power, their promises have gone up in smoke, leaving only the bitter bread of dictatorship. The old injustices continue, and administrative corruption thrives. Until well into this century the peasants lived in conditions no better than those of the Indian before Columbus crossed the Atlantic. Even today, tropical diseases, malnutrition, and lack of training prevent the common man from realizing his full economic and social potential.

Under a system of representative democracy these conditions would become a stimulus and challenge for their alleviation. The problem would be thrashed out in the press, in the legislative chambers, in the streets and the homes. Everyone would express his opinion freely, and the course of social evolution would be expedited. That is what is happening today in Mexico. That is the way it used to be in Colombia. For the time being, that is the way it is in Brazil. But under the dictatorships the expression of opinion is stifled. Gradually the dammed-up criticism and indignation of the people collect around a hard, explosive core of resentment and distrust. The lion's share of the budget, which could be used to combat the social evils that exist in all Latin American countries, goes to the army, the dictator's praetorian guard, and the police, really an instrument of the government party. Under these circumstances, those countries which in the new terminology are known as "underdeveloped" become highly developed breeding grounds of violence and revolution.

When the delegates to the 1948 Pan American conference arrived in Bogotá, the capital of Colombia, they paid slight, if any, attention to what appeared to be a routine maintenance of order by the army and police. But a long series of arbitrary government acts in the provinces had created between the people and the authorities a state of tension triggered for violence at any moment. At noon on April 9 the head of the opposition Liberal party was killed in downtown Bogotá, and in three hours the heart of the city was reduced to ashes. Foreigners who witnessed the scene said that on the following day Bogotá looked like London after an air raid.

One can easily point to a number of republics in South America that are sitting on volcanos. The case of Bolivia is tragic. In the presidential election of 1951, the Bolivians at the polls voted overwhelmingly for Victor Paz Estenssoro, who was in exile, who could not conduct his campaign in his country, and who embodies the traditions of a party that in its day was openly pro-Nazi, a party whose regime had come to an end in 1946 with its head, President Gualberto Villaroel, hanging from a street lamp in La Paz. That had been the verdict and judgment summarily exercised on him by his own people. What now impelled the Bolivian miner, the farmer, the people, to select as their leader a former official of that regime? What pushed them to that decision and all it implies of defiance, resentment, bitterness, and disappointment? There is the real problem. But the government of Bolivia resolved it by simply ignoring the vote of the people. The memory of the government of Villaroel, who ended his days dangling from a lamppost, has served to deflect the natural criticism of this procedure, which is clearly in violation of all constitutional guarantees. But no man who governs Bolivia today is going to feel the assurance of a patriarch leading his people. His feelings will be closer akin to those of a man about to straddle a wild broncho.

In many Latin American countries the masses have no arms and are practically naked. But this means nothing as far as the latent possibilities of explosion are concerned. The Mexicans who followed Pancho Villa against General Pershing in 1916 returned victoriously singing one of their ballads, or *corridos*, which went:

> *They've got airplanes by the dozens,*
> *But we've got what it really takes.*

The French, Russian, and Chinese revolutions, and the independence of India and Indonesia, like that of the United States and of Latin America, were achieved by the masses, by groups of ragged men who marched on empty stomachs and fought pitched battles, often with stones and sticks for weapons.

The problem of illiteracy raises some particularly interesting questions. Many of the civil wars in Latin America have been fought over a new constitution by masses who could not read. But this is not unprecedented. The North American colonies united around the figure of Washington and rallied to the signers of the Constitution in Philadelphia, but it should not be forgotten that even 100 years later, in 1870, more than 20 per cent of the population of the United States was illiterate. The industrial revolution in England, though undoubtedly headed by educated leaders, took place in a country in which the great majority of men could communicate only by word of mouth.

But along with the illiteracy of Latin America goes an astonishing amount of writing and reading. It has been a surprise to many people to learn that *La Prensa* of Buenos Aires was, until Perón murdered it in 1951, one of the largest and best-informed newspapers in the world. Throughout Latin America many dailies have circulations in the hundreds of thousands. Magazines attain sales of 300,000 an issue. *El Mercurio* of Santiago, Chile, is older than *The New York Times*. In most of the capital cities the dailies give fuller international news coverage than their opposite numbers in the principal cities of Europe and the United States.

But in addition to serving as news media, the Latin American newspapers are media of opinion. In countries with problems as complex as those which confront all the Latin American republics, the voicing of opinion is perhaps the most vital function of the press. That is exactly what complicates the situation, because those who read and write are the very persons who are gagged by government censorship and control.

9

The clearest—or at least the most notorious—threat to civil liberties in Latin America is that which has developed in the country with the lowest rate of illiteracy—Argentina. Leaving aside for the moment the closing of *La Prensa*, two excerpts from the report on freedom of the press in the Americas presented to the Inter-American Press Conference in 1950 will serve to round out the Argentine picture:

"Among the most recent developments affecting the freedom of the press in the Argentine, the commission would like to point out: The following newspapers remain closed: *Provincias Unidas*, *Tribuna Democrática* and *Vanguardia*. The last newspaper was closed because of 'defective sanitary equipment', but it still remains closed despite the fact that this condition has been corrected . . .

"At the beginning of this year [1950], 50 newspapers were closed down on a single day; subsequently these others have also been closed: *La Nueva Provincia* of Bahía Blanca; *El Intransigente*, of Salta; *El Día*, of Posadas; *Democracia*, of Junín; and the magazines *Que*, *Veritas* and *Semana Financiera* . . ."

One of the articles of faith of General Perón's doctrine is the suppression of freedom of the press. This doctrine is spreading to all parts of South America where there are dictatorial governments, and is being employed with new twists that improve on the formulas developed by the Peróns. In Peru the newspaper of the *aprista* party, *La Tribuna*, was closed without a semblance of legality and its machinery expropriated by the government. *La República*, a Peruvian newspaper published under the direction of Barrera Laos, former ambassador to Argentina and Uruguay and onetime Peruvian delegate to the World Court at The Hague, was also closed. In Colombia censorship is applied to every possible form of communication: the legislature was suspended for two years, when a favorable, homogeneous one replaced it. Correspondence is opened and read; telephones are tapped; radio broadcasts are subject to prior censorship; and a government corps of censors has been set up which enters the offices of every newspaper and reviews before publication all material, including news, editorials, advertisements, and photographs. The censors can tell the editor on which page to place any item. This system has been established for the express purpose of controlling *El Tiempo* of Bogotá, which has been the leading newspaper of the country and one of the best in America.

The restrictions on the freedom of the press are not limited to local publications. *Time, Life,* and several other magazines published in the United States, and the magazine *Bohemia,* of Havana, have been banned from circulation in Argentina, Colombia, Peru, Paraguay, Bolivia, Venezuela, the Dominican Republic, Nicaragua, etc. *The New York Times* has been repeatedly confiscated by the postal authorities in Colombia.

Latin Americans have reacted to this situation in characteristic fashion. The history of Latin American politics shows that those who refuse to give up their right to speak their mind have always sought refuge in neighboring countries, from which they may at least inform the world of what is taking place in their terror-dominated homelands. Today, just as in the days of the tyrant Juan Manuel Rosas, Argentines are voicing their protests from Montevideo in nearby Uruguay. At that time Montevideo was the refuge from which a host of Argentine emigrés, including writers of the importance of José Marmol and Esteban Echeverría, kept up a withering fire against Rosas. For twenty-three years Domingo F. Sarmiento, who later became president of Argentina, maintained a steady stream of criticism against Rosas from the columns of the newspapers of Santiago de Chile. Sarmiento was with the army of Justo José de Urquiza, which overthrew Rosas at the battle of Caseros in 1852, and his one item of luggage was a printing press. When the tyrant of Ecuador, Gabriel García Moreno, was finally assassinated in 1875, Juan Montalvo, a refugee in Colombia, exultantly cried: "I killed him with my pen."

Peruvians are making themselves heard today from Mexico or Chile, Colombians from Paris, New York, or Mexico. But the inescapable fact is that truth has become an article of contraband. Matters that are of the public domain in the rest of the world become known to many Latin Americans only when they go to New York. A substantial portion of the wire copy purchased by Latin American newspapers winds up in the censor's wastebasket.

The difficulties experienced by the masses in their attempts at self-expression are of still another order. Not only is there a high degree of illiteracy in Latin America, but there are regions where Spanish is not spoken. In Guatemala there are Indians who speak only one of the Maya dialects but have heard of a doctrine that offers them hope and is called Communism. In Paraguay the peasants take up arms and march to war to the sound of orders in Guaraní. In Bolivia the silent Aymará Indians slip like shadows along the beautiful avenues of La Paz.

It is practically impossible to preserve the spirit of the law in its application to those who speak only Quechua, Maya, Aymará, or Guaraní, when judgment is delivered in Spanish and the concept of justice is based on legal concepts brought in by the conquerors. To understand what is going on within those strata of Indian and *mestizo* (Indian-Spanish) population, in their economic as well as their human aspects, and to grasp the motives that inspire them to revolt, one must turn to the novel. In Latin America the novel is often a more accurate document than the history book. It has its origin at the points of greatest tension and sensitivity, and explains what goes on in the mind of the peasants and the masses. It escapes the limitations of the official report. And if at times the novel lapses into caricature or reflects a partisan viewpoint, these same weaknesses are often found not only in the official report, but even in statistics.

To plumb the tragedy of the Ecuadorian peasant one must

read a novel with an Indian title, *Huasipungo*, by Jorge Icaza. The shortest road to a knowledge of the Indians of Peru is the novel by Ciro Alegría, *El Mundo es Ancho y Ajeno*, whose very title (*Broad and Alien is the World*) is in itself an indication of the Indians' situation. The true story of the Mexican Revolution is to be found in such fictionalized accounts as Mariano Azuela's *Los de Abajo* (*The Underdogs*) or Martín Luis Guzmán's *El Águila y la Serpiente* (*The Eagle and the Serpent*). Alcides Arguedas, a distinguished novelist, wrote Bolivia's history in *Los Caudillos Bárbaros* (*The Barbarous Caudillos*). No better description of conditions in Colombia in recent years can be found than the short stories of Hernando Téllez, *Cenizas para el Viento* (*Ashes for the Wind*). The fundamental work on life in the Argentine remains Sarmiento's *Facundo*, subtitled *Civilización y Barbarie en la República Argentina* (*Civilization and Barbarism in the Argentine Republic*). It is well to read these titles twice: in themselves they paint a panorama in images of this difficult and contradictory world.

In many Latin American countries those who have been the leaders of the democratic movements are muzzled today. In Argentina it is a criminal offense to "show disrespect" for the chief of state, which, under present circumstances, includes the president's wife. Thus, any criticism, even if voiced by an elected representative on the floor of the legislature, can bring imprisonment, exile, or removal from office as a consequence. The constitutionally elected president of Peru, Dr. José Luis Bustamante, was overthrown by a military *coup d'état*, whose leader, General Manuel Odría, became president; now the ex-president cannot open his mouth in his own country. Neither can Victor Raúl Haya de la Torre, the leader of the *aprista* party, unquestionably the largest in Peru, who for over two years has been a refugee in the Colombian Embassy in Lima. In Venezuela a military *junta* forced the removal of Rómulo Gallegos, who had been elected president in the first free and popular election the country had ever enjoyed. Today the constitutional president is an exile. The same thing happened to ex-President Isaías Medina Angarita, who was also overthrown by a coup. Medina, who enjoys great popularity in his country, indicated his desire to return to Venezuela in May 1951, but the government denied him permission. Rómulo Betancourt, head of the Acción Democrática party in Venezuela, and also onetime president of the republic, is likewise unable to speak there. In Colombia all the former presidents are under the strictest censorship, particularly Eduardo Santos, whose term of office stands out as one of the freest and most upright in the memory of his country. Alberto Lleras Camargo, ex-President of Colombia, the present director of the Organization of American States, criticized at its very inception the dictatorship that now governs in Bogotá, and the dictatorship at once filed a protest with that body in an unsuccessful effort to silence him. In Paraguay Natalicio González, the constitutional president, was overthrown by a military plot, and today he is barred from addressing his fellow citizens publicly.

These are examples of how a fundamental condition of the democratic system is rendered void in those countries in which popularly elected, constitutional presidents, the leaders of majority parties, and all who criticize the actions of the government are silenced. In a large portion of Latin America today the clandestine press is as active as it was in occupied countries during the Nazi invasion. The parties of the Left have no alternative but to wage an underground struggle, and it is natural that they should consider the use of violence. Wherever democratic parties are "legally" stamped out, Communism finds fertile soil, for Communism has a long training in secret organization and in the technique of drastic action.

II

DOUBLE TALK

My promises to the countries where I have fought have been fulfilled: to achieve their independence and leave them free to choose their governments.
SAN MARTÍN's Farewell Address to the Peruvians

Liberty, the idol of free peoples, is still disdained by slaves because they do not know it.
SAN MARTÍN, To the Teachers of the Province of Mendoza

IN A WORK that has become a classic of English literature—*Green Mansions*—William Henry Hudson wrote these words of introduction to his novel: "Every nation, someone remarks, has the government it deserves, and Venezuela certainly has the one it deserves and that suits it best. We call it a republic, not only because it is not one, but also because a thing must have a name; and to have a good name, or a fine name, is very convenient—especially when you want to borrow money."

Hudson bore Venezuela no ill will. On the contrary, to him it was a magic place, primitive and wild. But if Hudson had been writing his novel today, he might have seen fit to alter his opening page, at least in one respect. *Green Mansions* was published in 1904, thirteen years before Venezuela first began exporting oil. Production that year was 1000 barrels a day. Today that output has risen to 1,600,000 barrels a day, and Venezuela is the second largest producer of oil in the world. A nation of 4,300,000 persons living in an area one third larger than Texas, Venezuela has so much money that it scarcely knows what to do. The government has an income of one million dollars a day and not one cent of foreign debt. Whether the world moves toward peace or war, it is impossible to weigh the future without reckoning Venezuelan oil in the balance.

The case of Venezuela is a dramatic example of the changes wrought in the economy of Latin America during the past several decades. With respect to the United States, Latin America has become a major world market for both purchase and sale. A fundamental difference between the United States and the Soviet Union is that whereas Russia is relatively self-sufficient in raw materials, the United States must lean heavily on raw materials from abroad. Among the things that the United States imports in large quantities is oil. Latin America was the source of 83 per cent of the oil entering the United States in 1950, and 42 per cent of that 83 was Venezuelan. At the same time Latin America supplied more than half of five other vital industrial and consumer goods imported by the United States: antimony, 97 per cent; copper, 63 per cent; tin, 53 per cent; coffee, 95 per cent; and sugar, 87 per cent. The flow of trade in the opposite direction saw 58 per cent of the machinery, 37 per cent of the chemical products, 40 per cent of the textiles, 30 per cent of the iron and steel, 36 per cent of the wheat, and 46 of every 100 automobiles exported by the United States destined for Latin American buyers.[1]

The world at large, moreover, is to a greater or lesser degree dependent on Argentine wheat, Chilean copper, Venezuelan oil, the tropical products of Brazil, and the tin of Bolivia. In 1900 Latin America was virtually in the backwaters of world economics and politics. Today the Panama Canal might be termed their epicenter. The new stature of Latin America in the world economic-political order must be recognized in any attempt to grasp the importance the Latin American republics may assume at any moment in the international assemblages.

[1] Business Report of *The New York Times,* April 1, 1951.

The General Assembly of the United Nations has sixty members: one-third of these are Latin American. While all of Europe can voice only fourteen votes, Latin America commands twenty. The United States and its forty-eight states have one vote. Russia and its satellites cannot muster a voting bloc one-third the size of the Latin American vote.

Among the European countries, Luxembourg has one vote, equal to that of Great Britain. In America, Nicaragua and the United States each has one vote. And though it is true that many deep-seated differences exist among the Latin American countries, they tend to act in unison on questions of international import. It has been well-nigh impossible to unite six European countries on a given issue. But in Latin America all the countries have nearly the same language, a similar historical background, and a community of interests that tend to join them in a common attitude toward the rest of the world. Just what this common chord is has been a point of controversy among observers of Latin America. Some believe that a general rejection of Communism is what knits the twenty nations together, others, that their unity is inspired by a fear of the United States. The greatest barrier to a satisfactory answer to these questions has been the "paper curtain" of censorship and deliberate misdirection which exists in many Latin American countries, impeding the free expression of public opinion.

The importance of Latin America's twenty votes in the General Assembly has already made itself felt in many matters of secondary importance and some of greater transcendence. Distinguished Latin American delegates man key positions within the world organization. The eminent Mexican, Jaime Torres Bodet, presides over the United Nations Educational, Social and Cultural Organization (UNESCO), the largest agency the world has seen for the encouragement and direction of activities in the fields of science, arts, letters, and the recognition of human rights. He has brought to his post the democratic spirit of his country. In the General Assembly of 1951, the second committee, known as the Financial and Economic committee, had as chairman a Cuban of democratic orientation. But in the same session the Political and Security, or first, committee, was presided over by a delegate representing the dictatorship of Colombia, while the *ad hoc* political committee sat under the chairmanship of a delegate from Peru, where a military government holds power.

In the Assembly convened in Paris in 1951, the strength of the Latin American bloc was demonstrated immediately. All the candidates for the presidency of the Assembly were Latin Americans, and Luis Padilla Nervo, the eminent Mexican internationalist, was elected. Thomas J. Hamilton of *The New York Times* summed up in December 1951 the incidents in which the leadership of the United States was seriously questioned. In effect he said that the United States suffered the following defeats and near-defeats during the opening sessions of the Assembly: on the Moroccan question, principally because Latin American votes inclined to favor France; in its desire to obtain a reduction in its contribution to the support of the United Nations (as favored by Congress), but toward the accomplishment of which it was able to muster only one vote besides its own, that of Nicaragua; in the election of a new member for the Security Council, in which it supported Greece against Byelorussia, and was on the point of losing because of the formation of a bloc of Soviet, Arab, Asiatic, and Latin American countries in favor of Byelorussia, so that only after nineteen successive roll calls did it succeed in electing Greece; and in its attempt to elect Sir Benegal Rau of India to the International Court of Justice—the Latin American nations were demanding the seat for one of themselves (four of the fifteen members of the Court are Latin Americans)— in which it won only after being at the point of losing.

It is not always easy to know the interests that inspire, or the objectives that guide, the delegates from the Latin American dictatorships. One of the Latin American delegations noted for its demonstrations in favor of the United States entered into direct conversations with the Russian delegation in the hope of gaining the secretary-generalship of the UN when it appeared that Trygve Lie might leave that post. It has been said that the Latin American votes in favor of a "softer" UN attitude toward Franco Spain reflected in every instance a desire on the part of those nations to mesh their actions with Washington policy. The fact is, however, that several of the delegations that took a most active part in this matter had come to an understanding with Madrid before sounding out Washington. The reservations toward the Franco regime held by the government of the United States stand in sharp contrast to the addiction shown toward that regime by the Latin American dictatorships. In Colombia, for example, it is patent that the overriding majority of the public is opposed to the Spanish dictatorship. In spite of this, former President Mariano Ospina Pérez, disregarding his nation's commitments to the UN, declared in a formal speech made months before the question was considered in the General Assembly and the new policy established that he would send an ambassador to Spain. When the Colombian ambassador appeared before General Franco, he addressed him in a fashion that broke all tradition of protocol: "Your Excellency has ceased to be simply the illustrious leader of the Spanish nation and has become the great Captain of the Race, who, by the light of the Scriptures, will lead the struggle to decide the fate of the world against the shadows of materialism."

What the Latin American governments are seeking with their pro-Franco policy is nothing even remotely connected with the Atlantic Pact or the defense of Europe. These questions are of little concern to them. *Franquismo* attracts them for what they see in it of doctrinaire justification for their official violence against the democratic forces in their countries and the civil liberties of their peoples.

The gravity of this situation becomes apparent when it is borne in mind that the Organization of American States[2] is the oldest international organization of a regional nature, and also the one that embraces the largest number of countries. A substantial number of the delegates who sit at the familiar round table of the Pan American Union today represent governments of a dictatorial character, military *juntas* that have defied the constitutional order in their countries or heads of state whose history has been one constant struggle against liberty. It is difficult for Latin Americans to see in the delegates of General Perón of the Argentine, General Odría of Peru, the military *junta* of Venezuela, General Rafael Leonidas Trujillo of the Dominican Republic, or Urdaneta Arbeláez of Colombia the type of representation calculated to foster the development of a free and democratic state of affairs in the hemisphere. With the collapse of two or three of the remaining constitutional governments of Latin America and the consolidation of the internal affairs of those countries in the hands of the neo-Nazi groups that have risen to power throughout the hemisphere, the Organization of American States may become the only international body in the world offering haven to proponents of the ideologies against which World War II was fought.

In a noteworthy article published in 1950 in the Mexican review, *Cuadernos Americanos*, Daniel Cosío Villegas, one of Mexico's intellectual leaders, wrote:

"There is not a decent man or woman who can contemplate the political panorama Latin America presents today without experiencing positive physical revulsion. Of the twenty countries that comprise it, seven (Nicaragua, Venezuela, Brazil, Argentina, Peru, Colombia, and the Dominican Republic) are indisputable tyrannies; nine, (El Salvador, Honduras, Costa Rica, Panama, Paraguay, Chile, Ecuador, and Haiti)

[2] The new name given to the Pan American Union at the Bogotá Conference of 1948. Both names are now in use.

stand on such a precarious political footing that any crisis—a presidential election or an economic dislocation—can plunge them into open dictatorship; and no one would put his hand in the fire on the faith that the remaining four (Mexico, Guatemala, Cuba, and Uruguay) are immune to tyranny, or even that their political progress in recent years gives much ground for optimism.

"The fact that sixteen of the Latin American countries are currently ruled by tyrannies, or are under threat of being so ruled, is in itself disturbing. But even more so is the magnitude or the relative importance of the nations involved. For in politics, as in so many other fields, mankind more readily tends to imitate the large evil than the small good. Of the three largest countries of Latin America, Brazil and Argentina have tyrannical governments, while Mexico alone enjoys liberty. Among the five nations of medium size, Venezuela, Peru, and Colombia have fallen under dictatorships; Chile is on the verge of so doing, and Cuba alone retains democracy, though in a form that leaves something to be desired."

Whether or not one completely agrees with Cosío Villegas's analysis, it points up a situation that cannot be denied. The fundamental fact upon which the *de facto* governments or outright dictatorships of Latin America postulate their existence is a semantic subtlety by which they maintain the outward semblances of a free democratic system for export purpose while a thoroughgoing despotism holds sway within their borders.

The rallying-cry of *peronismo* in its political conquest of the Argentine, repeated to the point of satiety in public demonstrations, the slogan under which the siege of the University of La Plata was carried out, was: "Shoes, yes; books, no." But this in no way handicaps General Perón when he turns his thoughts to what he terms the century of justice, and says: "We believe that here, from our Argentina, profoundly Christian and profoundly humanistic, we are working for a world ennobled by the exercise of those human virtues whereby hate will become love, selfishness turn generosity, and the passions of vengeance be transformed into forgiveness."

In March 1949 a new Argentine constitution was adopted with portentous solemnity. The preamble states that the constitution is destined "to establish national unity, further justice, maintain internal tranquility, provide for the common defense, promote the general welfare and national culture, and guarantee to all the benefits of liberty, for ourselves and for posterity and for all men who wish to live on Argentine soil." Its article 26 further states: "All inhabitants of this nation enjoy the following rights, within the laws that govern their exercise: to employment and the pursuit of all legitimate and useful business; to navigate freely and enter into commerce; to petition the constituted authorities; to assemble, to enter, reside in, travel through, and leave the territories of Argentina; to voice their ideas in the press without prior censorship; to use and dispose of property; to associate for useful purposes; to worship freely according to their beliefs; to teach and to learn."

In other words, an ideal constitution, under which the whole world would be delighted to live and work. A moment comes, however, when the governing party is hampered in the free play of its powers by the existence of newspapers like *La Prensa* and *La Nación*, two of the great dailies of the world. A labor dispute is trumped up between the government-sponsored Newsvendors' Union and *La Prensa*. And this confused account of the episode appears in the *peronista* newspaper, *La Epoca:*

"The labor incident involving *La Prensa* has given the Argentine people and all those who think without party labels the opportunity to assume the risk of a formal and definitive judgment. No one would venture to harm the moral spirit of the press in its mission as vehicle of humane and generous ideas. But we all share the belief that this enterprise, which employs as its emblem the word 'press' [*prensa*], is a deformation of that virtue of regarding one's fellow man with love, as intelligence directs when its purpose is to unite the collective emotions of a people and the aspirations of a republic . . . The Paz family [owners of *La Prensa*] belongs to the dynasty of those who, the world over, dedicate themselves self-righteously to plunder . . . For that reason *La Prensa* must be destroyed as a slave-trader . . . *La Prensa's* crime was not so much the money it made with its tricks of low cunning as the fact that it corrupted ten generations of Argentines . . ."

The publisher of *La Prensa* and its employees, exercising their right of petition as provided by the constitution of the new Argentine state, appealed to the government to permit them to return to work. The authorities gave them no answer. The workers decided to re-enter the plant and return to work. They were driven out with gunfire. The publisher and director, Alberto Gainza Paz, emigrated to Uruguay, exercising his right to leave the country. Shortly afterward the Peronist paper published his picture with this cutline:

"POLICE RECORD—Wanted. Dr. Alberto Gainza Paz, publisher of *La Prensa*, and incarnation of the highest manly and traditional qualities of the race according to the opinion of his friends and associates in the democratic farce they have perpetrated, to escape facing charges is a fugitive from justice, moved by cravenness and fear, like a common coward."

The Latin American dictator reserves the right to put his own interpretation on liberty. For him there are no fundamental rights of man, but only fundamental rights of the government party. Liberty is nothing more than the absolute liberty of his own party. Opposition to the dictates of the party places one outside the law. The liberty to dissent, to present a divergent point of view, does not exist. Justice is defined by the party. If the party decides to throttle a newspaper, justice is shaped to the desires of the government. The owner will receive compensation—or not—as the party decides. He has no recourse to a day in court. In this respect, a speech of which General Perón delivered himself on May Day 1951 is particularly enlightening. He said:

"Liberty in order to be true liberty must be what the public determines it should be . . . The struggle for liberty, in our eyes, is the one that leads to social justice, economic independence, and political sovereignty. We Argentines have our constitutional guarantees of liberty; but what would become of them with social injustice, economic slavery, and political vassalage? Those things would reduce our liberty to a form well-known to the workers of the Argentine: the liberty to starve to death.

"Therefore the fairy tale of liberty is too old a story for us to fall under its spell. It's not too different from the shell game or the money-making machine.

"I would like to take this occasion to tell you that the newspaper *La Prensa* has been expropriated by the government and will be turned over to the workers to do with it as they see fit.

"That newspaper, which for so many years exploited the workers and the poor, which was the refined instrument of all forms of national and international exploitation, which represented the crudest form of treason against the nation, will purge its sins by helping the working public to revindicate and defend its sacred rights.

"All this has been done by a free and sovereign decision of the Argentine people in protection and defense of the liberty it desires and in keeping with the laws and the constitution that it has freely adopted and upholds. It has been done without fear of what others may think of its free stand and sovereign attitude."

In any effort to grasp the dimensions of the political transformation that is attempting to fasten itself on Latin Ameríca today, the primary field of study must be the Argentine process. One must examine the events that have culminated in the government of General Perón and his wife. A brief biographical sketch is essential to plumbing the meaning of the "Justicialism" they proclaim. And the influence that the Argentine school of thought has had on the formation of the other Latin American dictatorships must be examined.

General Perón's grand illusion, in moments when his imperialistic fancy soars, has been expansion. In April 1949 he discreetly gave the continent notice of it in these words: "Keep before you the thought that this nation has given proof throughout its history that it is not content to proclaim liberty and independence for itself alone, but is prepared to carry these benefits the length of the continent for the greater good of its American brothers."

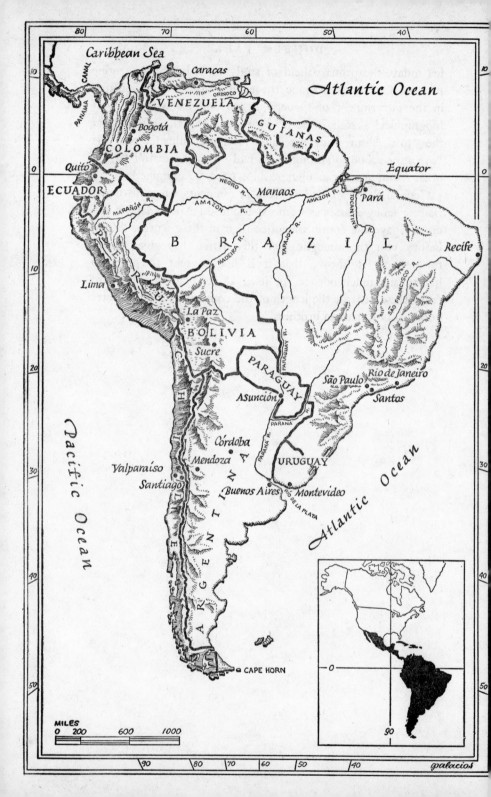

III

THE EGO WITH TWO HEADS: SINISTER

The arms of enlightenment were not in fashion under the government of that day; and the brilliant literary club had to lay them down before the brutal majesty of another club, that of the lash, organized to do away with every club of liberty. The only freedom of association that existed was in the form of the mazorca. *There was freedom of association to smite the Liberals, but association for the pursuit of liberty was treason against the nation. The "Literary Salon" was doomed to disappear because it was an open organization. It was then that we thought of the "Asociación de Mayo," or a secret lodge made of those we called the "Argentine Youth Generation. . . ."*

JUAN B. ALBERDI: *My Private Life*

LIKE THE double eagle on the Hapsburg coat-of-arms, the two heads of the Argentine dictatorship are joined in a single body. In this case the body is the firm of *Eva-Perón, Incorporated.* Perón is just a name. There is nothing unique about Perón's political personality; he belongs to the genus *dictator.* But Eva, Evita, is *species argentinensis.* She immediately calls to mind Encarnación Ezcurra, the wife of Juan Manuel Rosas. Rosas belonged to the type of Latin-American dictator which flourished in the nineteenth century, and for more than twenty years he ran Argentina, to quote one of his opponents, "as though it were his ranch." Juan Manuel and Encarnación ruled jointly, enjoying all the de-

27

lights of absolute power and pursuing a policy of terror without let or hindrance.

Rosas considered himself the Number One *gaucho* of Argentina, a role Perón enjoys too. Rosas maintained himself in power by terror. Argentines were either pro-Rosas or "traitors to their country." His picture was placed on the high altar in the churches, and people used to pull his carriage through the streets of Buenos Aires to show the measure of their devotion. Men wore red vests, and women a red rosette in their hair, because red was the dictator's color. It finally reached the point where the fronts of the houses were painted red. A modern admirer of Rosas, one of those who helped to prepare the way for General Perón's seizure of power, wrote a fulsome biography of the "Restorer of the Laws," as Rosas liked to be styled, in which he calls him a genius for having invented the forerunner of the Gestapo and the Ogpu, which was established in Buenos Aires over a century ago under the name of the *mazorca*. The *mazorca* was a highly efficient system of spying, informing, and punitive action. It has to its credit the first use of red pepper enemas to soften up recalcitrant opponents, a Creole formula that anticipated the castor oil of the Fascists. It was Rosas's ambition then, as it is Perón's today, to have a powerful, united Argentine to defy not only its neighbors, but other powers. To achieve this perfect union Rosas hit upon a very simple device: not to leave a single adversary alive.

Rosas's right arm in carrying out and perfecting this policy was his wife. There are episodes in the career of Doña Encarnación so similar to those in the life of Evita Perón that it almost makes one believe in the theory of reincarnation. It is impossible to consider the distaff side of Argentine politics without recalling Encarnación. Only then does one understand the opposition of any thinking Argentine to the idea of another woman in the driver's seat. No one can fail to shudder at the thought of a repetition of those barbarous incidents of the nineteenth century.

Manuel Gálvez, novelist and biographer of Rosas, an authority on the subject who makes no effort to conceal his admiration for the dictator, has painted Doña Encarnación in the following terms:

"The wife of the governor of Buenos Aires was all-powerful. Two years before, while her husband was on his way back from a campaign against the Indians, she had engineered against the government of [Juan Ramón] Balcarce a revolution that swept him from power. She manipulated generals and politicians, journalists and ward-heelers, distinguished men like Tomás Guido, and rabble-rousers. Determined, aggressive, fearless, shrewd, and possessed of boundless energy, she had accomplished what none of Rosas's friends was able to do. In her own home, ordering this one, upbraiding the other, insulting, goading, and keeping a watchful eye on all, she organized the revolution known as that of the Restorers, and brought down the government of General Juan Ramón Balcarce. This achievement, which, because it was the work of a woman, and moreover, a woman of the upper class, was unique in our history, conferred on Encarnación a renown and prestige without parallel. From then on she was known as 'the heroine of the Federation.'

"At her home in Biblioteca Street, Encarnación gave audience every morning. Men and women came to see her, for the most part those of the upper and middle ranks of society. The lower classes were looked after by her sister María Josefa in her house in Potosí Street, and these gatherings, which were frequented by Negresses, some of whom were fortune-tellers or pretended to have supernatural powers, were known as Witches' Sabbaths. Encarnación's visitors came looking for jobs or trying to ingratiate themselves with the government. They also acted as informers. All those with an axe to grind knew that Encarnación's influence was supreme with Rosas, who loved her passionately, a sentiment she completely requited. Neither his most intimate friends nor his generals, not his brothers, his parents, or even his daughter Manuelita, could get from Rosas what Encarnación could. She was flesh of his flesh and bone of his bone. She was a masculine type of woman and a complete despot. An unquenchable flame burned in her large, beautiful dark eyes. Her strong, firm features reflected the energy of her nature, which flinched from nothing, not even violence. She hated Rosas's enemies with an implacable fury perhaps even greater than his own . . ."

Before October 17, 1945—a hallowed date in the annals of *peronismo*—Evita was only a bit radio actress in Buenos Aires. After that date she became a world figure. Her trip to Europe in 1947 was one of the events of the year. General Franco sent a plane in which a suite befitting royalty had been installed so that she could travel in state on her visit to Spain. There she was cheered at bullfights, in the public squares, in the streets, by crowds larger than those which gathered to greet Franco. She was presented with a collection of costumes from the different regions of Spain which might have graced a museum. Franco was eager to show the world that he had an ally in Argentina, that his doctrine had spread beyond the Atlantic, and that his dream-empire of Hispanidad was on the way to becoming a reality.

At that moment Evita (who is really a beautiful woman), overblown with her new-found power and her sense of triumph, began to behave like a pampered child. She was late wherever she went, keeping ministers, ambassadors, and avid spectators cooling their heels for two or three hours. They were lent patience by the fact that at that moment Argentina was loading wheat for shipment to Europe. On one occasion Evita ordered the special train in which she was traveling held for several hours while her maids put the finishing touches on her toilette.

In Rome the Argentine Embassy spent a quarter of a million dollars furbishing up the house to receive her. The whole world buzzed over her visit to the Pope. All sorts of stories and anecdotes (many of them of the smoking-car variety) were told about her, as always happens with persons in the public eye. Protest meetings were organized, which the police had to put down with a firm hand. Europe was saying that Perón represented a neo-Fascism and that key posts in his government were held by high former Nazis or Fascists. In Switzerland Evita's automobile was pelted with tomatoes. The King and Queen of England used the pretext of a visit to Scotland to avoid receiving her. In Rio de Janeiro, at the meeting of the Foreign Ministers of America, when Evita walked into the assembly the president dismissed the session as a tribute to her and as a way to avert the possibility of her making a speech.

All these are the natural ups and downs of a public career that began by breaking all traditions. The cards seemed stacked against Evita. Argentine society, than which none is more aristocratic or exclusive, would have refused to admit a person of her background if she had attempted to enter it. The men of that country are not in the habit of taking orders from a woman. The president's wife traditionally plays a purely decorative role in the social life of Buenos Aires.

Shortly after Perón's inauguration, a newsreel showing the transfer of power was exhibited in the Argentine Naval Academy. Evita was prominently in the foreground. The students began to cough and clear their throats. The film was halted, the lights were turned up, and the commandant ordered those who had begun the demonstration to come forward. A dozen midshipmen stood up. They were expelled from the school and a number of others were severely disciplined. The cadets of the Military Academy pronounced themselves in complete accord with the midshipmen—a thing hitherto unheard of—and a navy officer's uniform was burned from one of the lamp-posts of the Plaza de Mayo in Buenos Aires. Those police who had not been on the alert to forestall this outrage were dismissed from their posts.

It began to be whispered that the army officers were planning to ask the President to curtail the political activities of his wife. Whereupon Perón announced that he was appointing her Secretary of Labor and Social Welfare. And, as the Spanish proverb goes, "The one who doesn't like soup will be served two plates." At the great military parade to honor the Year of San Martín (the hero of Argentina's War of Independence) in the reviewing stand with General Perón to receive the troops' salute was his wife.

To understand Evita's rise to power, it is necessary to see her against her early background in the theater world of Buenos Aires. In this field Buenos Aires can hold its own with Paris, London, or New York. The best Spanish, French, Italian, German, and Yiddish companies visit that city and present plays before crowded houses. The Comédie Française plays to an audience as appreciative as that in Paris. Toscanini has directed the orchestra at the Colón Theater, and the opening of the Buenos Aires opera season is a more sumptuous affair than that of the Metropolitan in New York.

Out of all this a tradition has grown up. There are great Argentine actresses: Camila Quiroga and her company a generation ago, Mecha Ortiz and Libertad Lamarque today, who are famous on both stage and screen throughout Latin America. There are comedy stars like Paulina Singermann. The same is true of radio. Success does not come easily in the Argentine theatrical world.

Evita—her name at that time was Eva Duarte—was born in the little town of Los Toldos in the province of Buenos Aires, and spent her early years in the provincial atmosphere of Junín, a town of about 35,000 people. She went to Buenos Aires with the ambition of becoming a radio and motion picture actress, and she achieved it. But she never quite reached the top. Critics said that she was still very young, that she showed promise, that she had a future . . . The pictures in which she worked have since been withdrawn from circulation. Her salary in radio was very small, though she received a sudden and substantial raise shortly before she rose to her present position. At that time she was going to work at the studio in an official car.

But if Evita's rise in the theater was slow, she was exploring other avenues with great success. She had been making the acquaintance of army officers and learning a great deal about politics. She was carried away by the ideas of Perón, who was already beginning to stand out as a leader in inner circles. The generals were engaged in a relentless conspiracy against the civilian government. They had been trained in the old Prussian school, and were unreserved admirers of the Nazi doctrine. They were bored with their humdrum existence under the command of leaders who wore no uniform, and they thirsted after power. They were on the alert for the opportune moment to bring off a coup. And they tried it once, and again, and again. The political atmosphere was charged with electricity.

Perón, who was the most powerful person in the dictatorship that General Edelmiro Farrell had set up, and who was fifty-three years old, fell head over heels in love with Evita, who was twenty-seven. So many things were happening offstage at this point that it is difficult to determine just what role the shrewdness and ambition of Evita played in the establishment of the machinery for tooling the new-model Argentina. But she knew that it was the hour of decision for her, and that her whole future hinged on it. She gave up her career as an actress and plunged into politics.

The reasons for the triumph of *peronismo* are not immediately apparent. Was it that in Buenos Aires industrial evolution had completed its cycle, and that in its wake had come social inequalities capable of engendering a revolution? Did Evita

Duarte, soon to become Evita Perón, have real influence in the officers' clubs where the deals for Perón's seizure of power were being made? Did the response of the masses come from an actual situation or was it skillfully incubated by Perón and harnessed at the decisive moment by Evita Duarte? Is she only collecting her rightful share of the spoils?

For years the struggle for power in Argentina had been carried on in the higher echelons of politics. The people had had nothing to do with it, had felt no pressing need to make it their concern. The Radical party, which represented the majority of the country, had had its hands tied by the state of siege imposed by the military dictatorship. The Socialists, very strong in Buenos Aires, were still thinking in terms of the theories that had informed their action during the nineteenth century, and had no working plan. But the liberation of France, the fall of Berlin, and the defeat of Japan encouraged public opinion to voice its protest and demand the restoration of civilian government and the return of the liberties suspended by Farrell's *junta*, dominated by Perón. There were great public demonstrations that the police had to curb, not without a considerable number of dead and wounded. The students were a prime factor in arousing the civic conscience, and the dictatorship cracked down on the universities. Sixty-four professors were dismissed from their posts for having taken part in the mourning ceremonies held by the students for their slain companions. Newspapers were closed, and over one thousand persons were jailed on political charges. But there was such a popular awareness that the triumph of the Allies represented the triumph of democracy and liberty that the people gathered in the streets again to demand the end of the dictatorship, that is to say, the ousting of Perón, the vice-president. The movement seemed so irresistible that Perón had to resign and was confined to the island of Martín García.

This was the triumph of the Radicals, the Socialists, of public opinion at large. The leaders had made no special appeal to labor. At this juncture, with uncanny foresight, Perón's friends—among them Cipriano Reyes, leader of the extreme Left, and at the moment one of Perón's supporters, and, above all, Evita Duarte—saw that *peronismo*'s hour had come. They visited the packing-houses, the factories, and the slums and egged the masses on to seize power. "Shoes, yes! Books, no!" and "We want Perón! Perón! Perón!" became the election slogans.

A program of such ambitious scope had never been presented to these people before. Perón had raised their wages. He promised to carry out only the people's will. He was going to strip the oligarchy of its wealth, which he would hand over to the people. Evita was busy day and night stimulating with frenzied vehemence the appetite these promises had aroused. Out of all this came the great march of the "shirtless" on Buenos Aires. This was diabolically superior to the march of Mussolini's Black Shirts on Rome, and recalled certain episodes of the French Revolution. The people were briefed thus: we are going to appear just as we are, without washing our hands, in dirty shirts or no shirts at all, so that they will see us as we are, and we will demand that they release Perón.

Preparations began on October 15, 1945, for the March of the Shirtless, which took place on October 17. It was the first great manifestation of the mob hysteria of *peronismo*. It was an impressive sight, arranged with all the fanfare and showmanship that are part and parcel of totalitarianism: huge portraits, flags, posters, slogans. Perhaps the crowd was not so large as that which had assembled to celebrate the defeat of the Axis or to demand Perón's ouster. But it was vehement, vociferous, almost brutal. One of the newspapers of Buenos Aires—which takes inordinate pride in its cleanliness, where even the lowest classes are always well dressed and the poorest child in the public schools wears an immaculate white smock—published a picture of the rally with a jeering caption about the bare-chested workers, the shirtless. The *peronistas* saw their opportunity and made the phrase their own: "Yes, we are the shirtless [*descamisados*], the underprivileged, who are demanding justice!" Since then Evita has never once addressed the people without beginning: "Dear shirtless ones."

It was Evita who unleashed this revolution. She duplicated the feat of Doña Encarnación Rosas, who carried out the revolution against Balcarce in favor of her husband. After a lapse of one hundred and twenty years, history repeated itself. For Perón's sake, Evita went down to the workers' districts and made the acquaintance of the local bosses. She visited the factories, and each visit was a one-man show. It was then that Evita found herself, discovered her true vocation. It was only a step from this to her rise to power, which she now exercises without consideration or scruple, demanding unconditional surrender from those who used to be above her in the social scale.

The march of these political events synchronized with the climax of the love affair. The March of the Shirtless took place on October 17, 1945, and on October 26 Juan Perón and Evita Duarte were married at a private ceremony.

It was the story of Cinderella in modern dress. The insignificant little screen and radio actress had become one of the outstanding women of her day. There is hardly a popular magazine in the world whose cover she has not adorned. *Time, Life,* and the magazine section of *The New York Times* have published feature articles about her. Even though her trip to Europe was not all a bed of roses, one fact stood out clear: Eva Perón was God's gift to news agencies. She even has her place among the heavenly bodies, for Captain Guillermo Walbrecher, director of the Observatory of La Plata, has given the name Evita to a new star discovered by his keen scientist's eye and his even keener sense of which side his bread is buttered on.

Evita has been transformed from a poor working girl into

one of the most sumptuously dressed women in the world. Chartered planes arrive regularly at Buenos Aires with the output of the best Paris designers to keep her wardrobe up to date. A photograph in *Life* showed her proudly displaying her collection of jewelry, which is kept in the drawers of a cabinet similar to those used for letter-filing. When, as a girl, she pored over movie magazines, she undoubtedly dreamed of the luxury life of the Hollywood stars. And suddenly she found that all this and more was hers. Although the salary of the president of Argentina is $576 a month, Evita spends $40,000 a year on Paris clothes. She owns newspapers and is the head of the largest enterprise in Argentina: the Eva Duarte de Perón Foundation. Her brother, secretary to the president, has amassed a large private fortune.

The setting in which this new Cinderella has her being is clearly reflected in the following report published in *La Nación* on August 24, 1950, of the gift presented to her by the members of Congress when Evita conferred diplomas and medals on the *peronista* delegates:

"The committee presented her with an artistic diamond bracelet, adorned with fourteen charms of platinum, sapphires, diamonds, and rubies. The charms represented: the national flag, the *peronista* shield, a flower-trimmed ship with her wedding date, the image of one of the shirtless, the dates of the president's birthday and hers, the dove of peace, Negrita, Señora Perón's cherished dog, the national coat-of-arms, the party emblem, the symbol of union, the insignia of the General Confederation of Labor, the name of the recipient, and the façade of the legislative palace."

It would be hard to find in history another example of such a meteoric rise by a woman. Josephine, a creole beauty from the island of Martinique, captivated Napoleon and became Empress of the French, but she made no attempt to wield power, and her name is associated principally with her love letters. Catherine of Russia, Catherine de' Medici, Elizabeth Tudor, were all to the manor born, and came to the throne by natural right. Perhaps the closest parallel to Evita is to be found in Theodora, the wife of the Emperor Justinian, who was known as the most beautiful courtesan of Byzantium, and who shared the throne with her husband. But there is no comparison between the work of Justinian, which is still a living part of our law, and that of Theodora, which is buried under the dust of history. Evita's antecedents are to be found in her own country, in Doña Encarnación Ezcurra.

Evita today has her hands on the controls of several of the most important branches of the administration. Her closest contact is with labor. The railroad workers' union has held out against her at various times. In 1950 posters appeared reading: "We want Perón, widower." Time went by. The labor unions' freedom had disappeared. And one morning the inhabitants of Buenos Aires woke up to find the billboards covered with huge posters displaying Evita's picture against the blue and white background of the Argentine flag, underneath it the caption: "Eva Perón, champion of the underprivileged, will be elected in 1951." A few months later new posters appeared. These were campaign propaganda for the coming election. "Perón-Perón." Which post was Evita seeking? The presidency? The vice-presidency? It brought to mind the motto of the Catholic Kings:

> *Tanto monta, monta tanto*
> *Isabel como Fernando.*[1]

Anything is possible. Despite the great opposition in Argentina to voting for a woman, so far it had seemed that Evita could get anything she set her mind on. She would probably be the vice-president. And it was not impossible that Perón might decide to make a tour of the world, in which case Evita would be president *pro tem*. She would thus

[1] Literally, Isabel is tantamount to Ferdinand.

be the first woman president in the history of the American republics.

Herbert L. Matthews of *The New York Times* (March 25, 1951) had this to say after a first-hand survey of the Argentine situation:

". . . in governments of this peronist type, foreign affairs are not directed by the foreign minister. It is General Perón, Eva Perón, and a small clique, mostly around Señora Perón, who control foreign policy . . ."

This is an accurate estimate. Evita has the power to determine changes of a very serious nature in Argentina's foreign policy. She holds no portfolio, but she has in her hands, among other things, what in Hitler's Germany was called the Ministry of Propaganda. And, above all, she completely controls the Eva Duarte de Perón Foundation. This Foundation did not come into being by law, but through a decree issued by General Perón. It is not under any council or directors or subject to controls of any sort. It is in charge of hospitals, low-cost housing projects, university developments, kindergartens, homes for the aged, vacation camps. Everyone must contribute to it, and liberally. The industrialist who fails to do so may find himself obliged to shut up shop, as happened to the Massone Pharmaceutical Company and to the Mu-Mu candy factory.

An Argentine congressman, Atilio Cattaneo, analyzed various aspects of the Foundation in a speech in which he said, among other things:

"It would seem that its aim is to monopolize public welfare, employing contributions and state funds. Not all the gifts received by the Foundation are voluntary, as might be imagined. The government has levied such a tax, as that on amusements, which has not gone through the normal channels of the law, and whose proceeds go to the Foundation . . . In the province of Santa Fe the government has floated a bond issue for the benefit of the Foundation. A business firm like that of Bunge and Born—and this is not an isolated case—which the President has described as 'an octopus of our economy,' has handed over a check for one million pesos. Nearly all agreements for salary increases carry clauses calling for the withholding of a percentage of salaries and wages, in spite of the fact that the law expressly forbids such withholdings on any grounds . . ."

Congressman Cattaneo was a lieutenant-colonel. He was removed from office, and, by a military court and a decree of General Perón, deprived of the right to wear his uniform or use his military title.

The *Bulletin* of the University of Buenos Aires for the month of April 1951 carries the following announcement:

"BUILDING FOR THE EVA PERÓN FOUNDATION. —On March 30, the following motion was presented and approved:

"To transfer to the Eva Perón Foundation title to the block belonging to the University of Buenos Aires bounded by the streets of Paseo Colón, Estados Unidos, Azopardo, and Independencia in the city of Buenos Aires, having a total area of 11,903.68 square meters, in keeping with the provisions of Law 13,992 passed by Congress.

"The reasons for the above motion are as follows:

"In view of the fact that the University Council in Resolution 120 of November 18, 1949, authorized the sale of the above-described property to the Eva Perón Foundation . . . etc. . . . the Congress of the Nation on September 29, 1950, passed Law No. 13,992, article 12 of which authorizes 'the gift to the institution in question of the aforesaid real estate for the purpose of amplifying its social activities,' the Rector of the University of Buenos Aires, etc. . . ."

Thus, in the interests of the Foundation a law of university reform and a resolution passed by the university council have stripped the University of Buenos Aires of an extremely valuable piece of property which formed a part of its holdings heretofore regarded as inalienable.

As for Evita's political ideas, they are very simple, almost rudimentary, but clear-cut, direct, and effective. They have brought about a radical change in the national point of view. The whole thing boils down to substituting for government by institutions the personal rule of her husband and/or herself. Where the term "public welfare" was formerly employed, "Evita" is now used. When a worker receives an increase of salary, a student a book, an old person relief; or when a clinic, a hospital, a gymnasium, or a playground is opened, it must be regarded as something done not by state or law, but by Evita or Perón. When wheat is shipped abroad, it is not sent by Argentina, but by Perón. An earthquake damages the city of Cúcuta in Colombia; Evita's airplanes immediately take off to bring Evita's aid to the stricken city, and the grateful city hangs out flags bearing the name of Evita. Help is to be found not in the law, but in Perón. There is fear not of the law, but of Perón. There is only one legal norm: Perón. Little by little the name of Argentina is falling into disuse; everyone speaks of Perón, of Evita. The task of building a nation, with its legislatures, congress, and executive branches, which involved a century and a half of arduous struggle, has now culminated in a single name. Evita repeats the same words every day to drive the point home. She stamps it on the mind of the party. She has imposed it, rubbed the nation's nose in it. Those who have ventured to oppose her, not doing as she wanted or not giving her what she wanted, have paid dearly for their integrity.

Behind this simple, elementary program there is a seething, dangerous passion and an unlimited capacity for work. Her radio training has stood her in good stead; she makes speeches to the nation in factories, in theaters, at public gatherings, before Congress, at banquets, on the national holiday, on Labor Day. Not a Christmas Eve goes by without a message

41

from her to her "dear shirtless ones" of the General Confederation of Labor, nor a New Year's Eve without her radio greeting to the republic.

Like Perón, Evita is an early riser, and between seven and nine in the morning she reads her correspondence. Then her office hours begin. Hundreds of people are already waiting for her. There are union representatives, working men, women who have come from far-off provinces, one to tell her that she has not the money to pay her rent, another that she needs help for her children, a poor girl that she wants a new dress. Evita receives them all, shakes hands with them all, and each one receives twenty, fifty, one hundred, two hundred pesos in crisp new bills that rustle "Evita" in their grateful hands.

At other times the queue is made up of army officers, ambassadors, and ministers, who often are made to wait two or three hours. It is not an uncommon experience for them to overhear the First Lady in her office describing them in the most unflattering billingsgate.

Evita's reception room never fails to amaze foreign visitors. Argentines are unpleasantly reminded of the audiences held by Doña Encarnación and her sister María Josefa Ezcurra, in Rosas's day.

At one o'clock Evita lunches with her husband. Then she signs her letters, and maps out her program for the afternoon: visits to factories, to Congress, to schools. She is wholly dedicated to her political career, to *peronismo*, and to the *peronista* republic. And she pulls more weight than a president.

Evita is not formulating an abstract theory of *caudillo* rule. Behind the bonfires of class hatred she herself has lighted a fierce passion burns. This is a paragraph from her May 1, 1951, speech:

"My dear shirtless ones: on this consecrated day for Argentine workingmen, on this marvelous May first when the workers celebrate the triumph of the people and of Perón against the eternal enemies and traitors to the nation, I come to address you, solely, absolutely, exclusively in the name of the shirtless."

Evita's words have the ring of the phrase Rosas's supporters invariably used when referring to their adversaries: "Death to the foul, savage, traitorous *unitarios!*" With feverish activity she keeps her own and her husband's fury constantly whipped up. Anything or anyone who opposes her must be crushed. Whoever is not with her is an *anti-peronista;* anyone who does not inform on a lukewarm colleague so that appropriate measures may be taken is also an *anti-peronista.* At a meeting (March 18, 1950) organized by the telephone employees, Evita said:

"The division of the country's rewards must be carefully scrutinized so that those who are insensible to the hour of Argentina, so that those who sell out their country or are indifferent to the exceptional moment in which we are living . . . must step aside to make room for right-thinking Argentines. I call upon the workers to point out the *anti-peronistas* because they are traitors to their country, and I call upon management to take steps against them, for if they do not, we will think that they, too, are traitors to their country."

Not a leaf or branch on the whole tree but shall quake with fear.

In the month of August 1951 attention everywhere was fixed on the Argentine elections. Once more biographical sketches of Evita appeared in newspapers and magazines all over the world. The ruling couple had set their gigantic publicity machine in motion to keep their names before the public. In Buenos Aires, in the stadium of Luna Park, a children's party was organized in honor of Evita. She was there to greet the children in person and to give them presents, a doll to the girls, a bicycle to the boys. As might have been expected, a horde of children like that which followed the Pied Piper converged on Luna Park to cheer the lady Santa Claus. In this youthful mob, children were trampled to death, suffocated. Evita's Christmas greeting to her faithful is a cake and a bottle of cider. The mails are clogged with these bulky Christmas cards. Could the Argentine nation withstand such temptation?

During the early weeks of the campaign there was a power shortage in Buenos Aires caused by lack of oil. The oil came from Iran, and the English were waiting for shipments of Argentine meat to be paid for with fuel oil. The Peróns had cut the shipments of meat to have food on hand for the two million Argentines who would be arriving to beg them to run. Everything was settled: Perón would be asked to accept the presidency, Evita the vice-presidency. Trains, busses, boats would give free transportation to the *viveros* (the name given to those who shout "*Viva Perón*," which constitutes a fairly lucrative profession). They would be given their meals in Buenos Aires. The theaters and the movies were reserved for them. Never had such a holiday been seen in Argentina. And this would be the final proof of the efficiency of the Perón method of learning the will of the people.

But the two million *viveros* who were expected failed to show up. Not even one million appeared. Figures vary as to the number; some say 250,000, some, 150,000. 250,000 people make up an impressive group, but compared with what had been expected, this was a mere handful. An icy finger seemed to have reached out to stop the wheel of fortune at an ominous point. Evita had addressed the people earlier to inform them that anyone who failed to support her was a rogue and an ingrate.

"I am taking this occasion to pray God to give light to those who lack sight to see Perón and understand him, so the coming generations will not point an accusing finger at them if they should learn that there were Argentines who were such ingrates that, in combination with foreign interests, they opposed a man like General Perón, who has sacrificed his life to open the way for the grandeur and happiness of his country. . . . I have never been in any way affected by lies and slander when they were directed against the person of this frail Argentine woman. On the contrary, I was very happy, my General, for I wanted them to spend their fury against my breast, which should be a shield to keep them from reaching you. But I have never been fooled. When I am attacked, my General, it is not I who am the target, but you. Those who do this are such traitors, such cowards, that they cannot bring themselves to say they do not want Perón. It is not Eva Perón they are attacking: it is Perón."

But it was no good. What happened after this took place behind closed doors. All that is known is that "Comrade Espejo," Secretary of the General Confederation of Labor, played his part without muffing a line: "You, *señora*," he said in his speech, ". . . you, comrade Evita . . . you have been and are our guide . . . you, who in the program of justicialism are a symbol and for the workers the leader and standard-bearer, should accept this new sacrifice . . ." Evita, on the balcony, in a choking voice, began: "My dear shirtless ones . . . do not force me to do a thing I have never wanted to do. . . . I implore you, give me at least four days to think it over . . ." "No! No!" shouted the *viveros*. "Right now!"

What had gone wrong? Why this hesitation, this semi-refusal? The newspaper of the city workers and employees, in reporting the rally, said:

"EVA PERÓN ACCEPTS. At the affectionate urging of those closest to her: 'Come on, *señora*, you can do it,' Eva Perón was unable to hold out against the love of the people. And so, when she said in a voice trembling with emotion that 'she would bow to the people's will,' the crowd gave free rein to its delight. Cheers rang out from every corner of the huge gathering. . . . The *peronista* ticket, in the form the people wanted it, had been set up . . ."

The Peróns withdrew to the presidential residence to size up the situation. After due deliberation, it was conceded that Eva would have to be scratched. It was a victory for the military. The superhuman moral and physical effort that Evita had made had ended in this.

"Eva is like a well-wrought figurine of stainless steel—smooth, hard, cold and beautiful," the North American journalist John Lear had written while all this was going on. Soon after this Eva Perón was no longer seen on the balcony. She had been taken to a hospital. Temporarily at least, the human machine had cracked up.

IV

THE EGO WITH TWO HEADS: DEXTER

Barbarians, you cannot slit the throat of an idea!
SARMIENTO

ON CHRISTMAS EVE 1950 Argentines gathered around their radios to hear Evita Perón's holiday greetings to the nation. This, in part, is the message that came to them:

"I raise my voice, humble as it is, united in purpose with him who loves you as no one else loves you because no one has given himself heart and soul to his people as he has: General Perón. My words are directed to the heart of every one of you, and on this night of hope I offer you my very life, if by so doing I can dry a single tear. I raise my voice to pour forth all my love upon the workers of the land, of whom I am and always shall be one, because they were the suffering and the downtrodden until God gave us Perón. I leave you with my love and my faith in Argentina and you. My joy tonight is your joy, as the sorrow you have suffered is also mine."

In Luján, the shrine of Argentina, where the cathedral commemorates the appearance of the Virgin most venerated in the lands of the Plate River, the crowds chanted: "Perón, King, Lord." The people speak of "Saint Perón," and Perón graciously accepts this popular canonization.

The identification of dictators with the deity is nothing new in the Latin countries. The Spanish peseta—once silver, now copper—bears the bust of Franco, ringed by an inscription that reads: "Francisco Franco, caudillo of Spain by the grace of God." Among the treasures displayed in the Cathedral of Toledo are two swords: one belonged to Ferdinand III,

47

known as the Saint, who in the thirteenth century brilliantly wrested much of Spain from the Moorish invaders and laid the bases of Castile's subsequent grandeur; the other is General Franco's. The battle-cry "God and Trujillo" has become famous in the Dominican Republic. In Colombia, following the elections that brought Laureano Gómez to the presidency on the crest of a blood-bath engineered by the dictatorship of Ospina Pérez, the retiring president greeted his successor with these words: "Before closing, I must offer thanksgiving to the divine providence that so plainly maintains a vigil over the destiny of our country."

Evita is a unique figure, but Juan Domingo Perón belongs among the rank and file of the dictators who have ruled the murky political fortunes of Latin Amercia. In Argentina itself Juan Manuel de Rosas ruled the provinces of the Plate River with a hand of iron for twenty-three years (1829–52). His simple formula of government was reflected in the slogans he utilized with an insistence and efficiency foreshadowing the modern propaganda machines: "Death to the savage *unitarios*" (the opposition party) and "Long live the Holy Federation" (his own party). It is not just coincidence that Perón's rise to power was preceded by the emergence of a school of Argentine political apologists for the acts of Rosas's government who painted him as a national hero. This meant a complete reversal of the nineteenth-century concept that saw in Rosas an example of the crassest tyranny. Perón takes his place in the gallery of those dictators of the past whose sorry distinction is the macabre role they played in the annals of Latin America's history—Dr. José Francia in Paraguay, Juan Vicente Gómez in Venezuela, Gabriel García Moreno in Ecuador, Rafael Carrera in Guatemala, and Porfirio Díaz in Mexico. His contemporary colleagues are Trujillo of the Dominican Republic and Laureano Gómez of Colombia, whose unbridled power puts them on an equal footing with Perón.

Perón and Evita followed different roads to power. His entrance into politics was the end product of a long and laborious military career. Step by step he arrived at the totalitarian convictions that reflect the ambiance in which he lived. Perón was born in the small village of Los Lobos in the province of Buenos Aires, where his father worked as a field hand. It is said that his grandfather owned a small drugstore in Buenos Aires, and was known in the neighborhood as "the doctor." The family may have been of Italian or French origin, and the story goes that Perón's great-grandfather was a Sardinian senator.

While Perón was still a child, his father pulled up stakes and moved to Patagonia, that sparsely inhabited southernmost province of Argentina, at the tip-end of the continent. This is a bleak, cold, wind-swept region where only a man of purpose and endurance would venture in search of a new start. The Peróns worked on the lands of Ivan Techudi, a Polish immigrant, and the children attended the country school. The family had been in Patagonia only a short time when the mother left her husband and children. She was next heard of on a farm in Sierra Cuadrada, in the neighborhood of the Commodore Rivadavia oil-fields, where she is said to have married a Chilean. In 1905 the family moved to Buenos Aires, where Perón finished his elementary and high-school studies and (1911) entered the Military Academy. In 1913 he was commissioned a second lieutenant in the infantry. His early advancements were in no way spectacular: in 1913 he became a first lieutenant, in 1924 a captain. In 1928 he married Aurelia Tizón, a schoolteacher, the daughter of a Spanish immigrant. She died in 1938, and Perón has always showed great reverence for her memory.

The military school in which Perón received his training has always retained a great admiration for Prussian organization. This is true of nearly all South America, where the guiding hand in modern military organization has been provided by German missions or officers educated in Germany. Hitler's rise was greeted as the dawn of a new political era for them by the majority of the Latin American military. They believed that Hitler's triumph, which they never doubted, would be emulated in America, and that their own political power would thus be assured.

In 1929 Perón was assigned to the headquarters of the General Staff, and in 1930, when the Conservative General José Francisco Uriburu led an insurrection against the legal president, Hipólito Irigoyen, Perón headed the troops that entered the capital and deposed Irigoyen of the Radical Party. From that time Perón's rise was rapid. First he was appointed private secretary to the minister of war; a short time later he became professor of military history at the War College; finally, he was named military attaché to the Argentine embassy in Chile.

A man of parts, an interesting talker, a good dancer, hardworking and sober, Perón won friends and admirers. It is said that Arturo Alessandri, then president of Chile, pointed out the fact that he was of *caudillo* timber. Perón was advanced to the rank of lieutenant-colonel while in Chile. Shortly thereafter, he was recalled from Santiago for reasons that have never come fully to light. In 1938 he was sent to Italy as military observer. There he first came into direct contact with the Fascist military organization. He was attached to the Tridentine Alpine Commission in the Tyrol, and this was followed by a tour with the infantry division of the Montagna Pinerole in the Abruzzi. After Italy, Perón visited Hitler's Germany, France, and finally Spain, still bleeding from the Civil War. Perón's widely circulated observation at the dawn of the new era in Argentina stems in great measure from those days of observation: "Mussolini was the greatest man of our times, but he made some disastrous mistakes. I, who have the benefit of his experience, shall follow in his steps while avoiding his pitfalls."

Perón returned to Argentina at a time when the political

structure of the country was on the verge of collapse as the result of a variety of circumstances. In 1940 President Roberto M. Ortiz's impending blindness forced him to turn over the government to the vice-president, Ramón S. Castillo, a Conservative characterized by his mediocrity and one deep-rooted conviction: that the Axis was going to win. When the foreign minister of Colombia made an official visit to Buenos Aires to attend the dedication of a statue of the Colombian national hero Francisco de Paula Santander, Castillo took him aside during the protocol visit and said: "Let us make no mistake about the outcome of the present war; the victory of Germany is assured, and it would be folly for us to be found in the other camp."

The German Embassy in Buenos Aires had been converted into a formidable arm of Nazi propaganda. It was the center of an active network extended throughout the continent. An investigation carried out by the Argentine congress brought to light the scope of its efforts. The Nazis had worked out for Latin America an elaborate master plan that became known at that time in rough outline and was later revealed in all its details.

Although the Nazi officials knew that they had the blind support of Castillo, his patent limitations were a constant source of exasperation to them. The Germans wanted to step up the timetable of their plan, and to have a freer hand for their operations. Perón seized on this situation and, wedding it to his personal interests, began to lay the foundations for a machine that might one day serve the ends of national totalitarianism. This had become his vision of a future Argentina. At that time Perón was in charge of troop training in Mendoza, a principal city of the interior, at the foot of the Andes, on the road to Chile. There his close friendship with General Edelmiro Farrell developed. Farrell was to play an important role in Perón's final triumph. It was also while in Mendoza that Perón founded the G.O.U. (Group of United Officers), a form of secret military lodge. The international ramifications of this group have given rise to much speculation, for it is possible that its principles have been highly influential among the military who have seized power in other Latin American countries.

The character and purpose of the G.O.U. are made clear in a secret manifesto that was distributed to its members in June 1943. It ran:

"Comrades: The war has clearly demonstrated that nations cannot defend themselves singly, and the result has been a system of alliances that mitigate but do not correct the danger. The era of the nation is gradually being replaced by the era of the continent. Yesterday the fiefdoms joined together to form nations; today the nations unite to form continental political unities. This is the aim of the war. Germany is undertaking the titanic effort of unifying the continent of Europe. On each continent the largest and best-prepared nation will rule the destiny of that continent in the new organization. In Europe that country is Germany. In North America the United States will be the monitor nation for the time being. But in South America there has not yet emerged one nation whose superiority is so manifest that its leadership can be accepted without discussion. There are only two nations qualified for that leadership: Argentina and Brazil. OUR MISSION IS TO BRING ABOUT OUR INDISPUTABLE PREDOMINANCE.

"The task is immense and the sacrifices are many. But nations are formed only through total sacrifice. The great leaders of our independence sacrificed their fortunes and their lives. In our own time, Germany has given life a heroic meaning. These will be our examples. The first step we must take to bring into being a great and powerful Argentina is to seize power. No civilian will ever grasp the true greatness of our ideal; therefore civilians must be eliminated from government and assigned to the only purpose for which they are qualified: work and obedience.

"Once we have acquired all internal power, our mission will be to be strong, stronger than all the rest of the countries combined. We must arm despite all internal or external difficulties. Hitler's struggle in peace and war will be our guiding star. The first step will be alliances. We already have Paraguay. Bolivia and Chile will be ours. Pressure can be brought to bear on Uruguay by the concerted weight of these four nations. Then it will be easy to bring Brazil into the fold because of its governmental structure and the large German element in that country. And with Brazil the continent is ours. Our leadership will have become a glorious fact without precedent, the achievement of the political genius and heroism of the Argentine Army.

"A mirage? Utopia? Consider the case of Germany. Defeated in war, in 1919 she was forced to sign the Treaty of Versailles, which placed her under the Allied yoke at the level of a secondary nation for at least fifty years. But in less than twenty years Germany staged a fantastic march to recovery and, still at peace, succeeded in annexing Austria and Czechoslovakia.

"When the war came, all Europe bowed before the will of Germany. But before the triumph came the sacrifices necessary for the realization of its great program. The steel hand of a dictator was needed to wring these sacrifices from the people. Our government will be an inflexible dictatorship, though at first it will make those outward concessions which are necessary to form alliances. We must win the people to us, but they must of necessity work, sacrifice, and obey. Only in this way will we be able to carry out the armament program that is indispensable to our conquest of the continent. As in Germany, we will use the radio and the schools to inculcate in the people the spirit that will impel them along the heroic road they must travel. Only in this way will they renounce the comfortable existence they now lead.

"Ours will be a generation sacrificed in the name of a higher ideal: the Argentine nation, which one day will shine with unmatched brilliance to the greater good of the continent and all mankind. Long live our country! Be of stout heart!"

Perón's seizure of power was the culmination of a series of events that can best be summarized as follows: Vice-President Castillo's deplorable administrative conduct, combined with several governmental scandals that came to light at the time, created an atmosphere of public opinion which made it possible for the military to march on the presidential palace and force Castillo's resignation. In this march on Buenos Aires the man at the head of the troops was General Arturo Rawson. The Army, just as when it had overthrown the Irigoyen government, assumed both the right to pass judgment upon the civil power and the responsibility of overthrowing the constitutionally established president. The reaction among the people of Buenos Aires was indifference, even satisfaction. Castillo in their eyes represented a form of dictatorship. He had violated the constitution by replacing the *Consejo Deliberante*, the principal legislative body, with a group of handpicked dignitaries who shared his political views. His foreign policy had been clearly in sympathy with the German cause, which, though it coincided with the position of the military of Perón's stripe, was hateful to the Argentine people, almost solidly pro-Ally. But what the public failed to see at the time was that behind Rawson stood the firebrand element of the Army, led by Farrell and Perón. The day of the march on Buenos Aires, the above-quoted manifesto was in the hands of the Nazi-Fascist officer group. This manifesto was made public by a military tribunal in Santiago, Chile, in December 1948, when a military plot to overthrow the Chilean president was discovered. Among the evidence presented were communications between Chilean and Argentine officers.

Castillo was not the man to cope with the situation. After taking refuge on a naval vessel, he finally signed away the presidency. Rawson now took over the government. But his tenure was brief—three days. He had retained General Pedro Ramírez in the post of Minister of War he had held with the Castillo government. It turned out that General Ramírez felt that his right to head the government was stronger than Rawson's. He brought pressure to bear, with the result that Rawson resigned and Ramírez became president.

General Ramírez appointed General Edelmiro Farrell, Perón's friend, minister of war. From June 7, 1943, to February 24, 1944, Ramírez remained in power. At one o'clock that February morning, General Farrell, who by that time was vice-president as well as minister of war, and a group of ministers appeared at the president's house and persuaded Ramírez to resign. Ramírez issued this brief proclamation to the nation: "Worn out by the taxing responsibilities of office, I am forced to take a rest. I hereby delegate the powers of office which I hold to the person of His Excellency, the Vice-President of the nation, Brigadier General Edelmiro Farrell." That was that. Of the thirty Spanish words comprising the message, nine are General Farrell's titles. Fourteen days later, Ramírez formally resigned and Farrell assumed office with all the outward manifestations of legality. And who replaced Farrell as minister of war? Perón.

The familiar cycle was about to be repeated. Perón simply followed the pattern established by his predecessors in the war ministry.

Farrell governed from February 24, 1944, until June 4, 1946. Actually, his interregnum prepared the way for the full flowering of the Peronist form of totalitarianism.

To the best of its ability, Farrell's dictatorship transplanted Nazi principles and Nazi organization to Argentine soil. If there had been a free election in 1944 the Argentine people would have overwhelmingly voted Farrell out of office. In those days, at any rate, public opinion was violently opposed to any political form that did not offer essentially democratic guarantees. The people still responded to the familiar lines of the national anthem:

> *Hark, ye mortals, the sacred cry*
> *Liberty! Liberty! Liberty!*

But Farrell usurped the government under cover of darkness. The people awoke the next morning to find their government in the hands of the officer clique that had stealthily organized the coup. For the moment a crude form of Nazism was put into operation: Perón later developed this into a program more directly suited to the Argentine ambiance. Daniel Cosío Villegas, who made a careful survey of these events in his book *Extremos de América*, makes these pertinent observations:

"At least two American governments have publicly and repeatedly denounced General Farrell's regime as Nazi: the United States and Mexico. When a Jewish newspaper was suppressed in Buenos Aires, President Roosevelt . . . pointedly declared that such an act branded a regime as unmistakably Fascist. And in Havana the Mexican foreign minister told Flora Lewis, a newspaperwoman, that he considered the Argentine government Fascist . . . and, as such, a threat to the continent and his own country. . ."

Farrell continued the state of emergency declared by his predecessors. Political parties were denied legal existence. The freedom of the press was subject to the government's discretion; the universities, were subject to governmental intervention. Behind the program was Perón's idea of restraining the free exercise of public opinion until the day when it became controlled public opinion. The establishment of a modern military system, coupled with the calculated use of violence and terror, was counted on to hasten the day when no one would dare oppose the will of the dictator. The masses were to be cultivated in order that the actions of the government should appear to respond to the public weal. This façade of mass acclamation would hide from the world the machinations of the officer in the presidency. If this seems surprising to anyone, the record shows that the same thing took place in Germany at a time when Germany was one of the most cultured countries in Europe.

Perón was the strong man in Farrell's dictatorship. He was Vice-President, Minister of War, and Secretary of Labor and Public Welfare. Politics, the army, and propaganda aimed at the workers were under his direct control. This last item is the most interesting because it represented a new departure in the history of Argentine dictatorship. Perón saw the opportunity for cultivating the workers by introducing a modern system of labor legislation and social benefits. But, striking deeper, he recognized the error his predecessors had committed in keeping aloof from the masses. If one is to make a political instrument of the masses, he reasoned, one must not only favor, but also flatter, them.

In less than one year Perón passed twenty-nine new labor laws and took part in 319 labor disputes and 174 settlements. This gives the measure of his activity. According to one of his panegyrists his name became a household word to 2,852,000 workers. He fixed wage rates at from 11 to 18 per cent above their previous levels. As these wage increases ran their course through an economy whose productivity remained static, prices were driven up, consuming the individual worker's purchasing power; real wages actually declined in the face of a rising cost of living. But among the workers the stratagem's initial effect was all that counted. They fell for the mumbo-jumbo telling them that all that had been done was for the people and by the people, that the inflation was the product of the obstructionism of the entrenched capitalistic interests. As Perón himself has said, the easiest thing in the world is to mobilize the masses against the "oligarchy"—that is to say, all those identified with the higher levels in industry, husbandry, commerce, the press, and the universities. In reality the forces unleashed by Perón were more closely allied to those utilized by Communism than those employed by the Fascists or Nazis. And as he encouraged them, he organized and educated them in a school of violence which was to play an important role in his ultimate conquests.

The leaders of Argentina's opposition forces apparently were blind to what Perón was doing. Their reaction was to lash out against the dictatorship, the state of emergency, and the humiliations inflicted on the universities—in a word, they adopted a purely defensive posture. Their attacks were launched in the name of such constitutional principles as freedom of the press, freedom of speech, the right to assemble, and the right of the individual to inform himself and make legitimate criticism of the government. They demanded only one thing: the resignation and imprisonment of Perón. Perón resigned and was ordered confined on the island of Martín García, but he did not leave the ministry with his tail between his legs. He made his exit through the front door, and before he left he strode to the balcony and spoke to the people—his people—jamming the plaza, the followers he had summoned to receive his instructions. And like a time-bomb—to borrow a phrase from one of Perón's biographers—Perón's now famous order for a Christmas bonus was a message of hope and a promise of return to his cheering supporters. Perón's imprisonment, as it turned out, was nothing more than the discreet absentation of the bridegroom on his wedding eve. Within the week Perón had returned to the capital in triumph. The "shirtless ones," spurred to frenzy by Evita Duarte, whose role of Juliet's nurse in this political courtship has been outlined in the previous chapter, seethed in the streets surrounding the Casa Rosada (Argentina's White House) and roared for their leader. Perón finally came to the presidential balcony—his balcony—and amidst a delirious ovation from the crowd received a warm embrace from President Farrell.

Two months before the presidential election of 1946, the

government recognized the legality of the political parties, and authorized them to organize their campaigns. Very generous, but a pure sham. The Perón machine was a high-powered instrument. It had the benefit of two years of official existence in power during the period in which all semblance of normal order had been disrupted. Despite the fact that official restrictions were lifted, all efforts to effect a free campaign were thwarted by Perón's unofficial tactics of intimidation and the employment of goon squads whose activities somehow escaped official notice.

One of the episodes most clarioned in the annals of Peronism was the march against the University of La Plata, the Cambridge of Argentina, located in a city only a short distance from Buenos Aires. Driven to exasperation by the dictatorship, the students barricaded themselves in the university buildings, and staged a sit-down strike. They were besieged for three days by mobs imported from the capital. "Shoes, yes! Books, no!" The mob shouted the slogans according to instructions. "Long live Perón. Forge the nation. Kill the students!" Resistance finally became impossible. The police took the buildings by storm, and several hundred boys and girls were forced to run a gauntlet of blows, insults, kicks, and canings by the infuriated *peronistas*. Nearly all were injured, some seriously.

The publication by the United States government of the Blue Book on Argentina only gave Perón another stick with which to belabor his opponents. The Blue Book was based on Ambassador Spruille Braden's report denouncing the hook-up between the Argentine government and the Nazis during the war. Nobody doubted that the wartime governments of the Argentine had favored the Axis cause, and no one ignored the fact that Perón's government was conceived along the totalitarian lines of Germany and Italy. But that an ambassador of the United States should be the one to point the accusing finger was, in the eyes of the Argentines, tantamount to interference on the part of the United States in the internal affairs of Argentina. This was obvious grist for Perón's propaganda mills. Argentina's national pride is a most sensitive thing, particularly where the United States is involved, for there is a strong sentiment of hostility toward "Yankee imperialism."

Perón saw his advantage immediately. "Perón or Braden" became the new slogan. The campaign ostensibly boiled down to these alternatives. Given this fine last-minute weapon, with the violence that had marked the early phases of the campaign and with the masses aroused to fever pitch by the demagogic harangues of Evita and Perón, the outcome of the election could not have been other than it was. On October 24, 1946, the official results were released: Perón—1,478,372 votes; Tamborini, the Radical candidate, 1,211,660.

Perón had to formulate a political philosophy—Justicialism—and give a name to his party. The idea of calling it the Labor Party was weighed, but was discarded because of the comparisons it suggested with the English party of the same name. The possibility of adding some qualifying adjective to the term "Radical" was also considered. At first Perón seemed the heir to the tenets of "Irigoyenism," which typified what might be called a wand-waving Radicalism. But finally the only possible formula was hit upon: "Peronism." The chorus of the *peronista* anthem, with which the workers open their meetings, runs like this (and the verses are in keeping with it):

> *Perón! Perón! Qué grande sós!*
> *Mi general, cuánto váles!*
> *Perón! Perón! Gran conductor,*
> *Sós el primer trabajador!*[1]

[1] Perón! Perón! how great you are!
My General, you are priceless!
Perón! Perón! Great leader,
You are worker Number 1.

In November 1951 the party machine was running in high gear. Everything was set for Perón's re-election. He would be the first president of Argentina to be honored by two successive terms in office. To this end the constitution had been amended. He could count on everything—except the backing of the country. In spite of the fact that Evita had been taken off the ticket, the military revolted. Perón managed to put down the rebellion, but many shifts in the General Staff and even in the lower echelons followed. General Arturo Rawson, former President, went to jail. The leaders of the Radical party divided their time between their political activities and jail. The Socialists suffered the same fate, and finally withdrew from the contest. The Communist candidate, Rodolfo Ghioldi, was shot in the back at a meeting in Rosario. Perón dragged out the "Braden or Perón" slogan, which he had used so effectively in his first campaign to arouse nationalist feelings. Nothing in the 1951 election could not have been forecast except the fact that the Radical candidate, Ricardo Balbín, polled over two million votes. The Radicals were not allowed even to have a printing establishment in Buenos Aires, not to mention a newspaper or radio time. There were towns that did not even know Balbín was a candidate. The only sound the air waves of Argentina carried, from the Bolivian frontier to the tip of Patagonia, was the chorus of the new anthem: "Perón, Perón, how great you are!"

V

PERON'S JUSTICIALISM IS FASCISM

I have been following closely and with increasing concern the development of the Argentine situation in recent months. This situation presents the extraordinary paradox of the growth of Nazi-Fascist influence and the increasing application of Nazi-Fascist methods in a country of this hemisphere at the very time that those forces of oppression and aggression are drawing ever closer to the hour of final defeat and judgment in Europe and elsewhere in the world. The paradox is accentuated by the fact, of which we all are quite aware, that the vast majority of the people of Argentina have remained steadfast in their faith in their own, free democratic traditions and in their support of the nations and peoples who have been making such great sacrifices in the fight against the Nazis and the Fascists.

FRANKLIN DELANO ROOSEVELT

PERONISM poses an immediate question to all who come to examine it: is this a new Fascism? The question is ticklish because it is threaded through with analogies to earlier Fascistic regimes which tend to distract from the real make-up of Perón's new Argentine state.

The New York Times in the spring of 1951 published a series of articles on Argentina by one of its editorial writers, former correspondent Herbert Matthews, in which he drew up a list of parallels between the government of Perón and the government of Mussolini. First Matthews points out the most obvious similarities: the march on Buenos Aires, the theatrical appearances on the balcony of the Casa Rosada, the anthem of the Youth Movement, *Muchachos Peronistas*, a Creole version of *Giovinezza*, and the use of the title *líder*, corresponding to *duce*. Matthews further establishes certain fundamental political parallels: the formulation of the Charter of Workers' Rights, which immediately brings to mind the *Carta del Lavoro;* the program of economic autonomy, a counterpart of Mussolini's autarchy; and the slogan "Neither Moscow nor Wall Street," which Mussolini might have been proud to have originated. Rounding out his argument, Matthews cites the control of the labor syndicates by the government, the conversion of the judiciary into a political weapon by the elimination of all non-Peronist judges, the manner in which the law has become an instrument of dictatorship, and the reign of terror, all typical of Italian Fascism.

To the above might be added Perón's indoctrination in Fascist Italy, and the presence within the inner circle of Peronism of two notorious Italian Fascists. Carlos Gregorio, the Italian labor leader, charged in July 1951 that Perón's social policies were in the hands of Vittorio Mussolini, the eldest son of the Duce, who has been living in Buenos Aires since May 1947, and Pietro Parini, former prefect of Milan and director of foreign Fascist clubs during Mussolini's regime. In Buenos Aires people at first called the *peronistas* the *peronazistas*.

In addition, there is Perón's own statement: "We will create a Fascism purged of the errors of Mussolini." This is precisely what is being attempted in Spain, where a school of Fascist thought has grown up the efforts of which are directed toward discovering the weaknesses that undermined Mussolini in order to avoid them in the successful regeneration of Fascism in Spain. It is startling to note the similarities between the manner in which Perón is developing his system in Argentina and the system as outlined in a recent study on Fascism published in *Claustro*, the Falangist university organ of Spain. According to this study, Fascism's great mistake lay in identifying itself with the industrial, mercantile, financial, and landowning interests "because Fascism", it states, "which did so many wonderful things failed to bring about the revolution."

But despite all these similarities, Peronism is not a carbon copy of European Fascism. Perón's system reveals distinctly native strains. It is a blend of Rosas and Mussolini, but something new has been added, its own original touches. It has its own label—Justicialism. Justicialism is Perón's own invention. It reflects the new state of world affairs, as is evidenced by its adoption of the so-called "third position," which Perón believes will eventually command the following of a majority of the world's peoples.

As Perón has said: "When I consider that we have been the first to proclaim this solution to mankind, and see, as I look about me, that we have been the first to bring it to realization, it can only confirm my faith in the high purpose to which God has seen fit to call our country; and my soul trembles with emotion at the thought that the day cannot be far distant when humanity, searching for a guiding star in the troubled night, will have to turn its gaze toward Argentina. We believe that here in our native Argentina, so profoundly Christian and so profoundly humanistic, we are working for a world ennobled by the practice of human virtues, where hate has been transformed into love, selfishness has been replaced by generosity, and vengeance has been converted into forgiveness . . ." [1]

The above words have been translated into all the languages of the world and distributed with the zeal that characterizes the propaganda ministry of a dictatorship. But there are simpler, more direct, less high-flown texts designed for internal consumption, and it is these which instruct the faithful. The

[1] *La Tercera Posición en la Prédica y el Ejemplo de Juan Perón* (Publicaciones de la Secretaría de Informaciones y de la Presidencia de la Nación, Buenos Aires).

question is, what is Justicialism in Argentina's own back yard? What manner of existence, this never-before-witnessed practice of the purest human virtues, based on love, generosity, and forgiveness? For the answer to this we must examine the facts of life in Argentina today.

On October 17, 1950, the anniversary of the March of the Shirtless on Buenos Aires, Perón stepped to the balcony of the Casa Rosada and harangued a multitude gathered for the celebration in the Plaza de Mayo. In closing his address he set forth the "Twenty Fundamental Truths of Justicialism," which run as follows:

1. True democracy is that in which the government carries out the mandate of the people and defends only one interest: the people's.

2. Peronism is essentially democratic. All political parties are anti-democratic, and therefore not Peronist.

3. Peronism works for the movement. He who serves a clique or caudillo in the name of Peronism is a Peronist in name only.

4. Peronism recognizes only one class of men: those who work.

5. In the New Argentina, work is a right because it brings with it the dignity of man, and a duty because it is just that a man produce at least as much as he consumes.

6. There can be nothing better for one Peronist than another Peronist.

7. No Peronist should feel himself more than he is or less than he should be. When a Peronist begins to feel himself more than he is, he is on the way to becoming an oligarch.

8. A Peronist's scale of political values is the following: first, the homeland; second, the movement; third, mankind.

9. Politics for Peronism is not an end, but the means of achieving the good of our country, which is the happiness of its sons and the national glory.

10. Peronism's two arms are social justice and social welfare. With them we shall give the people an embrace warm with justice and love.
11. Peronism seeks national unity, not division. It asks for heroes, not martyrs.
12. The only privileged members of the new Argentine state shall be the children.
13. A government without a doctrine is a body without a soul. Therefore Peronism has its own political, economic, and social doctrine: Justicialism.
14. Justicialism is a new philosophy of life, simple, practical, profoundly Christian, and profoundly humanistic, designed for all.
15. As a political doctrine, Justicialism establishes a balance between law and society.
16. As an economic doctrine, Justicialism upholds the development of a social economy, putting capital at the service of the economy, and economy at the service of the general well-being of society.
17. As a social doctrine, Justicialism brings about that social justice which assures to each his rights as a social being.
18. Our objective is an Argentina that is socially just, economically free, and politically independent.
19. We constitute a central government, an organized nation, and a free people.
20. In this world the best thing we have is our people.

Nothing could be clearer. This is the scale of values: first the nation; second the movement—that is to say, Peronism—lastly the individual. The nation and Peronism are one and indivisible: he who is not a Peronist—in the words of Evita—is a traitor. What motivates Peronism? The movement is its own justification. Everything that is not Peronist is thereby antisocial and should be uprooted and cast into the fire. There can be nothing better for one Peronist than another Peronist, or perhaps this might be paraphrased to say: to make two Peronists grow where only one grew before.

Essentially Peronism is a magic formula. Evita has always stated it with the greatest clarity, and today it has permeated all Argentine society. Institutions are the shabby invention of democracy, goes the formula; the only trustworthy force is the *líder*. For the future historian of the Argentine dictatorship Evita's speeches will be more illuminating documents than Perón's. Evita speaks with the inner voice of the movement; she scorns restraint, and the torrent of words she pours forth in her speeches wells from the depths of her soul, carrying all her hates and loves and resentments, everything that beats at the heart of the movement.

The average Argentine, shut off from the outside world, is traveling a frightening road of insecurity with only one signpost to guide him: Perón, Evita. These magic words are the open sesame to all doors—business, unions, government, journalism, the arts. This is Justicialism in action. The two rulers form a twin deity in the magical sense of those primitive societies which see themselves bound within a universe ruled by personal but irresponsible, rather than mechanistic, forces. The National Cultural Commission, for example, has adopted this magical interpretation of the New Argentine State and offered burnt sacrifice in the shape of two new prizes—the "Juan Perón" and the "Evita Perón" prizes for 1951 for two unpublished dramatic works informed with the spirit of Justicialism. This high opportunity to contribute to the glory of Argentine letters is garnished with a consideration of 30,000 pesos for each of the winners.

Reading between the lines of the "Twenty Truths," one discovers what is obvious from Perón's every action—a complete disregard for the sonorous constitution he himself drew up in 1949. This constitution begins: "The Argentine nation adopts as its own the representative, republican, federal form of government." But Article 19 of the "Twenty Truths" states: "We constitute a central government . . ." This latter is the truth. It has been Perón's one political concept; it is the essence of the dictatorship and the purpose that has guided Perón's every action.

For the Peróns, the history of Argentina pursued a hazy, chaotic, treacherous course until it reached one luminous point: October 17, 1945, the day Perón came to power. Evita expresses this thought in words that may be the echo of passionate scenes in tawdry romantic novels, or sincere, or the heady result of a moment of political intoxication: "We are in agreement, my General, that the real triumph is that of the nation and the workers; we agree that the workers, the humble, always stood with head high and embraced the just cause, and for that reason we embraced Perón's cause. We therefore give thanks to God for having bestowed upon us the privilege of possessing Perón, of knowing Perón, of understanding, cherishing, and following Perón."

Peronism's "third position" consists in sitting out the struggle between Communist Russia and capitalist United States, without being drawn into the conflict. Before his people Perón styles himself the umpire, judging and censuring the antagonists as he sees fit, until the day when he shall father forth the new era. "We will," he says, "arouse an interest in the world in our republic and its accomplishments, and make them known through the initiation of a new era in which our concerns and desires will no longer be ignored. At last we shall cease to be the anvil and become the hammer." But he emphasizes that to put this program into effect the Argentine people must place discipline and unity before all else.

It is Perón, moreover, who approves, rejects, and classifies the opposition parties. He accepts the idea of a controlled opposition. "Without an opposition there can be no democracy; but it is equally true that the opposition has responsibilities and duties that parallel those of the government;

therefore, when the opposition is neither responsible, enlightened, disinterested, self-controlled, objective, nor impersonal, but instead defeatist, sterile, negative, insolent, and obstinate, not only can there no longer be democracy, there cannot be even a semblance of civilized life."

The labor syndicates are helpless unless they support the Peronist organization. If the syndicate is considered Peronist, it will have more than it asks. If not, it will be starved out. "To him who hath shall be given . . ." Everything is controlled in an absolute fashion by the dictator.

Perón's favorite topic when addressing the workers is the struggle against capitalism. This is how he explained worldwide capitalist organization to the Transit Workers' Syndicate in July 1951:

"There are times when you step on a toe here and someone says 'Ouch' in London. Take the case of *La Prensa*, for example. We stepped on Gainza Paz, and a hue and cry went up all over the world. This proves that they are organized and stand up for one another. Workers mistakenly believe that they have international organizations. Those organizations have been undermined by the capitalists who have bought their leaders."

These premises established, Perón went on to tell the workers how they would never gain world dominance until they created "an organization superior to capitalism, which destroys, divides, poisons, and defiles everything it touches. It is apparent that workers everywhere are helpless before the prepotency and power of international capitalism."

Who is to organize this Workers' International called for by Perón? Perón. The New Argentine State should take the lead. The threat Perón sees in Communism is its possible infiltration into the ranks of the syndicates, perhaps wresting leadership from him, or at any rate weakening his influence.

Perón's ambitions to form an international Peronist labor organization go beyond his speeches and have been implemented by several tactical moves. He has created the post of labor attaché in Argentine embassies for the purpose of establishing contacts with labor organizations in other countries. He has organized a school for labor leaders in Buenos Aires, with international fellowships for study abroad. Labor leaders in other Latin American countries have been invited to go to Argentina to observe the model organization at work.

Nicolás Repetto, the Argentine Socialist leader, in a speech in February 1951, charged that there were only three countries in the world that provided no legal guarantee to strike—Russia, Spain, and Argentina. And, indeed, a careful reading of the new Argentine constitution, in which workers' rights are so minutely enumerated, reveals no guarantee of the right to strike. On the other hand, the secretary of the Argentine General Confederation of Labor, Peronism's Labor spokesman, declared at an international labor conference in Switzerland that "the liberty and right of free assembly are respected in my country, in full, positive and honorable fashion."

What is the significance of this contradiction? Perón explains the relations between the General Confederation of Labor and the government in words of hearty goodfellowship: "When the Confederation decides it wants such and such a thing done, it comes to me—the president of the republic—tells me about it, and I do it. And vice versa, when I want the Confederation to do something, I bring the comrades together and say to them: 'Look here, boys, it seems to me we should do it this way,' and they do it. This understanding is the product of our political and social system. I have already said on many occasions that in the normal course of national life and Argentine syndicalism, the Justicialist regime should operate with an absolute understanding and complete friendship, because, as I see it, Justicialism without the support of the Argentine working class cannot get very far, nor can Argentine syndicalism hope to attain its ends without the help of Justicialism . . ."

The manner in which this portion of the doctrine is applied can be appraised in the confiscation of *La Prensa*. The news-vendors' union set off the chain of events with a "boycott" of the paper, and then prevented the typographical workers from entering the plant. The typographical workers, in turn, sought the protection of Perón in order to return to their jobs. In the name of the President, the Minister of the Interior answered in this manner: "The President has turned over to this office the note you addressed to him asking his direct intervention in order that the employees of the paper with which you are associated might return to their work, which has been interrupted by the outbreak of a strike. It is my duty to remind you that the difference between the owners and the union upon which the publication is dependent for the distribution of its papers is purely of a labor-management nature involving wages . . . What you are really asking is the intervention of the police to break the strike, as was done in the days before the revolution . . ."

The events that followed are common knowledge. They were climaxed by Perón's speech closing the convention of the General Confederation of Labor. He devoted his whole address to the *La Prensa* incident, but not once did he refer to it as a labor-management dispute. "*La Prensa*," he said, "was one of the bridgeheads of capitalism in Argentina. Those institutions are like a tape-worm that reproduces itself if the head is not killed . . ." And he closed by expressing to the Confederation of Labor his thanks for its generous support of the government in the *La Prensa* difficulty.

One of the laws of social reform passed by Perón when he was Secretary of Labor and Public Welfare empowers the government to grant or deny the status of union to a labor syndicate. The international labor group visiting the Argentine in 1947 discovered that the government could ignore the labor laws when syndicates without union status are involved. For them there need be no enforcement of reforms in wages, hours, and working conditions, vacations with pay, and pension plans. Before these benefits can be assured, a syndicate must submit completely to the Peronist party, and then such favors as gymnasiums, sport centers, and other varieties of manna begin to fall into its lap. A "Committee of Defense against Treason" acts as a watch dog over the labor leaders reluctant to knuckle under. Perón himself has declared from the balcony of the Casa Rosada before a gathering of syndicate leaders: "Damnation to him who simulates friendship to our face, but in the hour of decision stabs us in the back." Anyone with ears to hear can catch the threat such words carry under a dictatorship.

The taxi drivers in Buenos Aires went on strike in October 1946. As there can be no strike, this was a subversive movement. So the government organized a strike-breaking corps of 200 taxis. From that day on the drivers who took part in the strike were refused licenses to purchase new cars. In the sugar cane region of Tucumán there was a strike among the workers. The price of sugar had doubled, the cost of living had gone up, and the workers were still receiving the same wages as the previous year. It would appear they had every reason in the world for seeking a wage readjustment. But the government declared the strike illegal; the labor leaders of the movement in Tucumán were ousted and replaced by a commission from the Peronist labor confederation. On the heels of this the government issued a decree granting a wage increase, not of the 18 per cent originally asked, but of 60 per cent. It should also be remembered that the prominent labor leader, Carlos Antonio Aguirre, died late in 1949 while being questioned by the government authorities. He was not seen for several days after being taken into custody, and no official report of his whereabouts could be had despite intensive inquiry. His body turned up later in a ditch in the province of Santiago del Estero.

Perón has set in motion a party syndicalism rather than a

state syndicalism. There is no disputing the tremendous political power he personally controls thereby. And this power is on the increase as industry is nationalized and private ownership replaced by state ownership. The eminent Socialist writer and leader, Americo Ghioldi, has made this observation: "One of the social transformations that I would call attention to is the extraordinary increase in the number of employees and workers directly dependent on the state for their livelihood. There are no recent statistics on this particular subject, but in 1943 there were 150,000 such employees and workers, while two years ago [1947–8] there were 600,000. Without a doubt, the number of workers and employees in all the divisions of the state (national, provincial, municipal, and others) reaches a figure of 1,000,000. With their families this means that approximately 4,000,000 citizens, or nearly a quarter of our population, are dependent on the state payroll. This figure, though based on a minimum estimate, is impressive enough when one considers that all those whose names appear on the government books have given up their economic, political, and cultural independence, and must be, or pretend to be, Peronists. The state has blotted out the political freedom of one quarter of the Argentine population."

Shortly after the inauguartion of his regime, Perón staged a spectacular ceremony in the main salon of the Casa Rosada. The United States ambassador, members of the cabinet, photographers, newsmen, were on hand to witness the signing of the first major act under the great economic decree of the new government: the program for the nationalization of industries. The railroads, power companies, shipping and air lines would belong to Argentina. Those who had fought against Britain's imperialistic ownership of the railroads could now gloat to their heart's content. For the moment, the matter in hand dealt only with the nationalization of the telephone service, but as the beginning of a new era it warranted the gala celebration.

This was denounced in the press of many countries as a Fascist move. There was some justification for this view, considering Perón's political record. But with greater reflection and wisdom the English viewed the matter in this light: there is nothing new in what Perón is doing, nor is it properly speaking Fascistic; it is simply the outgrowth of the nationalistic temper existing in Argentina; what is taking place there is similar to the events in Turkey at the time of Mustapha Kemal. Latin America is in that stage between colonial and independent status during which nations expropriate and nationalize major foreign enterprises.

The English hit the nail on the head. Long before the nationalization of the telephone and transport systems and public utilities, which is Peronism's greatest boast, similar acts of economic independence had been carried out in many Latin American countries. The nationalization of oil in Mexico represented a far more daring, radical, and revolutionary move than anything that has taken place in Argentina. Colombia, Venezuela, and Ecuador broke the shipping monopoly of the Grace Line and the United Fruit Company by creating the Great Colombia Fleet, which today is one of the most flourishing maritime enterprises in America. In many instances what has taken place in Latin America has been nationalization of a very different nature from that fostered by Perón. More often it has been a case of placing certain essential services, such as urban transportation, electric power, and telephone and telegraph systems in the hands of cities or provinces. In some instances mixed companies have been set up in which local private capital was allowed the option of entering into the municipal or state enterprise.

A curious feature of nationalization in Argentina is that there has been general satisfaction on the part of owners with the settlements, while the most critical group has been the Argentine Socialists and Radicals who had been the advocates of nationalization all along. The need of surrounding the nationalizations with a spectacular aura led to rash settlements by the government. Argentines could not fail to make the contrast between Uruguay's acquisition of its railroads and the purchase made by Perón. It becomes immediately apparent that Uruguay came off far better in its transaction. The Radical congressman, Silvano Santander, made a devastating analysis on the floor of Congress of the purchase of the Dodero shipping line. Americo Ghioldi sees a death blow to one of his Socialist party's most cherished dreams in the manner in which Perón has carried out the nationalizations. "When the country is able to learn," he has said, "the real state of the economy and the technical breakdown in industry, the deterioration of service and equipment in the transportation system under the pressure of rising costs and the weight of the bureaucracy (which is all a product of the government's witless administration) . . . the idea of turning utilities and services over to the government will have been discredited in the minds of the majority of workers and citizens." [2]

The Peronist view of nationalization is naturally based on the fundamental principle of the dictatorship—absolute control by the party. Local or regional control of services and utilities does not fit in with Perón's scheme of things because his interest is in the central government, not in the cities. His point of view is Stalin's rather than Hitler's. It would not be in his best interests, it would in fact do him harm, to share what he considers primarily as a source of political power with any other entities. Control of the telephone and telegraph systems and the means of transportation; concentrations of workers and employees who are directly dependent on and under the supervision of the government—these are

[2] *Los Trabajadores, el Sr. Perón y el Partido Socialista* (Buenos Aires, 1950).

more than steps in the economic evolution of Argentina. They are buttresses for the support of Peronism in power.

A man's worth is measured in Argentina first by whether he is a Peronist, and second by the function he performs within the system. In philosophical terms this is how Perón explains the doctrine: "The problem of future democratic thought is how to foster the fullest social development without losing sight of the individual, concentrating on attaining spiritual elevation while maintaining as a goal the general welfare."

Descending to less abstruse terms more in keeping with his military education, Perón expressed this same notion to a group of Argentine writers on December 11, 1947. He was announcing the creation of a new sub-secretariat of culture, which it was hoped would stimulate Argentine writers to take a more active role in the affairs of the New Argentine state. His speech on that occasion contains two essential paragraphs, one material, the other pertaining to the spirit. The one on the material aspect he let fall in a designedly off-hand manner: "I see no obstacle to appropriating 400,000,000 pesos for cultural pursuits . . ." The spiritual observations are couched in these words:

"Let us move forward shoulder to shoulder like noble percherons drawing the same wagon, who now and then give each other a kick, but all pull in the same direction. Gentlemen, I don't even criticize the kick. We can't all be saints or stoics in this life. There are different ways of seeing the same problem. But the important thing is that we haul this wagon to its ultimate destination, because on our arrival depends our felicity, whatever our way of thinking. And that is what we should never forget, and what we must strive to bring about . . ."

The matter is actually far more serious than might appear from the above. Some horses definitely had to be scratched.

During the first months of the dictatorship, 385 professors were dismissed and 630 more resigned out of professional solidarity. The most distinguished men in Argentina's scientific and literary circles are now barred from the universities. Ricardo Rojas, author of the best biography of the Argentine national hero, San Martín, so exalted by the Peronists during his centennial in 1950—Don Ricardo, the venerable patriarch of Argentine letters, has been absent for the past five years from the Institute of Letters in Buenos Aires, of which he was the moving spirit for two decades. His case is that of hundreds of other distinguished Argentines.

The university reform law now in force in Argentina has deprived the universities of the autonomy they previously enjoyed and has placed them under the direct control of the government. A man like Bernard Houssay, Nobel Prize-winner in Medicine and Physiology, was put out of academic life at about the same time the university conferred the degree of doctor *honoris causa* on Evita. Professor Rosieri Frondizi has supplied the following data: "The dismissals ordered by the President's political secretariat . . . together with the 'voluntary' resignations, stripped the Argentine universities, in the brief period of three months, of 1,250 members of their teaching staffs. The University of Buenos Aires lost 148; Córdoba, 333; La Plata, 245; El Litoral, 433; Tucumán, 57; Cuyo, 37. This number represents 70% of the university personnel in Argentina. In certain faculties, such as the School of Medicine of the University of El Litoral, the list included nearly the entire teaching and research staff: 339 members were removed from their posts. The almost complete lack of professors made it impossible, in certain cases, to organize examination committees at the end of the scholastic year. Among those dismissed from their posts were the most distinguished figures in Argentine letters, science, and culture, many of whom had more than twenty years of service to their credit. And these measures were not limited to Argentines alone; foreigners with democratic leanings had to pay with the loss of their positions for the sin of having a conscience that would not be bribed."[3]

The fundamental quality of Peronism in action is that everything culminates in Perón. He is represented as the embodiment of the ideals of the republic and the living finality of Argentine history. National tradition is a torch that has been handed down from San Martín, the founder of the republic, to Perón, who has revived it. If San Martín were alive today, so the interpretation goes, he would set his stamp of approval on the dictator. In closing the celebrations of the San Martín centennial, Perón spoke these solemn words in Mendoza:

"We feel that if he [San Martín] had lived in our times, he would have fought side by side with us for economic liberty. And, in conclusion, we feel that if he had lived in our times he would have fought as we have to free our land of all foreign domination, in other words, for our sacred sovereignty before all the nations of the world. We feel, comrades, that if he had lived in our times he would have cast [Spruille] Braden out of our land, and branded as harshly as we have the Argentine traitors in his pay . . ."

[3] "The Universities under Perón," *Cuadernos Americanos*, Mexico, 1948.

VI

THE MILITARY VS. APRISMO
IN PERU

Questing student, cherish your hope.
HAYA DE LA TORRE

In October 1948 General Manuel A. Odría, Minister of the
Interior under President José Luis Bustamante, started insur-
rections of the garrisons throughout Peru, including that of
Arequipa, overthrew the president, and set up a military government. For two years Odría acted as provisional president.
Then in July 1950 he arranged for elections, as a result of which
he was "elected" president. Visitors in Lima today find the
city outwardly normal. Odría has restored the order and balance that the forty most influential families of Lima have
been aiming for under the most varied forms of dictatorship.
There is no apparent opposition. On exceptional occasions the
President rides about the city without special escort. The
Apra, the largest party in Peru, has been declared illegal; its
leader, Victor Raúl Haya de la Torre, has been a refugee in the
Colombian Embassy in Lima since 1949. General Odría's government has been demanding that he be turned over to it
for trial on criminal charges. The government of Colombia has
been asking that he be given a safe-conduct, considering him a
political refugee protected by the right of asylum. In any case,
isolated as he is in the Colombian Embassy, the leader of the
opposition party can neither talk nor address his nation. Congress has been re-opened, a hand-picked, pro-government congress. The preceding legislative body was dissolved, and the
representatives of the majority party were jailed. The lead-

79

ers of congress took refuge in the Cuban Embassy. For eight months the Cuban Embassy tried in vain to secure them a safe-conduct. One day the refugees, at their own risk, left the embassy and managed to flee to Cuba. General Odría handed the Cuban chargé d'affaires his passport and broke off relations with Cuba. Thus, a simple, efficient order has been achieved by a process of elimination.

The Lima press reflects Peru's state of well-being. The traveler is unaware of any censorship whatever. The old conservative newspapers, which have always collaborated more or less sincerely and profitably with the dictatorships, continue as usual, and nobody interferes with them. The opposition newspapers have been closed down and their equipment has been seized. As a matter of fact, there is freedom of the press: freedom for those who have been allowed to survive.

There is a surface prosperity, for business has been good. General Odría did not rise to power single-handed; he had the backing of big business. To defend its gold reserve, Peru set up controls of foreign exchange. The exporters had to turn over to the state bank the proceeds of their foreign trade, and the bank adjusted the distribution of foreign currency according to imports and the purchasing power of the country. When General Odría came to power he removed these controls, and the cotton, sugar, and rice barons were free to use their dollars as they pleased. They found themselves rolling in wealth. Inflation followed, and Lima is more luxurious than before. The purchasing power of the Peruvian sol declined. But this really affected only the middle class and the workers. Haya de la Torre's forecast that "the rich would become richer and the poor poorer" has come true. Small wage increases were granted as a sop to the poor. The rich benefited not only from the higher prices Peruvian products commanded on the international market, but also from internal inflation. The Peruvian production that has increased most has been that of cheap money. Naturally this is very pleasant for traders on the exchange and for North Americans stopping at the Hotel Bol-ívar in Lima. But the situation is very different in the outly-ing provinces.

Peru is really two Perus, two nations, two histories, two peoples. One is the Peru of the ruling class, which has gov-erned the country from Lima since colonial times. The other is the Peru of the hinterland, the great rural masses of popula-tion, the Indian descendants of the Incas, many of whom do not speak Spanish and seem more like fictional characters than persons of flesh and blood.

Lima has had a brilliant history. Pizarro, the conqueror of Peru, found greater wealth there than Cortés found in Mex-ico. During the country's days as a Spanish colony—it was one of the most important—titles of nobility were distributed by Spain with a lavish hand, and the recipients of this distinction were in a special category. The annals of the city are paved with the names of counts and marquesses. The rule of the Incas was replaced by a refined, hypocritical viceroyalty. Un-der the tolling of the bells of the many churches could be heard the purling of a most mundane society, with its tales of the carryings-on of *tapadas* (literally, veiled women) and *limeñas* (women of Lima) like La Perricholi, who stole a vice-roy's heart and became the heroine of legends such as that which inspired Thornton Wilder's *The Bridge of San Luis Rey*. The viceroys were succeeded by the aristocrats of the repub-lic, but the social structure did not change. Today eighty-five per cent of Peru's population is rural workers. It is they who cultivate the cotton, sugar, and rice crops. Of Peru's seven and one-half million inhabitants, only 380,000 are industrial work-ers, most of these in small workshops. Only 40,000 are em-ployed in factories. At the top of the pyramid are the forty families, the heirs of the Spanish Crown. The passage from col-ony to republic was in the nature of a symbolic ceremony to them, the transmission of power into their hands.

"Over one hundred years ago," writes Felipe Cosío del

Pomar, the distinguished Peruvian art critic, "the republic came into being headed by a marquis as president. When Bolívar with his rude Venezuelan plainsmen and Colombian soldiers conquered the city, he was received under a gold-embroidered canopy by the aristocracy, whose deep genuflections could not hide their hatred of the democratic liberator. The brocades hung out in his honor on the carved wooden balconies and the republican festivities had a scent of exorcism. Hardly any change came about in the character and décor of the city. The holders of university degrees replaced the scholastic theologians . . ."

Peru's official history is easily written. It lends itself to brilliant, witty, courtly literature. It is probably the only republic of Latin America where marshals exist, their uniforms dazzling affairs. Its orators are silver-tongued. But the other history, the history of the people, has neither dates nor heroes nor silken uniforms nor plumed hats. The rich have taken even the feathers from the heads of the Indians. The Indian has become a theme of painting and poetry, spinning his wool on primitive spindles and playing the sad music of his *quena*—the Incan flute—as he tends his flocks of moist-eyed llamas in the bleak highlands. The oligarchy of Lima feels no urge to change a static economy under which it lives very comfortably. The principles of a democratic, representative government would set in motion all this stagnated multitude and create difficult problems for the dominant minority. It has preferred dictatorship.

Only about thirty years ago the first stirrings of a revolutionary movement began in Peru. The people were told that they, too, could have a history and speak their mind. From the bosom of the old aristocracy came the first revolutionaries, who broke the silence of four hundred years. Manuel González Prada, who belonged to one of the best families, became a friend of the people. He proposed to raise the Indian from the poverty in which he had been kept, and to elevate him to the status of a human being. A poet, writer, and speaker rather than a man of action, González Prada opened the eyes of the university youth. He was a typical product of the nineteenth century: radical, anti-clerical, anarchistic. He was followed by a generation that included the best of Peru. It was the generation of the Apra, the revolutionary party (*Alianza Popular Revolucionaria Americana*) whose leader, Victor Raúl Haya de la Torre, also came from one of the oldest and most conservative families. With the creation of Apra, millions of Peruvians began to dream that they might have a share in the history of their country, that they might speak, and—something their imagination could hardly grasp—that there might be those who would listen to them. Little by little a faith began to grow, a passion, a force determined to change the mode of Peru.

In the 1920's, without organizing into a party, the faculty and students of the universities approached the people. The Universidades Populares González Prada were inaugurated, centers for the education of workers, craftsmen, farmers. Instead of turning their back on the people, as had so long been customary, the students and their leaders turned their backs on Lima and addressed themselves to the people. A new method of writing history began. To appreciate the change it is enough to read a title that the Peruvian historian Jorge Basadre gave to a book: *The Masses, the City, and the Country in the History of Peru.* Moreover, the new writers realized that the novel was a better vehicle for the study of the Peruvian Indian than factual history. If they were to give an account of his restrained emotions, his frustrations, his hidden longings, they could do it more vividly, more accurately, in novel form than through the medium of texts and documents. The new tendency of the group can be grasped from the title of Ciro Alegría's great novel, *Broad and Alien is the World.*

A thoughtful scrutiny of this recent process reveals the fact that the rise of Apra really marks the beginning of the end of the viceregal colony in Peru. But the struggle today is more difficult than it was a century ago. The heirs of the crown have joined hands with the military caste; having common interests, they represent two forces in search of absolute power. United, their power of resistance is very great. The army has been immeasureably strengthened by the armament it received during the Second World War. Peru is a cogent example of what happens in Latin America when the army becomes a party instrument.

The army came into being in Peru to fight in the final battle that assured the continental independence of Latin America, the victory of Ayacucho in 1824. Rather than Peruvian officials, it was the soldiers from the lower walks of life who, allied with those of Venezuela and Colombia, made up the victorious squadrons. Bolívar saluted them with these words, which Peru would do well to recall: "The cause of the rights of man has, with your arms, won its terrible struggle against the oppressors . . . Peruvian soldiers, your fatherland will always reckon you among the first saviors of Peru."

One hundred years went by. General Luis Sánchez Cerro seized power in August 1930, and put civilian President Augusto Leguía in jail. What purpose animated this general in the presidency? "I want to see the point of each bayonet red with the blood of *apristas*," he informed his troops in a famous proclamation.

Nineteen years went by. General Manuel A. Odría, "fulfilling an imperative patriotic mission," as he said in a message to congress, "decided to depose Bustamante's government." What moved him to take this measure against the civilian president? He explains it clearly:

"The fundamental reason for the existence of the revolutionary government I head is to eliminate the sectarian danger that for more than twenty years, and under four political regimes, has done nothing but commit crimes of every order against all individuals and institutions. *Aprismo* has systemati-

cally threatened the individual, the family and the home, the
school and church, the military and civilian institutions, and
the nation itself. Apra threatens the fundamental bases of the
home, poisoning the mind of the child and the youth, setting
them up against their parents and their elders, filling them
with rebelliousness and insolence and contempt for the wisdom and experience on which the greatness of a nation rests."

General Odría was repeating the very words the Spaniards
had used to maintain their empire in America and to disqualify
the authors of the war of independence. He was referring to
the excessive tolerance of the last four presidents of Peru toward the *apristas*. These presidents were Sánchez Cerro, Oscar
Benavides, Manuel Prado Ugarteche, and José Luis Bustamante. Sánchez Cerro's attitude is clearly set forth in the
manifesto quoted above. The second president, Marshal Benavides, declared *aprismo* "an international sect," which automatically prevented it from putting forward its candidates for
election. The *apristas*, confronted with a choice between violence and the long slow road of peace, chose the latter and
supported the candidacy of a member of the Liberal Party, Luis
Antonio Eguiguren. Marshal Benavides had said: "I pray that
Peru, in perfect harmony and observing the principles and
norms of democracy, will elect the citizen who will succeed me
and to whom I will hand over the insignia of power." Eguiguren was elected by an overwhelming majority. Benavides
ordered the Election Board to halt the counting of votes, refused to recognize the election, and continued in power. The
third president was Prado, a civilian. His platform was the following: "My duty is to prosecute the *apristas* because they are
outside the law." The *apristas* had to go underground until May
15, 1945, when, with elections only twenty-five days off, they
were recognized as citizens once more and allowed to vote. It
was impossible for them to put up a candidate of their own,
but if they came to an understanding with one of the other
candidates, this would give them an indirect victory. They

supported Bustamante, and with their votes he won. Bustamante was a smooth, wily lawyer. As soon as his election was
assured, he made common cause with the enemies of *aprismo*,
double-crossing those who had elected him. Nevertheless, the
apristas won a majority of seats in congress and controlled the
provinces, the municipalities, the press, the university. Bustamante began to cut the ground from under them, encouraging
a strike by the congressional minority which made a quorum
impossible. Thus he assumed the legislative power. He did not
dare declare the party illegal, as the Minister of the Interior,
General Odría, demanded, and for that reason Odría finally
gave him his walking papers. This was the tolerance that the
four preceding governments had showed toward the *apristas*.

Aprismo has a strange history. It is the party of the Peruvian
people, yet it was founded not in Peru, but in Mexico. Haya de
la Torre, father of the movement, was an exile in Mexico in
1923. His founding of the popular universities, his sponsoring
of reform in the universities, and his brilliant speeches at popular rallies, had led the dictator, Leguía, to make the following
proposal to him: either accept a diplomatic post in London or
be declared an enemy of the government. Haya had chosen the
second alternative. A few days later, from his prison on the
island of San Lorenzo, Haya countered with a proposal of his
own to Leguía: release me from prison or I will go on a hunger
strike, and then I will carry on my resistance from the cemetery. And he went on a hunger strike. By this time he was the
idol of the people and the students. He came from one of the
old families of the escutcheoned city of Trujillo. Days went
by, and the doctors announced that Haya was on the brink of
death. The dictator took fright, and decided to exile him.
Haya arrived in Mexico, and before a gathering of students and
workers one night he announced the formation of a political
league—the A.P.R.A.—to defend the ideals he considered common to America: the struggle against dollar diplomacy and
all imperialisms; the nationalization of land and industry; the

inter-Americanization of the Panama Canal; the solidarity of the exploited classes.

The youthful outburst of enthusiasm that night in Mexico gradually became transformed into one of the most powerful movements in Latin America. From Mexico, Haya de la Torre embarked on a grand tour. He visited the United States, Russia, Germany, Switzerland, England, France. He spent two years studying at Oxford. In Peru the students and the people followed his movements with the keenest attention, even keener than that of the dictator. The year after the foundation of Apra was proclaimed in Mexico, it was organized as a party in Peru. It was a radical, left-wing party whose revolutionary programs were based on a passionate defense of liberty and justice, which put it at loggerheads with the totalitarian parties. When Roosevelt announced the principles of the four freedoms and laid the bases of the Good Neighbor Policy, *aprismo* at once accepted this new formula and pronounced it the basis for a continental understanding. As against the international European trends, Haya de la Torre clearly defined the position of the party: "Neither with Rome nor with Berlin nor with Moscow. *Aprismo* alone will save Peru."

In an instinctive movement of solidarity the old politicians of Lima—the heirs of the Spanish Crown—and the Communists joined forces against the democracy of *aprismo*. In 1929 Moscow branded *aprismo* as the party against which Communism must concentrate in America. That year the first Latin American Communist Meeting was held in Montevideo, and there the representatives of the Russian government imposed an agreement to combat *aprismo* openly. For his part, Haya de la Torre outlined his anti-Communist position in numerous documents, where such paragraphs as the following from a manifesto to the party in 1933, may be found:

"The campaigns of Communism against the Apra are well-known to all. Whereas *aprismo* wishes to fulfill the democratic cycle, organize the state constructively, educate, improve, defend, and train the producing classes of the country, Communism proposes, 'permanent agitation' among the workers of the mining and petroleum industries to slow down production and favor the development of similar industries in Russia. This profound difference between creole Communism—assisted in its propaganda by *El Comercio* [the Conservative newspaper of Lima]—and *aprismo* suffices to make clear our position toward Communism, and toward the hateful, negative labor of its evil agents in countries such as ours, which attacks the life and progress of the very classes it pretends to defend. For this reason we have noted that *El Comercio* and the representatives of civic authority in Congress call upon the creole Communists to attack *aprismo,* and our party—conscious of its mission to defend the people—is the target of the hateful attacks of this strange alliance."

Haya de la Torre's words in this message of 1933 could be repeated now. All along those forces which should have been sworn enemies joined hands. In parliamentary debates, in matters as serious as the oil question, the government supporters and the Communists voted alike. *La Prensa,* the sugar barons' newspaper, printed the Communist party newspaper on its presses. From presidential headquarters Bustamante made a deal with the Communists to enter a block of all parties against *aprismo.* Bustamante himself says this is his book *Tres Años de Lucha por la Democracia en el Perú (Three Years of Struggle for Democracy in Peru):*

"At this juncture [September 1947] I made separate appointments with the leaders of the anti-*aprista* political groups to persuade them of the advantage of putting up jointly approved lists of candidates to avoid unnecessary strife between themselves and the consequent scattering of votes, which on a previous occasion had given Apra an easy victory inasmuch as its members voted solidly for a single candidate, while the conservative and independent voters supported two or three candidates for the same office. I brought strong pressure to bear on the Communist leaders to dissuade them from insisting on the names of the two candidates they were stubbornly supporting. I made clear to all of them the decisive influence this election would have in the membership of the legislative houses, as the triumph or the defeat of the Aprista majority there depended on this, as did, consequently, the elimination of the threatened danger of a prolonged congressional recess, or, on the contrary, the coming of such a recess with all the serious consequences involved."

In spite of these presidential maneuvers, the *apristas* won the elections, and thereupon the minority and the presidency settled the problem in simple fashion: they governed without congress.

Although *aprismo* represents the majority of the Peruvian people, neither the civilians nor the military have permitted its legal existence except on rare occasions. Haya de la Torre has spent the better part of his political career either in exile or in prison or in hiding, wanted by the police. His first exile lasted for eight years. He returned in 1931 as a candidate for the presidency. Sánchez Cerro, by a barracks coup, had seized power, and was trying to legalize his position in rigged elections. He had to set up a powerful electoral machine to outweigh the popular vote. Shortly after taking office this second time, he put Haya de la Torre in jail. Not long afterwards Sánchez Cerro was assassinated. The new president, Marshal Benavides, promised a more liberal government. He released Haya de la Torre. But in no time he resumed the persecution of Apra. Haya de la Torre, to avoid being sent back to prison, had to live in hiding for three years. When the Marshal's term of office was drawing to a close, Apra won the elections and the Marshal declared them void. Once more Haya had to go into hiding, this time until 1945, when free elections were again scheduled. It was then that the *apristas*, unable to present Haya as their candidate, gave their votes, and with them victory, to Bustamante. This time the election was not declared void; the President was simply pressured to turn his back on those who had brought him to power and to oppose them. In 1948 Bustamante came out officially against *aprismo*, and Haya de la Torre had to seek asylum in the Colombian Embassy. Since then he has been waiting for a safe-conduct to leave the country, to avoid the risk of falling into the hands of a government that has restored the death penalty.

There is no strong party in Peru except Apra. The military and the politicians have traditionally made their deals in the clubs of the people who control Lima, and out of these agreements have come the presidencies, the dictatorships, the *coups d'état*. There are small organized parties, such as the Communists, but the masses have heard only one name: Apra. The dictatorships have obliged Apra to live underground. In its thirty years of existence it has known only four in which it could act freely. Of necessity it has perfected its organization in a form the opposition denounces as an imitation of totalitarian tactics. It would be more accurate to compare it with the organization of the Masonic lodges, which have formed a part of the Spanish-American tradition since the wars of independence. In these lodges at the beginning of the nineteenth century many of the threads in the fabric of Spanish-American freedom were woven. The lodges assisted José Martí in his fight to free Cuba.

Haya de la Torre is an idealist. He lacks the calculation, the wiliness, the iron hand, of the *caudillos* who have triumphed in Latin America. Whenever he has been faced with a choice between violence and peace, he has chosen peace. Neither his struggle against the dictatorships, nor imprisonment, nor his passion for transforming the political life of Peru has ever dulled his interest in music—he has played the piano from childhood —the theater, literature, and philosophy. His conversation abounds in quotations from Shakespeare—he can recite long passages by heart—or anecdotes about Beethoven, when a run-of-the-mill Peruvian politician would be flaying the skin off his fellow-countrymen, living or dead. He has been a friend of Romain Rolland, Walt Disney, Einstein, giving his intellectual curiosity the freest play. His years of exile, imprisonment, and hiding have afforded him the opportunity to read widely. While Peru was marshalling its forces against him, he was writing an essay entitled *El Espacio-Tiempo Histórico*, (*Historic Space-Time*), an original contribution to the philosophy of history. After talking with him one always comes away wondering if he will be able to prevail against the tricks and snares at which the old politicians are past masters.

On the other hand, the abnegation of a life devoted to a dangerous, apostolic crusade is inspiring to all who hear him, read him, or follow his activities. No other political leader of our day in Latin America has been the subject of so many articles, books, biographies, and essays, all voicing admiration and respect. He is more frequently called teacher than leader. In the United States, against which he has never abated his anti-imperialist, dollar diplomacy campaign, he has found his best friends. Some of his bitterest adversaries have succumbed to his moral integrity, as happened with President Benavides. Young *apristas* facing the execution squad have gone to their death with his name on their lips. When Haya was running for the presidency, the very stones proclaimed his name: the gnarled hands of the peasants painted his name on cliffs, rocks, and the old walls of the Incas.

Haya de la Torre organized a Tree Crusade in Peru. "Passer-by, you who raise your arm against me," ran the leaflet the *apristas* distributed among the Peruvian villages in the Tree Crusade, "before you harm me, take a good look at me. I am the warmth of your home in the long winter nights. I am the friendly shade that protects you against the summer sun. My fruits satisfy your hunger and slake your thirst. I am the beam and the rafters that hold up your house. I am the boards of your table, the bed in which you rest, your cradle and your coffin. I am the handle of your hoe, of your spade, of your plow, the yoke of your oxen, the sluice gate, the trough of your irrigation ditches, the door of your cabin. I am the substance and the goodness and the flower of beauty. I am the landscape. I am the material from which your ancestors built their aqueducts. If you love me as I deserve, protect me against the thoughtless."

Haya instituted the "Christmas for poor children." Fernando León de Vivero, former leader of congress in Peru, tells how Haya de la Torre and his fellow *apristas*, men and women, visited the tenements and poor quarters of Lima, giving the children toys, candy, and cakes in the name of *aprismo* at Christmas time.

In his message to Congress in October 1949, General Odría said: "Apra threatens the fundamental bases of the home, poisoning the mind of the child . . . It invades the schools, first winning over certain of the teachers to use them for its own ends to pervert the pure hearts of children and young people . . ."

A few months before the last campaign against Haya, I visited him in his country home beside a river half an hour from Lima, on the road leading to the mountains. The living room was a mass of books. His constant companion was his dog. On Friday nights busses brought hundreds of poor folk from Lima, artisans, workers, students. They erected canvas tents in which to spend the week-end. Haya talked with them like a friendly comrade, but in a paternal tone, for they looked upon him not exactly as a political leader, but as one who gave meaning to their lives. He was insistent that when they left on Sunday night or early Monday morning, not a scrap of trash should be left on the meadow where they had set up their tents. He climbed the mountains with them and swam with them, for he has always been devoted to sports. He would come back to the house sunburned and happy.

The military dictatorship that governs Peru today began with Bustamante. Although his election was fair and legal, his

determination to do away with *aprismo* led him to approve
the strike in Congress, and he assumed the legislative functions. He ruled by decree. Little by little he began to lose his
prestige. The *apristas* stood by as observers, waiting for the
next election. There were rumors, however, of a possible army
uprising that would prevent the *apristas* from coming to
power. The newspaper *La Tribuna,* directed by the secretary
of the party, Manuel Seoane, kept hammering this home in
every issue. "Elections," he said in one of his articles, "are the
cornerstone of democracy. The barracks coups have been proscribed by nations . . . The citizenry cannot and should not
think that there is any process better than that indicated by
constitutional norms."

Not everyone heeded these admonitions. A group of young
navy officers, who were not *apristas* but who refused to accept
Bustamante's dictatorship, demanded a return to constitutional order. They mutinied in the port of Callao on October
3, 1948. Lacking the support of *aprismo* or the army, they
were subdued in a few hours. President Bustamante had the
pretext he needed. Two hours after the revolt broke out he
declared it an *aprista* revolution and ordered all the Apra leaders imprisoned. The news ran through Peru like wildfire. Every
one knew what that meant. Those who were able sought refuge in embassies, others crossed the frontiers, and the rest
went to jail. The presses of *La Tribuna* were seized.

To the political bosses of Lima and to the military (which
was under the influence of Bustamante's former minister, General Odría) this seemed too little and too late. Previously
Odría had demanded that Bustamante declare *aprismo* illegal
on the grounds that it was an "international sect." Twenty-
four days after the uprising in Callao came the revolt of Arequipa, organized by Odría. In his proclamation of this date he
promised "that he would hang the *apristas* from the lampposts of Lima, and that his only regret was that there were
not enough to do the job properly." Three days later Busta-

mante had to step down from the presidency, and Odría took his place.

"One of my last measures before leaving the palace," writes Bustamante in his book, "was to demand a receipt for the files of the *aprista* party, which had been seized by the police when they took over the headquarters of the party, as well as for the papers found in the home of its leader."

The rest follows the natural process of dictatorships. When Bolívar, who had won his military titles in the greatest campaign of liberation the world has ever seen, came to the University of San Marcos in Lima, he removed his arms and insignia and symbolically bowed his head in the temple of science. "As I cross the threshold of this sanctuary," he said, "I am overcome by respect and fear. I feel abashed before men who have grown gray in their task of thoughtful, useful meditation, and who have deservedly risen to the rank they occupy in the fields of science. Despite my ignorance and lack of merits, you have gratuitously honored me with your kindness . . . I shall always recall this as the most honored day of my life . . . Whatever time is granted me after having fulfilled the obligations to which I am at present committed, I shall employ if not in an effort to reach the heights of learning you occupy, at least in imitating you."

When the military dictatorship of 1948 was proclaimed, the students of San Marcos protested against the overthrow of the civilian power. The president of the university, Luis Alberto Sánchez, who had raised learning to a new level in Peru, had to flee to Chile. To restore academic order the army, trained in ousting presidents, set up its batteries around the cloisters of the University, founded four hundred years ago. And the tanks Peru had received during the Second World War advanced, broke down the University doors, and literally and figuratively captured the University.

VII

VENEZUELA, OR THE MILITARY
IN OIL HEAVEN

Woeful the land where the man of arms becomes the lawmaker.

JOSÉ ANTONIO DE SUCRE

IN THE opening lines of an essay on the geography of Venezuela, Mariano Picón-Salas, the distinguished Venezuelan writer, says: "On the map the territory of Venezuela resembles a cow-hide of the Llanos dried in the sun of the torrid zone." This rustic metaphor of the geography of the country had its counterpart in the country's human product not too long ago. General Juan Vicente Gómez ruled Venezuela from 1908 until his death in 1935. A former cattle-rustler, swift and heavy-handed, given to few but trenchant words, he had the air of a barbarian patriarch and an amazing physical resemblance to Joseph Stalin. Like Juan Manuel Rosas of Argentina, Juan Vicente looked upon his country as his ranch. On his ranch he was boss. Those who thought of opposing him were thrown into underground dungeons where they suffered terrible tortures and rotted away in tropical dampness. The phrase "thought of" is used advisedly, for Juan Vicente could read what was going on in people's minds. Besides being a dictator, he was something of a wizard.

There had been a time, around 1810, when Venezuela was the leading country of Spanish America. Francisco Miranda, the precursor of the independence of all Spanish America, was a Venezuelan, as were Simón Bolívar, the Liberator; Antonio José de Sucre, Bolívar's finest general; and Andrés Bello, intellectual father of the Spanish American republics. But with the

95

use of independence and the abuse of freedom Venezuela's prestige disappeared. Its government became a dreary succession of strong men and dictators. The uniform became a badge of infamy. Contempt for the military became so great that it is told of an honest, self-respecting man whom someone called "General" that he answered in great indignation: "Don't you dare call me General. I haven't robbed anybody."

When Juan Vicente Gómez died in 1935, the new government confiscated his holdings, valued in the neighborhood of $200,000,000. His passing was hailed with rejoicing throughout Latin America, but particularly in Venezuela, and for good reason. There the feeling was one of rebirth. Hundreds of university students who had emigrated to Colombia, Chile, Argentina, Mexico, and Spain returned to their country. There was a lusty upsurge of democracy. One might say, enlarging on Picón-Salas's metaphor, that the dried cow-hide had come alive and was growing a fine, glossy new coat. And not only as regards the symbolic geography of Venezuela, but also on the world maps. For Venezuela suddenly became the leading exporter of oil in the whole world. It produces twice as much oil as the whole of Russia. Only the United States or the whole of the Middle East outstrips Venezuela's daily figure of 1,610,-000 barrels. Venezuela is the Iran of South America.

Juan Vicente Gómez, by milking Venezuela dry, made himself one of the richest men in the world. Today the republic of Venezuela is one of the richest countries. Its national income per capita is the highest in South America. If that income were divided equally among all Venezuelans, each man, woman, and child of the republic would receive 1500 bolívars (about $495 in 1951) a year. In terms of the same currency, the income of Argentina would give each inhabitant only 1,150 bolivars, and that of Uruguay, 1,100. One third of Venezuela's national income comes from oil. In peace or war, Venezuela today holds in its hands one of the oil-cans that lubricate the world machinery.

And that is not all. In the region of British Guiana deposits of iron have been discovered which are estimated at 125,000,000 cubic tons. The company called Iron Mines of Venezuela which has begun mining the ore, announces that it will be exporting 2,000,000 tons annually. The Orinoco Mining Company will be doing the same.

Venezuela is one example of the still-undiscovered possibilities of Latin America. Great surprises may be expected as the vast territory of the former Spanish colonies is explored, developed, and brought into communication with the rest of the world. The discovery of America is just beginning. This is not true uniquely of Venezuela or of the twenty southern republics. It holds true of the entire hemisphere. One has only to recall California before and after the discovery of gold there; pre-oil and post-oil Texas; Montana fifty years ago; or what the TVA has done for the Tennessee Valley. But the case of Venezuela calls for special scrutiny.

Like the rest of Latin America, Venezuela has its Achilles's heel: politics. When there is free play of public opinion, Venezuela gives an impression of vitality and security. When this is interrupted and repressed, everything becomes shrouded in reserves and "*¿quién sabe?*" If at times the map shows the glossy hide of a prize cow, there are times when it is like the dry, tense skin of a war drum. The superstitious rustics, the restless workers in the oil fields, and the bewildered students ask themselves if the spirit of "boss" Juan Vicente Gómez still walks the land.

All Venezuelans forty years or older knew and suffered from Juan Vicente. He is no myth to them. Some of them, too, enjoyed the benefits of his dictatorship, and in one way or another they are all the heirs of that shade. There were intellectuals who worked out a philosophy of dictatorship. The most eminent of them, Laureano Vallenilla Lanz, reduced Juan Vicente's practical approach to an ideal system, and wrote a famous book *Cesarismo Democrático* (*Democratic Caesarism*), an apology for what he called the "indispensable gendarme" and a negation of the Spanish American's capacity for self-government.

Vallenilla Lanz's book, which is still read by some of the officers of the Venezuelan army, was the Spanish American work most widely and enthusiastically read in Fascist Italy. The Italian edition was published in Rome in 1934. The translator, Paolo Nicolai, wrote a foreword to present it to the Fascist public:

"Vallenilla Lanz's greatest, his incomparable, merit in our eyes is to have steadily pointed out, with word and pen, the incalculable harm the republics of Central and South America have suffered in both the moral and material fields as a result of the principle of presidential alternation. This basic concept which he develops throughout the pages of *Cesarismo Democrático* . . . has brought upon him the title of 'apologist and philosopher of dictatorship' . . . From what we have said it is apparent, beyond the shadow of a doubt, that Vallenilla Lanz has every claim to be considered by us as an exquisitely Fascist spirit . . ."

Juan Vicente Gómez was succeeded by his Minister of War, General Eleázar López Contreras, a man of modernizing spirit, who took the first steps to liquidate the dictator's legacy. And five years later, General Isaías Medina Angarita, Minister of War under López Contreras, was elected by the Congress to succeed him in the presidency. These two generals were not blind, and they had seen how the people had demonstrated in the streets at the news of Gómez's death in an irrepressible manifestation of hatred toward the dictatorship, which nobody in Venezuela could forget. The problem was how to open the flood-gates to democracy, and to López Contreras it was a puzzling one. On one occasion, after he was out of the government, he said to me:

"It is not easy to judge from the outside the difficulties we encounter in Venezuela in trying to arrive at a representative democracy. In Colombia you people have had elections. That is part of your civil tradition. But to us they are unknown. When I was president, at a cabinet meeting where all the men were older than myself, I asked this question: which one of you has ever voted in a popular election? Not one of them had done so. Not a single living Venezuelan had had this experience. Now we have to start with what to everybody in other countries is the A B C of political life . . ."

Medina Angarita, a straightforward, well-intentioned, cordial man, took over the presidency in 1941, and the hopes of democracy rode with him. Anyone who saw Venezuela during his term of office came away with the impression that there was a firm basis on which to build a republic. At that time, one of the leading publishers of Buenos Aires said to me: "The best market for books in South America today is Venezuela." Schools and roads were built, attempts were made to find a solution to the country's most pressing problem: its dependence on a single product, oil. Oil has kept the value of Venezuela's currency at an excessively high level. In Caracas the cost of living is one of the highest in the world. For the moment agriculture holds no attraction for the farmer. Arturo Uslar-Pietri, one of General Medina's ministers, coined a phrase that has won great currency in Venezuela: "We must plant oil." That is to say, with the profits Venezuela is now receiving from its oil, improve the country and develop a sound basis for its future.

Unfortunately General Medina's administration found itself of necessity on the horns of a political dilemma: either the government was to consist of a succession of men selected by the President and approved by Congress or the choice was to be left to the will of the people expressed at the polls. Confronted with this dilemma, the military and the democratic party grew impatient, and General Medina, after a peaceful term of office, found himself in the thick of a fight. It was a crucial moment in Venezuela's history.

99

The military seized the initiative. The coups of Rawson, Ramírez, and Farrell in Argentina had showed them that the hour for barrack conspiracies had struck again in Latin America, and experience proved that whoever pulled off the coup came to power. The general staffs took upon themselves the right to judge the civil authorities. In the case of Venezuela, however, the situation was thornier than in Argentina. The army lacked any popular backing, and it was going to be a bloody business to overthrow the constituted authorities under these circumstances. Medina's government was popular. The army's only chance would be to associate itself with the Acción Democrática party, which had the support of the masses. So, as their plans to overthrow Medina began to shape up, the military made overtures to the leaders of Acción Democrática.

At first the leaders of Acción Democrática let themselves be wooed by the military, but did not follow their suggestions. If the party could count on enough support from the masses, and there was a possibility of their coming to power legally, why hamstring themselves, and have to include a group of ambitious officers in the future government? Elections were not too near. The government had made no definite choice of successor. The candidacy of the ambassador in Washington, Diógenes Escalante, was put forward, and it was not too far-fetched to think that by supporting him Acción Democrática could achieve its aim of establishing universal suffrage and insure peacefully the objectives the democrats were pursuing. The leaders of Acción Democrática did not commit themselves to the military. They went to Washington to confer with Escalante, and everything seemed to indicate the way to a friendly understanding.

But at this point Ambassador Escalante was stricken with a fatal disease. Congressional elections were approaching, and there was no possibility of an agreement between Acción Democrática and President Medina. The latter favored the candidacy of Ángel Biaggini, a mediocre figure. "President Medina had made up his mind to pick his successor, and set the clock back half a century," said the students. The alternative to Biaggini was ex-president López Contreras. "As the decision was not to be made at the polls, but at a cabinet meeting behind closed doors, the two generals hoped to handle the affair as a family problem, as though it were a question of succession in one of the old absolutist dynasties," to use the words of Alberto Carnevali, secretary of Acción Democrática. Feeling ran high, the democrats agitated in the streets and the newspapers, and at this point the military once more approached the leaders of Acción Democrática. Thirty-six hours later (October 19, 1945) the legal president was in prison, and there were forty-four dead in the streets of Caracas. The military who overthrew Medina were the very same who, before three years had gone by, were to serve President Rómulo Gallegos the same way.

Desultory shooting was still going on in Caracas at eight o'clock on the night of October 19, 1945, when the *junta* of army officers and leaders of Acción Democrática set themselves up as the new government. "The power was off in the presidential palace," Rómulo Betancourt—an eye-witness—relates, "and gasoline lamps lighted the memorable scene. Civilians and the military side by side, all with tense expressions, we signed the constituent act of the *de facto* government . . ." At this time the military did not venture to assume all the posts. The presidency of the *junta* was given to Betancourt, and the majority of its members were civilians: young lawyers of the group that had grown up in exile in the days of Juan Vicente Gómez. Major Marcos Pérez Jiménez, one of the most active organizers of the coup, returned to barracks. Major Carlos Delgado Chalbaud, at whose mother's home the meeting that decided the coup had been held, became the real representative of the military in the government. Delgado Chalbaud had been educated in France. He was agreeable and well-mannered and had been attached to the presidential staffs of López Contreras and Medina. Captain Mario Vargas also held a post in the government. He was much closer to Acción Democrática than the other officers.

The jails were filled with members of the defunct regime. A few days later some of the most prominent were deported. Rómulo Betancourt has written in his memoirs of these events:

"Generals López Contreras and Medina Angarita, and a group of less than twenty of their closest civilian and military collaborators were sent direct to Miami by plane, each with a check for $1000, the sum required by the immigration authorities. . . . History has showed that real revolutions, under whatever ideological sign they militate, always display great tolerance toward the defeated at the beginning. 'Monsieur' Guillotin's invention was put to work by Robespierre only after the emigré nobles, from their lair in Coblenz and with the support of all the crowned heads of Europe, had become a serious threat to Republican France. . . . In Venezuela we leaders of the popular and democratic revolution of 1945 made this same mistake in the first phases of our governmental action. The repeated experience of history should have warned us against this."

As can be seen, the style is out-and-out revolutionary. Lightning action was instituted to confiscate the property of those who, in the judgment of the revolution, had enriched themselves under the preceding governments. A *junta* ad-hoc proceeded to freeze bank accounts and put in escrow the property of those under scrutiny. It gave court clerks orders to legalize no deeds involving the transfer of such property. A civil court was set up to judge "individuals or corporations who themselves or through a third party, directly or indirectly, have committed deliberately or through negligence or lack of judgment acts or deeds prejudicial to the public weal, or have enriched themselves unjustifiably for their own benefit or that of others, through undue influence with those in public office . . ."

This radical approach characterized all the decrees that were signed by Rómulo Betancourt along with all the members of the *junta*, and Major Carlos Delgado Chalbaud's name led all the rest. A few lines will give an idea of the style of procedure:

"Art. 5. The court will determine the responsibility of those on trial, being guided by the dictates of justice and equity, as interpreted by its loyal knowledge and understanding.

"Art. 6. Until the court . . . hands down its final decision, the Minister of the Interior, by dictate of the Revolutionary Government *junta*, may order the seizure of the property of those affected by this decree.

"Art. 7. No appeal will be allowed from the measures and decisions of any nature handed down by the Court of Civil and Administrative Responsibility and its decisions will be considered final and *res judicata*.

"Art. 17. The responsibility referred to in Article 1 of this decree extends to the heirs as well."

To justify these measures on the part of a government that determinedly called itself revolutionary, Rómulo Betancourt cited as precedents not only the measures taken against the fortune of Juan Vicente Gómez, but also a ruling dictated by Simón Bolívar himself. When Bolívar became the supreme authority of Great Colombia in 1823 he issued a decree to this effect:

"Any employée of the National Treasury found guilty of fraud or the misuse of public funds or in any way involved in such an act will be summarily condemned to death, without necessity of further trial than the report of the court investigating the matter."

The list of those found guilty was an arbitrary one. Not all included on it were guilty, nor were all the guilty included, and the opportunity of the accused to defend themselves was practically nil. There were instances of torture in the prisons under the control of the military. It was a revolution with all that follows in revolution's wake.

For two years and three months the revolutionary *junta* governed Venezuela. Little by little the civilian manner was beginning to replace the military. What had been won by violence was on the way to transformation into a broad democratic formula. The state was able to undertake vast social transformations, thanks to tax reforms that enriched the treasury. General Medina had already initiated the oil reforms in 1943. Betancourt completed them with the surtax levied in 1945 and the income tax reform of 1946. In 1944 the nation received 5.60 bolívars on every cubic meter of oil extracted; in 1947, 11.77 bolívars. In 1944 the Treasury Department received 300,000,000 bolívars from Venezuela's oil; in 1947, 1,300,000,000. The oil companies made no objection to this; they could now, backed by the law, feel themselves safe in paying the government 50 per cent of their profits. The following is from the Creole Petroleum Corporation's last report:

"At the end of 1950 the oil fields of Venezuela produced 1,610,000 barrels daily . . . At the end of 1945 this figure was 960,000 . . . This spectacular growth of Venezuela as an oil-producing nation may be attributed to three factors . . . the favorable attitude toward the large capital investments required for the Venezuelan oil industry to reach its present magnitude."

The country was opened to immigration. Between 1941 and 1944 only 597 immigrants entered Venezuela; in 1948 the number was 20,351. A new power began to make itself felt in Venezuela: that of the labor unions. In 1946, 531 new unions were organized in industry and agriculture. In 1947 the number reached 950, and in November 1948, 1,014. In 1947 a congress was held which had as its primary objective the creation of the Confederation of Venezuelan Workers (C.T.V.). Foreign observers agree that conditions in Venezuela had never been so propitious for the free organization of workers as under the government of Acción Democrática.

Progress in every direction was apparent. In 1945, 300,000 children attended school; in 1948, 400,000. In 1945, 319 towns had electric power; in 1948, 606. In 1945, 1000 children ate in the state-sponsored school lunch-rooms; in 1947, 38,000. Venezuela, Colombia, and Ecuador organized a joint merchant marine, the Grancolombiana, which has become one of the most flourishing enterprises of Latin America.

But the essential problem still remained to be solved: that of finding a stable, democratic formula of government. Betancourt, wily and quick-witted, quashed the plots the military were already scheming to halt the march toward democratic solutions under the government of the *junta*. And finally, to the surprise of Latin America, Venezuela arranged for free, general, unrigged elections. Testimony of the most varied sort bears witness that it was an absolutely democratic election. It took place in December 1947. It was the realization of a dream of centuries for the Venezuelans. On that day in city and in village the people were up at dawn to take their place in the lines at the voting booths. There were enthusiasm, liberty, and respect. The ballots were of different colors, the only way voting could be handled in a country where a large proportion of the people is illiterate. The ballots of Acción Democrática were white; those of the Communists, red; of the *unitarios*, black; those of C.O.P.E.I., a party with reactionary, Falangist leanings, green. The majority voted for Acción Democrática. If nothing else, it gave hope of a state that favored the mass of the electorate. But the interesting thing is that the person elected to the presidency was a man who represented the other extreme from the self-seeking military. He was Venezuela's greatest writer, the novelist Rómulo Gallegos, a man above all party lines and contention.

How did it come about that a novelist was elected president of a country? What were Rómulo Gallegos's political credentials? In his novels he had presented the life of the lowly with tenderness and understanding. More than anyone else he had approached the small, intimate drama of the people. He did this without political design, out of a sense of human solidarity. In his works are to be found, in life-sized stature, the outspoken plainsman, the worker of the city, the frontiersman who measures his strength against the jungle, the poor Negro, the peasant bewildered by the oil gushing from his land. When Gallegos was inaugurated, one hundred men of letters from the entire Western continent went to Caracas to honor the event. Gallegos said to them: "It is one thing to wish, and another to do. Let us see what a man of good will can accomplish. It is one thing to move the puppets of fiction, and another to govern a people. As a Venezuelan song puts it:

> 'It's an easy thing to do
> To paint a dove.
> But for it to open its beak and eat—
> There's the rub.' "

In contrast to what usually happens at ceremonies of this sort, at Gallegos's inauguration the folk celebrations far outshone the diplomatic receptions. On three successive nights folk dances were presented in the bullring by people who had come from the four corners of Venezuela with their typical music, costumes, and dances. The folk had the leading role in this historic act, a role inspired by the strength and color of its traditions, not by violence, which was barred from the program. It was one of the most memorable festivities of Latin America.

But, alas, it was a short-lived flower! Nine months later the group of officers which overthrew Medina Angarita toppled Rómulo Gallegos from his post.

In a period of a little less than three years the military had seen that, against their will, they had been led to a civil form of government. What, in their ambition, they had believed to be a temporary solution was taking on permanent form. It was their idea that the army should be the deliberative body in Venezuela as it is in Argentina. Although they had followed a professional military career and did not owe their official rank to the vote of the people, they decided that they were qualified to pass judgment on the civilian authorities, and they had no intention of permitting Congress, the press, the courts, or public opinion to exercise this function, as in a democracy. And they had the example of the army in Peru, which had just taken this step, before them.

Major Pérez Jiménez, one of the moving forces in the plot against Medina, had learned much in a short time. He had just returned from a trip to Argentina, where he had been in close touch with Perón's general staff, after which he had gone on to Peru. "He and General Manuel Odría, a former teacher of his in the War College, undoubtedly agreed on a common plan of action," says a person who is in a position to know. Now all he had to do was to encourage his former comrades of the first revolution, and Major Delgado Chalbaud, Gallegos's Minister of War, to emulate the Argentine maneuver.

A last-minute development gave the conspirators the green light: Odría's recognition by the United States government. The army, like everybody else in Latin America, is always alert to see what course Washington will take. The recognition of Odría and Perón seemed an auspicious sign to Major Pérez Jiménez's clique. It was not only the recognition of Odría, but the marked enthusiasm with which United States Ambassador James Bruce renewed his expressions of friendship toward General Perón. Bruce, who at the beginning of his mission to Argentina had hailed Perón as "the great leader of a great country," in October 1948, on his return from a brief trip to the United States, sat down at Perón's table like one of the family. Newspapers carried the official account of the first interview between Bruce and Perón, which lasted three hours. Perón concluded his declarations with these words: "In my opinion the relations between the governments of Argentina and the United States will become progressively stronger. After thanking the Ambassador in the name of the Argentine people and government for his efforts on behalf of better and closer ties with the United States, I took the opportunity to praise the true American spirit, so abundantly demonstrated by its zeal to serve the cause of harmony among the American peoples, above every other consideration." These wooing words took on even more weight in the judgment of the Venezuelan officers in view of the fact that Ambassador Bruce's manifestations of solidarity had been made only a few days after Perón had delivered for home consumption a most offensive speech against the United States. It is doubtful that the United States will ever realize the repercussion that these attitudes of its ambassadors have on the general staffs of the armies of Latin America.

The officers presented President Gallegos with a devil-or-deep-blue-sea choice: either we share the government with you or you're out. Their real aim was to take over power and eliminate the leaders of Acción Democrática. The matter was not threshed out with the head of the state, but in the officers' clubs. However, the situation was common knowledge to everyone in Caracas, including the President. Gallegos called in the Minister of War, Delgado Chalbaud, who was one of the inner circle of officers, and Delgado Chalbaud's terse reply was:

"Mr. President, why don't you call in the military? They are waiting to hear from you."

Gallegos sent for the ringleader, Major Pérez Jiménez. The latter appeared with a document in his hand, which in the end he did not give to the President. Partial explanations followed, new interviews, meetings at the barracks. A kind of paralysis was felt in Caracas, which was aware that something was afoot without wholly understanding it. The President was confronted with a curtain of cotton. Gossip, words floating through a haze of cigarette smoke, canards . . . The Minister of War advised him to do nothing. The President finally decided to take the initiative. He called a meeting of the officers at the cavalry barracks. There he said to them: "Once more our country is undergoing the shame of seeing how ambition, lack of discipline and of military honor are bringing confusion into the life of the whole nation."

These were strong words. The president of the republic is the commander-in-chief of the army. The commander-in-chief was the only military authority that had been chosen by the people. He had the authority of his office and the representation of his country. The officers made no reply to his words, but their meetings continued, and they finally handed him a document. They requested that he remove from his post the commander of the one unit of the army which had proved its loyalty to him; that he change the aides-de-camp who sat at table with him every day; that he forbid the return of Colonel Mario Vargas, who was in the United States, and who was very devoted to the President; that he expel from the country the head of Acción Democrática and former head of the government, Rómulo Betancourt. Raúl Roa has reported Gallegos' answer in the latter's own words:

"I beg to remind you that by the terms of the constitution that I have sworn to uphold and defend, the only bodies to whom I am responsible for my political and administrative acts are, first, the legislative branch, on the occasion of my annual message or whenever this body so requests me, and second, the judicial branch, in the event that action of any sort is instituted against me. But never to the national army, an institution whose sphere of action is clearly defined in the national constitution. The army has specific duties and activities, which are not precisely those you have taken the liberty to exercise at this moment. I know that my fate has been decided. I urge you to measure the responsibility you are assuming. I have carefully weighed mine. If it is your determination to override the civil authority in its legitimate powers and rights, you should bear in mind that you will touch off a blaze of violence that will sweep Venezuela from one corner to the other, and the responsibility for civil war will be on your conscience."

Ten days later (November 24, 1948) President Gallegos was in prison, and Major Delgado Chalbaud and Major Pérez Jiménez had organized a governing *junta*, a government that was exclusively military. It was instantly recognized by the Argentina of Perón, the Peru of Odría, and the Dominican Republic of Trujillo.

The Speaker of Congress, Valmore Rodríguez, addressed a letter to the *junta*, saying, among other things: "I am writing by the light of a candle in my cell in the Model Prison where I have been jailed since the military uprising of November 24 . . . The thought of Venezuela's sufferings makes me forget my own, for after all, these walls are familiar to me, and nothing that happens in this struggle for the freedom and happiness of Venezuela can any longer surprise or perturb me. This letter is an appeal to the sense of responsibility of the military.

"In my cell-block there are also the President and the Vice-President of the House of Representatives, eight cabinet ministers, a judge of the Supreme Court, the Governor of Caracas, the presidential secretary, five congressmen, the President of the City Council of Caracas, the Governor of Aragua, the President of the Venezuelan Corporation of Development, the directors of other private institutions, and various political and labor leaders. Other sections of the prison are likewise filled with political prisoners. Throughout our land a similar spectacle is being afforded the nation and the civilized world. That is to say, almost all the members of Congress, the state legislatures, and the city councils, the governors of the states, mayors, judges—in a word, the total representation of public authority, is under arrest in every state and territory of our land, without the least consideration for

their robes of office. This is also true of the leaders of the political party to which the Venezuelans gave the mandate of
government in elections that the president of the military
junta himself publicly described on various occasions as model.
The picture is rounded out, now that you have achieved your
objective through your *coup d'état,* by the expulsion of the
president of the republic from the country after twelve days
of imprisonment in the Military Academy where the future
officers of the army are being trained . . ."

These were the beginnings of the military dictatorship that
has been in control of Venezuela since 1948. The government
of the United States, which had showered attentions on President Gallegos, was, naturally, distressed at the fall of his civilian government. In its note of recognition to the military
junta there is an appeal to Venezuela to adopt a representative form of government. President Truman, in his letter of
reply to the overthrown president, said: "I believe that the
use of force to effect political changes is not only deplorable,
but contrary to the ideals of the American nations . . ." For
its part, the military *junta* at once made a profession of its
friendship toward the United States, and, as is the habit of
dictatorships, loudly proclaimed its anti-Communist position.

The most conspicuous rectification of the measures taken
by Betancourt's government was a decree restoring to some
hundred persons the property that had been confiscated by
the revolutionary *junta.* The justification for this restitution
was "the need to insure the respect for principles and norms
that are indispensable to the proper functioning of Venezuela's institutional life." By an ironic twist of fate, it fell to
Delgado Chalbaud to sign both the decree of confiscation and
that of restitution.

The innovation introduced by the military *junta* was the
abolition of the national constitution by decree. Even in the
days of Juan Vicente Gómez, Venezuela had had a constitution that at times acted as a brake even on the dictator. It

was a constitution made to his order, but a constitution. There was a basic law of the land. Now the military decided not to recognize the constitution of 1947, and declared that they would observe that of 1936, but reserved to themselves the right to adjust it to circumstances. In this way universal suffrage was abolished. The members of the Supreme Court are appointed by decree. The military of Venezuela behaved even more highhandedly than Perón. Perón waited to be elected, waited to draft his own constitution. Moreover, there is an antecedent that cannot be overlooked in the case of Venezuela.

On October 13, 1947, the Minister of National Defense of the revolutionary *junta* made a dramatic entrance into the chamber of the National Constituent Assembly. He was in dress uniform, and carried a document in his hand. He had just one purpose in appearing before the body: it was rumored that the army was not loyal to the revolution, and he had brought with him proof of its fidelity. He made a brief speech, and handed the secretary the document. Addressed to him, it begins with these words:

"Citizen Lieutenant-Colonel, Minister of National Defense:

"We have requested of our superior officers the necessary authorization to request respectfully that, if you deem it desirable, you bring to the knowledge of the governing *junta* and the National Constituent Assembly, representative of the will of the people as expressed on October 27, 1946, in elections held under our supervision, and which, for this reason, we know to have been absolutely honest . . . We wish to go on record as stating:

"1. That we hold this National Constituent Assembly to be the genuine representation of the will of the people, and we are prepared to respect it and to see that it is respected;

"2. That we recognize the governing *junta* as the legitimate executive power inasmuch as it has been ratified in its functions by this Assembly and, in the manner stated above, we are prepared to accept it and to see that it is accepted . . .

"4. That we categorically and steadfastly condemn such citizens as endeavor to induce our companions in arms, by fallacious arguments, to conspire against the legitimate government."

The Minister who presented the document was Lieutenant-Colonel Delgado Chalbaud. It was signed by all the army officers, headed by the members of the general staff. The two first signatures were those of Lieutenant-Colonel Marcos Pérez Jiménez and Major Luis Felipe Llovera Páez. One year and ten months later the Assembly was declared illegal and the constitution abrogated. This was the action of the military *junta* composed of Lieutenant-Colonel Delgado Chalbaud, Lieutenant-Colonel Marcos Pérez Jiménez, and Major Luis Felipe Llovera Páez.

The great triumph of 1946 for Venezuela had been the establishment of universal suffrage. An outspoken opponent of the revolutionary *junta*, the leader of the Unión Republicana Democrática party, Jovito Villalba, said in reviewing the manner in which the electoral statute was drawn up:

"A month after the successful coup of October 18, a commission was appointed to draft the proposed law for the election of the Constituent Assembly . . . Together with Andrés Eloy Blanco, a member of the governing party—the only such member on the commission, but big-spirited and liberal beyond any doubt—there were Jesús Enrique Losada, a teacher; Nicomedes Zuloaga, a lawyer with a well-balanced, thoughtful approach . . . Germán Suárez Flamerich, a university professor and an accomplished parliamentarian . . ."

It is unnecessary to list the other names. They were the cream of Venezuela's law faculties and civilian experts. Now the military *junta* has disavowed all this and has done away with the electoral records. In April 1951 it came forward with a new electoral law, under the terms of which elections for a Constituent Assembly may be held in 1952. In this way the military government prolongs itself indefinitely. But the fundamental feature of the new law consists in declaring the Acción Democrática party illegal. That is to say, the party that won the majority of votes in a free election is now forbidden to present a candidate. By this ruling the majority of Venezuelans lose the most important of their political rights. In the elections won by Rómulo Gallegos the results were:

RÓMULO GALLEGOS (*Acción Democrática*)	871,752
RAFAEL CALDERA (*Christian Socialism*)	262,204
GUSTAVO MACHADO (*Communist Party*)	36,584

Under the new statute drawn up by the military *junta* these 871,752 votes for a democratic candidate would not be counted.

Major Marcos Pérez Jiménez, at the inauguration of the new Military Academy of Venezuela in 1950, said to the cadets:

"It is pertinent to point out that the Venezuelans trained for a military career in this institution will bring to their duties a broad, clear concept of the country's institutions which will impede the formation among us of oligarchies, would-be military castes . . . The dignity of life and of the civil organization of the republic, as well as respect for the rights of the citizen, will be considered sacred by the classes of officers prepared here."

What must the cadets have thought as they listened to this from the lips of a member of the military *junta?*

On November 13, 1950—two years less eleven days after the overthrow of President Gallegos—an admirer and friend of Major Pérez Jiménez, with the help of a group of accomplices, waylaid and assassinated the president of the military *junta*, Major Delgado Chalbaud. The assassin was Rafael Simón Urbina a strange, unbalanced person, whose life would have provided material for a dime novel. The police apprehended and killed him the same day.

Delgado Chalbaud was a man of finer clay than his associates in the *junta*. It seems that he took part in the conspiracies against his will. It was hard for him to say no. The other officers used him as a stalking-horse in carrying out their schemes. With Delgado Chalbaud gone, Caracas was gripped by terror. Would Major Pérez Jiménez make himself president of the *junta?* No. The murder of Delgado Chalbaud made a pause necessary. The members of the military *junta* had to choose his successor, as there was no congress or representative body in Venezuela empowered to take such a step. But this time the military were afraid to go too far, and they selected a civilian, Germán Suárez Flamerich, former dean of the Law School and sometime Ambassador to Peru.

Everyone's eyes were fixed on the new president of the *junta*. He was one of the authors of the electoral law the *junta* had abrogated. He had taught law. He knew what a constitution was. One hundred and fifty lawyers of Caracas reminded him of this in a message; the teachers repeated it to him, as did the university students, the mothers, wives, sisters, and daughters of hundreds of political prisoners. The students said: "If reprisals are to be the answer to this message, we will bear them with the firmness of those who are convinced that they have fulfilled their sacred duty as Venezuelans." The women, who are often bolder than men, called his attention in their message to the outrages that were being committed even against women, and told him that "they exceed those perpetrated during the grim dictatorship of Juan Vicente Gómez . . ."

It was all in vain. Suárez Flamerich sat back and watched the colonels at their work. Six months, eight months, went by. And then it was congressmen of Argentina, democratic opinion in Chile, writers of France, statesmen of Uruguay and Guatemala, the free press of all America that addressed themselves to the military *junta* and the lawyer to request the release from prison of former members of congress, of labor leaders, of students.

Ex-President Gallegos appealed for the second time to the Committee for Human Rights—the last time directly to Mrs. Roosevelt—saying:

"As a Venezuelan and as a man who feels human suffering, the fate of hundreds of my compatriots who at this moment are prisoners is a source of special concern to me. Some of them have spent more than one year in prison without having been brought before a judge, without having been given even the simulacrum of a trial. They are hostages in the Nazi manner, and they are treated as such. They are confined in separate cells, isolated from all contact with family or friends, deprived of all reading material, exposed to the abuse of their jailers, and some of them have been tortured . . ."

Anthony Boyle, representing the United Mine Workers of America; Serafino Romualdi of the American Federation of Labor; and Ernst Schwarz of the Congress of Industrial Organizations handed the Venezuelan Ambassador in Washington a letter in which they said, among other things:

"The three organizations which we represent, totalling a membership of more than 15,000,000 workers, belong to the Interamerican Regional Organization of the International Federation of Free Unions, with which the Confederation of Venezuelan Workers is also affiliated.

"We have received information to the effect that numerous union leaders have been arrested in Venezuela and confined in the Model Prison of Caracas and the penetentiary of San Juan de los Morros, without being charged with any offense, and without having been granted a hearing to learn the reason for their arrest. Among these prisoners are Bernardo Pérez Salinas, president of the Confederation of Venezuelan Workers, who has been in custody for six months, and Luis Tovar, president of the Federation of Oil Workers of Venezuela, to which, according to our information, 80% of the workers engaged in this industry belong."

At about this time an attempt was made on Rómulo Betancourt's life in Havana.

In October 1951 the governing *junta* decided to give the death blow to the autonomy of the University. The professors—men of all parties, among them the most illustrious men of letters now living in Caracas—sent a deputation to the head of the government, the former Professor Germán Suárez Flamerich. The reply was a brusque military order. Thus the University now receives the treatment it had under Juan Vicente Gómez. The professors were removed. And the flame of the lamp of wisdom appears to have begun to flicker over a barrel of gunpowder.

This is the way things stand. How sure of itself a country can be in which all the forces of public opinion are silenced is something only the future can tell. For the moment, as far as respect for human rights is concerned, international organizations have proved too weak to oppose the will of a man who successfully seizes power in any country or any continent.

There is in Venezuela a third party, that of the business men, and they are satisfied. Carlos Otto, a leading industrialist of Venezuela, says: "The economic prospects and administrative measures are excellent, and throughout the country there is evidence of progress and diligent activity, and an enviable state of prosperity . . ."

North American observers have come to the conclusion that in Venezuela—whose iron and oil and whose proximity to the Panama Canal give it a place of singular importance in the hemisphere's fight for democracy—democracy is doomed by a tradition of long standing. But they all point out the dangers in its present policy. Herbert Matthews of *The New York Times* wrote from Panama on April 26, 1951, after a visit to Venezuela:

"Venezuelan politics is at least as inflammable as the colossal and fantastic wealth of oil that seems to seep from every

117

rock . . . Economically the country is going through one of the most astonishing booms in world history, with more than $1,000,000,000 worth of oil being exported annually. That does not mean, however, that Venezuela is wealthy. Once the oil leaves the ground it does not belong to Venezuela but to the United States, British and Dutch companies, and all Venezuela gets is her royalties . . . The most optimistic estimate is that the oil reserves will be exhausted in twenty years. The question is how much of the cash returns are being used in satisfying such basic needs as the nutrition, clothing and housing of the people . . ."

VIII

BOLIVIA, LAND OF TIN, MILITARY, AND GALLOWS FRUIT

Every revolution in our countries is a backward step in their history and their political, material, and spiritual progress.

ALCIDES ARGUEDAS

WHERE THE Andes have their broadest base, where some of their tallest peaks lose themselves in the sky, lies Bolivia. It contains one of the most extensive stretches of tableland in the world. When the Germans dreamed of weaving an aerial net over South America—at the time they owned the most important or the only lines of aviation in Brazil, Bolivia, Peru, and Colombia—it seemed to them that this tableland was an airfield built by the hand of God, a rooftop from which to dominate a continent. The altitude of the plateau is 12,000 feet. Plane passengers are provided with oxygen containers, and for the first few weeks, until one gets one's "air legs," un- due haste or activity may bring on an attack of *soroche*, or mountain sickness, which makes its victim feel as though he were dying. The air is subtle, the sky a limpid blue; around the upland the beautiful mountain peaks are always visible, covered with snow the year round. To one side lies Lake Titi- caca, a fresh-water sea joining Bolivia and Peru, with islands, fine beaches, and swift motor launches that ply back and forth, as well as native reed canoes that antedate the coming of the white man. On the peninsula of Copacabana there is a famous shrine, once one of the richest in the world, and on the Tia- huanácu shore stand the ruins of a famous prehistoric city— already ruined when the Spaniards arrived—with a sun gate hewn from a single stone. On the other side, in a cleft, stands the city of La Paz, bright, clean, and modern, with ten-story buildings and, in the heart of the city, the University of San Andrés. To the east, in huge breastworks of color, the Andes descend to a semi-arid plain, with verdant oases dotting the red earth. This is the route to the Chaco, the green hell.

In the uplands the Indians speak only Aymará. As they herd their flocks they spin wool on hand-spindles, and their deadly slingshots are always within reach. From the women's backs, out of layers of bright-hued blankets, a *guagua* (papoose) rears its solemn head, and with the chewing of narcotic coca leaves—the national vice—the Indians lull the passage of the bleak, monotonous years. At fair time they drive their herds of llamas to market and dance at their festivities in devil masks with long silvered horns and teeth of little mirrors, to the music of their panpipes and *tonkories*. At night-fall they confide their age-old sorrow and desolation to the music of the *quena*. When there is trouble in La Paz the Indians slip silently into the city to see the bodies of the victims swinging from the lampposts of the main square. "Papa President has gone to the other world."

In the tropical lowlands the language spoken is Guaraní. The land is fertile, but there is no way of transporting the products that could be raised there. In the city of Santa Cruz the only illumination of the sand streets is the light of the moon. Santa Cruz was the point of departure for the soldiers who marched east to the Chaco War to fight, not the Paraguayans, but thirst. Battles were fought over a well, and to find a thimbleful of water they dug in the sand like madmen, with shovels, sticks, their nails, in a frenzy of thirst and rage. And they died of thirst.

From the vantage point of Bolivia, one can see clearly how full of absurdities the great southern continent is. Brazil is larger than the United States; Ecuador is smaller than Arizona or Nebraska. Bolivia is not especially large or small, just a little larger than France and Spain combined. But whereas Chile, which looks like the backbone of a fish, has fifty-seven sea ports and a coastline twice the length of the United State's Pacific coastline, Bolivia and Paraguay—the two South American Switzerlands—are walled in from the sea by Brazil, Argentina, Chile, and Peru.

More than four hundred years ago the Spaniards reached the present territory of Bolivia and founded its first cities. Since that time the white man has held the reins of power uninterruptedly in spite of the facts that as late as 1942 the census reported the population of La Paz as being only 14% "white or whitish," and that in the rest of the country the whites represent less than 2% and the "whitish" 37% of the total. The whites, the aristocracy of Bolivia, are cultivated and refined to the highest degree. A Bolivian writer-diplomat, Adolfo Costa du Rels, is the author of books in French which rank high in the literature of that language. The mines of Bolivia have created great fortunes. An Indian of humble origin, by name Simón Patiño, with a business sense comparable to that of the Rockefellers and the Morgans, became one of the multimillionaires of the world. Bolivia produces 97% of the world's antimony and 53% of its tin. But the Indians of the highlands still talk the language they spoke ten centuries ago, eat frozen potatoes as did their ancestors six hundred years ago, and huddle silently in the doorways of the great houses of La Paz. Those of the lowlands know that they live in the outer circles of the green hell. And the mine workers . . .

Foster Hailey of *The New York Times* visited the mines in June 1951. He has this to say:

"At the working face of the Pulacayo silver and lead mine in the Bolivian Department of Potosi the ore-breaking rock is so hot that it numbs the hand. Indians clad only in a G-string and rubber boots hack at the precious rock whose metals mean so much to today's industrial world. The temperature varies from 120 to 125 degrees. The humidity is 90 to 95 per cent. Rock dust fills the air and the lungs. Carbon dioxide bubbles from the freezing water that drips from the ceiling and runs down both sides of the tunnel.

"For eight hours a day, or longer, six days a week, 3000 to 4000 men, women and children ranging in age from 10 to 35 labor at cutting out the ore, hauling it to the surface and sorting it for shipment to the world's smelters. For this they receive wages that reach a peak, for the men, at 135 bolivianos a day. [The boliviano at current quotations is about 200 to $1.] These miners are the highest paid workers in Bolivia.

"When the day's work is done they leave the sweltering heat of the mine shafts and tunnels for unheated homes of unmortared stone. Outside in the clear, rare atmosphere of 15,000 feet altitude the temperature ranges from the low 50's in the day to below-freezing at night. Their meals are scant and lacking in vitamins, for all food has to be imported and the cost is high. Clothing also is costly and only a minimum can be bought. Fuel is used for cooking, not for the heating of water or for bathing, or for heating.

"Sixty per cent of the miners, it is estimated, have tuberculosis. Half are syphilitic . . . half the babies born die in the first year. Those who live have a life expectancy of 35. That is only about half what it is in the United States. Medical attention is scanty and few survive either a bad injury or major illness."

Once when I was in La Paz I got out of a car in the main square. It is a beautiful square in the Spanish manner, with the cathedral and the presidential palace flanking it on one side. La Paz has splendid street lights. I asked the chauffeur: "From which lamppost did they hang Villarroel?"

The man got out of the car, thought the question over carefully, and then answered, pointing with his finger: "Villarroel from that one; Vallibián, his aide, from that one; from that one over there Uría, his secretary; from that one, Roberto Hinojosa, one of those who write . . ."

He had a good memory. With the lampposts in view, one had only to close one's eyes to see what the square had looked like, each post with its dangling corpse, like grapes of wrath in a human vintage.

I asked a young woman of the upper class one day when I was talking with her: "Were you in La Paz when Villarroel was killed?"

"Yes. I had just gone out for a walk, with no particular place in mind. I saw all the people converging on the square, and I followed the crowd. There were the dead men; they had been stripped of their clothes. Months later the children were still playing a new game they had invented: if you don't give me that toy I'll hang you. One child lost his life playing it. Villarroel was a distinguished officer. I knew him well. He was not the way his enemies described him . . .

"Villarroel was killed on July 21. On September 27 an officer dressed in civilian clothes entered the presidential palace. He was going to kill the president pro tem, who was the chief justice of the supreme court. He made his way to his office, shooting down two of the guards. As he advanced on the president, the latter unbuttoned his coat, pointed to his heart and said: 'I am unarmed. Aim here.'

"The would-be assassin was completely disconcerted. He lowered his gun, and two attendants seized him. The news was broadcast by radio to the city. Everybody rushed into the streets. At that very moment Eguino and Escobar, the chiefs of police responsible for the killing in 1944 of the Minister of Foreign Affairs, Salinas Aramayo, Senators Luis Calvo, Felix Capriles, and Terrazas, and General Ramos, were being released from prison. The mob seized them and beat them to death. That night they were swinging from lampposts. On this occasion, too, the whole city paraded through the square.

A sudden storm came up, and a bolt of lightning struck near by, illuminating the scene with its macabre light. In two minutes not a soul was to be seen. It seemed like a warning from an irate deity. Many of the people rushed to the churches to pray for mercy . . ."

"That's Bolivia for you," I thought out loud.

"No, not exactly," she corrected me. "Do you know where the idea came from? A few weeks before, the newsreels of Mussolini's end had been shown. The people were very much impressed by the sight of the bodies of the Duce and Clara Petacci hanging for everyone to see. And they learned something."

She was right. In Bolivia there was Fascism under Villarroel. This was followed by anti-Fascism. And Bolivia has a terrible past.

Alcides Arguedas divided his famous history of Bolivia into four books entitled: *The Enlightened Caudillos; The People in Action; Dictatorship and Anarchy; The Barbarous Caudillos.* These last years have written new chapters that Arguedas did not live to record. One has only to turn the pages of these books to see that the actors in these bloody, drunken annals were, for the most part, colonels and majors. Several different histories could be written about Bolivia, as about any country. In its case they could be: the history of the people; the history of the hopes of the republic; and the history of the military. The last would afford examples of some of the most brutal dictatorships the world has ever seen.

In 1934 President Daniel Salamanca, who coined the bitter phrase "the pseudo-science of the high command" at the time of the Chaco War, was removed from office and replaced by Vice-President José Luis Tejada Sorzano. In 1936 the military threw out Tejada Sorzano, and Colonel David Toro assumed office. In 1937 the military threw out Colonel Toro, and Colonel Germán Busch took his place. In 1939 Busch shot himself. General Carlos Quintanilla, who succeeded Busch, ordered elections held; the winner was General Enrique Peñaranda. In 1943 the military overthrew Peñaranda; Major Gualberto Villarroel took his place. On July 21, 1946, Major Villarroel was strung up from a lamppost . . .

One of the required studies for the military is the art of killing. As a result these presidential changes have more the air of attack and counterattack than of democratic electoral choice.

Villarroel's 1943-6 presidency throws light on the events that preceded and followed his term of office. It is not exclusively Bolivian history. It is related to the Chaco War, which was set against a background of the international struggle for oil. The actual architects of German Nazism had a hand in the organization of the military lodges. Members of the Argentine army had close ties with the military of Bolivia. Thus, even though the local color is so strong as to seem completely to dominate the picture, it was really an international affair, for oil, tin, antimony, Nazism, Communism, and, more recently, Peronism, are all matters of world import.

Professor David R. Moore, author of a careful and well-documented compendium, *A History of Latin America* (revised, 1942), says, after pointing out the connection between certain aspects of the financial situation of Bolivia and the Chaco War (1932-5):

"Another factor held responsible for promoting trouble was the influence of foreigners. They were blamed for being behind the native politicians and generals. They had bought concessions. They needed facilities for getting oil and other goods to market. They could provide leadership. General [Hans] Kundt, a German, was placed at the head of the Bolivian Army, and a Belgian officer directed the Paraguayan. Foreign soldiers need not die in the jungle battlefields. The natives would supply the rank and file. The foreigners might expect, however, that they would share in whatever gains accrued from the newly acquired lands or transportation routes.

Foreign capitalists from the United States who had invested huge sums of money in Bolivia had to bear a large share of the odium that was heaped upon aliens in general in connection with the outbreak of the Chaco War. In 1922 New York bankers loaned Bolivia $33,000,000. In 1926, [the] Standard Oil [Company of New Jersey] bought approximately six thousand square miles of oil lands in the Bolivia side of the Chaco. In this same year an English firm advanced Bolivia $9,000,000. At the very time it required fully sixty-five per cent of the total Bolivian government revenues to keep up payments on money already borrowed. Much of this English loan furnished credit for purchase of British munitions. Two years later Dillon, Read & Co., of New York, placed another loan for $23,000,000. It was in this very year that war broke out in the Chaco."

Professor Moore goes on to say that these antecedents should be borne in mind, even though in the actual precipitation of hostilities the national pride of the two countries and lack of restraint on the part of the military played a great part. The casualties of this war rose to tens of thousands. La Paz was like a field hospital. The Paraguayans captured thousands of prisoners. Much of the disaster was blamed on General Kundt. Why was a Prussian directing the Bolivian army. Why had a Nazi party been formed in Bolivia, where there are only Indians?

When German industry was seeking and acquiring markets in South America, Bolivia opened its doors to the Germans. By the terms of a treaty of 1908 they were given commercial carte blanche: Germany was treated as a most-favored nation, and the establishment of German firms in Bolivia was encouraged. The French military mission was replaced shortly later by a German, headed by Colonel Hans Kundt and Captain Ernst Roehm. Kundt, as might have been expected, wanted to be top dog in Bolivia, and he tried, contrary to the constitution, to have President Hernando Siles's term of office extended. As a result he had to leave the country, but when the Chaco War broke out he was recalled, and though his military tactics were disastrous, he managed to inculcate in the younger officers a very Prussian and very Nazi state of mind. It is curious to note that as early as 1934 and 1935, when the Nazis had been in power in Germany only a short time, Bolivian officers who were prisoners in Paraguay laid the foundations for a military lodge based on Nazi principles and techniques. But it must not be forgotten that Roehm, too, was in Bolivia with Kundt, and Roehm later became one of the chief organizers of the Nazi party, and during its early days was Hitler's right-hand man.

After the Chaco War many of the Bolivian officers made a trip to Italy and to Germany. Major Elías Belmonte Pabón, who had been head of the police and Minister of the Interior, was sent to Berlin as military attaché. His Nazi sympathies brought him under suspicion by the United States, and the Washington government got hold of a letter he had written outlining a plan for seizing the government of Bolivia and implanting the Nazi system there. The letter was addressed to the German minister in Bolivia, who seems to have been the chief organizer of the Nazi party there. Not only were Nazi ideas rampant in the army, but the 8,000 German residents of Bolivia were for the most part Nazis, and very influential. A dozen German firms controlled business in La Paz. The government moved swiftly, handing the German minister his passport and declaring him *persona non grata*. But the military lodge went on, and played an important part as the center of operations of an international movement that had strong repercussions in many parts of America. The head of this lodge in 1943 was Major Gualberto Villarroel.

The military lodge was a highly secret organization that sought its members among the most daring and determined of the officers, and its objective was the complete control of the government. By the terms of its by-laws special meetings would be called when, for example, "it is imperative to change the head of the republic." In 1943 the colonels considered such a change imperative. The lodge gave the order. The night of December 20 President Enrique Peñaranda and his cabinet were in jail, and Major Villarroel assumed power.

The lodge, however, did not come to power unassisted. It was supported by the party of Victor Paz Estenssoro, Movimiento Nacional Revolucionario, which was organized in 1941. It drew its members from the ranks of writers, lawyers, young and belligerent pro-Nazis. It represented the frustrated and embittered of the post-war era. They viewed the humiliation Bolivia had received as a parallel to Germany's humiliation after the First World War—and, carrying the parallel farther, saw in Bolivian Nazism their hope of redemption. They were enemies of the Jews and of Yankee imperialism, and friends of Perón, one of their military brotherhood.

A book by a former Foreign Minister of Bolivia, Alberto Ostría Gutiérrez, carries in parallel columns the program of the Bolivian movement and that of the Nazis. It is interesting to compare them.

PROGRAM OF THE MOVIMIENTO NACIONAL REVOLUCIONARIO OF BOLIVIA

We proclaim the right of all Bolivians, men or women, as the basic principle and foundation of the organization of the state, the proper functioning of its institutions, and the application or reform of its laws. And we demand the cancellation of those privileges which permit non-Bolivians or foreign enterprises to exercise rights without being subject to the same obligations as Bolivians.

PROGRAM OF THE NATIONAL SOCIALIST PARTY OF GERMANY

We demand the union of all Germans to constitute a Greater Germany based on the right to independence which nations enjoy. No one who is not a member of the nation can be a citizen of the State. Only those in whose veins flows German blood, no matter what their religion, can be members of the nation.

We demand the elimination of all intervention by foreign stockholders or capital in newspapers, magazines, or other publications. We demand a law requiring all publishing enterprises or publicity agencies of any sort to file a statement with the civil or military authorities whenever they engage the services of foreign editors or correspondents, stating the salaries they receive and the nature of their services.

We demand the complete restriction of Jewish immigration and any other which does not contribute to the nation's productivity.

We demand the support of all in doing away with the great private monopolies, and putting all smaller enterprises in the hands of Bolivians exclusively.

We demand the death penalty for speculators, usurers, smugglers, those guilty of fraud or of corrupting public officials, and those trafficking in vice.

Faith in the nation must come to the rescue of the country. Thus we will be worthy of

We demand the adoption of legal measures against deliberate political imposture, and its diffusion by the press. To facilitate the creation of a National German press we demand: a) that all the editors and the staff of newspapers in the German language be members of the German nation; b) that no non-German newspapers may be published without special permission of the state; c) that the financial participation or the influence of non-Germans in German newspapers be forbidden by law.

All non-German immigration must cease. We demand that all non-Aryans who entered Germany after August 2, 1914, be obliged to leave German territory at once.

We demand the nationalization of all business enterprises that up to the present moment have been organized in the form of trusts.

We demand the pitiless persecution of all activities that are prejudicial to the common good. The sordid criminals who conspire against the well-being of the nation, the usurers, the speculators, etc., should receive the death penalty, whatever their race or creed.

The party leaders swear to devote themselves unremittingly—sacrificing their lives, if our destiny. We shall conquer through the irresistible strength of our movement, prepared for any sacrifice, including life it- the aforesaid objectives. need be—to the achievement of self, for Bolivia's sake.

How was it possible to accord recognition to the government headed by Major Villarroel, in view of these antecedents of the military lodge and the Movimiento Nacional Revolucionario, when the whole hemisphere was united for the defense of democracy? No country except Argentina did so. A memorandum drawn up in Washington in January 1944 expressed the uniform opinion of the other countries. With acid frankness it called attention to the links between Paz Estenssoro, founder of the Movimiento, and the German Legation, as well as the newspaper *La Calle,* which was subsidized by German money and characterized by its anti-Semitism and its Nazism. This anti-Semitism has a certain explanation in Bolivia because recent Jewish immigration had set up an unexpected competition to local business throughout the country.

In an official report to the State Department in Washington it was said that the conspirators in La Paz had been in close touch with their German sponsors through José del Castillo, Commercial Attaché of the Spanish Legation in La Paz, an active Falangist and defender of Fascist, anti-democratic theories and practices, who served as courier between La Paz and Buenos Aires. The report added that he happened to be in Buenos Aires when the revolt broke out, but that he then returned to La Paz at once. It also stated that through José Luis Aranguren, who occupied an important post in the Spanish Legation and was a leader of the Spanish Falange in La Paz, German and Argentine agents had contributed 3,000,000 bolivianos to the expense account of the coup.

Cordell Hull says in his memoirs:

"Six months had passed since the revolution in Bolivia had overthrown the government of General Peñaranda and installed that of General Villarroel. Throughout that time we were in constant consultation with the other American republics. These had taken the same step we had in withholding recognition from Villarroel. Naturally, the Argentine government had recognized the Villarroel Government very soon after it came into being with the aid of the extreme Argentine nationalists and Nazi agents."

The ideals they shared naturally created a link between the Bolivian movement and that of Argentina. A month after General Ramírez made himself ruler of Argentina, Paz Estenssoro visited Buenos Aires, entered into relations with the military and Nazi elements, secured arms for the coup against Peñaranda, and carried a message on foreign policy from General Perón to Bolivia. When Argentina clashed with the United States on the question of armaments, Paz Estenssoro's party sent him a message of solidarity.

Washington followed a vacillating policy. After five months it issued a new memorandum reversing itself. Major Villarroel achieved this triumph by playing on the candor of Ambassador Avra Warren. Warren had gone from Panama to La Paz as an observer, and before a week had elapsed, he sent a dispatch to Washington absolving the military government of guilt. Villarroel had purged the government without violence, removing members of the Movimiento Nacional Revolucionario, he had broken relations with Spain, and had expelled from the country a group of Japanese and Germans.

According to Alberto Ostría Gutiérrez, who has been a Bolivian foreign minister, Ambassador Warren submitted to the State Department in Washington, in June 1944, a report that said, among other things, the following: that when it had become apparent that the stigma of Nazism carried by the MNR was the chief obstacle to its recognition by the other American republics, Villarroel's group had quickly retired the members of the MNR from the cabinet; that the growing strength and prestige of the provisional government—

owing to the patience, firmness, and moderation of Villar-roel—had called forth manifestations of solidarity from other political groups and worthy independent elements in Bolivia; that, simultaneously with removing from office persons he considered dangerous to hemispheric security, Villarroel's government had begun to implement with deeds its declarations in favor of the United Nations; that the Bolivian production of materials vital to the armed needs of the Allies had gone ahead without interruption; that a decree providing for the expropriation and nationalization of Axis firms had been put into effect; and that in May 1944, with the arrest and deportation of 81 German and Japanese subjects, the government of Villarroel had irrevocably aligned itself with the cause of the United Nations.[1]

Other countries soon recognized Villarroel. Once he had been internationally recognized, he called for elections and legalized his presidency. The members of the Movimiento Nacional Revolucionario resumed their posts, and violence broke out afresh. The Supreme Court was abolished. Congressman Julio Alvarado's protests were silenced with a club. Five months after Ambassador Warren had made his report, a police communiqué, having to do with an uprising in Oruro, appeared in *La Calle*. It ran as follows:

"To date the following have been shot for their share in instigating the seditious movement: Lieutenant General Demetrio Ramos, Colonel Fernando Garrón, Colonel Eduardo Pacieri, Humberto Loiza Beltrá, Rubén Terrazas, Carlos Salinas Aramayo, Miguel Brito, engineer. Colonel Melitón Brito committed suicide in the town of Coquena, and Colonel Ovidio Quiroga, retired, managed to escape. Lieutenant Luis Olmos, Major Armando Pinto and Hector Diez de Medina are being held in Charaña for transfer to this city."

[1] Quoted in *Una Revolución tras los Andes*, by Alberto Ostría Gutiérrez (Santiago, 1944).

The story behind these executions reveals one of the blackest episodes in all Bolivia's history. The press of all America protested, as did cultural groups, universities, democratic organizations. Among the victims were men like Carlos Salinas Aramayo, Luis Calvo, and Rubén Terrazas. Salinas Aramayo had been professor of law and Minister of Foreign Affairs; in 1943 he had signed the declaration of war against Germany and Japan. Luis Calvo was a man respected by all for his moral calibre. Terrazas had been Minister of Education, dean of the Law School, professor of civil law, senator, and a distinguished writer.

The chiefs of police, Eguino and Escobar, who had been in charge of the executions, were promoted.

Fittingly to observe the New Year of 1945, Villarroel's government announced the formation of a new cabinet. It was headed by Paz Estenssoro, the head of Movimiento Nacional Revolucionario. The director of *La Calle*, Augusto Céspedes, was appointed an ambassador, as was one of Estenssoro's associates, Carlos Montenegro.

Paz Estenssoro was the brains of the new government. He represented it at the Conference of Chapultepec (1945), and it was he who, as Minister of the Treasury, directed its economic and social policies. He went to Buenos Aires to congratulate Perón on his triumph at the polls, and on this mission he was accompanied by the elite of the party. In his interview with the head of the Argentine state, as reported by *La Nación* of Buenos Aires, he observed with satisfaction "the identity of aims and action between the June revolution [Perón's] and that of Bolivia."

In February 1946 the University Federation of La Paz "in view of the fact that the titular head of Nazism in Bolivia, Don Victor Paz Estenssoro, still holds a chair in the Faculty of Finance of the glorious University of San Andrés . . . resolves: 1) To condemn publicly the intellectual author and accomplice of the murders of November of 1944, Victor Paz Estenssoro; 2) To request his resignation as professor of the University of San Andrés . . ."

Four months later a series of popular uprisings in La Paz overthrew the government. Paz Estenssoro and the other directors of Movimiento Nacional Revolucionario managed to escape, and with others who happened to be out of the country at the time, set up their headquarters in Buenos Aires. Villarroel and those closest to him remained to adorn the lampposts of the square.

Five years went by. Presidential elections were held in May 1951. Paz Estenssoro and his associates were still in exile in Buenos Aires, but from there they carried on an intense underground campaign. Movimiento Nacional Revolucionario and Partido Obrero Revolucionario—the name given by the workers to a semi-Fascist, pro-Communist organization—put up Paz Estenssoro's candidacy. The government refused to allow Paz Estenssoro to alight from the plane bringing him from Buenos Aires, and he had to return to his exile. He had no newspaper to back him, no radio time, and yet when the votes were counted, Paz Estenssoro led the government-backed candidate by 14,000 votes: Paz Estenssoro, 54,129; Gabriel Gonzalves, 40,381—this out of a total population of about 3,850,000.

These figures need interpretation. The totalitarian parties turned out to the last man, perfectly disciplined and defiantly aggressive. The opposition supported five candidates. Although Paz Estenssoro in reality won only 40% of the total vote, what he proved beyond a doubt was that he had the most powerful political organization in Bolivia. Moreover, Bolivia does not have universal suffrage. Paz Estenssoro's 54,000 votes, like those of his adversaries, represented only the voters who could read and write. The Bolivian masses are illiterate. If they had had the franchise, very possibly Paz Estenssoro would have had a much larger plurality.

The question one immediately asks is: how is it possible that men who escaped hanging in the revolution of 1946 by the skin of their teeth, who were outlawed for five years, could have achieved a triumph of this sort?

Paz Estenssoro told a North American newsman: "I am not pro-Nazi, or pro-Communist, or anti-American. I am only pro-Bolivian. I am not anti-capitalist. I ask only that the profits from Bolivia's natural resources be invested in Bolivia for the betterment of the country." He added that he would be delighted to receive technical assistance from the United States under the Point Four program, which has already been functioning in Bolivia under the auspices of the Institute of Interamerican Affairs. "My inauguration in the presidency," he went on, "will insure the steady flow of tin which is vital to the United States, and will even increase it."

Paz Estenssoro's message to the Bolivians, for home consumption, is much more drastic. He has promised the masses the nationalization of the mines, the distribution of land. The parties backing Paz Estenssoro have in common one thing that spearheads their action: the shibboleth of Yankee imperialism. This arouses an echo in Communists, Nazis, and just Bolivians. The nationalization of the mines in Bolivia has a more dramatic connotation than the nationalization of oil in Mexico or Iran. Bolivia has one product: tin: 70% of all Bolivia's exports is tin. If one day the mine-owners were to stop exporting tin, the government of Bolivia would be bankrupt. There would be no funds to pay state employees. The fortunes of the mine-owners are fabulous. According to *Moody's Industrials* (June 2, 1951), in 1950 the net profits of the Patiño Mining Corporation were $4,419,726 on a capital investment of $10,131,646. The tin deposits of Bolivia might have been looked upon as a gift from heaven. But the novel by Augusto Céspedes, former director of *La Calle*, which deals with this subject, is entitled: *El Metal del Diablo* (*The Devil's Metal*). The life expectancy of the mine-workers is one of the shortest in the world, and they lead a miserable existence.

When Villarroel and Paz Estenssoro took over the government of Bolivia, they signed an agreement with the mine-owners, allowing them to keep forty per cent of the dollars they received for their tin, while the other sixty per cent was to be turned over to the state in exchange for Bolivian currency at the official rate of exchange. It was an excellent deal for the mine-owners. On August 11, 1950, President Mamerto Urriolagoitia, who held office from May 1949 to May 1951, issued a decree by the terms of which the mine-owners were allowed to keep only twenty-eight per cent of their foreign currency. The owners protested to high heaven. They claimed they were being hounded, ruined. They halted the shipment of tin, and Bolivia was threatened with starvation. After two months the government had to rescind the decree and allow them their former forty per cent. Today when Paz Estenssoro says "nationalization of the mines" he has not only the mass of the people behind him, but even those who can read and write.

It was once thought that Bolivia was built on a tin mine. It is a powder mine.

Why, if the mines belong to an Indian (Patiño), blue-blooded Bolivians (the Aramayos), and a Jew (Hochschild), is the hatred of the political parties directed against Yankee imperialism? The fact of the matter is that the mines have their boards of directors in New York and their managers are North Americans: DeWitt C. Deringer for the Patiño Mines; George Tower for the Hochschild Mines; and Charles G. Bowers for the Aramayo. When the mine-owners refused to settle for twenty-eight per cent as their share of foreign exchange, a group of Socialists introduced a measure in the Bolivian congress to have the directors of the companies tried on criminal charges. So far these are nothing but words. The mine-owners have shielded themselves behind their North American associates.

Franz Tamayo, a Bolivian philosopher who occasionally descends from Olympus to view the political scene, and who enjoys an almost mythological prestige in his country, in July 1950 wrote in a prologue to a book entitled *Wheat, Tin, Sea,* which deals with Bolivia's three themes:

"The Yankee. Our powerful brother to the north is shedding his noble blood in defense of Korea's freedom. A noble destiny. After helping Cuba to free itself, they have now liberated Europe. But a melancholy thought assails me. If it were a question of Bolivia, I am afraid not one drop of the blood of a Yankee mouse would be shed for us . . ."

A few paragraphs from the programs of certain of the political parties of Bolivia will throw light on this bitterness of a nation that, from the depths of a mine pit, views the democracy of North America as something so remote and unattainable for the poor Bolivian that it arouses in him nothing but hostility:

"Yankee imperialism, implemented by the political piracy of the dollar, has made itself the economic and political overlord of the semi-colonies of America. Bolivia and the other Latin-speaking countries of the continent are mere factories for imperialism . . . Imperialism began by buying the governing oligarchies, which, without this economic backing, could not have remained in power . . ."[2]

"To the miners class struggle means one thing . . . the struggle against that sector of Yankee imperialism which is our oppressor . . . We denounce as declared enemies of the proletariat those 'Leftists' in the pay of Yankee imperialism who talk to us of the democracy of the North and its world supremacy. It is a farce to speak of democracy when the United States is controlled by sixty families, and when those sixty

[2] Program of the University Federation of Bolivia, approved in December 1938 and ratified in 1947. This program was drawn up by one of the present leaders of the Partido de la Izquierda Revolucionaria.

families live like leeches on the blood of semi-colonial countries such as ours . . ."[3]

"The governments are kept in power by the mine-owners and the agents of imperialism . . . If, by exception, a government comes to power which opposes their interests, it is quickly overthrown on orders from Paris, London, or New York . . . Our program cannot be fully carried out until a new type of state has been created which is no longer the expression of imperialism and feudal bourgeoisie, but becomes, on the contrary, the expression of the interests of the oppressed classes, that is to say, nine-tenths of our people."[4]

"The international contradictions of imperialism have resulted in its most powerful sector, the Yankee, linking the Latin-speaking semi-colonies of Indo-America ever closer to its expansionist and exploiting policy. Immediately following the end of World War I, which marked the replacement of England's imperialism by that of the United States, Indo-America, and with it Bolivia, has been unable to govern itself; it has become an appendage of imperialism; its nations have lost their political and economic sovereignty, and have become reservoirs of basic materials and a market for North American products. All this has been achieved by imperialism through its financial policies—dollar and pound politics—buying on the open market the oligarchies that govern us, and which have sold us out to imperialism, and which could not stay in power if it were not for the economic support they receive . . ."[5]

On the basis of the foregoing, it is easy to understand the Bolivian elections of May 1951. For a long time, and especially during the last five years, all these parties have been acquiring a growing foothold, not only among the masses, but also in the intellectual groups. It is not the newspapers of

[3] Program of the Syndicated Federation of Mine Workers of Bolivia, approved in November 1946.
[4] Program of the Partido de la Izquierda Revolucionaria.
[5] Program of the Partido Obrero Revolucionario.

La Paz that circulate among the miners, but mimeographed bulletins put out in Buenos Aires. In May 1949 some miners assassinated two American engineers and raped their wives. The Bolivian government sent in troops, and there were hundreds of casualties. Two delegates of the Interamerican Confederation of Workers who went to Bolivia as observers, made the following report:

"The majority of the mine workers unions are controlled by the Federation of Miners headed by Juan Lechín, who is in close touch with the totalitarian forces of the Movimiento Nacionalista Revolucionario and the Radepa Military Lodge, which was founded by the late dictator Villarroel. Juan Lechín has imposed a veritable state of siege in the mines, and the workers are working under the same kind of terrorism once imposed on the mine workers of Chile by the Communists . . ."

That fact is that as against the direct, radical solutions offered by Paz Estenssoro's supporters—who have gone so far as to propose dissolving the Pan American Union, forming a Federation of Socialist Republics of Latin America, internationalizing the waterways, and repudiating the national debt—the programs of the Liberal Party and even of the Bolivian Confederation of Workers hold little attraction for a proletariat now ripe for violence.

Paz Estenssoro's election posed the problem of whether he should be permitted to take power. President Urriolagoitia—who had been jailed under the dictatorship of Villarroel and Paz Estenssoro—conferred with the military, whose most capable leader is General Ovidio Quiroga, also a victim of Villarroel's dictatorship. They agreed that a military *junta* should take over the government, refusing to recognize Paz Estenssoro's election. This decision was made in May 1951. Anything can happen now. This is a moment of pause for a country hovering over an abyss. Nowhere else in Latin America is politics so definitely slanted toward an international conflict as in Bolivia. The workers who numb the gnawing pangs of their hunger by chewing coca see in the films made in the United States a workingman with shoes to wear, a comfortable house, and a car of his own, things that act as a bulwark against Communist penetration. It is hard to know just what goes on in their minds. But it is safe to say that as they descend into the mine pit, hand in hand with death, their feelings are not exactly those attributed to the dove of peace.

IX

PARAGUAY, LAND OF DILEMMA

In October 1550 some fifty Guaranís of the powerful Tupinamba tribe were in Rouen and, on the banks of the Seine in the presence of Catherine de Médicis and Henri II, gave an exhibition of their dances and war games. "Catherine de Médicis," relates the anonymous reporter of that singular spectacle, "who was making a progress with her usual pomp and magnificence, was entranced by the beautiful games and mimicry of the savages." The Indians, however, were not impressed by those sickly monarchs or by that glittering pomp against a background of squalor. Someone wanted to know the opinion of these Americans, and they gave it in succinct and disturbing words. "They said," Montaigne relates in a famous passage in one of his essays, "that they found it very strange that so many bearded, tall men, strong and well-armed, as made up the king's retinue, should submit to the will of a young boy. In the second place, they had observed that (in Europe) there were many people who enjoyed to the point of satiety every manner of comfort and wealth, while others begged for alms on their doorsteps, gaunt with hunger and poverty, and that it seemed strange to them that the latter could suffer such injustice and not strangle the others or set fire to their houses."

NATALICIO GONZÁLEZ

SINCE THE DAY in 1811 when Paraguay first proclaimed its independence, it has been forced to steer an uneasy course between Scylla and Charybdis: Buenos Aires and Hell. The fact that Paraguay exists as a nation indicates that it chose the second alternative. It has tried to defend its history, its culture, its tradition, and in so doing it has stopped at nothing. It has set up fiendish dictators, it has fought wars with all odds against it, it has turned a land of farmers into the most fearsome armed camp of the continent. This does not mean that Argentina has laid aside the natural temptation the proximity of this poor neighbor arouses, or that there are not those in Paraguay whose ears are open to the siren's song. Not long ago the role of the Lorelei was played by Evita Perón herself, and the spellbound mariner was President Federico Chaves of Paraguay. This happened in Buenos Aires, in August 1950, the year that had been officially designated in Argentina as "The Year of General San Martín."

President Chaves, who had legalized his presidency in the elections held on July 16, 1950, was inaugurated as constitutional head of the state—before that he had been *de facto* president—on August 15, and that same day or the morning of the following day he left by plane for Buenos Aires. There President Perón, who had arranged a kind of class reunion with certain of his comrades-in-arms of the neighboring countries— Peru, Chile, Bolivia, and Uruguay—received the new President warmly. Chaves represented a valuable piece in Perón's chess game. The group reviewed units of the fleet at Puerto Nuevo, and that night there was a splendid banquet. Here the Peróns brought off a master stroke. Instead of Juan, the President, presiding at the dinner, it was Evita who did the honors. All the speeches were addressed to her, and it was she who replied. The guests stood while she spoke. The President of Paraguay, who had visited hospitals and schools in the company of the First Lady, was more of a *peronista* that night than the lowliest of the "shirtless." His speech glowed with such phrases as:

"I am here to represent my country in this act of homage to the Great Captain of half a continent, to him who achieved the liberty of various nations of South America. But if he guaranteed the independence and sovereignty of half a conti-

nent, today it can be said that Argentina has another Liberator. In these times it is not enough to guarantee the political
independence of a country; economic independence and social
justice must be assured, as well. And, gentlemen, it can be
affirmed without the shadow of a doubt that this other Liberator of the Argentine nation, who has assured its economic
independence and its social justice, is the great leader of the
Argentine people, General Perón. He is a guide and leader who
does honor to the great Argentine nation, and who would be
an honor to the greatest nation of the world.

"But in all fairness it must be said that he has had a powerful
aid and collaborator: this great woman, this great lady who
. . . has revealed herself as the woman of America . . .

"As soon as I had assumed the responsibility of my constitutional office, I hastened to participate in the brilliant honors
accorded the American statesman and patriot; I hastened to
be present and to admire the great work accomplished by
peronismo, not out of mere curiosity, but to impregnate myself with it—as I have done in these all too brief days—for the
purpose of carrying out in my own country something of
what General Perón and his illustrious companion are accomplishing here . . ."

In her reply Señora Perón said many pleasant and enthusiastic things. Such as:

"The Honorable President of Paraguay has spoken words
which have moved me deeply as an Argentine, as a *peronista*,
and as the wife of the president of the Argentines . . . The
land the shirtless desire is the land Perón is forging . . . Tonight I speak, not as the wife of the president, but as an Argentine, and as such, I can only speak as a *peronista*. *Peronismo*
cannot be taught or studied: it can only be felt and understood. We shirtless ones are *peronistas* because we are of the
people, and because we know that *peronismo* stands for the
dignification of our children and our men . . ."

143

"I would ask the delegations of Bolivia, Chile, Peru, Uruguay, and His Excellency, the President of Paraguay, to carry a message from one American woman to all her sisters of America . . . and tell them that we must unite in spirit to fight for a just and happy America, and that on the bases of Justicialism and the Third Position of General Perón we can build our hopes . . . for a good life on American soil."

What is Paraguay's role in the international web President Perón is spinning? Does Argentine imperialism really exist? Where does President Chaves come in? How did he come to power?

Theoretically, Paraguay is a tropical paradise where people get up before dawn, work in the fields gathering the mate leaves from which the Argentine national beverage is brewed, and by noon are stretched out in their hammocks. It is a rural nation in which the bovine population exceeds the human. A recent census showed 1,304,000 inhabitants, and 4,500,000 head of cattle, plus uncounted pigs and sheep. One of the country's principal exports is attar of orange blossoms. Every bottle of eau de cologne is scented with the perfume of Paraguay. Asunción, the capital, with its low white houses and its streets shaded by a double row of orange trees, with its sky of Italian blue, and its garlands of brilliant green trees laden with golden fruit, recalls the terra cottas of Luca della Robbia. At nightfall the air is heavy with the scent of orange blossoms.

In Asunción's main square stands a monument to the flag. The pedestal of the flagpole is an armored tank, a souvenir of the Chaco War. I remarked to a Paraguayan friend: "You were not too badly off for equipment . . ."

"What a hope!" he answered. "That's a Bolivian tank. We began with nothing. But when our boys saw a tank coming they climbed into the trees, and as the tank rolled under them they dropped out of the branches, stabbed the Bolivians, and had themselves a tank . . ."

Hidden in the underbrush, they waited for the machine guns, and when they got close enough, roped them, just as they would cut out a calf in a round-up, and dragged them away. Just country boys.

In his book *Reportaje al Paraguay (Reporting on Paraguay)*, Luis Alberto Sánchez says: "The entire population of Paraguay is militarized. They all know how to fight. As with the people of the Balkans, a gun is part of the furnishings of every house. They know the secret of the '*piripipí*,' and they do not flinch from the '*pereré*' and the '*pororó*.'" The language of the people in Paraguay is Guaraní. Everybody speaks it at home, in the street, in the marketplace. It is an onomatopoeic language, and displays great ingenuity in coining words. A machine gun is known as *piripipí*; the rat-tat-tat of the cartridge belt is the *pereré*; the report, the *pororó*.

These details are typical of one of the bravest people in the world. When in 1865–70 Paraguay carried on a war single-handed against Brazil, Argentina, and Uruguay, at the end of five years of hostilities only 221,079 Paraguayans remained of its prewar population of 1,337,000, and most of the survivors were old men, women, and children. Even the women fought, and like Amazons. These were the women who in times of peace dance a charming folk dance with a bottle on their head, never dropping it as they move. They make a kind of lace called *ñandutí*—Guaraní for cobweb—that is even more delicate than that of Brussels or Venice. But when war comes . . . This is a description of a scene at the siege of Piribebuy, as told by the Paraguayan writer and diplomat, Juan E. O'Leary:

"The roar of the cannon had ceased, the crackle of rifle fire was no longer heard. The victorious Brazilians climbed over our breastworks. The sun glittered on their sharp bayonets. They thought the battle was over . . . A shriek, a long shriek of fury and despair, a deafening shriek greeted the vanguard of the oncoming Brazilians. And this shriek, which seemed to arise from the bowels of the earth, was followed by a rain of empty bottles and a cloud of sand that blinded the invaders. It was the women of Piribebuy!

"Crouching in the bottom of the trenches, intermingled with the dead, they had taken the enemy unawares. And now they rose up, their one thought to lie in death beside those they had loved in life . . . Armed with empty bottles, pieces of glass, their nails, and their teeth, they hurled themselves upon the Brazilians. The bottles shattered on the dark heads, the pieces of glass plowed furrows in the men's cheeks, teeth tore away pieces of flesh, fingernails scratched out the startled eyes . . ."

Such scenes from Paraguay's history nourish the imagination and the patriotism of its citizens.

This nation of warriors did not fight Spain for its independence in 1811. It simply turned its back on Spain and took up arms against Argentina. General Manuel Belgrano moved with his troops to incorporate Paraguay into the free Argentine Federation. The Paraguayans threw him back across the river, and the independence they proclaimed was in reality independence of Argentina.

The founder of Paraguay was a sinister, silent man who had begun to study for the priesthood and then changed his mind. He steeped himself in the French encyclopedists, and made himself *El Supremo*, the most rigid of all the dictators America has known. His name was José Gaspar Rodríguez Francia, and he ruled from 1814 to 1840. He carefully barred all the entrances to the country, and cut Paraguay off from the world, particularly from Argentina. Neither did he wish to have anything to do with Bolívar. This same tradition of haughty isolation was followed by the other Paraguayan dictators, the Lópezs, who governed the country for the next thirty years.

The laws they promulgated give the measure of these men. A Spaniard was permitted to marry only a Negress. The prop-

146

erty of any European who died in Paraguay could be left only to a Paraguayan or to the state. The church was nationalized; all its property, including places of worship, passed to the ownership of the state. Even today one of the items in the national budget is for religion. The members of the clergy are state employees, and no contributions are collected in the churches. One of the Lópezs opposed the founding of the Pío Latino Seminary in Rome on the grounds that the training of Paraguayan priests could not be entrusted to a foreign power.

Out of these inflexible forms of government came a passionate, violent nation. The ideological bases of what has been called the Liberal Party were laid by a group of the "Legionnaires," who in the war of 1863 favored Argentina. For this reason, the Liberal Party has been disposed to support a policy of compromise with Argentina, of recognizing economic and political direction by Buenos Aires. The recent speech of President Chaves in Buenos Aires falls far short of the professions of the Legionnaires to the other Argentine dictator, Rosas. Their statements contained such paragraphs as:

"Long live the Argentine Confederation! Death to the savage, foul *unitarios!* Death to the mad, savage *unitario* traitor, Urquiza! [These were the official formulas that headed every Argentine document during this period.] The province of Paraguay, beyond doubt the most distressful of all the unhappy lands on the face of the earth because of the cruelty, the despotism, and the irresponsibility of a ruler devoid of virtue, patriotism, or ability, is suffering a multitude of ills beyond endurance. . . The hearts of the Paraguayans thirst for the hour of their redemption, and await it from no other hand than that of His Excellency Don Juan Manuel de Rosas . . . With two thousand men moving through the Chaco on Asunción, that post could be seized, and all the Paraguayans are already yours . . . and we offer ourselves to join such an expedition in any capacity . . . bringing with us other of our countrymen who, like ourselves, see no hope of happiness for our province except through its reunion with the Argentine Confederation under the paternal rule of Your Excellency. . ."

In our own century Paraguay has swung pendulum-like between anarchy and dictatorship. The Liberals were in power from 1904 to 1931, and again in 1937. In thirty-one years twenty-two presidents rose and fell. One governed twenty-one days, another fifty-three. The average incumbency was nineteen months. By thirty-eight decrees issued over a period of fourteen years, the republic was maintained in a state of emergency. Then came the Chaco War, which united the Paraguayans and produced the country's usual quota of heroes. For the most part these were young officers who had familiarized themselves with the philosophy and techniques of totalitarianism in its different brands: Nazism, Fascism, Communism. The first to apply his learning was Colonel Rafael Franco; he seized power and proclaimed that "the liberating revolution in Paraguay is of the same nature as the totalitarian transformations of contemporary Europe." He was followed by General José Félix Estigarribia, who promulgated a constitution that did away with the senate, left the lower house subject to the president's discretion, and created a State Council of officials, army officers, the clergy, and representatives of agriculture and industry. One month after the new constitution had been proclaimed Estigarribia was killed in an airplane accident. He was replaced in 1940 by the minister of war, General Higinio Morínigo. Morínigo was a crafty peasant who could smell a plot as soon as it started, and knew how to nip it in the bud with a stern hand. He maintained himself in power for seven years. Like his predecessors, he kept the press muzzled. If the university students made trouble they quickly found themselves in concentration camps. He encouraged public works. Toward the end of his rule, in an effort to attract the people, he made overtures to the Colorado Party, which had been out of power for forty years, and which was the people's party. Morínigo made contact with Natalicio González.

Natalicio González was a writer, the best writer of Paraguay. He had been in exile for seventeen years, and had supported himself in Buenos Aires by founding a publishing house, where he published his own writings, and by opening a book store. He was astute and resourceful. He accepted the post Morínigo offered him, that of Minister to Uruguay. This caused an uproar in the ranks of the Colorados. Natalicio's defense of Morínigo left people bewildered. Was he unaware of the concentration camps in Paraguay? It hardly seemed possible. But he answered: let the journalists of Uruguay go there and see for themselves. Was this irony? Craftiness? The fact is that Morínigo respected and trusted him, appointed him Minister of Finance. Natalicio entered the government and persuaded Morínigo to restore political liberty. The exiles returned from Buenos Aires. Free speech became possible, so free that the old party leaders clamored to have Morínigo and his friends hung from lampposts like Villarroel in Bolivia.

Natalicio said nothing. And the people began to feel a growing admiration for this man of few words who got things done and within whom there burned a secret flame of love for his country. He had the support of the *pynandís*—the barefooted. At country gatherings Natalicio spoke to them in Guaraní. And they elected him president in 1948. At his inauguration, through the streets of Asunción marched 70,000 peasants, men and women, many of them from remote regions, who had walked days to get there. They practically danced as they passed before the reviewing stand of the new president to the sound of the *Polka Colorado*, their anthem. The women carried the provisions for the trip on their heads and their babies on their backs. A spirit of healthy rustic rejoicing animated the proceedings. Natalicio launched a vast program of rural rehabilitation, organizing colonies of farmers, building them habitable homes, supplying them with tools and machinery, founding a bank for them. A road-building program got under way. The dollar value of the currency went up. He achieved the miracle of organizing the country's finances. This writer, who in his youth had been a poet, was fired with the desire to build, to do things.

Natalicio stayed in power from August 15, 1948 until January 29, 1949: five months. The democratic revival he had set afoot was opposed by the Communists, who had organized themselves into a swift-moving, disciplined party; by the members of his own Colorado Party with international leanings; and by a certain military lodge of Argentina. Natalicio had become suspect to the Argentine rulers on three counts: because of the impulse he had given to the building of the highway that would link Paraguay to the port of Santos in Brazil; because he had built a river fleet to liberate Paraguay from the monopoly of the Argentine merchant marine of Dodero (since nationalized by Argentina); and because of his vigorous affirmation of Paraguay's sovereignty. Natalicio, who in his patriotic zeal has gone so far as to justify the dictatorship of Francia and the Lópezs because of its affirmation of the country's nationality, has an impassioned faith in Paraguay's national culture.

Natalicio was inaugurated in August 1948, and in September one Tavault Paz arrived in Asunción from Argentina to establish contact with the army officers and with the naval forces being trained by Argentine instructors. He had abundant funds and called himself an agent of Argentine politicians and army officers. Natalicio had him deported, and called the matter to Perón's attention in a confidential note. In December the military academy and the artillery division revolted. There was fighting for a day in the streets of Asunción. Two hours after the revolt broke out the Argentine ambassador presented himself at the Campo Grande barracks and, to his great surprise, found President González there. He had to return to the Embassy without being able to talk with the officers. That revolution fizzled out.

On Januray 29, 1950, another revolt broke out. Colonel Rogelio Benítez, Natalicio's most faithful supporter among the military, had been poisoned some hours earlier. The Minister of War, General Raimundo Rolón, seized the presidency. Natalicio, from the Brazilian Embassy, where he had taken asylum, resigned and left for Buenos Aires, the traditional refuge for Paraguayans in exile.

Rolón's uprising was not impromptu. The Minister of Education, Felipe Molas López, a dentist, had had a long interview with the Argentine Minister of Education, Dr. Oscar Ivanissevich. Molas López was a shrewd politician as well as a dentist, and in the police and the cavalry units he had a fine pair of forceps with which he could extract the President from his loyal followers when he gave the word. Molas had an understanding with Dr. Federico Chaves, the president-to-be; Chaves had an understanding with the Communists; Molas, Chaves, and the Communists had an understanding with General Rolón. Rolón accepted the presidency.

His term of office lasted one month. At the end of February 1950 he visited one of the barracks. There he was seized and removed from office. He was succeeded by Dentist Molas López who made a Communist leader, Epifanio Méndez, chief of police. This caused surprise, which the United States Minister took no pains to hide, but without results. In September 1950, the chief of police removed Dentist Molas López from the presidency, and replaced him with Dr. Federico Chaves. When Chaves, whom nobody had recognized as president outside of Paraguay, took the oath of office, there was one foreign envoy present at the ceremony: the Argentine Ambassador, who came forward and heartily embraced him.

And so everything is working out in normal fashion. The

Communists have kept their posts. Dr. Chaves is the welcome guest of the Peróns. The Paraguayan currency is quietly falling. The country folk have returned to their fields, to the green hell, and the women go on weaving their lace, the cobweb *ñanduti* . . .

X

COLOMBIA, OR HOW TO DESTROY
A DEMOCRACY

*Sámano, who, like all the Spaniards, had a withering contempt
for the patriots of Cazanare, whom he considered a bandit
horde whose destiny was the gallows, decided that the moment had come to punish and wipe them out to the last man.
The commanders, officers, and soldiers of the royalist army carried on the war in Cazanare with unlimited barbarity and cruelty. Sámano had issued orders to the commanders that they
were to destroy all the rural property of its inhabitants, that
they were to set fire to the houses, the sugar mills, the canefields, and towns, and to spare no man capable of bearing arms.
As destroying and killing in America gave the Spaniards great
pleasure during the war of Independence, Sámano's orders were
carried out to the letter, and from the year 1817 they gave no
quarter to anyone favoring independence who fell into their
hands. As a result, the inhabitants of the savannah, who had
always been patriots, were aroused to such indignation and
fury against the Spaniards that they took terrible reprisals
against their supporters in Pasto and against the Europeans
whenever the opportunity offered itself.*

JOSÉ MANUEL RESTREPO

In the pages that follow the reader will learn how the best
of the Latin America democracies could be razed to the
ground in a few months.

Well into the year 1951 it was announced semi-officially that
the end of the civil war was in sight in Colombia. The party in
power, the party of the dictatorship, had been victorious. This
was the first time anybody in Colombia or outside Colombia

153

had had news to the effect that there had been such a war and that it had been going on for two years. Not a single correspondent of the international news services had been at the battle sites. It had taken place in the immediate vicinity of the Panama Canal, and the United States government knew nothing about it. But the information was printed in the newspaper belonging to the head of the Colombian government, and it explains his rise to power. Reading between the lines, it becomes evident that one of the most staunchly democratic of the continental nations has become a totalitarian state. Within the Caribbean area, Colombia, the heart of the five republics created by Bolívar, occupying the uppermost corner of South America, next door to the Panama Canal, was a nation that had moral authority. It was an example of a large country basically American in its ethnic composition, with little immigration, that owed all its progress to its civilian, representative government. It enjoyed complete freedom of the press and the unrestricted interplay of public opinion. Overnight its liberties were snuffed out, and a new era began, that of the mailed fist.

The Conservatives, a traditional, democratic party, had come to power in Colombia in 1946 by the clear mandate of a general election. This was a fair, normal procedure. Then they decided to retain power by force. Why? Because their triumph had resulted from the division of the Liberal votes between two candidates. The Liberal Party continued to be an immense majority, and the only way to intimidate it was through terror. The way in which violence was organized and let loose can be explained only by the presence of foreign elements, surely Spanish Falangists. The peasant had to be made to feel that his loyalty to the Liberal Party could cost him his life, his worldly goods, the security of his wife and children. Starting out along this road, the regime went to extremes never before recorded in the history of any Latin American country, Colombia least of all. With open eyes, those in power entrusted their destinies to a reactionary, neo-Fascist group. The police were reorganized into a shock force, and the national army into a party militia with a belligerent general staff. As the majority of Colombia's population is rural, the countryside became the theater of violence. No less than 200,000 of the rural inhabitants left their lands or villages to take refuge in Bogotá or the state capitals, or crossed the frontiers into Venezuela or Ecuador. Many villages were destroyed, some completely wiped out. The crime of genocide was transplanted to the American continent. In less than six months a reign of terror had been established. The prisons became the scene of tortures. The Liberal Party, the party of the majority, was deprived of its means of communication. Former presidents of the republic, chosen in free elections, who had represented their country at the most important international assemblies, as well as ministers and ambassadors with records of thirty or forty years of honorable service to their credit were unable to address their fellow-citizens or to meet freely, as is the practice in other countries, as it had been in Colombia before this change. A more aggressive, more clearly defined system than that of Perón became the order of the day. The death toll from 1949 to 1951 has been estimated at 50,000 out of a population of about 11,000,000. The exact figure will never be known, for during this time the Colombian newspapers carried only such information as the government wished or saw fit to print. There is censorship of the mails and of telephone and telegraph communications. In Bogotá alone, a women's volunteer organization had to take care of 30,000 country people who had fled their homes in 1949. To justify the number of dead and displaced persons and a so-called presidential election, it has been stated, *a posteriori*, that there was a civil war.[1]

[1] The number of those who lost their lives in the wave of violence set off by the dictatorship has never been ascertained, nor can it be. The Government has given out no figures. The count of 50,000 is the estimate of Alfonso López, former President of Colombia, contained in a docu-

What had made Colombia different from the other Spanish American states? The republic was founded at the beginning of the nineteenth century by a young officer—General Francisco de Paula Santander—who had fought in the campaign of liberation to the last volley of the battle that made independence a fact in 1819. It was Santander who crossed the bridge at Boyacá in the action that turned the tide of war in the republic's favor. He was a man of university training, a lawyer. Bolívar continued the war southward, in what is today Ecuador, Peru, and Bolivia, while Santander, nine years his junior, forewent the glory that attends a soldier's career and devoted himself to establishing a civilian republic. He laid aside his sword, saying: "If arms have given us our independence, laws will give us our liberty." He threw himself into the founding of primary schools, grammar schools, high schools, universities, a national museum, libraries, academies, all the elements that for a century constituted the solid rock on which education rested in Colombia. He made these facilities available to the Indians as well as to the whites, to women as well as to men. It was in this field that he fought his hardest battle against the prejudices, entrenched privileges, and limitations of Spanish colonialism. In institutions where scholastic metaphysics had been taught, he introduced the social sciences that were just coming into being in England. Forty-five years before Domingo Sarmiento began in Argentina the great campaign on behalf of education which has made his name a beacon in all Latin America, Santander did the same thing in Colombia on a scale no less extensive and thoroughgoing throughout the

---

ment that was passed in its entirety by the official Colombian censor and published on June 2, 1951. Since then the violence has continued, and during the time the portfolio of war was held by Urdaneta Arbeláez, acting President and head of the dictatorship since September 1951, the bombardment of towns in the savannah and mountains of the state of Antioquia was ordered. Former President López is the only leader of the Liberal party with whom the dictatorship has consented to have any dealings.

whole country, from Bogotá to remote villages. At the same time he organized the public finances, supplying Bolívar with arms and funds without which he could not have carried out his campaign in upper Peru, and he made the laws respected.

In many aspects Santander was the most distinguished civilian Latin America produced in the first half of the nineteenth century. His accomplishments left a deep impress on the Colombian spirit. At present the statues in his honor are being dynamited. He stands for the "They shall not pass" that was Colombia's answer to attempts at dictatorship for a century. He broke with Bolívar himself when the latter, on his return from the wars of Peru, attempted to set up a military despotism.

Throughout the nineteenth century Colombia, like the rest of America, was plagued by anarchy, revolutions, civil wars. But its revolutions were headed by intellectuals seeking to change the constitution. The military caudillo did not flourish in Colombia. The office of president has been held by grammarians, academicians, men of letters. When I was a law student in Colombia, our professor of public law was elected to the presidency. He continued to give his course with one slight change: instead of his going to the university, the students went to the presidential palace for the class.

This was the basis on which Colombia's political culture was founded. In 1930 the Conservatives lost the elections to the Liberals. The Conservative president handed over his office to his victorious opponent with a handshake. In keeping with the Colombian tradition, a crowd of friends and constituents of the departing president came to the palace to accompany him to his home, on foot, down the middle of the street, without any official escorts, amidst the cheers of the spectators. At the same time, a similar crowd accompanied the new president from his home to the capitol, and from the capitol to the presidential palace, and the rooms of the official dwelling were thronged with crowds waiting to shake hands with him and wish him success.

The same thing happened in 1946. Liberal president Alberto Lleras Camargo turned over the presidency to Conservative Mariano Ospina Pérez. There were cheers for the departing president and cheers for the new incumbent. The democracy that Lleras Camargo turned over to Ospina Pérez's rule on that day was a free, representative, prosperous, safe government. Life and property were respected. Public opinion was freely expressed. Colombia had a congress, state legislatures, municipal councils.

In contrast to other Latin American countries, in which a single capital city tends to absorb the economic power and dominate the intellectual life of the nation, in Colombia there are provincial cities that vie with Bogotá in distinction, wealth, industry, and the degree of prosperity of their citizens. There are cities with a population of fifty, one hundred, two hundred, thousand in widely separated regions of the country which have a life of their own. Bogotá, the capital, which has grown by leaps and bounds during the last years, had in 1951 a population of not more than 800,000. Moreover, as the nation's principal wealth is agricultural and its chief export is coffee, the majority of the people live in the country or small towns. Colombia has a population of 11,000,000, the fourth largest in Latin America, only Brazil, Mexico, and Argentina outstripping it. Much of the cotton woven in the new industrial centers is grown in Colombia, enough to supply the internal demand and for export. In the Second World War many Allied troops wore uniforms of Colombian cloth and drank Colombian coffee.

In five cities the universities had complete academic autonomy. Members of all parties held chairs in them. The newspapers gave the most complete coverage to news from the whole world. *El Tiempo* of Bogotá was a counterpart of *La Prensa* of Buenos Aires in quality and standing. At any hour of the day or night one could go anywhere in the country freely without the slightest fear. In regions predominantly Liberal in their political affiliations, a Conservative could own a ranch and hire Liberal workers without the idea of possible danger crossing anyone's mind. Now many of these things sound like tales from a remote past. The war that began without being declared and without previous warning took place between government forces armed to the teeth and peasants taken completely off guard, and left the country drenched in blood and buried in ashes. It silenced every tongue, except those which speak for the dictatorship. As one of the ministers announced at the beginning of the dictatorship, "fire and sword" would be the order of the day.

In Colombia the majority of the voters belonged to the Liberal party. Liberalism there stood for a democratic ideology that had come into being under the influence of English liberal thought and the first French Republic, a party that adapted itself to the special conditions of Latin America. It stood for the defense of liberties and the principles of social justice. Although it was organized by intellectuals, it became the party of the people. From 1930 to 1950 it proved its majority in all the electoral contests, even though these were at times under Conservative auspices. In four fifths of the principal cities Liberalism had always had a plurality. But in the presidential elections of 1946 the Liberals supported two candidates as a result of a split in the party ranks. Therefore the Conservatives, who backed a single candidate, won, and their candidate, Mariano Ospina Pérez, came to power. The final count showed the following figures: Mariano Ospina Pérez, (Conservative) 565,489; Gabriel Turbay (Liberal) 437,089; Jorge Eliécer Gaitán (Liberal) 363,849.

At first Ospina Pérez governed with extreme caution. There was a Liberal majority in congress; the state legislatures were for the most part Liberal, as were the city governments. The leading newspapers were Liberal. So was public opinion in its majority, particularly the young people, farmers, and workers. And, above all, the Liberals had a great popular leader:

Jorge Eliécer Gaitán, who, though defeated at the polls, was the idol of the people and had behind him a mass of voters outnumbering the President's supporters by several hundred thousand. The President decided to form a coalition government of national unity. He invited Liberals to occupy half the cabinet posts. He said:

"A party government, and especially that of a group, invariably is actuated by and act on . . . the criterion of serving only partisan interests . . . Its programs always aim at imposing its political system, come what may, through oppression and exclusivism . . . It is impossible to serve two masters at the same time: the nation and the party . . . In Colombia's history we have eloquent examples of what a government along national lines stands for, its justice, its goodness, its excellence. Two examples will suffice: the admirable example of the administration of Manuel María Mallarino in the past century, and that which Alberto Lleras Camargo has recently left to future generations. Under my administration there will be no political reprisals on the part of the authorities against persons or their property; no one will be barred from public office for party reasons; I faithfully guarantee to all the exercise of their natural and civil rights, and I shall make it my care to see that public liberties are respected. Neither the head of the state nor his associates or agents will take any step that even remotely smacks of political reprisals against anyone."

Enveloped in this toga of words, the new president assumed office in 1946. Promising a national government, Ospina Pérez succeeded in not arousing the suspicions of the Liberal majority, which could well wait four years (the length of the presidential term of office in Colombia) to regain power in an election. That, however, was not the President's idea. His intention was to inspire enough confidence so that he could proceed behind the scenes to set up the machinery that would prevent the majority from exercising its political rights. Little by little, he began modifying the organization of the police force, which in the provinces was transformed into shock troops at the service of the Conservatives. The Liberals were forced to resign their posts in the cabinet. Thousands of country people stood by as their houses were burned down, many were killed, and part of Colombia's inhabitants began to move to Venezuela in search of peace. On the eve of the Pan American Conference that was to meet in Bogotá, terror reigned in the provinces. The leader of the Liberal party, Jorge Eliécer Gaitán—Gabriel Turbay had died —headed a rally at which 100,000 persons gathered in silence in the main square of Bogotá to ask only for peace and respect for human rights. Not a cry was uttered; the only sound was that of handkerchiefs waved in the air by the hands of peaceable, Christian people. Gaitán said:

"Mr. President, we are not here to present economic or political demands. All we ask is that our country desist from a line of conduct that puts us to shame in our own eyes and those of foreigners. We ask this in the name of mercy and civilization . . . We ask that this persecution on the part of the authorities come to an end . . . Put a halt, Mr. President, to violence. All we ask of you is the guarantee of human life, which is the least a country can ask."

Two months and two days after saying this, Gaitán was assassinated at noon in the heart of Bogotá.

Jorge Eliécer Gaitán had an immense popular following. No other South American politician can be recalled who had so strong a hold over the masses. His appeal for peace was made as the date set for the Ninth Pan American Conference drew near. Gaitán was bending all his efforts to seeing that the meeting took place in an atmosphere of peace. Backing up his appeal was the campaign he had carried on for pacification within the Liberal ranks. Thousands of country people who had taken refuge in Bogotá brought about a ferment of protest. The Conference was able to meet in an atmosphere of peace, but a chill wind of terror was blowing from the provinces. This was apparent to the delegates, the foreign correspondents, and to the international Communists who had gathered in Bogotá to turn to their own ends any circumstance that might arise.

On April 9, 1948, Gaitán fell, victim of an assassin's bullet, on the Calle Real, the street leading from the cathedral to Santander Plaza, and the masses went berserk. Their fury was fanned by a revolutionary group that seized the radio stations and ordered violence. The recipe for making "Molotov cocktails" was given over the air. The government took fright. The troops would not leave their barracks. The police handed out arms to the people. Inflammatory speeches by irresponsible persons egged on the arson and looting. The heart of Bogotá went up in flame. According to foreign newspapermen, it resembled sections of London after an air raid. General George C. Marshall, who headed the United States delegation, called it the work of the Communists. But the fundamental fact remains that the man whose prestige among the people constituted an insurmountable barrier to the dictatorship's ambition of continuing in power had been assassinated. His real rival, the Conservative leader, Laureano Gómez, who at that moment was the Chairman of the Pan American Conference in his capacity as Colombian Minister of Foreign Affairs, went into hiding, and then emerged to leave for Spain. He stayed there for one year, an honored guest to whom Franco was paying a debt of gratitude for the impassioned campaign carried on in the Caudillo's favor in the columns of Laureano Gómez's newspaper, El Siglo. He did not return to Colombia until it was time to organize his presidential campaign. In 1950 he became dictator of the country.

Laureano Gómez came home on June 25, 1949. He is a demagogue who had practiced the art of opposition for thirty years of political life. He has attacked presidents, archbishops, institutions. He has defamed great men of Colombia's past, including Santander. He has lashed out against the country itself, and is the author of a book, *Questions Concerning the Future of Colombia*, which supports the thesis that the country is unfit for habitation, and that its people are worthless. He has brought about a schism in the Church. The last two archbishops have been victims of his attack, and with the support of the most belligerent sector of the clergy he has formed a fiercely militant church within the Christian Church. Having been educated in a Jesuit school, he is much closer to this order than to the rest of the church in a country that is 100% Catholic. On taking office he entrusted the preparation of a new constitution for Colombia to, among others, an outstanding Jesuit, who had played a major part in bringing about the dictatorship, Father Félix Restrepo. There are reasons to believe that this constitution will be of a Fascist nature.

The last six presidents, Liberals and Conservatives, have been targets for Laureano Gómez's verbal violence. In his newspaper Hitler and Mussolini found the applause and support denied them by the rest of Colombia's press. His enthusiasm for Franco never declined. When Franco's agents visisted Bogotá in 1937, a great act of homage to the Falange was organized. Gómez spoke, saying:

"Spain, marching forward as the sole defender of Christian civilization, leads the Western nations in the reconstruction of the empire of Hispanidad, and we inscribe our names in the roster of its phalanxes with unutterable satisfaction . . . We bless God who has permitted us to live in this era of unforeseen transformations, and who has given it to us to utter, with a cry that springs from the very depths of our heart: 'Up Catholic, Imperial Spain!' "

The offices of Laureano Gómez's newspaper were the birthplace of the original cell of Black Shirts in Colombia. It was a tiny group, rash to the point of temerity, so fanatical that it could and did engineer situations of violence continually. The members of that original cell now hold high government posts: they are ambassadors, representatives to the United Nations, leading officials of the government. They hold all the keys of power.

The Conservatives, including President Ospina Pérez himself, realized that the man to cement their hold on the government was Laureano Gómez. When, on his return from Spain, he stepped out of the plane in Medellín, his first spoken words announced the storm that was to topple the country's democratic structure to the ground. He opened his speech with the Falangist salute: "Present." The argument he put forward as his opening gun against the Liberals, the majority party, was that they were Communists. It was the same tactics employed by President Prado in Peru to eliminate the *aprista* majority. If Liberalism is Communism, it can be outlawed at any time, and the majority of Colombians can thus be deprived of their political rights. The United States is not going to protest such action because it is put forward as a contribution to the international struggle against Communism. Laureano Gómez, as he himself admits, has arrived at this policy by a process of cold reasoning:

"In Colombia people still speak of the Liberal party to designate an amorphous, shapeless and contradictory mass . . . that can be only compared with or described like that imaginary creation of olden days, the basilisk. The basilisk was a monster having the head of one animal, the face of another, the arms of still another, and the feet of some deformed creation, all together forming a creature so frightful and dreadful that its mere glance caused death. Our basilisk moves with feet of confusion and stupidity on legs of brutality and violence which propel its immense oligarchic belly; with a breast of wrath, with Masonic arms, and a tiny, a diminutive Communist head . . ."

At another place in this speech Laureano Gómez said: "A cold, calm appraisal of the phenomenon will suffice . . ." In his turn, Augusto Ramírez Moreno, in a speech of welcome to Laureano Gómez, made "a cold, objective inventory" in which

he set forth the themes that would be developed to bring
about an end to the democratic system in Colombia. One by
one he listed the institutions against which the Fascist weapons
being forged there should be directed:

"The day the congressional majority attempts to take advantage of its power, the Conservative members, without
help from the government, are determined to close the Capitol . . . The Supreme Court is swayed by political hatreds
. . . The electoral college makes false returns to favor the
Liberals . . . The Council of State will accept and find in
favor of any proposal laid before it to nullify a Conservative
victory . . . The Confederation of Workers of Colombia . . .
is an instrument of revolution . . . which looks upon Colombia
as a stepmother because Russia is the real mother of that organization . . . Fortunately, the Conservatives number one
million stout-hearted, determined men who are moving ever
more swiftly toward power."

The speaker had been one of the Black Shirts of the first
Falange cell in Colombia a few years before. The program he
outlined was quickly put into effect. A few months later Congress, the Supreme Court, the Council of State, and the
Confederation of Workers had been done away with or made
to knuckle under. Ramírez Moreno became Colombia's ambassador to France.

A study of the methods employed to bring the Colombian
Congress and the other institutions under control by the
totalitarian system is rewarding. It is a swifter, bloodier, and
more radical system than that employed in Argentina. The
campaign against Congress began before it convened. The
speeches at Medellín took place in June 1949; Congress was
scheduled to open in July. Not more than ten sessions had
been held when Congressman Alvaro Gómez Hurtado, director
of *El Siglo*, Laureano Gómez's son and his right arm in the government, passed out whistles to the minority members, who
used them to prevent the Liberal members from being heard.

Six days later Laureano Gómez declared that Congress should be considered outside the law. Congress had been studying a proposed law to move the election date forward with the object of shortening the reign of violence that was bleeding the country. Laureano Gómez decided that such a measure was not to his interest and declared the law unconstitutional. "The measures it [Congress] is attempting to put through are null," he said, "and those who have taken part in the discussions will be punished according to law if the measures are passed." The procedure in Colombia is that if a proposed law is held to be unconstitutional, it is brought before the Supreme Court. The law was passed, it was laid before the Supreme Court, and the Court upheld it. Whereupon Laureano Gómez turned on the Court:

"The Court has been drawn into the orbit of politics. The Court has lost its impartiality. Unfortunately, it would seem to have lost its dignity as well. It is not, it cannot continue to be, a tribunal. It has become a political committee, a contemptible political committee."

The procedures employed in Congress itself reproduced the tactics of Fascism in its palmiest days, without excluding even the assassination of Matteotti. A few days after Laureano Gómez's speech, on September 8, 1949, Conservative congressmen fired on Liberal members. Some hundred shots echoed through the legislative chambers. Gustavo Jiménez, the Liberal congressman who had the floor, was killed where he stood. Jorge Soto del Corral, the most distinguished figure in the younger ranks of Liberalism by reason of his broad legal training, former Minister of Foreign Relations, former Ambassador to France, sometime Rector of the National University, suffered wounds that completely eliminated him from the political scene. Immediately Congressman General Amadeo Rodríguez was accused of having fired on Soto del Corral. A few days later Laureano Gómez was nominated for the presidency of the republic, and at the banquet held in his honor

General Amadeo Rodríguez was seated at his right. The young Falangists, who that day paraded in the manner of their confreres of Spain, mingled with their shouts of acclamation of "Caudillo" Gómez a joyous "Long live Amadeo's pistol!" When an indictment was sworn out against General Rodríguez, he left for Ecuador. After a while he returned to Bogotá. The indictment against him lies buried in the court files.

In the following months things began to speed up. In the outlying regions the death toll rose to the thousands. The cards allowing the peasants to vote in the elections were taken from them by force, and they were pressured into forswearing their Liberal affiliation. The governors of the states are appointed directly by the national government, and these posts were filled by men who could be counted on to carry out the new policy. The following is a copy of the safe-conducts that were issued to the peasants (a photograph of Laureano Gómez adorns the upper corner):

"The undersigned President of the Conservative Directory CERTIFIES: that Mr. Guillermo Saldarriaga Restrepo, bearer of card No. 2379991 issued in Carmen (Chocó) has sworn that he does not belong to the Liberal party. Therefore his life, property, and family are to be respected.—Carmen, Chocó, October 29, 1949.—Alfonso Orrego, President."

In many instances this forswearing is performed in the presence of the parish priest, who signs the safe-conduct. When the Archbishop of Colombia received proof of this activity on the part of the clergy, he issued a pastoral letter to the effect that priests engaged in such coercion would be suspended from their duties. In this pastoral letter he said, among other things:

"We order all priests under our jurisdiction . . . to abstain totally from furthering, encouraging, or supporting, directly or indirectly, all activities designed to obtain by means of violence or deception the accomplishment of determined political aims, bearing in mind that the Church is the first to condemn any attempt against the rights and liberties of man, and that the end, however good it may be, never justifies the use of illicit means . . . They are likewise to refrain from demanding or advising those affiliated with a given political party to renounce their errors openly . . . By virtue of c. 2222 No. 1° we threaten with penalty of suspension A DIVINIS IPSO FACTO INCURRENDA those priests who subsequently venture to act contrary to the mandates of clauses 2 and 3 of this circular . . ."

This pastoral letter of the saintly Archbishop, one of the first victims of the new Caudillo's fury, was later suppressed by the censorship in Colombia. It is in keeping with the best tradition of the country. It is a reflection of the halcyon days of democracy and the Church, and at the same time testimony of the Church's horror at what was being perpetrated in the provinces. Nevertheless, everything continued, on a rising scale, in accordance with the plan outlined in Medellín by those acclaiming the leader returning from Spain.

On October 31, 1949, the Director of the Pan American Union, Alberto Lleras Camargo, addressed a letter to his fellow Colombians. He had been the preceding president of his country. When, during his term of office, the struggle as to his successor had assumed a violent aspect, he had formed a bipartisan cabinet to guarantee the honesty of the elections and to make them the faithful expression of the will of the people. Thanks to this, he was able to hand over, together with his office, a country in an unquestionable state of civil democracy. Three years later not a trace of this remained. The aspirant to dictatorship had made up his mind that the Colombians were Communists, and that the situation called for fire and the sword.

"The explanation invariably advanced," said Lleras Camargo, "is that Communism was threatening the republic. I ask myself in amazement how it is possible that in three and a half years the most discredited and smallest party, which never caused even a ripple on the surface of Colombian political life, has suddenly become a source of danger to ten million Colombians whose basic religious unity, whose social solidarity, rendered them immune to the doctrines of the extremist parties . . . Out of this violence, which is shrouding the republic in mourning and shame, which discredits it and lowers it in the opinion of the rest of the world, nothing just, equable, or upright can come to the country. I know there are those who hold that Colombia can be governed by force. My experience is wholly contrary to this belief. Nobody, not a majority party, and even less a minority one, not any group of civilians or of the military, nor all the armed forces combined can ever hope to govern a country whose one, invariable, and steadfast tradition, aside from its Catholic faith, is liberty . . . The Liberal party, which governed Colombia for sixteen years, cannot be outlawed or proscribed from the country's public life, and I gravely fear that only this can be the logical consequence of such a crusade, if the effort continues to identify it with Communism. It is a terrible mistake and a fatal error that will give less satisfaction to the handful of opportunists and Communist fanatics of Colombia than to the directors of this international movement . . ."

The answer of the Colombian government to this solemn warning was to lay a charge before the Organization of American States, through its Washington Embassy, accusing Lleras Camargo of undue intervention in matters of Colombia's internal affairs. Lleras Camargo was obliged to present his resignation as director of this organization, which, after a unanimous decision by the body, he withdrew.

The state of uncontrolled violence led several members of congress to draw up a plan for impeaching the President in the Senate. The Colombian constitution provides for such cases, and the procedure has been followed on other occasions. The president is under obligation, if the senate calls upon him, to present himself before this body and defend himself against charges. This is the maximum juridical function of the legislative body and the test of the president's loyalty to his oath of office.

The news that such a step was contemplated was answered with threats against the leaders of both houses. Attempts were made against various congressmen. The leader of the lower house and one of the congressmen went in person to talk with the Minister of War. They handed him a note for the President, to the effect that the house was going to study the matter to see if he should be brought before it. They asked for police protection so the deliberations could go forward peaceably.

This took place on the morning of November 9, 1949. When these members returned after delivering their message they found that the police were already driving their colleagues from the Capitol and had seized the building by presidential order on the grounds that public order had been disturbed.

The following are examples of the decrees issued that same day:

"Owing to the disturbance of public order, a state of siege is declared throughout the nation . . .

"All regular sessions of the National Congress are hereby suspended until such date as the government decides that the state of the nation permits their resumption . . .

"Likewise, all sessions of the state legislatures, as well as of the municipal councils, are suspended . . .

". . . all assemblies and public meetings throughout the nation are forbidden . . ."

"For the duration of the state of siege the governors are empowered not only to exercise their functions as agents of the executive power and heads of the regional administration . . . but also to take such measures as they deem necessary for the maintenance of public order . . . Consequently they may, without being bound by existing ordinances, create posts, fill them, assign them definite obligations and duties, do away with them, draw upon public funds . . . and perform such acts as they consider necessary for the aforesaid purpose . . .

"A censorship over the press and radio will be established throughout the country. The local authorities and the heads of police will see that this measure is carried out. . .

"The ministries of War and of the Interior, and the governors . . . are empowered to suspend any publication when, in the opinion of the agent of the government, it is impossible to establish a satisfactory censorship over it . . ."

"The decisions of the plenary sessions of the Supreme Court with regard to the validity of the decrees issued by the national government will be governed by the vote of three fourths of the judges . . .

"The norm set forth in the preceding article will be applied . . . to the decrees issued by the government during the state of siege . . ."

This was only the beginning. All existing provisions for exercising any sort of controls on the government were done away with. Public opinion was gagged. When the modification of the structure of the Supreme Court was made, empowering a few of the judges to nullify any action against the government, that body tried to defend itself. The majority of the judges sent the president a letter saying, after adducing cogent legal precedents: ". . . with all due respect we beg to inform Your Excellency that we consider the procedure employed by Your Excellency's government toward the Supreme Court entirely unacceptable and illegal because it undermines the juridical order provided in the Constitution of the Republic."

The President's reply was a withering blast: "First I wish to express the surprise of the government in the face of this unexampled occurrence in the history of the country, to wit, that a group of magistrates of the highest court of justice should express an opinion on a juridical matter that has not yet been submitted to the consideration of the said tribunal ... I do not know whether you have realized that in writing me the letter to which I refer you have already disqualified yourself to pass judgement in this matter if it should be brought before you."

The structure of the Council of State was modified by decree. The Council of State controlled the legality of the government's decrees. Its members were elected by Congress as provided in the Constitution. The dictatorship decided to increase the membership of the Council and to appoint its members directly in order to insure itself a political majority and thus remove this control. Congress appoints the comptroller-general, who heads the organization that supervises disbursements under the national budget. The dictatorship removed the comptroller named by Congress and put in its own. And thus, without Congress, without freedom of the press, with the roots of free public opinion hacked away, the date of the presidential elections approached. In documents signed by the country's ex-presidents, university professors, justices of the Supreme Court, and members of the Council of State, all these facts were pointed out. These documents had to be circulated clandestinely. The government forbade their publication. But Laureano Gómez had unlimited opportunity to carry on his propaganda, to set up his electoral machine. The governor of every state was his agent.

As one views the steps in this process, which seems to lead inevitably to the establishment of a totalitarian state alongside the Panama Canal, it is nothing if not surprising to read the opinion of Willard L. Beaulac, former United States Ambassador to Colombia, on the man who set up the play for the dictatorship, Mariano Ospina Pérez. In his book *Career Ambassador* (1951), Mr. Beaulac says:

"Democracy's greatest heroes on April 9 [the date of Jorge Eliécer Gaitán's assassination] and succeeding days were Pres-

ident Ospina and his wife, doña Berta. Their courage was freedom's shield. With a hysterical mob storming the doors of the
palace and firing into it, with the radio screaming that the
president must resign, that the liberal party must 'assume
power', President Ospina never once thought of surrendering
Colombia's precious democracy. He had issued guns to the
civilians in the palace, including Mrs. Ospina, and they were
prepared to use them if the palace were invaded. He himself
had no weapon. He told me later that he had decided, should
the enemies succeed in entering the palace, to await them
seated at his presidential desk. He fully expected, in that
event, to be killed. He would die, then, in action. The only
arm he would carry would be his investiture as civilian, constitutional, elected president of Colombia. This would not save
his life, but his assassins would be branded as enemies of Colombia and of democracy. He had full faith in Colombia's democracy. He was prepared to die unresisting in order that
democracy might fight through and live."

That is all. With regard to the dictatorship that followed,
the ambassador has not a single word of reproach. As a matter
of fact, he does not even mention it.

The transfer of the dictatorship from the hands of its in-
itiator, President Ospina, to those of Laureano Gómez was
effected via "elections," the elections whose date Congress
had moved forward in the hope of shortening the months
of violence. The manner in which the government prepared
and carried them out can be gathered from this excerpt from a
letter addressed to the president of the republic by the head
of the Board of Registry. The Board of Registry is the
agency directly responsible for the issuing of certificates at-
testing their holders' right to vote.

"It is useless to have a complete census and responsible, upright registrars and a system guaranteeing the impartiality
of the officials in charge . . . if the electors of certain political groups are unable to reach the office where the voting

permit is issued because of police intimidation or because their neighbors holding opposing political views wound or assassinate them under the very eyes of the registrar or with the indifference or approval of the mayor . . . Incidents of official violence against the members of the Board of Registry are set forth in document No. 2 appended to this letter . . . the outrages committed by the civilian authorities and the police against the Boards of Registry, as well as the confiscation on the part of many of them of the Liberal voters' registration certificates without any other pretext except that they are not Conservatives, are set forth in Document No. 3. The National Board of Registry cannot guarantee the normal issuance of voting certificates because the municipal authorities of 120 municipalities (one seventh of those of the country) not only do not uphold it, but, on the contrary, forcibly interfere with the execution of the function for which it was created."

The protest was ignored, and the Registrar resigned. Some days later the members ex-officio of the Supreme Electoral Court, three former presidents of the republic and the rector of the National University, likewise resigned. "Inasmuch," they said, "as electoral campaigning in its most popular and democratic aspect has, for all practical effects, been suppressed, and, as a result of violence on the part of the authorities, a major part of the registry board members have been driven out; with a policy of terrorism in full sway that stops at nothing, with the complete support of the police and authorities; with local power in the most partisan hands that could be found, and a general policy of depriving the most humble of their electoral certificates: all that remains is the most unbridled violence whose object is to increase the votes in favor of one side and reduce or eliminate those of the opposition . . ."

The members of Liberal party, unable to speak, write, establish communication with one another, or call meetings of the party's presiding committees, decided to abstain from vot-

ing. Two days before the "elections," the Liberal candidate
for the presidency, Darío Echandía, sometime Ambassador
to the Holy See, a scholar and a man of outstanding civic virtues, set out with a small group of friends for the center of
Bogotá. As they were walking along one of the main streets,
the police ambushed them. Dr. Echandía's brother fell dead
at his side from bullet wounds, and four others of the group
were killed. One of the party has described what took place:

"As we were about twenty steps from 31st Street, a group
of police officers leveled their rifles at us. I called out: 'We are
with Dr. Echandía; be careful!' And then a shot rang out . . .
we all threw ourselves on the ground. The police continued to
fire in all directions, toward the ground where we were lying,
above us . . . The fusillade lasted for about two minutes. Behind us several of the men were groaning with pain. We got
up and with our hands in the air walked toward the police
squad. Dr. Echandía . . . called out: 'We are unarmed. Don't
murder us; you can arrest us if you want to!' "

Two days later the "elections" were held. Laureano Gómez
was elected by a unanimous vote. President Ospina Pérez that
same night made a radio address to the nation:

" . . . the electoral campaign and the atmosphere of tranquility in which it was carried out are proof that the authorities took measures to insure complete neutrality . . . The
members of the National Police Force, who were called on to
carry out an exceptionally difficult and stern task, which society has not always understood and appreciated, and has at
times repaid with injustice and ingratitude, have on this occasion, too, been worthy of its trust . . . the presiding genius
of the Liberator [Bolívar], whose profound teachings have
always been the lodestar of my spirit and the incentive to
my acts, can take credit for a part of this republican victory . . . I cannot conclude . . . without giving thanks to
Divine Providence, which so manifestly continues to watch
over the destiny of our nation . . ."

The most striking feature of the speech is the omission of the slightest reference to the assassination of the Liberal leader's brother by the police.

When it came his turn "President-elect" Laureano Gómez made a speech concluding with these words:

"I bless God a thousand and a thousand times for having filled my heart with this burning love for my country and for having made my mind grasp a sublime doctine whose lofty principles remove from the soul every selfish or impure interest. I praise God because he has permitted me to walk through the fires of hatred without allowing my heart to become contaminated by it, and has kept it happy, free from the dark shadows of vengeance, pure, without the dregs of bitterness. I glorify Him because my mind is serene and recognizes the good cause that it must serve and the evil that must be exorcised. We need peace, the happiness of our people, prosperity for the home and for the individual, generous and glorious freedom, inviolable security, easy access to the riches of the earth and to the achievement of well-being, and, as the crown of all these beatitudes, the growing greatness of our mother Colombia."

Life magazine sent a special correspondent to cover the elections in Colombia. This is his report (December 12, 1949), which was illustrated by a number of photographs taken on the scene:

"For decades Colombia was one country in Latin America which never chose its governments with bullets instead of ballots. But by last week, in the election shown here, her liberty-loving people lost their precious heritage through a relentless power play by the minority Conservative party . . . the Conservatives (who held the presidency although the Liberals had a majority in Congress) played rough from the beginning. They recalled strong man Laureano Gómez from voluntary exile in Fascist Spain as their candidate. The main feature of his campaign was a reign of terror in the interior.

Liberal towns were shot up. In the last two months 2,000 Liberals were killed, hundreds jailed and other hundreds fled their towns. Seven thousand Liberal families fled to Bogotá alone. There Conservative president Mariano Ospina Pérez declared a state of siege and exercised heavy-handed censorship. Troops took possession of the capital and patrolled the streets . . ."

The New York Times, which sent correspondents and staff members to verify at first hand what was happening, concluded its editorial comment (November 19, 1949) with these words:

"There has always been the danger that the Fascism we crushed in Italy and Germany would prove hydraheaded. We destroyed organizations; we killed, imprisoned and punished some men. We did not kill Fascism, and it seems only too likely that we have another striking proof of that fact in Colombia."

La Prensa of Buenos Aires sent one of its editors, Quiliano Anta Paz, to cover the elections. As happened with Milton Bracker of *The New York Times,* he had to leave the country to cable his information. He filed from Lima, Bracker from Quito. The censorship would not allow them to send their reports from Colombia. All copies of *Life, The New York Times,* and *Time* carrying this information were confiscated by the Colombian postoffice. Certain students who attempted to distribute mimeographed copies of a translation of *The New York Times* editorial were jailed. The representative of *La Prensa* said, among other things:

"Lima, December 10.—Foreign journalists visiting Colombia . . . were confronted with an increasingly drastic censorship that threatens to suffocate the country's press, and as a result the wildest rumors are given credence. We had no choice, if we were not to fail completely in our assignment, but to exercise the greatest caution and reserve in our reports. Even so, several of us ran into difficulties. But this detail, harmful as it is to the freedom of news-gathering, is only one aspect of this censorship, which can be criticized on other grounds such as mutilating the text of reports, blocking the new agencies' means of communication, and even suggesting that they use only government-controlled communication channels. And, above all, there is the relentless pressure of an atmosphere charged with passions, fears that no one can dispel. The official attitude, instead of attempting to remedy this situation, seems to foment it . . . Sunday's election took place in a moment of eclipse of democracy . . ."

The *Atlantic Monthly* summed up the situation in these brief lines: "On November 27, under the most rigid dictatorship in modern history, Colombia elected Gómez president . . ."

Before the end of his term of office President Ospina Pérez performed several significant acts. One was to raise the Colombian Legation in Spain to Embassy rank in spite of the resolution adopted by the United Nations in 1947, which was still in force. The Dictator followed the example of Argentina. The ambassador appointed to the post was Roberto Urdaneta Arbeláez, who, as president of the Colombian delegation in the UN, had worked hard though unsuccessfully to improve relations with Franco. Among the last acts of the retiring Dictator was an exchange of decorations with the governments of Argentina, Spain, and the Dominican Republic.

On August 7, 1950, Laureano Gómez assumed office, taking his oath before the Supreme Court. This should have been done before Congress, but Congress had been dissolved by force. When he received Gómez in the palace, Ospina Pérez said: "I leave with a glad heart because the country is in the best hands Colombia possesses." To which Gómez replied: "My gratitude is boundless. I hope to be able to imitate the proofs of courage and virtue so amply displayed by Your Excellency, which saved Colombia."

One month after his inauguration, Laureano Gómez issued

a decree disqualifying the Vice-President, Eduardo Santos. In Colombia the vice-president is elected by Congress. Santos, who had been president of the country, and whose selection as vice-president was applauded even by President Ospina Pérez, is one of the most eminent figures of America. The system of congressional election of the vice-president has existed in Colombia since 1863. Santos was elected vice-president in 1949 for a term of one year. His term of office was coming to an end, and Congress had to choose a successor, but the government kept the body dissolved by force. The Constitution, however, provides: "When for any reason congress has not elected a vice-president, the previous incumbent shall continue in office." The dictatorship chose to ignore the Constitution on this occasion, as it had done many times before in instituting changes.

The violence that was rending the country continued unabated. Laureano Gómez had rewarded the most active firebrands with cabinet posts. Alfonso López, a former Liberal president, and a distinguished leader of the Liberal party, though, curiously enough, a personal friend of Laureano Gómez—he is a cold, objective person—estimated the number of deaths from 1949 to 1951 at 50,000. As has been pointed out, it is impossible to know the exact figures. The victims are buried secretly or thrown into the rivers or converted into handfuls of ashes. In one village the priest was asked for a death certificate, and this was his reply:

"The undersigned, parish priest of Our Lady of Carmen, certifies that in the parish registry there is no record of the death of Manuel Carvajalino Peña. The reason for this is that when the aforesaid Mr. Carvajalino was shot, the former priest, Nervardo Salazar, was not here in the parish, and the body of Mr. Carvajalino, together with those of many others, was buried in a common grave without the rites of the church. —El Carmen, April 1, 1951. Luis Antonio García, parish priest."

The violence has followed a vicious circle. The government

cannot control its own agents, who were given carte blanche and appointed to the police force. This was true particularly of the rural districts, where many of these agents were recruited from criminal ranks. The country people who have had their houses burned down, their lands confiscated, and their wives and daughters violated, have taken refuge in the hills, have gone to other regions where they can better defend themselves, and have initiated guerrilla warfare, retaliatory raids. Popular heroes have come from their ranks, men resembling "El Campesino" in the Spanish Civil War.

Laureano Gómez appointed as his Minister of War Roberto Urdaneta Arbeláez, a diplomat who studied at the Jesuit University in Spain, and who hoped to succeed Gómez in the presidency. It was he who, at the beginning of Ospina Pérez's administration, organized shock troops of police. Urdaneta Arbeláez had held various diplomatic posts; he was the first Ambassador to Franco Spain, and until recently, President of the Political and Security Committee of the United Nations. As Minister of War he announced that he was going to exterminate the bandits. What constitutes a bandit? The military force sent to fight the refugees in the Llanos—a region the size of one of the larger states of the United States—defines such malefactors in a "Warning to All Citizens" that contains paragraphs such as these:

"As of this date [October 20, 1950], the following will be considered bandits and so dealt with by the army:

"All persons 16 years of age or older who hide or flee from the armed forces in any place.

"All persons, whatever their age or sex, who circulate by land or water between 11 p.m. and 5 a.m. or who go out or move about any town or its surrounding countryside during curfew hours;

"All civilians issuing orders differing from those normally in force for work without special authorization signed and sealed by a military authority;

"All civilians who at any time or in any place carry firearms without certificate of registration, authorization, or other form of safe-conduct issued by some military authority within the last five months . . ."

And so forth.

As though this were not enough, planes subsequently flew over the Llanos and dropped leaflets ordering their evacuation. Families who had lived there for generations tending their cattle, who had been born there, whose relatives were buried there, had to pull up stakes and leave, journeying for days to seek refuge in other localities and to begin a new life. As the leaflet had warned, the extermination got under way. Many villages were burned. A special target of these attacks was the Protestant religion, which had small missions or chapels in many of these places. A group of young men between the ages of eighteen and twenty professing the Protestant faith appeared in the city of Sogamoso several days after this campaign began. Their right hands had been chopped off. This has been going on since 1950. In the State of Cauca Valley alone since April 27, 1951, the Protestant chapels and schools of Andinápolis, Betania, Ceilán, Betel, Belén, San Francisco, Colorados, Tulia, Galicia, La Cumbre, Moralia, Restrepo, and Palmira have been razed or burned. The violence has been carried out in the name of religion, against the will of the Catholic Church, to which the fanatical clergy paid no attention, as happened in Spain. The pogrom in the city of Río Negro has been recounted by Father Jairo Mejía Gómez, a priest worthy of his cloth:

"It was approximately eleven o'clock at night . . . when a loud shout brought me to the window of the parish house . . . I saw a group of some fifty people shouting *vivas* to the Conservative party and the Catholic religion . . . When I heard them shout 'Long live the Catholic faith,' I called out at the top of my voice from the window: 'Listen to me, all you men and citizens of Río Negro: as a priest I forbid you to shout

"Long live the Catholic faith," for the Catholic religion does not sanction violence.' "

This is not an isolated case. There are clergymen like the Bishops of Manizales and Antioquia who have suffered the most offensive threats, and whose pastoral letters on behalf of peace are not allowed to be published. This diabolic confounding of religion with politics is one of the most sinister features of the situation in Colombia under the dictatorship. It is impossible to describe the incidents of violence to which this has given rise, or the many others which reveal the barbarous instincts that are released when the government, instead of restraining and punishing, stimulates them. The example of what took place in Germany goes to prove that the cultural level of a nation has no bearing on the case. An eminent Colombian sociologist, Luis López de Mesa, whose life has been devoted to his studies, has summed up in a phrase the accomplishment of this neo-Fascism which the dictatorship has imposed on Colombia: "The revolution of 1949 began with the casting overboard of the principles of the Christian religion."

In its latest phase the Colombian dictatorship has employed the tactics recommended and employed by Goebbels: the big lie, so big that it admits of no answer. The violence, says the government, is the work of the enemies of the regime. It occurs in the country—says the Minister of the Interior—"but the plans and programs are worked out in the city, with cold-blooded, sly calculation to bring about their desired results." Minister of War Urdaneta Arbeláez went even farther: he laid the responsibilty for what was happening at the door of former President Eduardo Santos. Commenting on a telegram sent by Dr. Santos, which had been artfully cut by the official censorship, Urdaneta Arbeláez accused him openly of egging on the trouble-makers, and added:

"If the pacification of Colombia is the real objective, the first thing to do is frankly and courageously to disavow and condemn the delinquency, withdraw from the malefactors all material and moral support, and open the way for the return to work of those who bear no share of the guilt for the shocking crimes that have been perpetrated. Let us all join forces to the end that the criminals may feel the stern hand of justice."

The ministers make their accusations over the radio and through the press, bringing them to the knowledge of the whole country. The accused are denied all possibility of a public defense.

The following are excerpts from Eduardo Santos's telegram, barred from publication by the censorship:

"The country thirsts for peace, is horrified by the violence and blood-letting and the thought that Christian civilization is threatened with destruction among us . . . we have always been unalterably opposed to violence, not only because it is contrary to the fundamental principles of Liberalism, but because our people have been and are its victims, because it has brought mourning to thousands of our constituents' homes. We beg that violence be combatted and eliminated because we know that violence can never be cured by violence, by extermination and the scorched earth policy, by the method of 'pacification' launched by the terror of 1816 [during the War of Independence] and bearing such abominable fruit in the Llanos today. Violence is the greatest evil that afflicts the country . . . one must avoid partisan and unfeeling generalizations and distinguish between those in whom horrible experiences give rise to a desire for revenge or those harried like wild animals by implacable enemies and those who would profit from the state of confusion to seek infamous advantages or satisfy their base instincts . . . Violence can never be contained or eliminated on the basis of partisan vengefulness or by persecuting political opponents. This only encourages and spreads it. It must be dealt with from the standpoint of statesmen and Christians, with the support of all the responsible elements of the country, as one proceeds in the case of a mortal illness, not as one attacks a hated personal enemy. And if in connection with all this there is the desire to fix responsibility, clearly, precisely, seriously, Liberalism will go all the way along this road. Let this be determined, especially as concerns those who, because of the positions of authority they occupy, are most responsible. To the end of achieving national conciliation let understanding, mercy, and justice go hand in hand."

By cutting out two-thirds of this telegram, the Minister converted it into a message inciting to violence, and tried to use it as a means to stir up public opinion to the point of endangering the ex-President's life. Santos addressed a letter to the Minister: "The right of legitimate defense," he said, "is one of the basic concepts on which justice rests . . . I am being denied this right . . . I trust that you, as head of the censorship, will not persist in barring the defense of those unjustly offended . . ." The Minister did not allow this defense to be published. Like the political opportunist he is, the Minister today defends the dictatorship without reserve. But when Santos was president and Urdaneta Arbeláez one of his ministers, he presented him with a gold plaque on which was engraved: "To the eminent president, Eduardo Santos, apostle of justice, of right and of peace among nations, to whom all Colombia owes a debt of eternal gratitude."

It is difficult for those who did not know Colombia before the dictatorship to realize what this situation, compounded of violence, cowardice and totalitarianism, signifies for that country. No one there can believe that the systematic destruction of liberty, the undermining of the structure of the state that has been going on there, is the work of foreign inspiration. Perhaps this is the manner in which Fascism adapts itself to the soil of South America. The liberal systems, loosely-knit, open to free discussion, more eloquent in the field of philosophic speculation than apt in matters of economic change, are an easy prey to surprise attack, to tactics of direct action with a gun held at their head. Trusting in its long tradition of legality, Colombia walked confident and unguarded. The change was lightning-like. All Latin America has been the loser. The continent has lost, no one can say for how long, one of its strongest democracies, what might have been a bulwark against totalitarian inroads. The new state has not been proclaimed in the name of a caudillo like Franco or Perón. The triumph has been that of totalitarian absolutism, imposed by fire and sword, on the best of democracies.

Laureano Gómez is a sick man. He had no sooner assumed the presidency than a heart attack brought him to the brink of the grave. A decree was quickly passed invalidating the succession of Vice-President Eduardo Santos, and thus insuring that, in the event of Gómez's death, he would be succeeded by one of his own group. In October 1951 a second attack left Gómez permanently bedridden. Congress was quickly convoked to elect a vice-president in a show of legality, and the choice fell on the man who had ordered the massacres in the savannah, Minister of War Urdaneta Arbeláez. Urdaneta Arbeláez, in his speech of acceptance, implored the aid of Divine Providence to the end that under his government not a drop of blood should be shed.

The Congress that elected Urdaneta came to office in keeping with the strictest Nazi technique. Laureano Gómez appointed a committee to choose the candidates for Congress throughout the country. There was not even the simulacrum of a party convention for that purpose. When this body convened, it was found that the great majority supported the new leader, Gilberto Alzate Avendaño, a member of the original group of Black Shirts, an ardent Falangist. He is a fiery young man who follows the Perón line against Wall Street and favors even more extreme totalitarian measures.

At times the pretense of attempting to arrive at a peaceable solution is put forth. When the Government was seeking a loan from the Import-Export Bank, it proposed talks to this end with the Liberal Party, taking advantage of the circumstance that with Eduardo Santos out of the country, the acting leader was Alfonso López, the only person in the Liberal ranks with whom Gómez and Urdaneta Arbeláez will have any dealings. The talks had hardly begun when a fresh wave of violence broke out, and they were broken off. The Liberal leaders have withdrawn to let the conflicting personal ambitions of the Conservatives bring about a dog-eat-dog situation. But so far main dish at this grisly banquet has been the nameless peasants of the Colombian countryside.

XI

THE COLOMBIANS IN KOREA

It is necessary to kindle the cult of sincerity, even to the point of indiscretion. Liberty is conscience. That man is free who knows the law that governs him. And public freedom is public conscience. That nation is free which knows the reasons for the laws that govern it. The greatest enemy of liberty, therefore, is secrecy—worse, even, than violence. Despotism, which is the rule of secrecy, is worse than tyrrany, the rule of violence. It is better to be a man who recognizes the injustice of the violence done him than a barnyard animal who is ignorant of the reason why it is fattened and cared for. The worst slave is the one who is happy with his enslavement

So devote yourselves, you young men, to doing away with secrets. Democracy is publicity. And I do not know whether fools—whose number, according to the Scriptures, is legion—will call this a paradox. For, to them, everything their dyspeptic minds cannot digest is a paradox.

MIGUEL DE UNAMUNO,
in a letter to Joaquín
Maurin, January 4, 1918

WHEN the Korean War broke out only one Latin American government, implementing its words with deeds, offered and dispatched one thousand soldiers and a corvette to the fighting front. This was the government of Colombia.

Just what induced Laureano Gómez, head of the dictatorship ruling Colombia, to take this step? Was it generous sympathy with the democratic cause? Was it close ties with the United States? Was it obedience to a mandate of the Colombian Congress? The answer to these questions will be most

187

helpful to an understanding of the international politics of this hemisphere.

Laureano Gómez assumed the dictatorship of Colombia on August 7, 1950, under very special circumstances. To insure his "election," the government that preceded him had broken with constitutional procedure by closing the Congress and unleashing a wave of violence that took a greater death toll in Colombia than all the casualties suffered by the troops of the United Nations in Korea up to that moment. The new President, who had no intention of modifying this situation, decided that it would be a shrewd move to court the favor of the United States government and investors. Even before taking office, he began to give North American journalists interviews in which he professed boundless admiration for the United States and stated that he would introduce a constitutional amendment giving maximum guarantees to all who wished to invest capital in Colombia. Once in power, he made every effort to interest American companies in his public works program. To make this even more convincing, he dismissed Colombian engineers or assigned them subordinate positions and put the administration and technical direction of this work in the hands of North Americans.

There is a strange story behind all these protestations. This is where an account of what happened to the Colombian launch *Resolute* must be inserted.

Early in 1942, as the *Resolute* was sailing Colombian Caribbean waters in the vicinity of the port of Cartagena, a German submarine that had managed to slip through the outer defenses of the Panama Canal fired on it, and a considerable number of inoffensive Colombians became food for the sharks. The incident caused the greatest indignation in the country. Eduardo Santos was President at the time, and the matter was laid before the Senate. A debate was scheduled, with a view to declaring a state of war against those responsible for the outrage, the Hitler government.

But the matter did not prove simple. Even though public opinion was solidly behind the government in condemning this wholly unwarranted attack, Laureano Gómez and José de la Vega, respectively owner and editor of the newspaper *El Siglo*, were members of the Senate. Following the frankly pro-Nazi line of their newspaper, they made vehement speeches opposing a break with Germany.

The explanation of the incident given in Laureano Gómez's newspaper was that the affair had been trumped up by the North Americans: it was not true that a German submarine had torpedoed the launch. North American ships, *El Siglo* maintained, had fired on the *Resolute* and sunk it in order to create in Colombia an atmosphere of hostility against the great German nation.

The handling of this incident was only one of a series expressing a policy of long standing. *El Siglo* had flatly opposed taking any action that might directly or indirectly align Colombia with President Roosevelt's policies. There were two reasons for the editors' taking this stand: their campaign against Yankee imperialism and their sympathy with the German cause.

At that time the government was in favor of spending 30,000,000 pesos for improved armaments. Among other things, there was the problem of keeping better guard over the Panama Canal. Colombia's proximity to the Canal laid upon it a special responsibility in the defense of the hemisphere. Months before Pearl Harbor, President Eduardo Santos declared that Colombia would guarantee that in no event would it allow its territory to be used as a base for an attack on the Canal, and that his country would assume this responsibility itself as a primary obligation.

The position taken by Laureano Gómez's paper is apparent from the following excerpts from an editorial of September 7, 1940:

"The reaction produced in us by the Anglo-American pact is

very different [from that of the Santos government]. The journalists closest to the government have hastened to declare that the proximity of the canal lays upon us the duty of defending it, and that if we do not, 'the United States will do it, whether we like it or not.' This is unconditional surrender in advance; and this is the meaning and aim of the plan that orders the squandering of thirty millions on the purchase of armaments of—it hardly seems necessary to point out—North American manufacture. This is the sad, the depressing truth, and we have no intention of concealing it from the Colombian people.

"The country is moving slowly but inevitably toward ruin and dishonor in order to worm itself into the good graces of the power that mutilated our national territory.

"The government of the country is playing with fire. No matter what turn events take, no matter what the collaborationism of our authorities, the Conservative Party, which is half the nation, will oppose this shame by all legal means."

The editors of *El Siglo* went even a little farther. In the Senate they raised with almost brutal frankness the question of who should have control of the Panama Canal.

There was a great change since 1940 and 1950. Laureano Gómez, the dictator, felt very strongly about the war in Korea. It is a war, he says, in which Colombia has a direct stake. He wants Colombian soldiers to go to fight in Asia, and he has dispatched a corvette, the pride of the tiny Colombian fleet. But in 1940 he was of the opinion that it was preferable for the Panama Canal to be in the hands of England, Japan, or Germany rather than in those of the United States. The following paragraphs from editorials in *El Siglo* are from speeches pronounced on the floor of the Colombian Senate by the co-director of the paper. They were later collected in a book that ironically enough bears the title *The Good Neighbor:*

"There is talk of the dangers to the Panama Canal in the event of the war spreading to the American continent. So what! Is the Canal ours? Are there not certain past events that would hardly incline the patriotic Colombian to become greatly exercised over a route that was built at the cost of our territorial integrity? Would we have cause for alarm or regret if tomorrow, when the spoils of the conquerors are divided up, the zone of which we were plundered were to pass under the control of England, Japan, even of Germany? The loss of the Canal would be a catastrophe without precedent for the United States, but not for us. We are only human."

"Do you think the life of a single Colombian should be sacrificed so the United States may continue to hold possession of the Panama Canal?"

"The people of North America should realize that to seek us as an ally when a foreign enemy is knocking at their gates is to ask of us a sacrifice that is an offense to our dignity, that is a path of abjection for us . . . Colombia and Mexico are the two despoiled republics which, for the deepest historic reasons, can offer North America nothing but a strict neutrality."

Without doubt the Department of State in Washington has a complete dossier on these earlier attitudes of the dictator of Colombia. But another side of the affair is equally interesting. The icy dignity with which Gómez's paper advocated Colombia's neutrality went hand in hand with a mounting admiration for Nazi Germany. *El Siglo* reported the fall of Paris with satisfaction because France was rotten and had been corrupted by the Masons. Laval was hailed as the genius of the hour. Churchill was held up to ridicule. Many editorials, comments and notes were devoted to the Jewish question. Those who shaped the policies of the democratic government of Colombia "were misled by the pernicious influence of Jewish propaganda in the United States." Laureano Gómez cherished the hope that the triumph of Hitler would wipe the Jews off the face of the earth.

"Hitler has proved," he said in an article, "that it is possible to wage a long, difficult, and immensely costly war without money. The Jews thought they could boycott Germany by removing all the gold and transferring it to the United States. They were mistaken. The Führer has made a truly miraculous discovery: he has found that he and his people can get along on the 'work standard'. . . In Great Britain, as in the United States, the government is practically controlled by Semitic elements that feed the flames of conflict. All this will redound to the good of Latinity, or specifically of *hispanidad*[1], because it is uncontaminated."

Laureano Gómez has now, somewhat hastily, tried to efface this part of his past. He would like the files of the State Department to record, not the name of that ill-fated *Resolute*, but that of the corvette *Padilla*, which he sent to Korea to fight for democracy shoulder to shoulder and heart to heart with the United States. The corvette and the thousand men have gone as his personal contribution, without prior consultation with congress. To be sure, it is impossible for him to consult Congress because there is no Congress: it was dissolved by force two years ago. Neither can he consult public opinion: the press is censored. Strangely enough, the newspaper *El Tiempo* of Bogotá was closed down for twenty-four hours for having published a photograph of the entrained soldiers waving to their families from the windows of the train as they left Bogotá.

This is inexplicable. The soldiers were going of their own free will. Recruiting one thousand volunteers for Korea was not a difficult undertaking. Colombians have a reputation for endurance and bravery. It is an opportunity rather than a trial to be sent out of the country today when life,

---

[1] At the beginning of his regime in Spain, General Franco made "*hispanidad*" one of the fundamental themes of his political program. It was a promise to reconstruct the Spanish empire in America. The idea has persisted, extending to the Falangist groups in Spanish America. Today it would represent the imposition of a regime analogous to that of Franco in Spain and would give political unity to a world as extensive as that dominated by the successors of Philip II.

particularly in the rural areas, has become unbearable. The Colombian has always showed himself willing to fight for a cause he considered worthy of his sacrifice. Colombian troops formed a large part of Bolívar's army. Colombian units fought in Cuba for Cuban independence. The Colombian is glad and willing to serve in the Korean war, proclaimed as the fight of democracy against Communism, and the idea of adventure in foreign parts appeals to him.

The government could recruit not one thousand, but ten thousand, Colombian peasants for the front—where their lives would be in no more danger than in their own country. And by sending this expeditionary force, the dictatorship rids itself of a number of democratically inclined officers whom it was finding troublesome.

At the 1951 Meeting of Foreign Ministers in Washington, Laureano Gómez's delegates played an outstanding role. None more vigorously supported the position that the continent should arm itself for joint action on a broad scale both here and in Asia. Naturally, the day after the meeting negotiations got under way to obtain arms for Colombia. These are not to equip the thousand peasants who have been sent to Korea. These arms are for home consumption. We have no way of knowing how many Reds the Colombians have killed in Korea up to this moment, but we do know that there have been in the neighborhood of 50,000 casualties in Colombia since 1949.

The government now needs arms to wipe out these refugees. As is only human, these people thirst for vengeance and are moved by the elementary need to continue existing, even though they have lost everything they had. They have been driven to desperation and crime. This is the war in which the dictatorship of Laureano Gómez is really interested. This is the war for which it is obtaining arms from the United States on the pretext of using them in Korea.

Anne O'Hare McCormick said in *The New York Times* at the time of the Meeting of Foreign Ministers in Washington:

"There is no guarantee that the arms that will be allocated by the Inter-American Defense Board to carry out the twenty-one nation security pact may not be used in border disputes or to maintain local dictatorships in power." Their use in border disputes is highly problematical, given the Pan American system, but as for their employment for the other purpose Mrs. McCormick mentions, there is no question. And it should be pointed out that a few weeks before the meeting in Washington, the Colombian Minister of War, who is not a general, but a politician who has succeeded Laureano Gómez in the dictatorship, sent army planes over the areas where the refugees are hiding out to drop the following leaflets:

"Army Headquarters of Colombia. National Army. Military Institutes Brigade. Infantry Battalion, No. 21. 'Vargas.'

WARNING TO CIVILIAN POPULATION

All law-abiding citizens of the region included between Paratebueno, Barranca de Upia, El Secreto, Agua Clara, El Iguaro, Monterrey, El Porvenir, and Tauramena are hereby notified that beginning March 8 army troops have orders to deal with everyone who has not left the above listed regions as outlaws. The Avianca and Afrypesca airlines have been authorized to evacuate all those so desiring.

Apiay, March 1, 1951."

The zone covered by this order is as large as Nebraska. The Minister of War who directed this small war is Urdaneta Arbeláez, a former member of the Security Council of the United Nations. The slaughter that followed this evacuation order is one of the most horrifying chapters in recent Colombian history.

Nobody any longer remembers the launch *Resolute*. Everyone's attention is fixed on the corvette *Padilla*, now in Korean waters. But the democracy-loving people of Colombia shudder with fear at the news that the dictatorship is continuing to arm.

Aside from this, the thousand Colombians sent to Korea have served with distinction. All the officers in the lower echelons are young men with Liberal leanings who represented a threat to the government of Colombia, and who are the cream of the army. The troops are made up of Colombian peasants, to whom a rigorous life is nothing new. In the camps of Korea the Colombian soldiers, when off duty, get out their guitars, and the other soldiers gather around to listen to music they have never heard before, and which delights them. The North American commanders say there are no better battle troops. According to the official communiqués they have inflicted losses on the enemy at the rate of fifty to one. As human material they are first-class and worthy of a better fate; if nothing more, they deserve to be treated with a little Christian tolerance in their own country.

XII

BRAZIL: A CONTINENT WITHIN
A CONTINENT

*Oh Brazil, that immense continent, which unveils itself more
and more to my knowledge.*

> GOETHE, in a letter to C. F. L. Schultz,
> September 5, 1822

IT IS NOT ACCURATE to say that Brazil is a nation: Brazil is a
continent still waiting to be discovered and brought into
production. The scope of its possibilities is enormous. For
years it was the leading producer of diamonds, which were
discovered by accident. An observer's curiosity was aroused
by a boy playing with some pieces of crystal, which on investigation proved to be diamonds. When the Kimberley
mines were discovered in Africa they were found to be better
than those of Brazil, and the latter disappeared from the
precious-gem map. By 1924 the name of Brazil was associated not with diamonds, but with coffee. It produced enough
to supply the entire world and leave a surplus of millions of
sacks, which were burned. At that time 75% of Brazil's exports
was coffee. Twenty-one years later, in 1945, Brazil had come
up with other products for foreign trade, and coffee represented only 35% of its exports.

David R. Moore says in his *A History of Latin America*
(1942): "By 1700 Minas Geraes was reported to be a veritable 'hell on earth'. Even the secular priests bore a reputation
for villainy and debauchery." In 1950 Minas Geraes had
transferred this fire to its steel mills. Now Brazil manufac-
tures its own railroad equipment: Brazilian-made rails span

the country, and the rolling stock bears the stamp "made in Brazil."

In *New Worlds Emerging* (1949), Earl Parker Hanson wrote: "Regardless of ownership, whether state or private, local or foreign, few Latin American nations have truly national railroad systems; Volta Redonda [a rich Brazilian mining region] means in part that Brazil is planning to create one . . . As a symbol of achievement, an inspiration, and a signpost for the future, Volta Redonda has meaning to the Brazilians—and so also to all the Latin Americans—very similar to that which the Dnieper Dam had to the Soviets in the early days of their industrialization . . ."

And so it goes. If Far Eastern rubber is lost to the American market, Ford raises it in Brazil. When the orange crop of Spain or Portugal fails, or even if it does not, Brazilian oranges are eaten in London.

In 1951 Brazil had a population of 53,000,000, larger than that of all the rest of South America. It is only now beginning to colonize a country larger than the United States, a territory that produces coffee, cotton, sugar, a subcontinent that has coal and oil, the largest manganese deposits in the world, and a hydraulic potential of 20,000,000 h.p. But its most valuable natural asset is its 53,000,000 inhabitants. They have been badly fed, badly housed, badly dressed, and diseased. But they are now emerging from the barefoot state to that of wearers of shoes, and they will consume more with every day that passes. An industrialized Brazil is possible because there is a great consumers' market there. Its progress in the field of tropical medicine, a recognized fact in the scientific world, which, among other things, protects the health and life expectancy of the new-born, preparing them for a productive life, is the most important thing that is happening in South America today. These 53,000,000 will grow in number as living conditions improve, and they have a continent of their own, ready, waiting for them. In which di-

rection will they move? Toward democracy? Toward the
burying-ground of freedom?

Brazil has the shape of a rough triangle, not unlike the
contour of the whole map of South America. This coincidence is significant, for the Brazilian is more like his South
American brothers than is the Argentine. He is more Negro,
more Indian, more tropical. He comes from the same coffee
groves, the same canefields, the same jungle, has the same
approach to life, the same ways, the same problems. And
Brazil has common boundaries with all the countries of the
continent except Chile and Ecuador, which last was its neighbor too until a frontier dispute stripped it of its Amazon forests.

So far, however, Brazil has not been a leader of South
America. Only in recent years has Rio de Janeiro become a
factor in international assemblies and arbitration settlements,
and it is a matter for interesting speculation as to which will
have the upper hand in the coming years, the Brazil of
Vargas or the Argentina of Perón.

If Brazil has been terra incognita to the Brazilians, it has
been much more so to the rest of the South Americans. Rio
de Janeiro has been much closer to Paris than to the capitals
of its ten neighbors. Only with the Plate River cities—Montevideo and Buenos Aires—has it had a superficial intimacy. In
the attempts at fostering closer relations with Brazil, the
Spanish Americans are motivated partly by curiosity and
partly by necessity. In the contest of personalities the choice
is between Perón, who, for the time being, is imposing his will
on an Argentina overpowered by colonels, and Vargas, with
his wily old gaucho's paternal smile, who has made a come-back
from his equivocal past, returning in triumph on the crest of
a wave of overwhelming personal popularity. Today it is a
treat to hear Vargas talk about democracy.

Up to the present moment Portuguese America and
Spanish America have been two separate Americas. Their

different tongues had placed a barrier between them. To be sure, Portuguese is closely related to Spanish, and Spanish Americans do not bother to study it because, with a little effort, they can read it, understand it, and almost speak it. By the same token, Brazilians do not study Spanish. This apparent advantage has in reality kept them apart. On the level of daily living, the person who speaks Portuguese also reads Portuguese, and the person who speaks Spanish reads Spanish. The great achievements of Brazil in the scientific, literary, and historical fields are not well known in Spanish America. And in Rio de Janeiro, apart from Portuguese literature, people given a choice between a French or a Spanish American writer have chosen the French without hesitation.

The history of the two peoples has been different. The Portuguese came to this hemisphere pursuing objectives diametrically opposed to those of the Spaniards. They were a seafaring people with a long mercantile tradition, and where they landed there was no important Indian civilization. The Portuguese had no incentive to push into the interior. They established themselves on the Atlantic coastline of what is now Brazil—the longest of any country in the world, over five thousand miles. Those who were put in charge of the *capitanias* were authorized to explore inland as far as they wished within the two parallel lines on the map that marked the limits of their jurisdiction. A feudal economy developed which was to leave a profound impress. Putting all Brazil under the authority of a governor-general or a viceroy was merely a legal expedient. The country lacked the basis of a prior native organization such as had existed in Mexico or Peru before the Conquest. The real rulers of Brazil were the great landholders or plantation-owners, who had many Indians first, then many Negroes, and always great land grants. And the Jesuits played an important role, too.

In their colonies the Spaniards established themselves inland, following the pattern of Spain with Castile as the heartland. The Portuguese settled themselves along the coast, as Portugal had done in Europe. For this reason the early history of Brazil has points of resemblance to that of the English colonies in North America. Even today three quarters of the population of Brazil inhabits a coastal zone not more than one hundred miles wide. But the extension of the frontier inland assumed different characteristics than in the United States. The Portuguese Brazilians entered the backlands at lance-point in widely scattered areas, not in a mass movement, and without destroying the native population. Instead they fused with it.

The geography of Brazil has conditioned its history. The tropical heat of the country affected the laws, human relations, and social ideas that had come in from Europe, the very structure of the Church. On the one hand there came about a kind of slackening in the severity of justice, of the marriage bond, of the clergy, of customs in general; on the other, a tolerance and flexibility in human relationship. United States visitors to Brazil find it hard to accustom themselves to the indifference that exists there in the matter of color. No one pays any attention in hotels, on the beaches, at the places of amusement, and in the government to variations on the chromatic scale which would raise insoluble problems in many regions of the United States, and difficulties everywhere. If one were to trace a huge S on the map of America, beginning in the islands of the West Indies, curving along the Caribbean through the Gulf of Mexico, Central America, and around the Brazilian coast, one would find that in the area embraced by this S the human product is permeated with the heat of the tropics. Life there is noisier and gayer, friendlier, taking less thought of the morrow. The words that originated in the Iberian peninsula have been set to the music of Africa. One example of this is the Mardi Gras, which, in New Orleans, Panama, or Rio de Janeiro, is one of the grandest shows in the world.

The process of racial fusion began immediately in Brazil. In 1580, Father José de Anchieta gave the population figures as 25,000 whites and 13,000 Negroes. In 1800 the figures were 430,000 whites, 1,500,000 Negroes, and 700,000 Indians. But these statistics are completely misleading. They give the idea of delimited groups, whereas in reality all were ingredients of a melting-pot. Life was centered in the plantations, not in the cities. Brazil's history falls into four economic cycles: dye-wood, sugar cane, mining, and coffee—that is to say, four rural ages. In the "big house" the plantation owner lived like a Biblical patriarch surrounded by vast numbers of legitimate and illegitimate offspring all living under the same roof, all enjoying his fatherly protection.

The slave was a slave, but was not outside the orbit of his owner's life. He shared his master's problems and struggles. Gilberto Freyre, who has analyzed the social processes in Brazil with singular penetration says:

". . . sugar . . . was for the large, closely-knit families: for the prolific families of the 'big house.' It must be borne in mind that the slaves, too, were members, culturally and sociologically, of these families. Not only did they take the names of the first families . . . but also their way of talking, walking, their manners, their amusements, their religious attachment, even their political stand or obligations . . . The slaves of Captain Machado, a devotee of Our Lady of the Conception, for example, were at daggers drawn with the slaves of Colonel Mendonça, who professed the cult of a rival virgin, Our Lady of Guia, out of loyalty to the house or family of which, sociologically, they formed a part . . . Or they engaged in bloody battle on behalf of the Conservative party (to which their master belonged) with slaves who fought with knife and lance to insure victory for the Liberal party (whose cause their masters, in turn, upheld) with a fervor, according to reliable witnesses, never displayed by mercenary troops . . . a fervor that came from the complete identification of the slave with the feelings, interests, and obligations of his master or of the family he regarded as his—his sociological home or family . . ." [1]

This situation made it possible for this Negro world to give Brazil artists, teachers, bishops, and prime ministers of His Highness, the Emperor. Also society people, men of wealth. Freyre quotes the following lines from a book by Thomas Ewbank, published in New York in 1856, and entitled: *Life in Brazil, or a Journal of a Visit to the Land of the Cocoa and the Palm:*

"I have passed black ladies in silks and jewelry, with male slaves in livery behind them. Today one rode past in her carriage, accompanied by a liveried footman and a coachman. Several have white husbands. The first doctor of the city is a colored man; so is the President of the Province . . ."

The Negroes came to Brazil in the eighteenth century, the whites in the nineteenth. In the second half of the last century a spate of European emigrants poured into South America, especially Brazil and Argentina. The Europeans took root in Brazil more easily than in Argentina. According to the United Nations Economic Survey of Latin America (1948), of the 6,780,000 who reached Argentina, only 53.5%, or 3,630,000 settled there for good, while of the 4,732,000 who made Brazil their destination, 74%, or 3,500,000, became Brazilians.

And just as there was a Negro republic in Brazil in the sixteenth century, of runaway slaves who founded their own state from the *quilombo,* the fugitive slave settlement in the backlands to which they had fled, so in the twentieth the Germans of South Brazil, numbering some 800,000, without actually setting up an independent government, lived their own life, with schools where their children were educated in

[1] *"O Bangüê nas Alagoas"* (*Cultura,* Rio de Janeiro, September-December 1948).

German, and the cult of the swastika flourished. But the general rule in Brazil has been a free and friendly association among all peoples. It is on this that the Mexican writer José Vasconcelos has based his theory of a future "cosmic race" compounded of all existing races and all colors.

Peace has been Brazil's watchword. It achieved its independence without war, by the simple procedure of inquiring of a member of the royal house of Braganza if he would like to be emperor, and when he answered *"Eu quero"* (I do), crowning him forthwith. In this fashion the only real monarchy that has existed in this hemisphere since the fall of Moctezuma and Atahuallpa came into being. The Mexican experiments with Agustín Iturbide and Maximilian were makeshifts doomed to failure, and Haiti's "black emperors" were only flashes of sheet lightning in the night. But the Empire in Brazil, which lasted from 1822 to 1889, was authentic. Dom Pedro II's enlightened rule (1834–89) was a real contribution to the history of monarchy, and deserves the same study as that given to the reigns of Frederick the Great and Catherine of Russia. But in 1889 the monarchy ended as it had begun: with exquisite courtesy the Emperor was handed a first-class ticket on a liner bound for Europe and politely wished God-speed. The proclamation of the republic was made in the press. To those recalling the fall of the monarchies in France and Russia or the upheaval that followed the abdication of Alfonso XIII in Spain, this Brazilian courtesy is bewildering.

Brazil's great territorial conquest was the territory of Acre, which in 1903 was transferred from Bolivia to Brazil without the slightest violence. With velvet glove the Viscount de Rio Branco performed the operation, handing Bolivia a check for £2,000,000 sterling.

More danger-fraught than the termination of empire might have been the abolition of slavery if this step had followed the pattern that led to the Civil War in the United States. In Brazil the affair was handled in parliamentary debate and through the press, and a decree put an end to slavery.

And thus we come down to the history of these last decades, with the figure of Getulio Vargas holding the spotlight.

The economic crisis of 1929 hit Latin America with the force of an earthquake. The following year the governments of Bolivia, Peru, and Argentina were thrown out by military coups, and in Colombia the Conservatives, who had held power for forty years, were swept out of office by the voters. Brazil, too, had its revolution, the bloodless revolution of Vargas.

It was the year for a presidential election. President Washington Luis had selected his successor, Julio Prestes. Political tradition in Brazil had established the alternation of candidates from the two great states of São Paulo and Minas Gerais. This time it was the turn of the *mineiro*, but Washington Luis was backing a *paulista*. This sat badly with the *mineiros*, and they proposed a deal to the state of Rio Grande do Sul: they would jointly support a candidate for the presidency from the state of Rio Grande do Sul, Getulio Vargas, and defy the government's political machine. Vargas accepted, and winning the election was the main plank of his platform.

Vargas came of old gaucho stock. He was born in 1883 in the village of São Borja, near the Argentine border. Like his father and grandfather before him, he was a rancher. Vargas studied law, was elected to Congress, and became a leader there. He carried in his political equipment the lessons he had learned on the pampa—when to speak and when to keep quiet—and this carries conviction. He can hear the grass grow. He is unpretentious, affable, cordial. Someone wrote a book entitled *Getulio's Smile*. He would like to conduct his people as one drives a herd, and with a rancher's proud, paternal eye, watch it fatten and grow sleek. When he made his debut in politics the ceremonies and protocol of the Braganzas still prevailed, and Vargas was like a country bumpkin at the emperor's court.

In 1929, as candidate for the presidency, Vargas had already selected as his minister of the interior a fellow gaucho, resourceful young Oswaldo Aranha. On the eve of the election, Vargas retired to his ranch, and left Aranha in charge of affairs. When the returns were in, President Washington Luis telegraphed the official results to Aranha: Julio Prestes had won. Aranha answered him as follows:

"The Honorable President of the Republic, Cattete Palace, Rio de Janeiro: I want to thank Your Excellency for your telegram, which I shall have published so the public mind will be at ease knowing that the first magistrate of the country has confirmed the fact that the people of Brazil will be governed by the man of their sovereign choice. We were animated by no other idea when we stepped into the electoral ring, confident that the culture and integrity of our people and its leaders would decide the issue. To close the ballot-boxes, to refuse to give out information or set up polling places, to remove watchers, falsify the returns, leave the booths exposed to police aggression, buy votes, discriminate against voters, tamper with or confiscate the registry books, rig the elections, prevent the voter from casting his ballot, or bring pressure on him to vote against his convictions—these are all degrading procedures which we were sure could not happen here and invalidate the returns, for they are abhorrent to anyone who has an ounce of decency, and should be condemned by all Brazilians.

"Unfortunately, I have a great number of proved complaints that just such things have taken place in many states, especially São Paulo, Maranhão, Ceará, Pernambuco, Rio Grande do Norte, Santa Catarina, Paraná, and Sergipe. I shall transmit them to the proper authorities . . .

"As you have requested, I hereby inform you of the election returns so far counted in Rio Grande do Sul: Getulio Vargas, 287,321 votes; Julio Prestes, 789 . . ."

A rumor began to spread from one end of Brazil to the other: revolution was on the way. Aranha approved. Vargas approved, but with the proviso that it was not to affect the normal life of the country. At Pôrto Alegre, the state capital of Rio Grande do Sul, things went on as usual, but in leisure hours plans were made for the revolution. Aranha pronounced a fiery speech at party headquarters. The people rushed into the street shouting: "Getulio! We want Getulio!" Getulio appeared on the balcony; he did not say a word, he just smiled. One day he went to the bank and borrowed a sum of money for a trip to Rio. In a little while the word went around: It's the march on the capital! The seizure of power! The revolution!

The march of Getulio, the Generalissimo, was made by rail. At every stop he was cheered by the crowds. In Rio a crowd stormed the train, shouting with one voice: "Getulio." Vargas' chief-of-staff, Goes Monteiro, had set up his headquarters the night before in the beautiful Ponta Rosa Club. The light ladies of the neighborhood swarmed into the building, and it was like carnival time. Everybody danced. Getulio danced, and between dances the news came: Washington Luis had resigned, overthrown by the military. He had put up no opposition. What for? Vargas had come to Rio and installed himself as dictator.

The forces that had backed Vargas's presidential campaign, that had supported him in his revolution, represented a motley group known as Aliança Liberal. It was a combination of strange bedfellows—army officers, Fascists, liberal democrats, students, and Communists—who had one common denominator: "No." They were solidly opposed to what had gone before. Vargas, like a careful gardener, cultivated these opposition flowers with a green thumb. With his gaucho wili-

ness he must have thought that with this monosyllabic program of the Aliança Liberal another word would go very
well: "Getulio." It would lend it a more affirmative quality.

When Vargas drew up his program he said (and this por-
trays him perfectly): "The program is more the people's than
the candidate's."

The military had put him in the presidency provisionally,
until a new Congress could decide on the course of action to
be followed. For the time being he had a free hand. He dissolved the existing Congress, state legislatures, and municipal
councils. He abolished customs barriers between the states.
He declared a moratorium on the payment of Brazil's foreign
debts. He called an international meeting of coffee-growers,
forbade further coffee-planting, and to keep up prices ordered the surplus burned. In 1932 twelve million sacks of
coffee went up in smoke.

Was this what the Aliança Liberal wanted? Definitely not.
In 1932 the opposition began to marshal its forces, starting
in Vargas's own state. São Paulo later became the center.
Bertholdo Klinger, former prefect of police, who controlled
the military forces of São Paulo, assembled 32,000 soldiers
and took command. Under the federal system of Brazil, the
states have their own armies. 120,000 bullets a day were
manufactured so that there would be no shortage of ammuni-
tion for the revolution. São Paulo demanded a return to the
constitutional order. Vargas replied that measures had already been taken to convoke elections for a new Congress
that would decide the matter, but he would not capitulate
to those who took up arms in rebellion or yield to the threat
of violence. With great tact he strategically deployed his
troops, which were those of all Brazil. The revolution ground
to a standstill, and in two months was dead. Borges de
Medeiros, the leader of the revolt, was advised by Vargas to
take a rest in Recife; it would be good for his health and
would save him from falling into the temptation of stirring up

trouble if he returned to his own state. Borges de Medeiros's associate, Otelo Rosa, was offered an apartment in the Hotel Flamingo, one of the best in the world. No reprisals would be taken against São Paulo. In his proclamation Vargas said:

"Having been informed of the shortage of wheat in São Paulo and the resulting scarcity of bread, the government is prepared to transfer at once to that city a shipment from the wheat stores of the capital . . . The provisional government will do everything in its power to see that there is no lack of foodstuffs . . . So let everyone return to his peaceable occupations and live in harmony with the other states, which will always take pride in the progress and civilization of São Paulo!"

That was the end of the rumpus.

If the old members of the Aliança Liberal wanted a Congress, they should have one. And if they wanted a constitution, they should have that, too. In 1931 Vargas informed the steering committee named for this purpose:

"The old political formulas upholding the rights of man would seem to be in a state of decline. Instead of individualism, synonymous with too much freedom, or Communism, a new form of slavery, what we need is a perfect co-ordination of all initiatives under the control of the state and the recognition of class organizations as collaborators in the public administration . . . The felicitous remark of a distinguished statesman can be very opportunely quoted in this connection: 'A government may be provisional, but the revolution is permanent.' It will, therefore, pursue its unwithstandable cycle of evolution, accomplishing its work serenely, without hatreds, and with constancy . . ."

In 1934 Vargas announced that what had been demanded had been done: he had called a constituent assembly, which drew up a constitution and elected him president of the republic. He had allowed his former associates of the Aliança Liberal to draw up "their" constitution—theirs, not his. And he received it with all the ceremony employed by the Spanish colonial governors when they received a royal order, kissing it, laying it on their heads in sign of respect, and then, with a deep genuflection, placing it under the royal seal, and adding: "To be accepted, but not observed." Vargas received the constitution and smiled. He would give it rope enough to hang itself. He would continue as a man without a party. The first plank of the Aliança Liberal, the "No," was being chopped away. The second plank, "Getulio," was filling the gaps.

Brazil was a hotbed of foreign ideologies. From one end of the country to the other Communists and Nazis were working with might and main. The Communists had a splendid organization and a great leader, Luis Carlos Prestes, who exercised a magnetic attraction over his followers. They are Communists not because of Karl Marx or Stalin, but because of Luis Carlos Prestes.

On November 27, 1935, the Third Infantry Regiment of Praia Vermelha hoisted the red flag over its barracks. The Guanabara Palace, the president's home, was, so to speak, a cannon-shot away. A group of officers of the School of Aviation in Alfonsos Field had risen, too, and had murdered in their sleep those officers who did not side with them. It was believed that the governor of Rio Grande do Sul, who was unfriendly to Vargas, would support the rebels with his troops. Exactly the opposite happened. The attempted revolt was quickly snuffed out. By November 28 it was over, and the leaders who had not fled to other countries had been jailed.

On New Year's Eve 1936, on the heels of the greetings, kisses, and popping of champagne corks, Vargas's voice came over the radio:

"Brazilians: all over the world, in this hour of comradeship, everyone lays aside for a little while the toil and cares of the day and lifts up his heart and spirit to proclaim his faith in a better future . . . We Brazilians, whose hearts are always open to the gentle voice of peace and brotherly love, are hearing many voices in this momentous hour . . . Trained in a materialistic conception of life, Communism has become the most dangerous enemy confronting Christian civilization. In the light of our spiritual formation, we can see it only as the agent of destruction of all the achievements of occidental culture, as the triumph of the base appetites and lowest passions of mankind, a return to primitivism, to the primeval forms of social organization, characterized by the predominance of the instincts of the herd, whose outstanding examples are to be found among the ancient tribes of the Asiatic steppes. In flagrant opposition to and unadaptable to the degree of culture and the material progress of our day, Communism is fated to maintain an attitude of permanent violence . . . In the discharge of my solemn duties as head of the state, I am not in the habit of haggling over responsibilities or consequences . . ."

The outlawing of the Communist party gave wings to the Nazis. They had a powerful party behind them. Hitler had turned his eyes on Brazil as the bridgehead for the Nazi domination of South America. There was a solid base from which to work in the large German population of São Paulo. In 1933 Plinio Salgado had launched his *integralista* party, whose green-shirted legions were receiving Nazi military training. They offered Vargas their support, and Getulio smiled. A green shirt, says Azevedo Amaral, was an "open, sesame" to many privileges, just as being a Communist was dangerous. Many Communists joined the Green Shirts. The *integralista* coffers were full to overflowing with contributions from the German embassy, the German colony. The whole world got word of the new Nazi-Fascist Brazil.

Vargas had many irons in the fire. He harped on the Communist danger; he encouraged Nazi-Fascism; he pointed out the bankruptcy or incapacity of the liberal constitution. It all added up to anarchy. But there was a solution: a strong state, "*O Estado novo*," a democracy having authority. The revolution makes no sense unless it can provide new institutions in the place of those it rejects.

On November 10, 1937, Vargas read a proclamation to the Brazilian people from the Guanabara Palace. The substance of its content was: the constitution of 1934 is dead. Long live the constitution of 1937! The constitution the people heard of in this fashion was Vargas's this time. Over the radio he announced it, promulgated it and put it into effect, to be accepted and obeyed.

The Vargas constitution starts off with: "The president of the Republic of the United States of Brazil, to fulfill the legitimate aspirations of the Brazilian people . . . with the support of the armed forces and yielding to the weight of public opinion . . . is determined to insure the unity of the nation, respect for its honor and independence . . . by drawing up the following constitution, which will as of today go into force throughout the country."

These are representative articles from the constitution:

"Brazil is a republic. Political power comes from the people, and is carried out in its name and in the interest of its well-being, its honor, its independence, and its prosperity." (Article 1)

"The president of the republic, the supreme authority of the state, will co-ordinate the activities of its highest representative bodies, direct its internal and foreign politics, initiate or guide the legislative policy of national interest and be responsible for the country's administration." (Article 73)

"The legislative power will be exercised by the National Congress, in collaboration with the Council of National Economy and the President of the Republic, by the former in matters having to do with its advisory capacity, and by the latter in putting forward and ratifying laws and issuing legal decrees authorized by this constitution. The congress will be made up of two chambers: the Chamber of Deputies and the Federal Council." (Article 38)

"The Chamber of Deputies will be made up of representatives of the people elected by indirect suffrage." (Article 46)

"The Federal Council will be made up of representatives of the states and ten members appointed by the President of the Republic. Their term of office will be six years. Each state, through its legislature, will elect a representative. The governor of the state will have the right of veto over the person selected by the legislature. In the event of a veto, the person in question will be confirmed in his post only if supported by two thirds of the votes of the members of the legislature.

"The Council of National Economy will be made up of representatives of the various branches of the national economy . . . designated by professional groups or unions recognized by law, guaranteeing equal representation to labor and management. The Council will be divided into five sections . . ." (Article 57)

"The presidency of the Council of National Economy will be vested in a minister of the government to be designated by the President of the Republic. The President will also designate up to three members to each section of the Council of Economy . . ." (Article 59)

"At all times, by a plebiscite to be provided for by law, power to legislate on certain or all matters coming within its scope, may be conferred on the Council of National Economy. The authorization of such a plebiscite resides with the President of the Republic . . ." (Article 63)

"The proposing of laws, in principle, resides in the government. In any case, proposals for new laws or amendments brought forward by either of the two chambers will not be authorized for discussion if they deal with tax matters or in any way presuppose an expenditure. No member of either house is empowered to propose a law. Such a step can be taken only with the support of one third of the congress or of the members of the National Council. Any proposal put forward by one of the houses will be held up for discussion until the government communicates its intention of presenting another covering the same matter . . ." (Article 64)

"In addition to the cases provided for by martial law in time of war, the law can establish the death penalty for the following crimes . . . d) any attempt, with the help or financial support of any foreign power or organization of international character to bring about a change in the political or social order established by the constitution; e) any attempt to overthrow the political or social order by violence to the end of seizing the state and establishing the dictatorship of a social class . . ." (Article 122)

"All citizens are free to express their thoughts, verbally or in writing, in print or in pictures, in keeping with the conditions and limitations provided by the law. The law may provide: a) censorship of press, theater, motion pictures, radio for the purpose of insuring peace, order, and public security, empowering the proper authorities to forbid the circulation, broadcasting, or performance . . ." (Article 122, clause 15)

"A state of emergency is declared throughout the country." (Article 186, Temporary Measures).

The enthusiasm of the *integralistas* knew no bounds. Germany, Italy, and Spain received the joyous news of the setting up of a totalitarian state in Brazil. The new constitution was proclaimed on November 10, 1937. On November 14 Vargas dissolved the Nazi-Fascists by declaring the *integralista* party illegal. As a matter of fact, Article 2 of the constitution already foreshadowed this: "The flag, the national anthem, the Brazilian seal and coat-of-arms are the only ones that may be used throughout the nation. No other flag, anthem, seal, or coat-of-arms will be permitted . . ." From the day he assumed office, Vargas had declared: "The government will not allow itself to become the prisoner of any party, class, or faction, being responsible only to the Brazilian people, the final judge of its acts."

Vargas had used the malcontents for his own ends. He smiled on them and, in the end, threw them into the street. He loves authority; he likes to impose order, his own concept of order, in the Latin American, the Brazilian manner, not the dramatic, hysterical fashion of Hitler or the cold cruelty of the Führer's henchmen or the pomposity of Mussolini's balcony scenes. Nobody in Germany ever thought of calling Hitler Adolf. Mussolini was not called Benito in Italy. In Brazil Vargas is always referred to as Getulio. His dictatorship had much more in common with that of Porfirio Díaz in Mexico or that of Antonio Guzmán Blanco in Venezuela than with the European varieties. Getulio's "Estado Novo" flirted with the innovations of the corporate state, but what he was really seeking was a strong central authority to control his vast country, in which sociologists claim there are at least eight great nations, all of which Vargas wanted to hold in his gaucho grip.

Vargas's political thinking differs radically from that of Hitler, Mussolini, Stalin, Franco, or Perón in that he has not founded a party or sought to govern in the name of a party.

Vargas, who had his hours of amorous dalliance with Germany, and who governs a country in which there is a strong German element, gradually began to slip gracefully out from under the diatribes against Yankee Imperialism and into the Good Neighbor fold. Roosevelt commanded his warm admiration and lay much closer to his heart than Hitler, was much more in keeping with his manner. In one of his earliest speeches in Congress, on the occasion of the Allied triumph in 1918, he had said:

"The outcome of this war proves once more that all violence is sterile, all oppression but temporary, and that tyranny breeds only hatred. There is only one enduring and constructive force: love."

And acting on this principle, Vargas sent his fellow gaucho, Oswaldo Aranha, to Washington to weave the web of solid friendship with Roosevelt. In his turn, Roosevelt emphasized more and more the relation between the problems of the United States and those of the Brazilian and Spanish American world. In May 1941 Roosevelt, speaking before the Council of the Pan American Union in Washington, said:

"Adolf Hitler never considered the domination of Europe as an end in itself. European conquest was but a step toward ultimate goals in all the other continents. It is unmistakably apparent to all of us that, unless the advance of Hitlerism is forcibly checked now, the Western Hemisphere will be within range of the Nazi weapons of destruction . . . I am not speculating about all this. I merely repeat what is already in the Nazi book of world-conquest. They plan to treat the Latin American nations as they are now treating the Balkans. They plan then to strangle the United States of America and the Dominion of Canada . . . The Nazis are taking military possession of the greater part of Europe. In Africa they have occupied Tripoli and Libya, and they are threatening Egypt, the Suez Canal, and the Near East. But their plans do not stop there . . . They also have the armed power at any time to occupy Spain and Portugal; and that threat extends . . . also to the Atlantic fortress of Dakar, and to the island outposts of the New World—the Azores and Cape Verde Islands. The Cape Verde Islands are only seven hours' distance from Brazil by bomber or troop-carrying planes. They dominate shipping routes to and from the South Atlantic. The war is approaching the brink of the Western Hemisphere itself. It is coming very close to home . . . It is time for us to realize that the safety of American homes even in the center of our country has a definite relationship to the continued safety of homes in Nova Scotia or Trinidad or Brazil . . ."

In June 1942 the third meeting of the Ministers of Foreign Affairs of the American Republics was held in Rio de Janeiro. In his opening address Sumner Welles said:

"I know that Hitler's representatives have said to some of you that Germany has not the slightest thought of dominating the Western Hemisphere. All that Germany wants, they have told you, is complete domination over every part of Europe, of Africa, and of the Near East, the destruction of the British Empire, the enslavement of the Russian people, the overlordship of the Far East, and when this is accomplished, only friendship and peaceful trade with the Americas. But Hitler's representatives have omitted to mention that in such a fateful contingency we would all of us then also be living in a Hitler-dominated world. You may remember a few days ago Hitler publicly denounced President Roosevelt as the greatest war-monger of all times, because the President has declared that the people of the United States 'did not want to live in the type of world' that Hitler wished for . . ."

Not long after this Brazil declared war on Germany. In July 1944 Brazilian troops landed in Italy and took an active part in its liberation.

The year 1943 was more propitious for Nazism in Spanish American Buenos Aires than in Rio de Janeiro. President Ramón Castillo had maintained diplomatic relations with the Axis. More than that, he was pro-German. Hitler's agents set up propaganda headquarters in Buenos Aires, making it the center of their spy ring and efforts at penetration. In the Blue Book on Argentina published by Washington in 1946, certain details having to do with Brazil are revealed:

"In the summer of 1943, the Nazi SD agents in Argentina established direct cooperation with two Integralist figures then living in exile in Buenos Aires, Sr. Jair Tavares and a Dr.

Caruso. There followed several months of efforts to draw
Brazilian Integralists into a conspiracy, designed to undermine the Brazilian war effort and to obtain for the SD intelligence from Brazil useful to Germany. When the latter efforts
proved unproductive because of communication difficulties,
Becker arranged a meeting between Caruso and Tavares,
Cols. Perón and González, and a SD agent. At this meeting
the Argentine officers offered to aid the Integralists in line
with the Argentine plan of framing an anti-United States
bloc, and to make available the courier service of the Argentine military forces for communications with the Integralists in Brazil. The results of this meeting were conveyed to
Dr. Raimundo Padilha, the principal Integralist leader who
was in hiding in Brazil, with the result that Padilha
despatched to Buenos Aires a Major Jaime Ferreira da Silva,
whom he had authorized to negotiate with the Argentine officials and with Becker. Ferreira arrived in late December
and promptly conferred with Becker and the local Integralists . . ."

Vargas had to be on guard against snakes in the grass, but
a gaucho is used to that.

In 1945 Vargas completed fifteen years in power. Rio wondered if he would ever give it up. Little by little he pulled
up his horse, as though he were going to dismount. In February of that year he announced that elections would be held.
On March 11 he said that he would not be a candidate. Two
days later, the candidacy of his Minister of War, General
Enrico Gaspar Dutra was launched, and Vargas offered him
his support.

Everything seemed to indicate that the *"Estado Novo"* had
been Vargas's personal creation for his own use. When he
left the presidency, Brazil would go back to the old state, to
the system of representative government. That was Dutra's
platform. But Vargas knew that this was just the end of the
first act—these fifteen years had been only the first act, and

he still felt very young. With his habitual smile and silence, always delighted with applause, he did his best to leave no disagreeable memories of his rule. He threw open the doors so that the exiles could return, and set the political prisoners free. Luis Carlos Prestes, the Communist leader, was released after nine years in jail. There were critical voices: the Supreme Court accused Vargas of certain abuses of power, as for instance, illegally seizing the presidency in 1937. But nobody knew for sure whether he was giving up his office or not. In August his name was put forward by others as that of a presidential candidate. He allowed the period for accepting to expire, and did nothing about it. In September he declared amnesty for all Brazilians who had attacked him or the state. In October 100,000 people gathered to acclaim him, and he said to them: "I do not choose to be a candidate." Nobody believed him, not even his former Minister of War, the general who had helped him to power in 1930, the presidential candidate he was backing, Enrico Gaspar Dutra. "You never can tell about Getulio . . ."

In that same month of October, fearing that at the last minute Vargas might order the election halted, a group of officers, headed by the Minister of War who had succeeded Dutra, obliged him to hand in his resignation. The Supreme Court assumed the presidency. It was another of Brazil's bloodless revolutions, the kind of revolution Getulio liked, one that did not interrupt the march of public affairs. Elections were held in December; the voting was the heaviest and freest Brazil had ever seen. (Wily Getulio knew that five years later it would be even larger and freer.) General Dutra won. The Communists polled 568,000 votes, to become the fourth largest party in Brazil. They seated fourteen members in congress. They represented one of the largest Red groups in the world.

In keeping with his promise, General Dutra called for a constituent assembly, and in 1946 Brazil had a new constitu-

tion with a warmed-over taste. The old freedoms once more,
the representative system of government . . .

Dutra had the support of the Social-Democrat party and
the Catholic bloc. People recalled that as Minister of War in
1936 he had reorganized the army along the lines of the German *Wehrmacht*. The Spanish *franquistas*, who have had a
finger in all the Nazi-Fascist pies in Latin America, thought
the moment had come when they could resume with Brazil
the business they had started under the presidency of
Castillo in Argentina, and which was going ahead full sail
there under Farrell and Perón. Franco appointed Eduardo
Aunós as his ambassador in Rio. Aunós's antecedents were of
the very worst, as set forth in the Blue Book published in
Washington. It was he who, as head of the Spanish Embassy
in Buenos Aires, had collaborated in the plan to arm Argentina with German arms shipped from Spanish ports. This
was the Nazi master plan.

But Franco had reckoned without his host. Dutra refused to
approve his choice, and Aunós did not go to Brazil.

In 1950 Dutra's term of office came to an end. Once more
the figure of Getulio, the gaucho, loomed on the political
horizon. This time Dutra did not back him. His candidate
was Cristiano Machado. It has been said that not less than
$10,000,000 went into Machado's campaign fund. But this did
not bother Getulio. The country was turning thumbs down
on General Dutra, and the word was "Getulio." Getulio could
hear his prestige growing the way he could hear the grass
grow. When the votes were counted the results were:
Vargas, 2,500,000; Machado 900,000; Eduardo Gomes, "independent candidate" of the União Democratica Nacional,
300,000.

Vargas has always been chary of words, prodigal of smiles.
He would not talk about his election until it was an accomplished fact. Then he announced that his government would
follow the lines of the English Labour Party, the Scandina-

vian socialisms. He turned his back on the patterns of the
South to emulate those of the North. He would continue to
be a friend of the United States, an advocate of the Good
Neighbor policy. The warm relations between Brazil and the
United States of the Roosevelt-Vargas days have suffered a decline. There is a feeling of resentment against the United
States because of a loan of $125,000,000 to Perón's Argentina
in 1950. All Brazil felt this as a slap in the face, especially inasmuch as, among other reasons, the country now has to
spend money strengthening its military garrisons along the
Argentine frontier in case of any eventuality. This loan has
done more to harm the United States in Brazilian eyes than
all the Communist propaganda. Possibly Getulio can erase
these unpleasant memories.

The Dean of Columbia University's School of Journalism,
Carl W. Ackerman, visited Brazil immediately after Vargas's
election. He was eager to see how freedom of the press stood
there and what its future prospects were. Vargas was at his
ranch in Rio Grande do Sul. Assis de Chateaubriand, who
owns thirty-two newspapers and a chain of radio stations and
travels about Brazil in his own planes, and who is a personal
friend and political opponent of Vargas, said to Ackerman: "Let's go to Getulio's ranch; I'll take you in my plane
and you can ask him your question."

Vargas replied to Ackerman:

"I give you my guarantee that under my government there
will be as much freedom of the press in Brazil as in the
United States . . . I cannot tell you how honored I am
that so distinguished an educator and journalist as you should
have taken the trouble to come out here to greet an old
cowhand . . ."

The new feature Getulio has announced is that his will be
a government of evolution, not revolution. The Labor party
has elected him its leader. To be sure, the party has pointed
out the need of certain constitutional reforms . . .

XIII

CHILE, ECUADOR, URUGUAY: A TRIANGLE ABOVE A VOID

Let the citizen-soldier
Lay aside the livery of war;
And on the altar of country
Place the laurels of his victory,
And glory be merit's sole award.
Then peace, my native land,
Will see its longed-for triumph,
Peace, whose presence fills
The world with quiet and delight.
Let man, with heart aglow, resume his tasks;
Let the ship weigh anchor, and to the friendly
Zephyrs entrust its certain course;
Ring, anvils, and for the bountiful sheaves
May the sickles of the reapers be too few.

ANDRÉS BELLO

WITH REPRESENTATIVE DEMOCRACY done for in Colombia, there would seem to be only three countries left in Spanish-speaking South America on which democracy can pin its hopes: Chile, Ecuador, and Uruguay.

Uruguay is, in more ways than one, the Switzerland of America. The banks of Montevideo today are international safe deposit boxes, containing funds from many countries, near and far. Uruguay is a land of security. It has solid democratic, civilian underpinnings. Its intellectual influence has made itself felt throughout the Latin American world. A Uruguayan writer, José Enrique Rodó, was the teacher of a whole generation of Latin Americans at the beginning of the century. From Rosas to Perón, Argentine dictators have come up against a stone wall in the free city of Montevideo, which they have never been able to subdue either by wile or by force of arms.

A large part of Spanish America owes its civil structure to Chile. It was in Chile that the Venezuelan, Andrés Bello, drew up legislative codes to replace those of the Spanish monarchy. In Spanish America codified law is the beginning of order. What South America owes Bolívar and San Martín in the military field, it owes to Bello (and Chile) in the field of republican organization. It was in Chile that the civil, penal, and international codes were worked out, as was Bello's monumental grammar "for the use of Americans." With these instruments, independent Spanish America had the tools to begin its national life, with law, language, and a basis for dealing with other countries. Chile was a laboratory of democracy, and this gave its political life a distinctive stamp.

Ecuador's position in these past years has been one of democratic firmness and respect for liberty in marked contrast to that of its neighbors, Colombia and Peru. President Galo Plaza Lasso stands out not only by reason of his intrinsic merits, but also by comparison. Ecuador occupies an area the size of Sweden and its population is that of Norway, but instead of bordering on the North Polar region it lies squarely across the equator, between the Amazon jungle and the hottest coast of the Pacific, where the Andes rear their snow-capped peaks above plateaus and the upland Indians still do not speak Spanish. In this fistful of country, a simple, sturdy President has—so far—fought and won the battle of civil democracy.

What is the significance of this triangle resting on three widely differing countries, one on the upper, one on the lower, end of the Pacific coast, and the third midway along the southern Atlantic? What can be expected of them? Have they the economic solidarity, the political consistency to insure stability? Can they defend themselves against the fifth columns that are boring within their political life? Are they true democracies? Do these three frail hopes offer a solid support for the triangle, the sacred tripod, of freedom?

I CHILE

WHEN, during the first half of the nineteenth century, Rosas was harrying his political opponents, Sarmiento, the greatest of the Argentines, took refuge in Santiago de Chile, where he worked as a teacher and journalist. There he wrote the book that is a classic of Latin American literature: *Facundo, Civilization and Barbarism in the Argentine Republic*. The title tells the whole story. And in the twentieth century, when Juan Vicente Gómez set up his dictatorship in Venezuela, those Venezuelans who refused to abandon the cause of freedom found in Chile a place where they could talk and write. Today, as twenty years ago, it is in Chile that the persecuted *apristas* of Peru find a haven.

The greater part of Chile's population lives in a central valley running parallel to the coast. It is a kind of canyon that in the spring resembles a flower garden. The best grapes in Latin America are grown there. The Chilean never says bread and wine, but wine and bread. Wine comes first. The valley is a reproduction on a small scale of the map of Chile, and is well protected on all four sides. To the north stretch deserts where it almost never rains and where only nitrate- and copper-miners live. To the south, toward the Straits of Magellan, it rains the year around. Punta Arenas, the southernmost city of the world, is a center of the fur trade in nutria skins. President Pedro Aguirre Cerda even went so far as to declare the Antarctic Chilean territory. To the east stands the barrier of the Andes. Even today San Martín's crossing of the Andes with his army is considered one of the greatest exploits ever performed in South America. And to the west lies the ubiquitous Pacific Ocean.

In Chile there has not been the particular racial mixture characteristic of the rest of America. The Negro never became acclimated there. The Indians of Chile were the warlike, indomitable Araucanians. The Spanish settlers of Chile were in a large degree Basques. With the Independence came Irish, Scotch, and English immigration. Today in the leading families one finds names like Errázuriz, Yrrarazabal, or Eizaguirre interlarded with MacIver, Edwards, and Mackenna. Toward the end of the nineteenth century the Germans came. On this racial map none of the so-called "inferior races" is to be found; on the contrary, there is a superiority complex.

Benjamín Subercaseaux has baptized his country with the title of one of his books: *Chile, a Geographic Extravaganza* (1943). Truly nature must have been in a sportive mood to set a country on a terrace of land 3,000 miles long and, at most, 250 miles wide. But Chile's problem is neither geographical nor racial. It is the old, old problem of rich and poor. Chile has sometimes been called an inverted California. California's deserts are to the south, those of Chile, to the north; California's forests in the north correspond to those of Chile in the south. The central regions of both California and Chile are fruit paradises. There are no better peaches in the world than those of Chile. California itself is, in part, the creation of Chileans. Thousands of them went to San Francisco at the time of the gold rush, and their names still persist in certain families and in the names of streets and towns. And just as California has the poverty-stricken inhabitants described by Steinbeck in his books, so in Chile, not far from Viña del Mar, the playground of the rich, one finds in the country the *huasos* and in the cities, the *rotos*, two of the most submerged groups in America.

The first families of Chile comprise an oligarchy. Sixty per cent of the country's arable land is in the hands of six hundred people. To these can be added those who have made their fortunes in industry. Chile is the industrial nation of South America. It produces more coal than Mexico or Brazil. It has large deposits of iron, which it has been mining and manufacturing since the beginning of the century. North American capital has been invested in its mines, especially the copper mines, not in industry. In 1938, 75% of its industrial capital was Chilean. Chile has one of the highest percentages of factory- and mill-workers in Latin America. Only 33% of its working population are engaged in agriculture.[1]

In Santiago, the beautiful capital, with its 1,200,000 inhabitants, the families of the upper class still live largely in the French manner, as a result of the strong influence exerted in Latin America by France at the turn of the century. The rural areas abound in those "bluff and gentle, serious and light-hearted, democratic and feudal" country gentlemen described by Eduardo Barrios in his famous novel *Gran Señor y Rajadiablos* (*Fine Gentleman and Devil's Disciple*). The city slums house the *roto*; his rural counterpart is the *huaso*. These are the disinherited, having all the virtues and vices that go with poverty, and showing a wry wit and resourcefulness that recall the rogues of Spanish picaresque novels. A better idea of their character can be gained from fiction than from sociological studies. Joaquín Edwards Bello has written two novels *El Inútil* (*The Good-for-Nothing*) and *El Roto*, and Eduardo Barrios is the author of *Un Perdido* (*A Ne'er-do-well*), which deal with this sector of society. These titles are a preview of the books' contents.

Chile has produced the greatest American woman poet of the twentieth century, Gabriela Mistral, who was awarded the Nobel Prize in 1945. Gabriela grew up in the south of Chile,

[1] Report of Office of Development of Production for 1943 (Santiago, 1946).

where the mountains withdraw from the valley, where the fields are barren, the winters hard, and the people long-suffering and frugal. The title of her first book of poems, which made her reputation, is significant. It is *Desolación*.

The cruelest poverty is to be found in the mining areas. According to a report of 1946, 15% of the copper miners suffer from silicosis, 65% of the coal miners are afflicted with intestinal parasites. Poverty is a product of the countryside, rebellion of the city. It is in Santiago that the political pot boils. It is stirred by the students, the intellectuals, the poets, the representatives of entrenched wealth, the industrialists, the old radicals, the Communists, the neo-Nazis. In 1941 twenty-two parties were represented at the polls. They all have their leaders and speakers. In thirty years of Communism Russia has not produced so notable a poet as the Chilean, Pablo Neruda, author of an ode to the heroic defense of Stalingrad.

The Colombian journalist, Roberto García Peña, has described the human element of Santiago de Chile in these words:

"Chile pours the full store of its varied social gamut into Santiago. There its land-owning aristocracy rubs elbows with its bold, witty *rotos*; its *siúticos*, the hard-working and creative, if slightly pretentious, middle class, and the *huasos*, who lay the foundations in the country of the nation's modest wealth. Retired seamen, winegrowers, cattlemen, soldiers, workers, government employees, and old-clothes men make up Santiago's urban population, giving life there its mobility, crowding the old streets—Ahumada, Moneda, Monjitas, Huérfanos, Bandera, Estado—filling the movie houses, the restaurants and stores; those who in the late spring and autumn afternoons, when the caress of the sun stirs the well-springs of sensuality, climb the slopes of Santa Lucía hill, the sacred grove of lovers, whose protective foliage sends the vital statistics soaring . . ."

Until 1913 Chile lived on its nitrates. 95% of all the nitrates used for fertilizer came from Chile, supplying 75% of the country's national income. Then synthetic nitrates were discovered, and with the close of the First World War came economic disaster. The nitrate age was over. The result was the political upheaval registered by the elections of 1920. Liberals and conservatives, landowners and aristocrats formed the Unión Nacional bloc. Against them were ranged the masses and the middle class in the Alianza Liberal, headed by Arturo Alessandri. Alessandri was the first orator to use a balcony to talk to the people of the people and to promise them a government for the people. Up to that time politics in Chile had been confined to the realm of abstract ideas, lofty and high-sounding concepts. Now for the first time it made its appeal to the *huaso*, the *roto*, the *siútico*, in words that had a direct bearing on their everyday life and problems. Alessandri won.

In his first term of office (1920–25), Alessandri, whom an economic crisis had brought to power, was confronted with many serious problems. When he had completed his mandate, he left behind him a new constitution, that of 1925, which modified that of 1833, and a series of labor laws. Chile was the first country to adopt a code of social laws in keeping with the recommendations of the Labor Office of Geneva. But Alessandri's star was declining, and another was rising which augured very different things, that of Colonel Carlos Ibáñez. Ibáñez had the backing of the army and a sector of the people. During his first presidency he moved on a plane diametrically opposed to that of Alessandri. He had come in on a wave of prosperity. That was the time when the United States banks were handing Latin America loans for the asking. Ibáñez had all the money he wanted and could do many things, but this blissful state was of brief duration. In 1929 came the crash, and South American governments began to fall as quickly as stocks on the New York Exchange. The revolt against Ibáñez was touched off by the students, and the Colonel was obliged to take to his heels and seek refuge in Argentina. His exile lasted until 1936. In his wake came chaos.

In the elections to choose Ibáñez's successor, his former minister of the interior, Carlos Montero, was chosen president. He lasted eight months in office, when he was overthrown by a military coup that put Carlos Dávila, former Ambassador to Washington and a distinguished journalist, into the presidency. He ruled for one hundred days. Another barracks coup, and new elections. For the second time Alessandri was elected president. This was a period of prosperity during which social legislation considered the most advanced in Latin America was rounded out.

But Alessandri's presidency was set against two new world phenomena: Russian Communism and Nazism. The people had organized a Republican Militia to combat all tyranny "Communist, civilian, or military," and it was being trained as infantry, artillery, and cavalry. When it was dissolved the records showed that it had had some 50,000 members. Against this, the Nazis organized their own force, Acción Nacional, smaller, but more aggressive and more closely knit. To the military instruction the Nazis added uniforms, flag, salute, Hitler's technique. Congress had to pass special measures in 1936 against both Communists and Nazis. In the elections of 1937 the Communists, who had had three seats, returned six congressmen. For the first time the Nazis had representatives in congress; they had won three seats.

As the election of 1938 approached, Alessandri favored the right-of-center Liberal candidate, Gustavo Ross. Radicals, Socialists, and Communists, following the example of France, formed a Popular Front supporting Pedro Aguirre Cerda. The Nazis put forward their own candidate, Colonel Carlos Ibáñez, who had returned from exile an ardent National Socialist. Alessandri had forbidden the marches of the Black Shirts, the Fascist salutes, and so forth. The shock troops of Ibáñez and his supporters got ready for drastic action. When Alessandri went before Congress to read his message a Nazi sympathizer fired a shot into the air, a bomb was set off, and finally, after a march of 20,000 Nazis through the streets of Santiago hailing Ibáñez, the more daring organized an attack on the presidential palace. The affray cost sixty lives. The public reaction was swift and decisive. Ibáñez withdrew his candidacy, and the Popular Front won the elections.

Pedro Aguirre Cerda took office on December 24, 1938, but died on November 10, 1941. New elections were called, and once more the Popular Front won with Juan Antonio Ríos. He governed until 1946, when Gabriel González Videla was elected to succeed him.

The years of Aguirre Cerda's and Juan Antonio Ríos's terms of office, 1938–46, were full of agitation. Labor disputes multiplied like weeds. The Communists, who in 1945 had seven congressmen, won seventeen seats in the 1946 election. The Nazis had been stirring up trouble since the outbreak of the war, their activities directed in large part by the German Embassy.

Chile had not received the influx of immigration that landed in Argentina and Brazil. The Europeans had tended to remain on the Atlantic coast; by and large, the countries along the Pacific had not attracted them. But there had been one exception in Chile: the Germans. Around 1850, at the invitation of a president interested in the colonization of the southern part of the country, they had come to the region of Valdivia. The colony soon grew, and was somewhat outside the government's control. The settlers were progressive, industrious, well organized. They established their own schools, where the teaching was in German. They amassed sizeable fortunes, and it was not long before their influence made itself felt in industry and commerce. The Chileans had entrusted the training of their army to a German mission. Chile's fine army still goosesteps in its military parades.

"On January 31, 1941, the police of Chile secured their first concrete information concerning the functioning of the German National Socialist party, and revealed the threat to national security this implied. These activities were headed by Walter Boetch, attached to the Germany Embassy staff, and their purposes were strictly military . . . and exclusively in the service of the Reich. A year later, in 1942, new revelations having to do with the fifth column in Chile gave rise to the sensational trial presided over by Judge Mewes, of the Court of Appeals of Valdivia, who, among other things, ordered the imprisonment of sixty Germans on the basis of the following findings: 1) The German Nazi party in Chile has assumed government functions; 2) Its military organization gives it the character of a foreign armed force; 3) German Nazi propaganda methods employed in the schools have as their object to substitute Germany for Chile in the minds of the students; 4) The German Nazi party in Chile controls the life and acts of those Chilean citizens whom the NSDAP regards as Germans . . . The spy organization, details of which have been sent to the Army General Staff together with the list and plans of secret bases and air fields . . ." [2]

The subsequent history of these activities is to be found condensed in the Blue Book of Washington:

"In late 1943, German officials in Berlin were informed by their agents in Argentina that representatives of the Argentine military regime [that of General Ramírez] were fostering wide-spread agitation among Chilean, pro-Axis nationalists, within and without the Chilean armed forces, for a revolutionary overthrow of the Ríos Government—with the expectation of achieving thereby a pro-Argentine, pro-Axis policy in Chile. The chief Argentine plotter was Colonel Perón, who, it should be noted, had served as Argentine Military Attaché in Chile from 1936–1938. Perón was closely supported in Argen-

[2] Alberto Ostría Gutiérrez, *Una Revolución tras los Andes* (*A Revolution behind the Andes*), op. cit.

tina by such GOU Colonels as Saavedra, Mittelbach and González, and his agent for these purposes in Chile was Captain Juan B. Chavarria, an Argentine officer. A German official in Berlin, kept fully informed of the progress of this plot, has stated that, as about January, 1944:

' . . . following the return of one of the agents sent to Chile by the Argentine General Staff, Colonel Perón decided to give the Chilean revolutionary movement financial support in the amount of one million U. S. dollars, the first payment of which would amount to one million pesos. Following the unfavorable reception of the Bolivian revolution, however, the Argentine interest gradually ceased . . .' "

Argentina began inching itself into the Chilean political picture, and in 1945 the North American journalist, John W. White, summed up the new developments:

"Colonel Juan D. Perón, the recognized leader of the present regime in Buenos Aires, has told the people of Argentina on repeated occasions that it must prepare for total war . . . The Chilean government has showed great alarm at the possibility of an attempt on the part of Argentina to occupy and annex a part of its territory. This fear was touched off by a report turned in by the Military Attaché of Chile in Buenos Aires to the head of the Chilean General Staff last June, in which he told of a conversation he had had with Colonel Perón in the latter's capacity as Minister of War when he had been called to his office for this purpose . . . Colonel Urizar, the Chilean Military Attaché, states that Perón told him that Chile should join with Argentina 'to form a single country.' Perón's argument was that in the world today there is no place for small, weak nations because they cannot defend themselves against the methods of modern warfare. Perón added that a great nation 'like Argentina' needed an outlet to both oceans and declared that an 'Anschluss' would couple Chile's mining economy to the industrial, agrarian economy of Argentina, thus forming a perfect whole. United, he said, Argentina and Chile could control the South American continent, and even become a world power . . . The Chilean Minister of Foreign Affairs has confirmed the existence of the aforesaid document to certain prominent members of the diplomatic corps in Santiago, who, in turn, have informed their governments of its content . . ." [3]

In 1946 the Popular Front won again. Its candidate was an experienced Radical legislator, Gabriel González Videla, who came to a cordial understanding with the Communists, by this time an important political force, who backed him with their votes. González Videla, a man of great ability, took office on December 24, 1946, and has been running the range—or perhaps one should say the gauntlet—of the political spectrum. He began with a cabinet composed of Radicals, Communists, and Liberals. Then he weeded out the Communists and the Liberals, and, as he says, "for the first time in Chile's history the Radical party assumed full governmental responsibility." Following this, he formed the Democratic Front. Then he wooed the Right. Finally, without being able to bring about an understanding among the various groups, he formed a cabinet of a purely administrative nature. In successive messages to congress he has described these steps with startling frankness:

Message of 1947. "Because I fully understood the serious situation with which the country was confronted . . . the very night the political forces of the Left elected me to office, I asked . . . all parties . . . to collaborate in the formation of a national government . . . I regret and I shall always regret that my appeal . . . went unheeded . . . Under the circumstances I was obliged to limit the make-up of my first cabinet to the two parties whose efforts, abnegation, and sacrifice

[3] John W. White, *"El Nazismo en América." Revista de América,* Bogotá, February 1945.

had made my election possible, that is to say, the Radical Party and the Communist Party, and I asked and obtained the collaboration of the Liberal Party . . ."

Message of 1948. "You are all aware of the disturbances set afoot by the Communist Party this past year through the labor unions that control the country. These conflicts, which express a political aim rather than real labor problems, continued, with slight variations, up to September 1947, when the government launched its legal attack on the intrigues of the Soviet government . . . After the resignation of my cabinet, I tried once more, again fruitlessly, to organize a national government . . . I realized that the country faced a new and more imminent danger: the subversive activities of the Communist Party, which had become an instrument of Russian expansion. I was unsuccessful and my attempts failed . . . I organized an administrative cabinet made up of men outside party factions . . ."

Message of 1949. "Together with the Radicals, on March 6 the other groups of citizens who uphold the action of the Executive triumphed. The understanding of the country's needs stimulated the civic generosity of the Liberal, Conservative, Socialist, and Democratic parties, which have with such great sacrifice backed the regime I defend . . ."

Message of 1950. "Until a few months ago, I had a cabinet of a different complexion from that of the one that now surrounds me. Several of the parties whose members formed part of that cabinet are now opposed to my government. They are in their right. But I am not overstepping mine when I ask of them the understanding that comes with a firsthand knowledge of the problems we face in the present political combination . . ."

Message of 1951. "In view of the split between the major parties that supported the previous cabinet of national coalition, the present political combination, which I now present to you, is the only possible one in view of my failure to organize a national government . . ."

The changes of cabinet are not too important. They are in the country's tradition. They represent the reaction of congress or of the parties against the President in matters of passing significance. But the crisis to which he alludes in his messages is deeper and more serious.

On his election in November 1946, González Videla announced that his administrative program would be based on four points, the first of which was the fight against inflation. After four years he made the following report: "The country continues in the grip of the inflationary process, which for many years has been threatening the foundations of its economic life and its social stability." And a year later, in his 1951 message: "The efforts of my government to check the inflationary process have been constant and unremitting . . . With great sorrow I have seen the inability of all the measures I undertook to this end to halt the advance of this appalling scourge . . ."

The problem was that of empty stomachs. As the President stated, all salary- and wage-earners were faced with the steady decline of their purchasing power. An investigation carried out by the United Nations[4] found that the actual wages in agriculture and mining today are below the level of 1940. This has given rise to a state of dangerous insecurity. In the hope of coping with this the government has had recourse to drastic measures such as "the law for the defense of democracy," declaring a state of emergency, and martial law. When strikes broke out in the coal mines in 1947 they were put down in the manner indicated by the following notice:

"This is to summon . . . living at . . . that he present himself at the regular place of work on October 10, at 8 a.m., under penalty that, if he does not do so he will be considered a viola-

[4] *Recent Facts and Trends in the Economy of Chile*, 1951.

tor of the army draft law and punished with a sentence of a minimum of three years and a day, to be served in full. Signed . . . Zonal Military Commander." [5]

When González Videla made his report to Congress on this strike, he did not present it as a local Chilean situation, but as part of the international picture, to which he always devotes many pages in his messages. "The Soviet plan of penetration must come to an end . . . This is no time for cowardice or hesitation."

However, the agitation of workers and employees did not come to an end. When, in 1949, bus fares went up to twenty centavos in Santiago a movement of protest was headed by the students. The government declared a state of siege, and the resulting casualties amounted to eighteen dead and three hundred wounded. When, in 1951, the railroad workers went on strike, the government immediately ordered troops under General Urizar to take over the shops and roundhouses. The Communist leaders among the workers were sent to Pisagua, a kind of concentration camp set up in 1947. Among those to whom punitive sanctions were applied were one of González Videla's former ministers, Miguel Concha Quezada, Congressman Juan Vargas Puebla, and the poet Pablo Neruda.

The law for the defense of democracy only built up pressure at the center of Chile's social problem. Put forward as a weapon against Communism, it gradually spread to many other fronts. Even the Radical party has showed itself distinctly cool toward giving the President further support along these lines. It is hard to see the connection between the problem of living wages for the people and a war against Russia. In his message of 1951 the President presented the case in schoolmasterish terms that failed to carry conviction:

"Recently, when irresponsibility and discouragement over

[5] *Latin American Facts* (published monthly by Latin American Research Bureau), September 1951.

the rising costs of living were being utilized by the anti-democratic and anti-patriotic groups to provoke the workers and employees to defy the legal order, going over the head of the national organizations and its responsible leaders, in my conviction that salvation lay in the maintenance of democracy, I have, day after day in interminable exhausting sessions, used advice and persuasion to convince the employees and workers that they, too, were responsible in large measure for the inflationary process and that it was urgent that they, through responsible action, co-operate with the government to halt it . . ."

Chile is the world's second largest copper-producing country. Today the national finances are as dependent on copper as they were a generation ago on nitrate. In the vicinity of the mines, settlements of between ten and twenty thousand workers have grown up. Among them social unrest is an occupational disease like silicosis, and the United States is constantly in the foreground. United States companies control 95% of the production. The Chileans resent the fact that their fate is determined by the boards of directors of three North American companies that are among the most powerful in the world. At the head of them stands the Anaconda Copper Mining Company. Anyone who is aware of the power that Anaconda wields in the state of Montana will have no trouble understanding how it operates in Chile. Following is a summary of what Anaconda means to Chile, and what Chile means to Anaconda:

"In 1950 almost half of Anaconda's net profits came from foreign operations. From their Chilean subsidiary, Chile Copper Company, they got 36% of their entire net profit. In 1949, before Korea, when business in general was bad, 67% of their profits came from foreign holdings. From the Chile Copper Company came more than half (56%) of their total net profit. This is in the table below:

NET PROFITS OF THE ANACONDA COPPER MINING CO.:

1950		% of the total
Consolidates (i.e. Total)	$46,689,645	100.00
Foreign	23,125,556	49.5
Chile Copper Company	16,977,277	36.4"[6]

After a long fight Chile, in 1951, managed to secure better market conditions for its copper, concluding an agreement with the United States by the terms of which Chilean copper would be tax-exempt and its price would be raised three cents a pound. The workers at once requested a wage increase. The petition was followed by a strike, the strike by repressive measures. The government declared the strike illegal, pronounced it of a revolutionary nature, and decreed martial law.

This is the back-drop of the social question in Chile.

The proximity of Argentina, or to be more exact, of Perón's Argentina, further complicates the situation. Chile needs Argentine meat, and in return offers nitrates and steel. Perón is busily at work undermining Chile's civil institutions. In 1947 González Videla paid Perón an official visit. An agreement was signed whereby Chile was to keep a permanent stockpile of 15,000 tons of nitrate in Argentina and Argentina agreed not to build synthetic fertilizer plants. There was a short spell of cordial relations, which the Argentine President seems to have regarded as an interlude to be turned to advantage while he waited for the plum of a Chilean-Argentine union based on a military entente to fall into his lap.

In his 1951 message to the Argentine Congress, President Perón said:

"The price-protection of our products has been of major importance in bringing about a favorable balance in our for-

[6] *Latin American Facts*, September 1951.

eign trade. Our position has been greatly strengthened by the importance we have been able to give to other buying markets. A few of our foreign trade figures will bear out my words: Our exports to the United States alone have increased by 232% over those of 1949; to Chile, 121% . . . In a word, good business."

As far as Chile is concerned, President González Videla said in his 1951 message that the figures for imports as compared with those of 1949–50 were:

COUNTRIES OF GREATEST IMPORTS:

	1949	1950
4th. Argentina	$64,718,125	$65,071,549

On the basis of these figures the percentage calculation of the present Argentine government is too complicated to be easily grasped. It is simpler to understand this business in political terms. This was pointed out by Foster Hailey of *The New York Times* in a despatch dated from Buenos Aires in September 1951:

"A change for the better in the relations between Argentina and Chile, which have been strained for several years, is not so evident. The Chilean Ambassador here is not the welcome guest at the Casa Rosada that Señor Luzardo is [Luzardo is the very pro-Perón ambassador Vargas sent to Buenos Aires in 1951]. But Señor Perón has spoken of Chile in some recent speeches, the chief of the Chilean Army was warmly received in Argentina a few weeks ago and there have been charges made in Chile that Argentine funds are being used there to promote the presidential candidacy of General Ibáñez del Campo, a fervent admirer of Señor Perón."

With regard to the protection of Chilean nitrate on the international market, the former Ambassador of the United States to Buenos Aires, Spruille Braden, said in an article published in *Look* in September 1951:

"We have also been guilty of failing to keep our word. One such occasion concerned the synthetic-nitrate plants which we built during the war. To Chile, a leading producer of natural nitrates, the plants were of great importance. Formal assurance was given the Chileans at the Mexico City conference of 1945 that the plants would not be sold without our consulting Chile. We should never have made such a promise. But having given our word, we should have kept it. We did not. Several of the nitrate plants were sold to American companies without a word to Chile until I intervened and insisted that we honor our pledge."

II ECUADOR

THE president of Ecuador, Galo Plaza Lasso, has drawn up this balance sheet of politics in Ecuador during the past twenty-two years: from 1925 to 1947 Ecuador had twenty-seven presidents, seven constituent assemblies or extraordinary sessions of Congress, six constitutions, and countless revolutions, some successful, some abortive.

What happens to the Ecuadoreans? What is the reason for these explosive changes? I visited Quito once in December, during the Christmas holidays. Nowhere in the world have I breathed such pure air. At 9,300 feet above sea-level, directly on the equator, the mountaintops are white as salt, the tablelands the color of emeralds. During this season, by special privilege granted them by a Spanish king, the Indians begin sweeping the streets before dawn. In the old homes the novena to the Christ child is made before mangers adorned with images of polychromed wood, miniature masterpieces of the anonymous artists who have been making them in Quito for the last three hundred years. Midnight Mass on Christmas Eve in the Church of the Company of Jesus is like a scene from an Oriental tale. The façade of the church is elaborately carved in stone, and inside everything glitters with gold, worked as though it were foam. How is it possible that among this snow, this sky the color of the Virgin's robe, these mangers, and these golden temples the body of President Eloy Alfaro was dragged through the streets in 1912? Is there some strange witchery in the air of Quito?

In *Ecuador and the Galapagos Islands,* Victor Wolfgang von Hagen wrote: "Almost everything in Quito is ascribed to the air; it is renowned throughout the Republic as the healthiest in the world, as celebrated as the waters of Vichy or the mud baths of Carlsbad are to Europeans. There are, it is true, a few unacclimated travelers who have denigrated this Quito air and have actually said (out of the hearing of the Quiteños, of course) that the quality of Quito air and its weather depends on the time of the day and on the side of the street: on the sunsplashed side, it is spring; on the shady side, autumn; when the sun goes down, winter."

The same thing may hold true of politics. The Liberals walk on the sunny side of the street, and it seems to be spring; the Conservatives in the shade, and it is autumn. But as the sun moves, so do the people. And there are frigid nights, with shadows and a wild moon.

Ecuador has the youngest president and, with the exception of Uruguay, the smallest territory in all South America. On maps of today it is only half the size it was in nineteenth-century atlases. Now, almost as large as Italy, it looks diminutive on the map of South America, bordering, or almost bordering, as it does, on Brazil. But with its bright green fields, its diaphanous sky, its delicious fruits, its perfect old corners, it has something of the intimate charm of Florence.

Not far from Quito is the town of Otavalo. On market day all its squares and streets, which are empty during the week, are thronged with Indians who come down from the neighboring hills by a road that skirts a crystal lake lying at the foot of a snow-covered peak. They have traveled many miles. They wear colored ponchos that reach to their ankles. The rich ride horseback, their saddles studded with silver. It is like a fabulous ballet with twenty thousand dancers, all of whom seem to have stepped out of the colored pages of an illustrated magazine. None of them speaks a word of Spanish. The cloth they wear was woven on their own looms, and the dyes are of their own manufacture. When they dance to the music of their home-made harps, it is willows swaying in the wind. These Indians, the women with babies tied in shawls on their backs, have paved the roads, planted the fields, cleaned the church until it gleams like a silver platter.

There are old and wealthy families in Quito who are pure white. It is said that the population of the uplands is 28% white. It looks less. The Indians and half-breeds make up the remainder. There are no Negroes there. It is said that on the coast the population is 15% Negro (it seems more) and 27% white (it seems less). The remainder is a "coffee-and-cream" combination, sometimes more coffee, sometimes more cream.

Leopoldo Benítez has written a book entitled: *Ecuador, Drama and Paradox*. It is a good title. President Galo Plaza has said: "Ecuador is a rich country inhabited by a poor people." To visiting Mexicans Ecuador seems, even as regards its history, like a state of Mexico that somehow got lost.

In the beginning, after the country was able to shake off the dragons' teeth crop of caudillos the war of independence had sown, a great liberal statesman arose, Vicente Rocafuerte. He made a good start and left a legacy of liberty, but he was engulfed by the reactionaries. He was succeeded by the nightmare of Gabriel García Moreno, an iron-willed despot who made the country his small, theocratic empire under the spiritual rule of the Jesuits. It was one of the starkest, cruelest, and strangest dictatorships in history. An assassin's bullet finally ended his career in 1875. A revival of liberalism followed, its standard-bearer a courageous man of action, Eloy

Alfaro. Alfaro finished out his final term of office (1907–11) in prison, from which he was dragged by a fanatical mob that in 1912 quartered him, dragged his remains through the streets of Quito, and burned them on the Ejido. After this came a period of anarchy, and to add to its misfortunes, this was when Ecuador lost part of its territory. Alfredo Diez Canseco, the Ecuadorian writer, calls Ecuador the Poland of America.

During the financial crisis of 1929, Isidro Ayora' was president of Ecuador. He tried to weather the storm by introducing a series of changes in the financial and banking structure of the country, but in 1931 he was forced out. Between August of that year and the end of 1935 Ecuador had four presidents. In 1935 Federico Páez made himself dictator with the support of the army. In 1937 Páez fell and General Alberto Enríquez took his place. In 1938 Enriquez fell and Aurelio Mosquera Narváez succeeded him. Mosquera Narváez died in 1939 and was followed by Carlos Alberto Arroyo del Río. In 1944 a Revolutionary *junta* overthrew Arroyo del Río and chose José María Velasco Ibarra to succeed him. In 1947 Velasco was ousted and Colonel Mancheno assumed the presidency. This happened on August 24; on September 2 Mancheno was out and Mariano Suárez Veintimilla was in. On September 17 Suárez Veintimilla was out. It is very unlikely that the reader can keep these names straight. Neither can the Ecuadoreans.

To succeed Suárez Veintimilla a provisional president was elected, Carlos Julio Arosemena, a man who had not been involved in the preceding tugs-of-war, and whom the leaders had sought out in the hope of getting a respite from them. Arosemena restored order and freedom and arranged for elections. These were held in June 1948. Everyone agrees that they were the freest and cleanest ever held in Ecuador. The victorious candidate was a wealthy young rancher who is a fine amateur bullfighter. He was the son of a Liberal president. He hates striped pants diplomacy and protocol and is a splendid dancer. This is Galo Plaza Lasso. He was educated in the United States, where part of the time he studied agriculture in a western university, and part of the time sold apples on the streets of New York. His football days are over; he is still a bullfighter, but in the political ring. Before his election he was Ambassador in Washington. Then he returned to Ecuador, where he organized his following in Congress as one trains a football team. Its colors were Liberal.

The first thing to do, thought the new President to himself, is to eliminate the revolutions. The thought had hardly come to him before the first one broke out. Colonel Mancheno, who had been Minister of War under President Velasco Ibarra, seized a tank and said to a group of young officers: "Follow me. We'll overthrow Galo." They did not follow him. Colonel Mancheno tried to surround the presidential residence with a handful of half-hearted supporters, and the revolution was put down in half an hour. A few days later the President appeared before Congress, and after making a statement that neither the President of Peru nor the President of Colombia, his neighbors, nor the Presidents of many other countries could repeat—that is to say, that he had been elected by the people, added:

"I am convinced that when the citizenry . . . and the parties . . . reach the conviction that the only path to power is the broad and legal road of free suffrage, they will no longer try to secure it by house-breaking methods . . . The people of Ecuador and its armed forces know there are no magic formulas . . . and that the fight against poverty will never be won with the empty words of false apostles or the cowardly adventures of rebellion and coups."

Ten months after Galo Plaza had spoken these words, in July 1950, Guevara Moreno the former Minister of the Interior under President Velasco Ibarra came to an understanding with the police of Guayaquil, seized the government building there, the airport, and the telegraph lines. It was a complete victory that lasted three hours. This time, too, the army said "No" to the rebels. At the end of the three hours the ex-Minister was cooling his heels in jail. From Carcacas former President Velasco Ibarra, onetime professor of constitutional law and now a fervent Peronist, made this pronouncement: "Guevara Moreno represents a hope for the country." The government decided to lock this hope away in a safe deposit vault, and sent him for a year to the "Black Heaven," the penitentiary where the despot García Moreno used to send his enemies.

Ecuador has either to be made or to be made over. On the country estates in certain regions people still live in the Middle Ages. One need only read the novels of Ecuador to confirm this. There are scenes in Jorge Icaza's *Huasipungo* or *Media Vida Deslumbrados* that make those of *Tobacco Road* seem mild indeed. If at times the coloring seems laid on with a trowel, that is because of the frantic longing for a new life. The great poet Jorge Carrera Andrade writes: "Quito, the bare-footed city, as an intelligent woman of Venezuela has aptly called it, has done everything it could to shoe itself in a hundred attempts that have been called revolutions . . ." The president has said "Of 512,000 children of school age, 216,000 are unable to attend school because of the lack of buildings and teachers . . ."

This people, so scourged by neglect, anarchy, and dictatorships, is singularly gifted. The cloth the Indians weave on their primitive looms is eagerly bought up by tourists. George Wythe, who has studied the industrial panorama of Latin America says: "The manufacturing industry of Ecuador is much more developed than might have been expected." This industry is the product of some factories having modern equipment, but it is in the hand or home industries that the Ecuadoreans are matchless. They have preserved for generations a tradition that gives their work unique artistic quality.

The campaign against illiteracy has been carried out in

keeping with the Laubach plan[7] combined with local methods. Miguel Albornoz, one of Ecuador's distinguished journalists, describes it:

"The newspapermen started their campaign last March [1945] with an impressive mass meeting in Quito's biggest bullfight arena. They recruited volunteer teachers and had 5,000 sets of illustrated cards printed. Newspapermen gave wide publicity to the campaign. By November the UNP [about 100 newspaper editors, reporters, and future writers] had more than 4,000 volunteers at work, and about 9,000 illiterates were taking daily instruction. Around 5,000 people had already learned to read and write at a cost of 17 U. S. cents per person. The Quito journalists took the highlands and the Amazonian provinces for their territory, while the Guayaquil group of intellectuals, LEA ("Read"), took the coastal provinces and the Galápagos Islands . . . The journalists plan in five years to eliminate the illiteracy that afflicts 2,000,000 of Ecuador's 3,500,000 people . . ."

In a country with Ecuador's social problems, unless the machinery of democracy is quickly put in motion, Communism or Creole Fascism will find good fishing in troubled waters. The literature of Ecuador, with its decidedly Leftish trend, can easily lead the way toward Communist solutions. The only way to counteract them is a rapid, unequivocal implementation of democracy with deeds, not words. When Galo Plaza spoke by invitation before a joint session of the United States Congress on June 21, 1951, he did not mince words:

"The battle for freedom and the rejection of poverty and

[7] Frank Charles Laubach (1884–), an American missionary and educator, is the sponsor of a widespread method of teaching primitive and illiterate peoples to read by means of phonetic symbols and pictures. He himself has taught it in the Philippines, Malaya, Ceylon, India, Egypt, Syria, Turkey, Mexico, Haiti, and elsewhere. One of its principles is "each one teach one," *i.e.*, each person who can read teaches someone who cannot, thus setting up a chain of increasing literacy.

injustice should not have any geographical limitations. It should be carried out everywhere and, in the case of Latin America, it is wise to recall how near we are to you. We practically live in a wing of the same building, but if we overemphasize the good will and intentions and the patience of the peoples below the Rio Grande, we might be giving too much of a headway to the forces that, moving in the dark, with the weapons of falsehood and deception, intend to undermine our spiritual foundations. To meet this threat, we must give our masses the opportunity to work and to seek their betterment, and we must do it now . . . Freedom and political ideas mean little when you are walking around on bare feet with an empty stomach . . ."

On one point Galo Plaza has been adamant: freedom of the press. His attitude is a stinging rebuke to his neighbors. His formula is very simple: a free press for a free people. And under his government there has been no gag on the press.

There has been a certain international concern about Ecuador. The World Health Organization, the Pan American Bureau of Sanitation, the Institute of Interamerican Affairs, the Kellogg Foundation have all made effective contributions. Today Ecuador and Mexico are the only countries in Latin America that have instituted general anti-tuberculosis inoculation. 650,000 children have been immunized. The aid of the Scandinavian Red Cross has been invaluable in this connection. In 1949 the Mexican government sent a commission headed by the Secretary of Hydraulic Resources to collaborate with the engineers of Ecuador on an irrigation plan.

But in the background walks the unlaid ghost of the dictator García Moreno. There is an unceasing effort on the part of the reactionaries to bring the Catholic Church into the belligerent Conservative front, following the pattern set by the dictatorship in Colombia.

Shortly before the outbreak of World War II the German colony of Ecuador—some two thousand closely united persons—undertook to set up a Creole brand of Nazism. They established schools inspired by Nazi doctrines. Hitler shrewdly appointed a Catholic Ambassador, who knew how to make Nazism palatable to the reactionary groups of Ecuador. The German airline, Sedta, operated at a considerable loss, but this did not matter. It was a link in the aerial web Germany was spinning over South America.

Today new Black Shirts have sprung up in Ecuador. They hike into the mountains and scrawl the party emblems in huge letters on the rocks. Catholic unions have been organized to carry the religious conflict into labor problems. Lay schools, which have been the norm in Ecuador for many years, have become the target of attack. The sons of aristocratic, conservative families are being sent to Spain to study. Franco has begun a strong drive to attract Spanish American students by establishing scholarships for them. Spain recognizes the work done at Latin American schools that follow a plan of studies analogous to that of Spain, and there is the advantage of the language, which means a saving of time and effort for the students planning to study abroad. Moreover, with the Spanish peseta at its present low value, they benefit by the exchange. No country is taking fuller advantage of all this than Ecuador, and the neo-Nazi reactionaries are counting on these students as shock troops for use in the not-too-distant future.

It must not be forgotten that Ecuador is a small country sandwiched in between two centers of reaction, Colombia and Peru. Or that General Odría is making use of tactics employed by former military dictators in Peru: border incidents. There is nothing like a frontier clash to focus international attention and arouse nationalist feeling, always a trump card.

III URUGUAY

In Uruguay the army scarcely exists, and least of all for barrack coups. What exists is schools, and everybody adores the school. In 1919 a constitution was drawn up along the lines of that of Switzerland. It was set aside in 1934 under the dictatorship of Gabriel Terra, but it seems to have resurged now with greater strength. In 1952 Uruguay will be a republic without a president. The president there is to be replaced by an administrative council.

How is such a thing possible in Latin America? Are the Uruguayans of a different clay; do they belong to a different race? No. They are like the others. In Argentina it is often difficult to tell whether a person comes from Montevideo or Buenos Aires. The common denominator *"rioplatense"* (from the Plate River) still exists. Uruguay's history follows the standard Spanish American pattern. From its independence until 1904 its presidential succession was by revolution. Chaos was the order of the day. Uruguay had to work out its salvation by bitter experience during the nineteenth century, and even suffered a relapse of dictatorship from 1933 to 1938.

Uruguay's evolution follows a familiar course. We know from the Bible that in the beginning was chaos. Today Denmark is pointed to as a model state. Yet it had its barbarous days and its villainous kings—"there's something rotten in the state of Denmark." And the same thing happened in Switzerland, in Sweden, and in Norway. Free, representative institutions are the outcome of a long process, and they can be named because a point of comparison exists.

When José Batlle y Ordóñez assumed the presidency of Uruguay in 1903, the usual revolution followed. Don José overwhelmed it by force of arms at first, and then by reason, and the latter won the day. In Latin America it is not the people, but the caudillo that is savage. When the caudillo winds the horn for the kill, the people eagerly follow him. Killing is something man has never been averse to, as Europe's history proves. But when the leader or the head of the government sets a standard of decency, the people are decent too. The head of the state is more responsible, more of an example, more of a guide in Latin America than in other places. Vague but deep-rooted in the people is a tendency to follow the lead of authority and of the priest. Subconsciously they still feel that power comes from God. When the president hands out knives and carte blanche to slit neighbors' throats, a primitive drama is staged. But when he upholds the law and teaches it by his example, the people not only learn it, they even apply it.

Uruguay, the smallest republic of South America, is almost five times the size of Switzerland. It is sparsely populated. There are more inhabitants per square mile in Ecuador and in Central America. Salvador, Guatemala, or Costa Rica has several times its ratio of population. Montevideo is its large city, but not so large as to absorb everything. In 1951 of Uruguay's 2,353,000 inhabitants, only 770,000 lived in Montevideo. "Uruguay is a pastoral country. About three-fourths of the area is turned over to grazing, and the country's prosperity rests primarily on livestock breeding." [7] The national hero is José Artigas (1774–1850), a gaucho. In Montevideo's main park the most beautiful bronze statue is not dedicated to any general; it is a covered wagon drawn by three yoke of oxen. Some writer has said that the first age of Montevideo was the leather age: the houses were made of hide, as were the doors, beds, trunks, ropes, clothes. The gauchos enlivened the first hundred years of the republic with their campaigns. They had to defend themselves against the Brazilians, by whom, on occasion, they were overrun. They fought in the

[7] George Wythe: *Industry in Latin America* (1949).

war with Paraguay. Rosas intervened in Uruguayan politics; he supported the *blancos* against the *colorados*. There was never any lack of fighting bands on one side or the other.

Onto the native gaucho stock the European immigrants were grafted. They were the same as those who went to Brazil and Argentina. Not so many, because Montevideo did not have the drawing attraction of Buenos Aires. Uruguay's character did not change. Life went on in the country on the primitive ranches or the rich *estancias,* but the gaucho continued being the gaucho. In summer the beaches of Montevideo are a South American Riviera. But Montevideo is more a city of Uruguay than a universal center.

In 1931 Gabriel Terra became president. As this was still a depression year, he launched a great program of public works to take care of the unemployment situation, and he clashed with the Administrative Council. He was attacked in Congress by the Socialists, and his answer was to make himself dictator. He dissolved Congress, set up a military government in many places, and imposed a censorship of the press. Baltasar Brum, former President of the country, an eminent jurist and a member of the administrative council, committed suicide after opposing Terra. In 1934 Terra called a constituent assembly that drew up a new constitution and re-elected him. In 1938 Terra turned over power to his brother-in-law, General Alfredo Baldomir, who in 1942 dissolved Congress once more. All this was a kind of parenthesis that today seems like an episode of the distant past.

When Uruguay recovered its balance, its position was like that of Switzerland, an oasis surrounded by bonfires. There it stands, proud of living in peace and freedom with its cows, its sheep, and its horses that look like English thoroughbreds. And with its schools and a concern for education that also reminds one of Switzerland. The essayists whom Uruguay produces generation after generation—Rodó, Vaz Ferreira, Zum Felde—uphold generous, elevated, pure ideals.

In 1947, on the death of President Tomás Berreta, he was succeeded by Luis Batlle Berres. In his inaugural address Batlle spoke to his fellow-citizens in simple, rustic language like that of Old Castile. He said:

"Allow me to speak to all in the simple, homespun words I use with my family . . . Let my first thought be directed toward Tomás Berreta, who until a few hours ago was President of the Republic. I was attached to this man by intimate ties of long standing; his parents had clasped my grandfather's hand in friendship . . . I have come to work, to fight and to dream—because to govern is also to dream—but I come prepared to turn into reality everything that means improvement and progress. Government is action . . . I prefer to make mistakes as I move forward rather than mark time . . ."

The geographic (it might be better to use the term geopolitical) situation of Uruguay has made it a battleground of ideologies. There are political refugees there from many countries, particularly Argentina. Communists and Fascists have set up organizations in Montevideo, and they have their followings. The freedom of the press that exists there is a source of irritation to the Argentine dictatorship, which sees in the newspapers across the bay the news that it suppresses. In 1944 the Farrell-Perón government sent a note of protest to the Uruguayan government complaining of the information printed in Montevideo. It was necessary to explain to the Argentine dictators the meaning of a free press in a free country. In 1945 the Russian chargé d'affaires made a verbal protest on the same subject and received the same answer. But the Russian Embassy refused to accept this, and sent a formal protest. The Uruguayan Minister of Foreign Affairs handled the matter with meticulous care: he turned it over to the Minister of the Interior to study it from the juridical point of view. The latter, after making his report, handed it to the Attorney-General to give it legal form. Thus they were able to give the Russian Embassy a lesson in the

A B C's of the rights of citizens in regard to the press of a free country. The following are excerpts from the Minister of the Interior's report:

"The government is not responsible for the ideas expressed in the newspapers, on the radio, or through other mediums. It has no authority to control the political views of the press or to impose ideas on it. Nor to prohibit it from dealing with certain themes. Intervention of this sort, which is contrary to law, would be considered by national public opinion, which is well versed in the theory and practice of democracy, an act of tyranny . . . In our country the government has no monopoly over the mediums of expression . . . The diplomatic relations between the U.S.S.R. and the republic of Uruguay do not depend for their existence or their endurance upon what this or that newspaper says. They depend on the sovereign will of the state expressed through appropriate channels: the executive branch, whose ministers are responsible to Congress . . . a representative body of society . . . which moves in obedience to the dominant ideas of public opinion arrived at through the free play of a free press, without arbitrary controls, and without administrative orientation or censorship . . ."

The exercise of these liberties and the daily complications of its international life have led Uruguay to play an active role in international conferences attempting to arrive at a common ground in the defense of human rights. In November 1945 the Minister of State, Eduardo Rodríguez Larreta, sent to all the governments of the American continent a note that implied a modification of the traditional principle of nonintervention. If this principle, on the one hand, constitutes a defense of national sovereignty, on the other, some way must be sought to keep it from becoming "the shield behind which acts of violence are perpetrated, laws are violated, the agents and forces of the Axis are given protection, and solemn obligations are flouted." Before this, in San Francisco, Rodríguez

Larreta had spoken out clearly: "The world will never enjoy peace and security . . . until juridical order prevails in all countries to guarantee the rule of justice and make the basic rights of man a reality . . ."

The Uruguayan formula has not been accepted. The dictatorships have no intention of opening the way for collective action to restore the existence of human rights. But neither has Uruguay desisted from supporting its theory. Nor is it possible to sustain indefinitely the two-faced attitude of so many countries that vote without reservations in favor of every principle in defense of human rights at the international conferences and ignore them in their national conduct of affairs.

In the light of the foregoing it is easy to understand Uruguay's plan for reforming its own constitution. It was President Andrés Martínez Trueba who, on taking office, proposed the plan of the reform. His plan is that in 1952, after he has been in office a little more than a year, a system will be instituted which will eliminate the office of president and substitute for it a council to be called the National Council of Administration, made up of nine members directly elected by the people for a term of four years without re-election. The presidency of the Council would be rotating, for a term of one year. Comparing this government plan with the former "strong man" regimes, it seems as though centuries had elapsed between the barbarous armed factions and the highest form of pure, civilian authority.

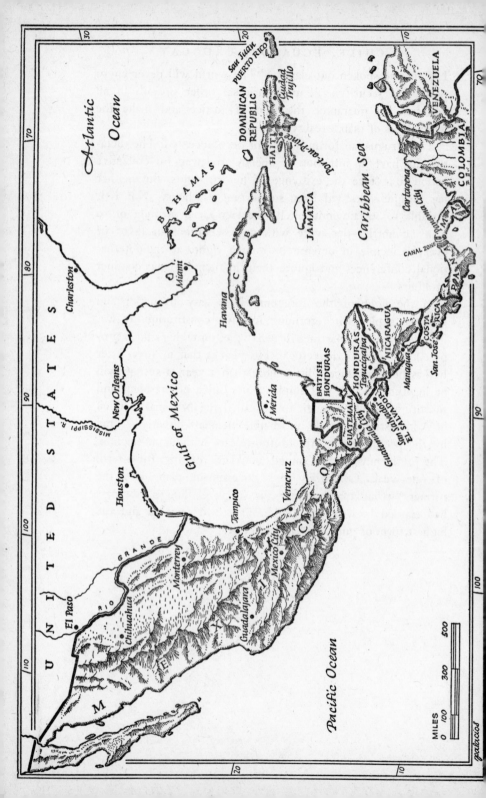

XIV

THE CARIBBEAN, WORLD
HURRICANE CENTER—1

*Let no one deem the likeness his, but think rather that there
are many devils who resemble one another. Whoever finds
himself begrimed, let him wash himself clean, for this matters
more than criticizing and tearing apart my thoughts, my expression, my ideas, or the other shortcomings of this work.*

TORRES VILLARROEL

*Christ wanders gaunt, forlorn, and feeble,
Barrabas boasts slaves and wears gold braid,
And the lands of Chibcha, Cuzco, and Palenque
See panthers in purple robes arrayed.*

RUBÉN DARÍO

THIS IS neither Latin America nor Spanish America. This
is Caribbean America. It is a patchwork of colonies, semi-
colonies, protectorates, republics, pseudo-republics, democracies, and anti-democracies. In Central America there are five
independent countries, a zone belonging to the United States,
and a colony that is a bone of contention between Great
Britain and Guatemala. Opposite it to the east lies a be-
witched archipelago. Curaçao belongs to Holland, and the
language spoken there is *papiamento*, a mixture of Spanish,
English, and Dutch amalgamated with an African pronuncia-
tion. Martinique, which is French, speaks Creole. There is a
group of islands that the Danish government sold to the
United States, and which are still called Virgin. In Trinidad,
a colony of the British Crown, one finds Hindu temples and

Jewish synagogues—and its name comes from the Holy Trinity. Cuba's Havana is the most Spanish of American cities, while the towns of Haiti seem to have been transported from Africa. Puerto Rico is a Spanish island that has been halted midway on the road to independence. Venezuela owns islands, Colombia owns islands, and Honduras owns islands that it has leased to the United States. The island of Hispaniola is divided in two: one half is the Negro republic of Haiti; the other, which preserves the greatest wealth of tradition of the Spanish discovery, has lost even the traditional name of its capital city, Santo Domingo.

These observations will be limited to the eight states that are listed as independent nations, plus Puerto Rico. Of necessity they will be only an aperitive, an introduction, to a fascinating subject. Some observers not too familiar with Latin America judge its ability or vocation by what happens in the Caribbean and lay the responsibility for the local despots at the door of the citizenry. They forget that the Caribbean is a frontier zone where North America and Latin America mingle in such strange and variable proportions that it is not easy to fix the responsibility of either one.

The great tragi-comedy of the Caribbean is known as "T.T.T." That is to say, Tacho Somoza, Tiburcio Carías and Trujillo: Nicaragua, Honduras and the Dominican Republic. The type of dictatorship these men have set up in their respective countries has a strong feudal flavor. Tacho is principally a rancher; it is estimated that he has an annual income of $1,000,000. Trujillo is a dairyman who also controls other enterprises that make him the richest man in the Caribbean, in a much higher bracket than Tacho Somoza. Tiburcio Carías is a fancier of blue-blooded cattle. He is proud of his herds, as well he may be: he and his wife have a contract to supply the Honduran army with milk, not to mention other necessities, including even the wood to bake its tortillas. The idea the members of the cast of T.T.T. share is that God gave them each a republic for his ranch. Their paternalistic governments are established on absolutist principles. Their authority comes from God. In their realms there are no citizens, only peons. The difference between their governments and that of Spanish colonial rule is that the Crown governor had to submit to an investigation of his term of office and the land grantees were under the authority of the Royal Tribunal. Not Tacho, Tiburcio, nor Trujillo has to give an accounting to anybody.

I SOMOZA'S NICARAGUA

UNTIL 1838 Nicaragua formed part of the United Provinces of Central America that was headed by a great leader, Francisco Morazán. Progressive, liberal, imbued with the best ideas of his day, Morazán nationalized the holdings of the Church and assigned them to public education. With the battlecry of "Long-live religion! Down with the foreigners," Rafael Carrera took up arms against Morazán, and in 1839 the union of Central America terminated. From then on Nicaragua was a bone of contention between English and North American interests. It was the best route to the Pacific, better than Panama, where yellow fever grew wild. The rivalry between England and the United States for the control of the Isthmus of Nicaragua ended in 1850 with the signing of the Clayton-Bulwer Treaty. Gradually the United States strengthened its hold with the help of outright adventurers like the filibuster William Walker and businessmen like Commodore Cornelius Vanderbilt. An English accent crept into the history of Nicaragua.

Vanderbilt signed a contract with President Frutos Chamorro for a transportation service, by ship and omnibus, from the Caribbean to the Pacific via the San Juan River,

Lake Nicaragua, and an overland route. When the gold rush to California began, the Commodore extended his service to include boats sailing from New York. The omnibuses of the line were painted the seraphic blue and white of the Nicaraguan flag.

Walker was a journalist, a lawyer, and a doctor, though the title by which history knows him is filibuster. He left San Francisco in May 1855 with a party of three hundred set-tlers for Nicaragua. The first thing he requested of the government of Nicaragua was permission to arm them. He had no more than set foot in Nicaragua when he organized the "American Falange" and started a civil war. The one objective of the Falange was to fight, always to fight. "Nothing tries so much the firmness of men like those constituting the Falange as inaction," Walker wrote in his history, *The War in Nicaragua*. "The roving and adventurous life of California had increased in them the thirst for action and movement characteristic of the American race . . ."

In March 1856 Walker was in command of 600 members of the Falange organized into two battalions. Nicaragua proved too small a theater of action, and he invaded Costa Rica. A few weeks later he issued this proclamation to the people of Nicaragua:

"With such accumulated crimes—conspiring against the very people it was bound to protect—the late provisional government was no longer worthy of existence. In the name of the people I have, therefore, declared its dissolution, and have organized a provisional government, until the nation exercises its natural right of electing its own rulers."

Shortly after Walker installed himself as President of Nicaragua and was recognized by the United States. One of his first decrees reads:

"Art. 1. All acts and decrees of the Federal Constituent Assembly, as well as of the Federal Congress, are declared null and void.

"Art. 2. Nothing herein contained shall affect rights heretofore vested under the acts and decrees hereby repealed."

Walker was a Southerner and a fervent advocate of slavery. Nicaragua, like all Central America, had abolished slavery shortly after winning its independence. This seemed stupid to Walker. He restored slavery.

"The Spanish American States," he wrote, "after their independence, aimed to establish Republics without slavery; and the history of forty years of disorder and public crime is fertile in lessons for him who hath eyes to see and ears to hear . . . The decree, re-establishing slavery while it declared the manner in which the Americans proposed to regenerate Nicaraguan society made them the champions of the Southern States of the Union in the conflict truly styled 'irrepressible' between free and slave labor. The policy of the act consisted in pointing out to the Southern States the only means, short of revolution, whereby they can preserve their present social organization."

The subsequent course of events is common knowledge. Walker invaded Costa Rica on the one hand and confiscated Commodore Vanderbilt's holdings on the other. Vanderbilt joined forces with the English in Belize (British Honduras) to attack him. They all assisted the Costa Ricans. Walker, defeated, returned to the United States for a breathing spell, and then went back to Nicaragua with the aureole of a hero. For a second time he had to abandon Nicaragua. Central America wanted none of him. He tried it a third time, and in September 1860 was captured by the English, who turned him over to Honduras, which tried and shot him. This all took place between the years 1854 and 1860. Thereafter, in a life and death struggle, Nicaragua came to the year 1909, when Adolfo Díaz became president.

Adolfo Díaz had been a bookkeeper for the house of Fletcher in Pittsburgh. He started a revolt against President José Santos Zelaya, and won with the support of the United

THE STATE OF LATIN AMERICA

States, which supplied him with arms. President Taft hastened to give him fatherly approval. "That Republic," he said in a message to congress, "after so many years of governmental maladministration, interspersed with internal disturbances and followed by civil war, has at last established a government on a constitutional basis, which finds itself, unfortunately, with a depleted treasury. . . ." Taft proposed a loan, and an agreement was signed whereby Nicaragua put its customs under United States control. Díaz's government could stay in power only as long as it had United States support. Not long after he took office, a revolution broke out and the rebels seized the railroad and cut some electric wires—that is to say, they damaged American property. Díaz's answer to the protest of the United States Minister was: "I can do nothing. If the Minister wishes to protect the citizens of the United States residing in Nicaragua, let him send in troops, who at the same time will do me the favor of protecting Nicaraguans as well . . ." In *The Political and Economic Solidarity of the Americas* (1941), Laurence Duggan, who was adviser for Latin American affairs to President Franklin D. Roosevelt, summed up subsequent events in these words:

"In 1912 factional warfare broke out in Nicaragua. American marines were landed at Corinto and defended the conservative government against the anti-American liberals. For a number of years the marines remained in Nicaragua without treaty justification, upholding a government sufficiently complaisant to do the bidding of the United States. Finally a treaty was ratified by the Senate on February 18, 1916, which granted to the United States in perpetuity the exclusive right to construct a canal by way of the San Juan River and lake of Nicaragua and leased to the United States for 99 years a naval base in the gulf of Fonseca and also the Great Corn and the Little Corn islands as coaling stations. In return for these favors, the United States paid Nicaragua three million dollars to be expended in ways that would meet the approval of the American Secretary of State. Costa Rica and Salvador protested that the granting of naval stations in the gulf of Fonseca violated an agreement previously made by Nicaragua about the construction of a canal. These two states brought their claims before the Central American Court of Justice, which decided against Nicaragua. Nicaragua refused to carry out the decision of the Court and was upheld by the United States. The Court had been formed in 1907 for a period of ten years and was to be renewed at the end of that time and had been set up with the special benediction of the United States. As a result of the action of Nicaragua, it was not renewed and ceased to exist. For the destruction of an institution which had real possibilities of service, the United States must share the blame. It might have advised Nicaragua to abide by the decision of the Court. All the circumstances surrounding the matter justify the belief that it encouraged her to disregard the decision."

The Marines remained in Nicaragua from 1912 to 1925. In 1924 a Conservative president and a Liberal vice-president had been installed in office. As soon as the Marines left, the Conservatives rebelled, President Carlos Solórzano took flight, the revolutionary troops drove the Liberals out of congress, and Adolfo Díaz once more resumed office. This implied non-recognition of the vice-president, Juan Bautista Sacasa. In *A History of Latin America*, David R. Moore analyzes the situation succinctly:

"Dr. Sacasa rebelled. He claimed that upon the resignation of President Solorzano, he, as vice-president, should have succeeded. Congress, especially a rump assembly from which Liberal members have been expelled, had no right to deprive him of succession to the office to which he had been constitutionally elected. Moreover, it was evident that he represented the majority of the voters. Costa Rica, Guatemala, and Mexico recognized his claims . . . President Coolidge, however, immediately recognized Adolfo Díaz and sent down a formidable force of battleships and soldiers to suppress Sacasa and his followers. He declared that American lives and property and even the canal rights were in danger; that England and Italy had asked him to protect their nationals; that Díaz was the choice of Congress while Sacasa was in league with Mexico and Communism. It must be remembered that Díaz had sold the canal site to the United States during his first presidency and was still most friendly to Washington officials and Wall Street capitalists . . ."

In his message to Congress on January 10, 1927, President Coolidge said:

"I am sure that it is not the desire of the United States to intervene in the internal affairs of Nicaragua or of any other Central American Republic. Nevertheless it must be said that we have a very definite and special interest in the maintenance of order and good government in Nicaragua at the present time, and that the stability, prosperity and independence of all Central American countries can never be a matter of indifference to us. The United States cannot, therefore, fail to view with deep concern any serious threat to stability and constitutional government in Nicaragua tending toward anarchy and jeopardizing American interests, especially if such state of affairs is contributed to or brought about by outside influences or by any foreign power . . ."

On this occasion the marines remained from 1926 until 1932. More foresighted than in 1925, they took a decisive step toward bringing about a new order before they left. They fused the police and the army into a single body, the National Guard, with Tacho (Anastasio) Somoza as its commander.

And who was Tacho Somoza? A boy who knew English, an English with all the four-letter words he had learned when his father sent him to a business school in Philadelphia. Growing tired of school, he became an automobile salesman.

He returned to Nicaragua, an expert mechanic, and then got a job with the Rockefeller Foundation in its campaign to rid Nicaragua of malaria. The North Americans found him very entertaining because he danced well and because of his taxi-driver English. He was made Undersecretary of Foreign Affairs, and then Commander of the National Guard. "The United States Minister, Hanna, and his wife," writes William Krehm, "were enchanted by Tacho's effervescent personality." [1]

During the years of the second American occupation, the Nicaraguans, exasperated by the continued presence of the marines, had organized guerrilla bands under the command of Augusto César Sandino. When the marines left, Sandino dissolved the guerrillas. Everybody applauded this. In Managua a banquet was organized in Sandino's honor at the presidential palace, but as he left the banquet, Somoza's guardsmen seized him and dispatched him to the other world. The National Guard immediately moved in on the rest of Sandino's men, whom they surprised at their camp. From this to becoming president was but a step for Somoza. He organized a coup in 1936 and was inaugurated president on January 1, 1937. Washington's recognition followed immediately. Since then Tacho has been boss in Nicaragua. He exports cattle to Costa Rica, Panama, Peru. These business enterprises have played no small part in the revolutions in Panama. Tacho is the owner of pasteurizing plants, a gold mine, a cement factory. When Krehm was in Nicaragua he found that fifty-one ranches and forty-six coffee plantations belonged to the hustling dictator. He does not permit freedom of the press on the grounds that he wants to keep the country orderly.

[1] William Krehm, correspondent of *Time*, is the author of a book, *Democracies and Tyrannies in the Caribbean*, which is highly informative and entertaining. The Spanish edition, translated by Vicente Sáenz, has been brought up to date with ample foot-notes (1949).

As far as possible, he avoids bloodletting. His son was sent to West Point to be educated. According to *Time* (November 15, 1948), when Roosevelt received him in Washington—it was a kind of dress rehearsal for the visit of the King of England—Tacho told Roosevelt: "I want to treat everybody good. Democracy in Central America is like a baby—and nobody gives a baby everything to eat right away. I'm giving 'em liberty—but in my style. If you give a baby a hot tamale, you'll kill him."

In San Francisco a consul asked Tacho: "How is it possible for you to leave Nicaragua? Won't they steal the presidency from you?" And Tacho answered: "They're fools. There's no one there who could do it."

Nevertheless a day came when Somoza had to allow elections. This was in 1946. Tacho's man, Leonardo Argüello, was elected. Argüello, however, took his role in earnest. A few days after becoming president he ordered a change of officers of the National Guard. Tacho, who considered the Guard his private property, objected, whereupon Argüello notified him that he had twenty-four hours to get out of Nicaragua. Tacho asked for three days. In those three days he deposed Argüello and took over the presidency himself. A few months later he set up his uncle, Victor Román y Reyes, as president. Uncle Victor spent his time doing nothing. If Nicaragua were as large and as important as Russia, Uncle Victor's position would have been like that of N. M. Shvernik, President of the Supreme Soviet Council, who is President of Russia. And following out the parallel, Somoza would have kept for himself the modest post held in Russia by Joseph Stalin. But in 1950 Uncle Victor died and Tacho was elected president for six years. The person who gives the presidential interviews in 1951 is Tacho Somoza, who among other things, is profoundly interested in the defense of democracy in the hemisphere, like all the dictators, and has proposed the unification of the armies of Latin America under one general staff, with

identical arms and code of rules, as the best way of collabo-
rating with the United States "in the defense of those precious
ideals we share."

II HONDURAS UNDER CARÍAS

HONDURAS is a republic of bananas and cattle. The bananas
belong to North American fruit companies, the cattle to
Tiburcio Carías. The most illustrious figure of Central American liberalism was born in the capital of Honduras, Tegucigalpa. This was Francisco Morazán, who in 1830 was president of the federation of Central America. At that time
Honduras occupied an outstanding position; today it is an
utterly obscure little country. Its politics and national economy are standing on a banana skin. 65% of Honduras' exports
is bananas. It is beginning to export rice. All the hope of
Honduras is centered on some day having railroads, which are
indispensable for the bare necessities of its development.
Tegucigalpa, its capital, is a city whose inhabitants know a
locomotive only from pictures. But in the banana zones the
American companies have built railroads, sometimes with
government permission, sometimes without. When the banana trees were attacked by disease, the United Fruit Company hauled away the rails of the Puerto Castilla-Iriona line.
The Hondurans felt as though the twentieth century was being carried away as junk, to leave them once more in pre-
Discovery days. In 1923 the Cuyamel Fruit Company backed
the presidential candidacy of Miguel Paz Barahona, and he
won; the United Fruit Company backed Tiburcio Carías, and
he lost. This does not prove that the Liberals were stronger
than the Conservatives, but that Cuyamel was stronger than
United. The same thing happened in 1928, only this time a
balance of power was struck, with the President of the Re-

public backed by Cuyamel, and Carías, the leader of congress, by the United Fruit. Then an even more nearly perfect solution was reached: United Fruit bought Cuyamel, and Carías became president.

Just before Tiburcio Carías took office, the Central American patriot, Vicente Sáenz, paid him a visit. He found Carías busy with inaugural preparations. Soldiers with blue ribbons on their hats were scurrying about, setting up machine guns and mortars. "I am sure, General," Sáenz said to him, "that you will uphold the prestige of Honduras and demand a revision of the treaties with Washington . . ." Carías answered: "This is a very difficult moment . . . We are confronted by so many pressing problems . . ." Sáenz says Carías looks like a strong, healthy man who gets up at daybreak. And this healthy man, after evading an answer four times, suddenly hit upon a solution worthy of a great statesman. Turning to his Minister, Pineda, he said to Sáenz: "I can say that I am in favor of closer ties with our sister republics of Central America. Isn't that so, Pinedita?" Then, tightening his belt a notch, he shook hands with his visitor and took leave of him cordially.

Some years earlier Carías had introduced a novelty in Honduras and in America: the bombardment of rebels from the air. This was to be used later by Laureano Gómez in Colombia, but when Carías did it in 1924 it was really a trail-blazing innovation. On assuming the presidency in 1933 he used it again. He employed the planes of a famous company that was organized in Honduras, the TACA—Transportes Aéreos de Centro América. In a country where gold was hauled by mules, a New Zealand pilot, Lowell Yerex had found an ideal spot to develop an enterprise that carries gold, coffee, machinery, live-stock, and even bombs by air.

Even though Carías looks like a prosperous rancher, he studied law, and to make things legal, in 1934 he introduced an amendment to the constitution to have himself re-elected.

In 1936 he rewrote the constitution completely, and all power is now in his hands. Municipal autonomy, which had existed in Honduras since the days of Spain, has been abolished.

Honduras and Nicaragua are the two most sparsely populated countries of Central America. Honduras has 1,500,000 inhabitants, mostly rural. Tegucigalpa, its capital, is a diminutive city, but it has about three hundred political prisoners who drag heavy iron balls chained to their ankles. Until 1944 Carías maintained a state of lowering peace, but that year the people's indignation exploded. Women assembled in the cathedral, and carrying flags of Honduras and the United States went out in the street shouting: "Down with Carías!" Shortly afterward the same thing was repeated in San Pedro, the second largest city of Honduras. This time the troops handled the matter. The streets showed pools of blood. But governments were toppling in America, and, like Somoza, Carías thought that it would be better to let someone else occupy the spotlight. He arranged for elections, and for them to be won by Jose Manuel Gálvez, a former lawyer of the United Fruit Company. To what extent Carías can go on ruling under this arrangement is not clear. Gálvez has changed many of Carías's policies. He is a man of initiative, who values material progress and tries to give his government a democratic appearance. He pays attention to problems of water-supply and highways. Still—is there a possibility that Carías wants to be elected again? Or will Gálvez be the spearhead of Honduran resurgence? These are the question marks of the moment.

III THE DOMINICAN REPUBLIC
UNDER TRUJILLO

THE third "T" in the triangle of despotism in the Caribbean stands for Rafael Leonidas Trujillo Molina of the Dominican Republic. Several biographies of him have been published. Trujillo is a generous Maecenas of literature of this sort, the only kind permitted to circulate in his country. A Spaniard in his service wrote one entitled *Trujillo, or The Restoration of a Nation*, in which passages like this may be found: "God help Santo Domingo the day General Trujillo is no more! . . . Who would there be capable of carrying on the work of nation-building initiated by this great patriot? . . . The continental dimension of Trujillo, allowing for differences of time and distance, is as strong as in Bolívar. Like that great Don Simón of Venezuela, this Don Rafael of Santo Domingo cannot be confined within the narrow limits of his nation . . . It has been said that he has had as the theater of his astounding labor only a little island of the Caribbean . . . The size has nothing to do with it; from the little corner of Greece that was Athens came the patterns of the spiritual life of all the Western world." This is writing as practiced in the Dominican Republic. What has happened is that the country where Spain founded the first university of the new world, the home of the first historians of the discovery and of men who have been the glory of Spanish letters for centuries, men like Tirso de Molina and the poet Bernardo de Balbuena, has become a no-man's land. Santo Domingo, the capital, is the oldest city of America; Christopher Columbus' remains are buried there. Its name has now been changed to Ciudad Trujillo to make it a monument to despotism in the New World. Not even the hurricanes have wrought such havoc.

This is the only country in America whose name officially includes the word "republic." In the atlases, in the publications of the United Nations, in the *World Almanac,* one always reads "Dominican Republic," which goes to show how unreliable official language is. And yet it is a nation of good people, who, according to Sumner Welles, have fought like no other for their freedom.

What this nation of good people has had to suffer as it has been tossed back and forth like a ball in an international game can be divined by following the zig-zags of its history. When the whole island of Hispaniola was a colony of Spain, pirates, corsairs, and buccaneers often landed on its shores. Drake entered its capital and carried off even its bells. The French, for their part, took Port-au-Prince, and by the Treaty of Ryswick (1697) the island was cut in two: the eastern part remained with Spain, the western with France. In 1795, by the Treaty of Basel, the entire island went to France. In 1791 revolutionary France dictated a decree favorable to the freedom of the Negroes. The whites protested. There was a rebellion on the island, and the English and the Spaniards who entered to impose order were thrown out by the indomitable Negroes. In 1806 the Dominicans rebelled against the Haitians and offered to become a Spanish colony again. Spain raised its flag over half of the island—with some timidity, because by then it was, as has been said, a "foolish Spain." In 1821 the Rector of the University of Santo Domingo, Núñez de Cáceres, proclaimed independence, which lasted one year—for in 1822 the Haitians invaded the eastern half of the island and hauled down the Spanish flag.

Until 1844 the Haitians dominated the country. In that year Santo Domingo declared its second independence. The president elected in 1845, Pedro Santana, was the first to surrender. In 1861 he asked the Spaniards to take control of the island, and in payment received an appointment as senator of the monarchy and the title of Marqués de las Carreras. The country had to declare its independence for the third time in 1865, only to lose it in 1905 through American intervention. At first this intervention was only control of the customs, but in 1916 everything passed into the hands of the United States. The supreme authority in the island was Vice-Admiral Thomas Snowden. Not until 1924 did Horacio Vásquez become president. Just as the lamps of a fourth independence were going up for Santo Domingo, it fell into the hands of Trujillo in 1930. And there it remains. When will the fifth independence be proclaimed?

Briefly this phrase of its history can be summed up as follows: in November 1916 Secretary of State Robert Lansing outlined to President Wilson the reasons why, in his opinion, the Dominican Republic should be occupied militarily. The Secretary said that the President of the Dominican Republic had called elections for senators and congressmen, and that the majority of those returned favored General Arias. "This new phase of the situation coupled with the fact that the provisional Government will not meet the views of the United States in regard to the establishment of financial control and the constabulary, brings the Government of the United States face to face with a serious problem." President Wilson, perplexed, but trusting in his Secretary's judgement, accepted his recommendations. The Secretary issued instructions to a captain of the Navy, H. S. Knapp. On the 29th of this same November, Captain Knapp anchored his warship in the harbor of Santo Domingo, took the orders he carried out of his brief case, and issued them. Among other things, they said:

"Whereas, a treaty was concluded between the United States of America and the Republic of Santo Domingo on February 8, 1907, Art. III of which reads:

"Until the Dominican Republic has paid the whole amount of the bonds of the debt its public debt shall not be increased except by previous agreement between the Dominican Government and the United States . . .

"Whereas, the Government of Santo Domingo has violated the said Art. III on more than one occasion . . .

"Now, therefore, I, H. S. Knapp, Captain, United States Navy, Commanding the Cruiser Force of the United States Atlantic Fleet . . . acting under the authority and by the direction of the Government of the United States, declare and announce to all concerned that the Republic of Santo Domingo is hereby placed in a state of Military Occupation by the forces under my command, and is made subject to Military Government and to the exercise of military law . . ."

Among the instructions issued to Captain Knapp there were some like this:

"For malfeasance in office or for other proper and sufficient cause the Military Government will remove any Dominican judge or other court official and will appoint his successor in office."

Certain improvements were carried out under the military occupation, but the principles of representative government were undermined. The military personnel sent there left something to be desired. The occupation took place at a time when the United States was sending its best men to Europe, and the Dominican Republic received the short weight. Sumner Welles has written a book dealing with this episode entitled *Naboth's Vineyard*. A few paragraphs selected at random from this important work throw light on the situation:

"While it is . . . difficult to reach any definite conclusion as to the actual extent and number of the more flagrant outrages perpetrated, it is a fact that a policy of repression was carried out by the forces of occupation over a protracted period in the eastern Provinces of the Dominican Republic which was inherently unwise, which reacted primarily upon peaceful civilians, and as the result of which many atrocities were undoubtedly committed . . ."

Welles cites certain shocking incidents uncovered by an investigation carried out by the United States Senate. Then he gives information of this nature:

". . . the Military Governor of the Dominican Republic, with its cabinet, constituted a dictatorship whose actions there was none to criticize. The censorship of the press in the Dominican Republic had become so rigid that the slightest criticism of measures adopted by the Military Government was stringently punished, and comparative freedom of speech had long since become a thing of the past . . .

"In a memorandum [this was on November 12, 1919, three years after the occupation] addressed to the Military Government it was recommended first that the electoral law then in force be replaced by a new act guaranteeing more fully the liberty of the electorate; second, that the act providing for the organization of the communes be amended so that the 'ayuntamientos,' or municipal governments, would acquire the measure of independence from the control of the National Government guaranteed them by the Constitution of 1908; third, that the act of conscription be replaced by a new act devised to compel the military authorities to conform with fixed rules and regulations . . .

"The action of the Military Governor . . . in imprisoning a Venezuelan citizen for having published an article containing photographs showing alleged injuries inflicted upon Dominican citizens by American marines, intensified the growing bitterness of feeling in Latin America, since the report of the action was widely published . . ."

When Trujillo came to power he found that the stage had been set for him by the military governors of the occupation.

Few self-respecting persons would collaborate with the forces of occupation or have a share in what was regarded as the murder of public liberties. Only Rafael Leonidas Trujillo came forward. On December 9, 1918, he presented himself and asked for a post in the National Guard. He was accepted, and he distinguished himself in action against the patriot guerrillas. In 1921 he fought against the rebels in La Noria, and his name was mentioned in the official communiqué: "Participated in engagement with bandits in La Noria . . . His conduct prior and during the engagement was exellent . . . Calm, even-tempered, forceful, active and painstaking." Some time later, no one knows how, a Major Lora was found dead. One of Trujillo's official biographers observes: "On February 23 Major Lora was killed, and that marks the beginning of Trujillo's brilliant military career . . . Not that we attribute to the sad demise of Major Lora the later success of his brilliant military career . . ."

When the marines were withdrawn, Horacio Vásquez became president. He promoted Trujillo to the rank of lieutenant-colonel and chief of the general staff. Later he made him chief of police. Trujillo brought the police into splendid discipline, and two years later, in 1927, held a review that created a very good impression. President Vásquez named him brigadier-general. Mussolini sent him a decoration. Shortly after this there was an uprising against Vásquez. Trujillo did not move his troops, and the President was ousted. Estrella Ureña succeeded him, with Trujillo as the strong man of the government. Trujillo began to organize elections, and in 1930 was "elected." He had already begun a reign of terror.

Trujillo organized the Partido Dominicano, of which he was the sole leader, and all other parties disappeared. He has a huge army, which is in the nature of his personal guard. The members of Congress, whom he selects, before entering office leave with him their resignation, signed but undated, as do the judges, members of city councils, and other public officials. Each morning government employees and congressmen read the paper to find out whether they still have jobs. Not a single independent person but has served time in prison. The students are always having to seek asylum in foreign legations to get out of the country. Many people have disappeared. Albert C. Hicks has written a terrifying book on Santo Domingo under Trujillo, entitled *Blood on the Streets*. The press of Latin America has published hundreds of accounts of this reign of terror. Trujillo is the author of a civic primer, which today is required reading in the schools, defining to the children at an early age what constitutes an enemy of the government:

"The president works unceasingly for the happiness of his people. It is he who maintains peace, supports the schools, builds the roads, protects all forms of labor, helps the farmers, favors industry, keeps up and improves the harbors, supports the hospitals, encourages learning, and organizes the army for the protection of all law-abiding citizens.

"If you should find in your home a man who wishes to disturb order, see that he is handed over to the police. He is the worst of evildoers. Criminals who have murdered a man or stolen something are in prison. The revolutionary who plots to kill as many as he can and steal everything he can lay his hands on, your property and that of your neighbors—he is your worst enemy."

In 1937 Trujillo ordered the extermination of the numerous Haitians in the frontier zones. Quentin Reynolds says in his introduction to Hicks's book that between 15,000 and 20,000 Haitians were killed, and Hicks quotes Trujillo's own words when he ordered the operation: "I found that Dominicans would be happier if we got rid of the Haitians. I will fix that. Yesterday three hundred Haitians were killed at Banica. This must continue." On the eve of these events, the University of Santo Domingo had sent to the Swedish Academy a proposal that concludes with these words:

"In view of the above-outlined facts, which prove that the present President of the Dominican Republic, His Excellency Generalissimo Rafael Leonidas Trujillo Molina, has, by his acts during the year of 1935, showed himself worthy of the Nobel Peace Prize to be awarded in the year 1936, the undersigned professors of the Law School of the University of Santo Domingo, in keeping with the provisions of the statutes of the Nobel Foundation, recommend to the Norwegian parliament that the Nobel Peace Prize for the year 1936 be awarded to His Excellency Generalissimo Rafael Leonidas Trujillo . . ."

The killing of Haitians wore Trujillo out, and he took a vacation, leaving Jacinto "Mozo" Peynado as his replacement in the presidency, but keeping his hand on the wheel through the National Guard. It was at this time that Trujillo's son, Ranfis, nine years old, was raised to the rank of brigadier-general and that a great neon sign was put up in the city of Santo Domingo reading: "God and Trujillo." Refreshed by his rest, Trujillo returned to the presidency and went to work stirring up a revolt in Haiti. In 1950 the government of Haiti laid a protest against the activities of the Dominican Republic before the Organization of American States. It charged that the Secretary of the Dominican Legation in Port-au-Prince was supplying the conspirators with funds, that subversive leaflets were being printed there, and that the Dominican radio was broadcasting propaganda.

At the time that this was happening in Haiti, Dominican patriots in exile were attempting to organize a revolutionary force to return their liberties to the Dominicans. The situation was similar to the days when Bolívar was working in the West Indies to organize his army of liberation, or when Martí was agitating in Central America to form his "*Cuba Libre*" forces. Dominicans have taken refuge in Havana, in Central America, in Venezuela. As a matter of fact, Cuba is a kind of general headquarters for Dominicans in exile. And just as the Haitians carried their protest against the Dominican Republic to the Organization of American States, so Trujillo laid before it his complaint of the revolutionary activities of the Dominicans scattered through the Caribbean.

The Organization of American States took a leaf from King

Solomon's book. It recommended that the Dominican government take immediate and effective measures to stop its officials from tolerating, instigating, stimulating, assisting, or fomenting subversive or seditious movements against other governments. It requested Cuba and Guatemala not to allow the organization in their territory of armies having as their objective the liberation of the Dominican Republic. And it concluded by saying that in view of the fact that the conflict arises because on the one hand the principle of nonintervention is appealed to, and on the other the exercise of representative democracy is banned, the thing to do is "to reaffirm the principles of representative democracy . . . as the fundamental bases of the inter-American system."

IV EL SALVADOR IN THE HANDS
OF A MERLIN

EL SALVADOR is only a little larger than Belgium and has a population of 2,150,000. It is the most densely populated country in Latin America. Its products are coffee and cattle. San Salvador, the capital city, is small, and the country is a rural community whose calendar is divided into the time the coffee plantations are weeded and the picking season. It is a land of rich planters and poor peons. It has a refined, educated class, and ignorant, credulous masses.

From 1931 to 1944 Salvador was governed by a wizard. His name is Maximiliano Hernández Martínez. In 1931 he was Minister of War under President Arturo Araújo. In Salvador, as everywhere else, this was a time of crisis. Coffee was a drug on the market, and poverty was widespread. The President came to grief in the storm. A military coup brought Martínez—General Martínez—to power. He was a Theosophist, and issued magic formulas that awed the ignorant masses. It was a moment of desperate problems, with no rational solution in sight, and people followed the "conjure man" blindly. He had new formulas for planting corn. He filled green, red, yellow bottles with water and set them in the sun on the roof of the presidential palace where they became transformed into philtres to cure rheumatism, cancer, heart disease. He said: "It is a greater crime to kill an ant than a man, for when a man dies he becomes reincarnated, while the ant dies forever." For this reason he never killed ants. People, that was a different story . . . The educated Salvadorians smiled and paid no attention to him. But the wizard soothed the peons; he gave them hope. The Communists cherished the hope that they could light a bonfire in this little country, so plagued by poverty. And they did. They organized a Red army of desperate peons, and in the vicinity of the town of Izalco they began to kill the plantation owners and take over the land. Martínez quickly caught up with them, and not one lived to tell the tale. The number of dead has been estimated, probably with exaggeration, at 10,000. The plantation owners heaved a sigh of relief.

With magic formulas Martínez changed the constitution. Without anyone quite knowing how, he had himself elected over and over again. Thirteen years of Martínez. Finally the opposition organized and put up a candidate, Arturo Romero. He was a distinguished young doctor who had studied in Paris, and he had an apostolic calling. He carried on his work quietly, from house to house. The revolution he had been preparing broke out in December 1943, but was unsuccessful. The wizard was too powerful. Romero had to take flight. At the frontier, guards, without knowing who he was, slashed him half to pieces with machetes. It was not until he was taken to a hospital that his identity was discovered.

A dramatic tug of war began, the authorities trying to hold Romero, his followers to rescue him. When he finally managed to escape he was transformed into a symbol. Martínez pitilessly kept the execution squads at work: "Let my enemies reincarnate when I am dead." As many casualties as war might have occasioned occurred in Salvador, when, after the revolt, which lasted a few hours, the wizard began his reprisals. One day a Mass was announced for those who had died. To the crowd of black-dressed women who thronged the church the priest had to say from the pulpit: "Official orders have forbidden us to celebrate the Mass."

In May 1944 Martínez decided that a change might be advisable. He turned the power over to General Andrés Ignacio Menéndez, his alter ego. Menéndez took a liking to the presidency, but the people threw him out. The Chief Justice of the Supreme Court took his place, and elections were scheduled. The name on everybody's lips was Doctor Romero. His candidacy aroused a frenzy of enthusiasm. Just a few days before election day the military brought off a coup, and a colonel with Falangist leanings seized the presidency: Osmín Aguirre, director of police. His government was recognized only by Carías of Honduras, Somoza of Nicaragua, and Franco of Spain. It was purely a family affair, and El Salvador was cut off from the rest of the world. The ostracism was so marked that new elections had to be scheduled, and General Salvador Castañeda Castro became president. In 1949 a coup unseated Castañeda and Major Oscar Osorio took his place. In March 1950 Major Osorio was constitutionally elected and initiated a period of honest reconstruction.

The density of its population makes El Salvador a focal point for international agitation. From Costa Rica the directors of the workers' organization "*Rerum Novarum*" have tried to penetrate El Salvador. On the other hand, Argentina has a labor attaché at its legation in San Salvador, and the president of the syndicate of railroad workers visited Buenos Aires in 1948 as a guest of the Perón government. That same year, a representative of the CIT (Interamerican Confederation of Workers) visited Salvador, and said in his report: "The

future danger lies in the fact that the working class, inex-
perienced in politics and confused as it is today, might believe in the Communist leaders." [2] When, under a new constitution, the Salvadorian unions were able to organize and
hold a convention in October 1951, they said: "Salvador must
adopt a position consonant with the Declaration of the Rights
of Man . . . Both totalitarian systems of the extreme left
(Communism) and those of the extreme right (Fascism,
Falangism, Peronism, etc.) must be eschewed . . . And as a
patriotic ideal the hope of a Central American Union must be
maintained . . ." [3]

V PANAMA UNDER THE DICTATORSHIP
OF ARIAS

MANY of the circumstances attending Panama's birth have
weighed on its subsequent existence. When it seceded from
Colombia under the armed protection of President Theodore
Roosevelt, it leased the Canal Zone to the United States for
ninety-nine years. It received an annual rental of $250,000,
which in 1936 was increased to $430,000. Workers from all
parts of the world were brought in for the building of the
canal. The French had used Chinese labor; the United States
preferred West Indian Negroes. The Negroes were paid in
silver, the white workers in gold. Today all payments are in
greenbacks, but the discrimination still exists. At the postoffice there is one window for the "gold workers" and another
for the "silver workers," and there is the same segregation in
schools, hotels, housing, and transportation. Paul Blanshard
discusses this situation in his book *Democracy and Empire in*

[2] Signed by Luis Alberto Monge, Vice-President of the CIT.
[3] Cited from *Informativo Obrero Interamericano* (Havana).

the Caribbean (Macmillan, 1947). One could hardly say that the United States had set up a model school of democracy in the heart of the Republic of Panama, where most of the people are cinnamon-colored.

The Canal Zone is a strip five miles wide flanking the Canal on both sides, not including the cities of Colón and Panama, which are only under American sanitary control. The territory of Panama, thus split in two, stretches from the Colombian border to that of Costa Rica. Its area is twice that of El Salvador, but its population barely reaches 746,000. One fourth of its territory is uninhabited jungle. Life in the country continues primitive, but the city of Panama is like the vast foyer of a luxury hotel. Panama, which was once the breeding ground of yellow fever, is now advertised as the healthiest country in the world.

The introduction of Oriental workers at the time of the building of the Canal has given rise in the city of Panama to some of the most attractive and luxurious shops in the hemisphere, shops dealing in products from China, Japan, India, and Persia. When sailors of the American fleet come to town, the city is flooded with drunks, jazz, and greenbacks. Carnival still keeps all the fire and color of its traditional observance. Dancing goes on all night in the *tamboritos* to the sound of voluptuous music. The regional costume of the women of Panama is of the prettiest in America.

The Panamanian descendants of old Radical families of Colombia preserve a republican tradition at war with opposing ideologies. The struggle is a difficult one because it is not easy to uphold principles in such a noisy, restless atmosphere. In the Academy of History, in the University, in the field of politics itself, there are nevertheless outstanding figures who staunchly support the ideal of a representative democracy.

In 1940 the government backed the presidential candidacy of Arnulfo Arias. Arias, a graduate of the Medical School of

Harvard University, found himself more in affinity with the ideals of Hitler than with those of Franklin D. Roosevelt. He came to power by manipulating the electoral machine. Once President, in 1941, he introduced a new constitution that extended the president's term of office from four to six years. He sponsored an anti-Negro policy; he prohibited Hindus and West Indians from engaging in any but domestic work. He deprived naturalized Jamaicans of their Panamanian citizenship. Panama became a happy hunting ground for Nazis and Fascists from Hitler's dominions. As a defense against German submarine attack many merchant ships had taken Panamanian registry and flew the flag of Panama. Arias forbade this, a move directed principally against United States shipping. By one of fate's little ironies, the United States had cherished a viper in its bosom. This distinguished gentleman, educated at Harvard, born in the republic brought into being by Theodore Roosevelt, president of the vital area around the Panama Canal, turned out to be a German sympathizer, a champion of Hitler's racial doctrines, a partisan of white supremacy, a man animated by a burning desire to wipe out representative government in Panama.

But Arias is a man of volatile temperament. One day he left Panama by plane. A love affair? A political adventure? He landed at one of the Caribbean airfields, and Panama drew a sigh of relief. Aníbal Ríos was elected president, and war was declared on Germany. Ríos was followed by Enrique Jiménez, who sponsored a new constitution to put an end to the totalitarian one Arias had imposed on the country. But Arias was still alive, and under the presidency of Daniel Chanis he worked out his plans with the chief of police, Colonel José Remón—"Chichi" Remón, as he is familiarly known. They overthrew the President, and on November 24, 1949, Arias was back in the driver's seat.

In no time he was conducting business along the old familiar lines. The characteristic touch this time was nepotism.

Four of his relatives were appointed to the cabinet. Although the law provided for the organization of labor unions, the Minister of Labor denied them legal status. Arias attempted to take over the Panama Trust Company, a private bank, and its directors were forced to close it. The newspaper *El País* openly attacked Arias, and he shut it down. Mass meetings were held in the city square to voice demands for a general strike of protest. Six former presidents and many distinguished men spoke, condemning the dictatorship. They were clapped in jail. One of them, Ricardo Adolfo de la Guardia, had to go to the hospital to be treated for the wounds he had received when he was taken prisoner. Arias ordered Congress dissolved and restored the totalitarian constitution of 1941. He was encouraged to take these steps by the example of Colombia, where the government had been ruling without Congress and where the constitution had been suspended in favor of a dictatorship.

But Panama is a small country without an army, and the people rioted in the streets. Women marched at the head of the crowd—one of them the wife of former President La Guardia, who was still a prisoner in the hospital. Colonel Remón, who had brought off the coup that put Arias in power, nevertheless liked to stand well with the people. Although he had worked out a splendid racket giving him a monopoly on the sale of meat in Panama, he was chief of police. And with Remón the revolution broke out. There were shots, deaths, skirmishes between the supporters of Arias and the police and the great mass of the citizenry that had mobilized. Arias barricaded himself in his office in the presidential building until Major Lescano Gómez and Lieutenant Juan Flórez of the police force managed to get in. They had come to inform him of the decision of the people. Both fell dead of bullet wounds. It is said that Arias himself killed one of them. The President's study looked like a battleground. The room was a shambles, with blood stains on everything including the President's white suit. Arias was taken to jail. Two weeks later he was tried and deprived of his rights as a citizen by the National Assembly. As sentence was pronounced, the women present sang the national anthem.

At the time that all this was taking place the current issue of a magazine called *United Nations World,* came out in New York with a fulsome article on Arias. Arias had told the writer of the article, Victoria Bertrand, who had visited him a few weeks before:

" 'Panama is a democracy, that you can see readily. Once I was called a dictator', he smiled, thoroughly amused, 'it was the fashion then. Now no one denies I am giving full liberty —and the opposition takes plenty of advantage of it, as you can easily see . . . Yes, Panama is a full-fledged democracy . . .'

" 'During your first administration you granted equal rights to women . . .'

" 'I did. Woman's intuitive intelligence is essential for good government.' "

And Miss Bertrand summed up her impression of Arias in these words:

"This charming 'guest at the palace', whose political and romantic adventures have occasionally crashed the international headlines, views the world situation with the measured wisdom of an experienced politician. The much-publicized impulses of an attractive and exuberant man of the world sometimes mislead his critics into underestimating his ability. His course is well defined. While his relations with the outside world are steadily kept in happy equilibrium, the bulk of his knowledge and energy, as well as the warmth of his devotion, is concentrated on the development and improvement of his country. It is this correspondent's impression that engraved deeply in Arnulfo Arias' heart is one word: Panama."

In 1951, the chief of police, Colonel Remón, who in 1949 had installed Doctor Arias, dis-installed him. The powers of

the president were assumed by the head of the supreme
court, Alcibiades Arosemena. Remón went back to the police
barracks and his business. He controls the meat industry, as
well as some other businesses, in Panama. In handling meat
he works as an associate of Tacho Somoza. Tacho sends him
cattle from Nicaragua, and Remón processes them and sells
the meat in Panama. Remón appears to have entered the
antechamber through which Somoza and Trujillo rose to
power—that of police commanders. In 1951 he launched his
candidacy for the presidential chair . . .

XV

THE CARIBBEAN, WORLD HURRICANE CENTER—2

The pivot of America lies in the Antilles. If enslaved, they would be nothing but a pontoon between an imperialist republic and a jealous, superior world resentful of its power, a mere outpost of the Rome of America. But if free, and worthy of so being by the existence of a just and effective freedom, they would be a guarantee of the stability of the continent, of the independence of Spanish America, still in danger, and of the honorable intention of the great republic to the North, which would find more enduring greatness in the development of its own territory than in the ignoble conquest of its weaker neighbors and in the feral struggle their possession would engender with the forces of order for the domination of the world.

José Martí

I COSTA RICA

Costa Rica is only a little larger than El Salvador. Its population is white and sparse. On the north it borders on Nicaragua, populated by Indians and half-breeds, on the south on Panama, a cocktail shaker of many races. Its chief products are coffee and bananas. It was in Costa Rica that the United Fruit Company peacefully started, to spread out later through the rest of Central America, becoming the symbol of Yankee imperialism.

In 1936 León Cortés Castro, a former schoolteacher, a liberal, was elected president. William Krehm says of him:

"When Cortés left the presidency in 1940, a congressman accused him of having appropriated for his own use a lamp from the presidential dwelling. Cortés denied this, and produced a receipt from the Minister of Finance to prove that he had paid for it. His adversary came back at him, this time referring to two hens and two roosters Cortés had received from the National School of Agriculture. Cortés finally admitted that he had done wrong to accept the chickens, but argued that the fault lay with the director of the School who had made the gift."

In 1940 Cortés was succeeded by Dr. Rafael Ángel Calderón Guardia, whose position was that of a Christian Socialist, and who had the support of the Catholic Party. He drew up a Labor Code, founded a Social Security bank, and encouraged the labor unions. Toward the end he became unpopular. The government was accused of corruption. Calderón Guardia approached the Communists, and finally began to work with them. The Communists, who had been organized since 1925, had as their leader a brilliant, disinterested intellectual. In 1936, out of a total of 86,898 votes they polled 4,538, a very high proportion in Latin America. At that time President Cortés advised Congress to prohibit the use of the mails for the circulation of Communist literature. In 1943, when Russia dissolved the Comintern, the Communists disappeared as a party, to re-emerge as the "Vanguardia Popular." They organized belligerent meetings and, together with President Calderón Guardia, opposed Cortés's candidacy for a second term. This paved the way for the election of Teodoro Picado in 1944.

Picado is Polish on his mother's side. During his regime, the power of the Communists grew. In the 1948 elections they backed the return of Calderón Guardia. In opposition to them the newly founded Oposición Nacional put forward as its candidate Otilio Ulate, and Ulate won. His election was recognized by the electoral tribunal, but Congress, intimidated by the Communists, demanded that the election be nullified. The result was civil war. Ulate's supporters started their campaign with the six old rifles mentioned above. For the first time the government of Costa Rica had arms: those lent under the Good Neighbor policy: fourteen jeeps, twenty-four tommy guns, six machine guns, two armored trucks, two hundred tear bombs . . . The leader of the rebels was young Pepe Figueres, the son of Spanish parents, who since his university days had been a leader of student agitation.

During March and April 1948 an exchange of shots occurred in Costa Rica. The *ticos* (Costa Ricans) refer to the episode as the War of National Liberation. A journalist of San José, the capital, gave his coverage of it the Churchillian title "Blood, Sweat, and Tears." In reality the war was fought in the cozy confines of a group of hills. The casualties were reported, not by numbers, but by name. The communiqués did not conclude with "casualties, forty thousand," but with "killed in action, Eloy Morúa," "killed in action, Rolando Aguirre." When the war broke out someone asked: "Where are the arms?" and they showed him six old rifles like six hollow reeds. The first proclamation issued by the generalissimo of the revolution—whom everybody called Don Pepe—begins in this fashion: "Costa Rican: Are you doing all you can for the triumph of freedom? The army of National Liberation is fighting brilliantly in the theater of war. You can render great service to the patriotic cause by piling logs and stones in the roads, cutting telephone and telegraph lines, seizing police headquarters or precinct stations, and doing everything in your power to disorganize and isolate the usurping government."

This, which Europeans, accustomed to carnage on a large scale, find highly amusing, is deadly serious in Costa Rica, and has a heroic quality. Costa Rica has been a country of peaceful evolution. There is no smell of gunpowder about its history. It has always had more schoolteachers than soldiers. The presidency has gone from Don Cleto, M.A., to Don Ricardo, M.D.

—from Professor León Cortés Castro to Doctor Rafael Ángel Calderón Guardia. The news of its independence from Spain came to Costa Rica through an item in the newspaper, not by war. Not long ago the president of Costa Rica was a practicing obstetrician. His time was divided between his professional calls and his official duties. It was not unusual for him to have to interrupt a cabinet meeting to usher a new Costa Rican into the world.

Despite the fact that Costa Rica has been called a nation of lawyers, the medical profession has supplied a large proportion of its presidents. The national librarian is one of the most respected and loved figures of Latin America, Joaquín García Monge, who has given most of his time and energy to the publication of the best literary weekly in Latin America, *El Repertorio Americano*. Its politicians have for the most part been venerable old men, patriotic and devoted to the good of their country. The typical features of the neat, carefully tended countryside of Costa Rica are the heavy painted carts drawn by ponderous, sleepy-eyed oxen and the scented coffee groves.

Within this peaceful, bucolic framework one can understand the religious tone of the words of President Figueres when the parenthesis of war was closed: "Let us observe a moment of silence in tribute to the dead who have fallen in this national campaign . . . May their bodies and their blood fertilize this land so that the lilies of civic virtue may never cease to flower here . . ."

It should be said that tiny Costa Rica, with these battles which ended leaving no more than fifty-six dead in the army of Don Pepe Figueres, appears on the Spanish-American scene as a moral symbol and guide. The gunfire of 1948 will appear in its history as a war, its most bloody war. When the country took arms to expel Walker from Central America, the number of dead reached 200. In 1948, however, if only fifty-six men in Don Pepe's ranks fell, the government lost more than fifteen hundred! In a population of 870,000, this is a major tragedy, as if tomorrow two thousand persons should die in a borough of New York. The Costa Ricans fought their war in order to win liberty. Don Pepe was a student, a farmer: he was extemporaneously made a general to assure Costa Ricans the rights they had always had: to speak freely, think freely, and be free men. For Latin Americans this symbolizes the astonishing capacity of the unknown student, of the anonymous citizen, who can suddenly spring up like a David and deprive the giant of his head. Bolívar assured the independence of Colombia at the Battle of Boyacá, one of the decisive dates in the history of Spanish America. Colombia regards that battle as the birth of the republic. It lasted two hours, and the liberating armies lost thirteen men. Don Pepe Figueres's war was another small symbolic epic.

Figueres had three small planes, confiscated from TACA, which made nineteen trips to Guatemala, bringing back arms, cotton, gauze, and other supplies. The great military strategy was known as the "Corn Plan," the deployment of troops as the "Ghost March." The capture of Puerto Limón with the aid of the "terrible" Caribbean Legion largely decided the outcome of the war. The history of the Caribbean Legion is well known: it has fallen as a terrible shadow to frighten all the dictators of the Caribbean. In the taking of Puerto Limón it was represented by one man, a Dominican. The total number of foreigners who formed the legion at the beginning was seven. At the end of the war this number had risen to nineteen. But *Time* published a fabulous report of its derring-do, and the specter of the Carribbean Legion began to haunt Trujillo, Tacho Somoza, and Tiburcio Carías. Somoza gave his full support to Picado and Calderón Guardia. Between them they concocted a Communism *à la nicaragüense*.

The archbishop of Costa Rica, Monsignor Sanabria, flew from the capital to Pepe Figueres's headquarters to propose peace terms. Figueres answered that he would accept only unconditional surrender. Picado finally yielded. Figueres entered San José with his troops. Government was to be in the hands of a military *junta* until the scars of war had healed. Figueres presided over the *junta*. The first thing he did was to abolish the army. Certain persons were to be allowed to keep a machine gun in the house, but there would be no army. The old army barracks was turned into a Museum of Fine Arts. The Communist party was outlawed. A few days before the date he had agreed to, Figueres handed over power to Otilio Ulate. From Nicaragua, Somoza tried a pot shot at Costa Rica, organizing an army of invasion. The President of Costa Rica reached the Organization of American States in Washington on the phone. The Organization went into action, and the threat of war was over.

Today the workers in Costa Rica are divided into two groups, one that is the heir to the Communist legacy, the other representing *Rerum Novarum,* a labor organization that is making itself increasingly independent of the Church. Archbishop Sanabria is a new-style Catholic, an ardent advocate of social justice whose face is firmly set against all types of totalitarianism. Under his protecting mantle stands Father Benjamín Núñez, who studied at a seminary in the United States, and to whom the Church does not represent a reactionary group at the service of capitalism. When the United Fruit Company tried to win over Father Núñez, he put it severely in its place. He was interested in only one thing, the fight for justice.

Under the presidency of Otilio Ulate, Costa Rica seems to be returning definitely to the democratic way of life which has been traditional in this small country. If Costa Rica guards its liberties and complements them with a program of social justice, it will remain one of the most secure refuges of civilian life in the Caribbean.

11 WAS THERE SOMETHING ROTTEN
IN GUATEMALA?

BETWEEN 1840 and 1944 Guatemala was ruled by four dictatorships, with brief interludes of anarchy. The dictators were
Rafael Carrera (1840–65), Justo Rufino Barrios (1873–85),
Manuel Estrada Cabrera (1898–1920), and Jorge Ubico
(1931–44). Their combined years in power totaled seventy-
two, seventy-two years during which Guatemala was the despots' football. Carrera's despotism was of the reactionary
stripe. In the name of religion he seized power and destroyed
the union of Central America that Francisco Morazán had
constructed on liberal bases. He was profoundly ignorant and
completely authoritarian. Even the Church felt his heavy
hand. Barrios was an enlightened despot. He imposed com-
pulsory public education, built the first Guatemalan railroad,
introduced the growing of coffee, confiscated the holdings of
the Church. He attempted to extend his dictatorship to all
Central America. He was killed while riding his battle horse.
Estrada Cabrera was a provincial despot. His formula for
keeping order was terror. He was liberal in his dealings with
foreign companies to secure funds, and he inaugurated non-
existent public works for the sake of publicity. Ubico was a
mad despot. He resembled Napoleon in appearance, and this
was a contributing factor to his derangement. He was in the
habit of making triumphal visits to terrified towns that had
been ordered to set up welcoming arches of colored tissue
paper.

Seventy-six years of despotism and forty spent in fruitless
efforts to restore a normal way of living have maintained in
poverty and ignorance the country with the proudest past in
all Central America. The Mayan ruins of Petén, which John

Lloyd Stephens brought to the attention of a wondering world
in the nineteenth century, stand as a mute background
against which their builders' Indian descendants weave bright-
hued blankets. The "ghost" city of Antigua is a testimony to
the Spanish ambitions of colonial days, which hoped to find in
Guatemala a second Mexico. All this was being engulfed by
nothingness until the fall of Ubico in 1944.

Of Guatemala's 3,000,000 inhabitants in 1951, 60% are Indians who preserve their languages and their customs. In the
west are the Toltecs, to the east the Aztecs, in the north the
Maya-Quichés. Illiteracy is their most tangible inheritance.
Education is a difficult problem because the teachers must
either know the Indian tongues or be Indians who can bridge
the gulf between the native and the *ladino*. The *ladino*—the
word is a corruption of *latino*—who may be a Negro, a North
American, or a Chinese, is one who knows about the non-
Indian world and speaks a European language. Eighty-six per
cent of Guatemala's Indian population speaks four principal
Indian languages. The rest is divided into small groups among
which eleven different languages have been identified.

But the greatest stumbling block for the person who does
not know Guatemala is the Spanish language. Words take on
a local meaning there. The *Indian* who becomes rich is
white. The *white* man who has no money is an *Indian*. The
dictators are called *democrats*. *Communist* means one who
opposes the *dictator*. When Juan José Arévalo arrived from
Argentina he was called a Nazi, when he was in the presidency, a Communist. Ubico began mass killings of "Communists." Just how far each of these expressions coincides with
its universal significance is a problem in semantics the answer to which lies in the inner recesses of the Indian or
ladino mind.

Guatemala produces coffee, bananas, chicle, sugar, cattle,
and Indians. Until Pearl Harbor, coffee was in the hands of
the Germans and the plantation-owners of Guatemala. The

property of the Germans was confiscated by the state, and today it is a national enterprise employing 200,000 workers. It is an experimental station for the improvement of coffee and an electoral reserve. The bananas have been in the hands of the United Fruit Company. The cattle and Indians, for the most part, are the property of the land-owners.

Jorge Ubico ruled Guatemala from 1931 to 1944. Elizabeth J. Velsmann, a North American journalist, optimistically remarked in *The Pan American* (December 1949): "If Guatemala resembled a prison, it was an efficient, model one." In 1944 the prisoners of this model jail rioted. The lawyers and teachers protested. The students marched through the streets with locked arms shouting: "Get out! Get out!" Ubico's answer was to have them fired upon. The foreign embassies could not hold all the people seeking refuge. The people had been encouraged by the overthrow of the wizard Martínez in El Salvador. The business houses, the motion picture theaters, and the university closed down. General Federico Ponce saw his opportunity, forced Ubico's resignation, and set himself up in power. The people waited to see what would happen, and the stores, theaters, and university re-opened.

Without letting the grass grow under his feet, General Ponce, who was well-versed in the history of Guatemala, put a pistol to the head of Congress and had himself elected President. His personal affairs began to flourish most satisfactorily. He obtained the recognition of the United States, and the opposition pinned the Nazi label on him. At this time Juan José Arévalo, who had been teaching in Argentina, returned to Guatemala. The students had put him forward as a candidate for the presidency. Guatemala did not know Arévalo, nor Arévalo Guatemala. He had been living in Argentina for years, where he had studied and was teaching at the University of Tucumán. Guatemala selected him the way one buys a lottery ticket. The government termed him alternately a *peronista* and a Nazi. The masses followed him without knowing why. As his campaign progressed, the government applied the usual bloodletting tactics. But every death won him new supporters. As an answer to General Ponce's terrorism, the students secretly allied themselves with a group of young army officers. One day, about two o'clock in the morning, the shooting began. By noon a huge column of smoke was rising from the government munition dumps. That afternoon General Ponce took refuge in the Mexican Embassy. His rule had lasted about one hundred days. Ubico moved from the Spanish Embassy to the British, and thence to New Orleans. The victors organized a *pro tem* governing *junta*, and two months later elections were held. Arévalo received 85% of the votes.

Juan José Arévalo set out to accomplish a revolution in administration and in the life of the people of Guatemala. The undertaking was not without its risks. At the end of his six-year constitutional term of office he had survived twenty-seven attempts to overthrow him. He had said: "I shall not remain in office one day beyond the limits established by the consitution, but not one day less, either." He raised the schoolteachers' salaries, he organized a school system for the Indians, he demilitarized education, he made the university autonomous, he created the faculties of Humanities and Agronomy, he built one hundred thirty-five schools, he published thousands of volumes in a series of books by the world's great authors at prices everyone could afford. He built an Olympic center with a great stadium, a sports palace, and tennis courts, initiated a vast health and sanitation campaign, and erected seventeen hospitals.

The United Fruit Company, which prefers to do business with the weak republics of Central America—its dealings with the British islands and the American possessions are negligible—suddenly found itself confronted by a man who said: "If I am elected president, I shall see that our workers are treated with the consideration shown to foreigners." United Fruit translated these words into: "Arévalo is a Communist." United States Ambassador Richard C. Patterson, Jr., was a man not overendowed with tact, and as between Guatemala and the United Fruit Company, he was unequivocally with the latter. "Unofficially, Mr. President," he said to Arévalo one day, "I want you to know that as far as I am personally concerned, your Government will never get a dime or a pair of shoes from my Government until you cease the persecution of American business." [1] In turn, Arévalo said to Samuel Guy Inman, who reported it in *A New Day in Guatemala* (1951): "You do not have an ambassador of the United States here, but a representative of the United Fruit."

Patterson made friends with the enemies of the government. Relations deteriorated to the point where as the different entries in the Olympic Games passed the reviewing stand to the sound of their respective national anthems, when the American flag came by the band broke into *"La Cucaracha."* Arévalo finally informed Washington that Patterson was *persona non grata*, and he was recalled.

The social reforms carried out by Arévalo are those which have been put into effect in much of Latin America by governments of the most varied political complexion: a labor code, social security, plans for stimulating production. But in a country where everything had been solved by the magic formulas of dictatorship, this was subversive. During Ubico's rule labor was denied the right to organize. The North American journalist, C. H. Calhoun, who visited Guatemala in 1951, said in his report to *The New York Times:*

"The responsibility for a situation that threatens not only the future of Guatemala but also hemispheric solidarity cannot be placed entirely on the Communists, who get their orders from Moscow, nor on the complaisance of the Government. Responsibility must also be shared by the fourteen-year

[1] Quoted in *The New York Times,* June 30, 1950.

dictatorship of General Jorge Ubico and also by some of the Guatemalans who now shout loudest against the menace they face . . . President Ubico abolished the peonage system that enslaved the humble Guatemalan Indians, but he also prohibited labor unions. During his regime, any worker who asked for higher pay or shorter hours was branded a Communist. The same label was pasted on anyone who opposed his dictatorship . . ."

Guatemala's thorniest problem was its dealings with the United Fruit Company. United Fruit protested the Labor code and considered illegal a strike justified by law, invoking the special status it had been granted under Ubico's dictatorship. In 1951 the controversy had become so hot that United Fruit announced that it was withdrawing from Guatemala. The manager declared that the demands of the workers were intolerable. "The company," he said (*The New York Times*, dispatch from Guatemala dated August 23, 1951): "has been charged repeatedly with exploiting the country and the people despite the fact that last year it paid $9,712,143 in salaries and wages, of which almost 93% went to Guatemalans . . ." These figures need to be broken down. *The New York Times*, where these declarations appeared, published shortly afterward a letter saying: "Nine million dollars is certainly an impressive amount of money for one company to have poured into the economy of little Guatemala. Yet, when 93% of this sum is divided among 97% of the 37,000 workers, we find the average yearly income of the workers, including 'salaried employes,' to be $251.66 . . ."

Which way is Guatemala heading? When Vicente Lombardo Toledano and his associates—who in labor matters are considered the spearhead of Russia in Latin America—went to Guatemala, they were given an official reception, attended by four of Arévalo's cabinet ministers, Lieutenant-Colonel Jacobo Arbenz, and the leader of Congress. Serafino Romualdi, the leader of the Interamerican Regional Organization, which represents the most vigorous anti-Communist labor group on the continent, remarked this fact, and at the same time has said: "We have had occasion to deplore such stupid handling of the Communist issue on the part of the American interests in Guatemala." Naturally the politics of Guatemala are affected by all these factors, which, though extraneous to the country, put stumbling blocks in the way of a normal working out of its destiny. When Arévalo turned over his office to the new president, Jacobo Arbenz, on March 15, 1951, he summed up his position in a speech from which the following is an excerpt.

"I entered upon my office bent upon giving the people what they awaited from me . . . It was necessary to begin with the first article of the new constitution which says: 'Guatemala is a free, sovereign and independent republic, organized for the primordial purpose of insuring to its inhabitants the enjoyment of liberty, culture, economic well-being, and social justice. Its system of government is representative democracy' . . . At that time I was convinced—as I still am—that there can be no freedom for a nation as long as its individual inhabitants, each and every one, are not free, and that the dignity of a republic rests upon the sum total of the dignity actively and effectively operating in each individual inhabitant of its soil. To achieve this in Guatemala we came into conflict with the peculiar economic and social structure of the country, where the culture and the political and economic control were in the hands of three hundred families who were the heirs of colonial privileges, or employees of foreign overlords, or members of an administrative caste. Creole feudalism . . . reacted in an outraged manner against the way my government understood democracy and emphasized freedom. The banana barons, Roosevelt's fellow citizens, rose against the insolence of a Central American president who dared to put his compatriots on a footing of equality with the honorable families of the exporters. Hitlerism has not died . . . After the grueling, enlightening experience of the past six years, during which I have plumbed the depths of this tragicomedy of man's inhumanity to man, what I can say is that contemporary democracy is losing ground at a dizzying speed to the Punic doctrines of Hitlerism."

III CUBA ENCHAINED AND CUBA FREE

THE history of Cuba can be, and has been written from many points of view. Fernando Ortiz has made it revolve about two contrapuntal factors: tobacco and sugar. These have determined the island's economy. From the moment it sprouts, tobacco demands the most exacting care. It is cultivated by superstitious Negroes and smoked by dreamers. Its leaf holds equal sway over the hours of thoughtful leisure and those of vice. Sugar is Cuba's economic life: and as goes sugar, so goes Cuba's prosperity. Sugar cane falls under the swing of machetes, the syrup boils in the refineries, and it is behind sacks of sugar that the Cubans barricade themselves in their struggle for survival.

There is another way to write Cuba's history: around its relations with the United States. This is the approach Herminio Portell Vilá, the Cuban historian, has used. Of the former Spanish colonies which today are independent nations, Cuba was the last to free itself from Europe. It finally achieved its freedom with the help of the United States. The peace treaty was signed in Paris in 1898, and in 1899 the Cubans awoke to find that they had an American governor. It was not until 1909 that the United States troops withdrew from Cuba. In 1901 Cuba was obliged to write into its constitution the Platt Amendment, Article 3 of which reads as follows:

"That the government of Cuba consents that the United

States may exercise the right to intervene for the preservation of Cuban independence, the maintenance of a government adequate for the protection of life, property, and individual liberty, and for discharging the obligations with respect to Cuba imposed by the treaty of Paris on the United States, now to be assumed and undertaken by the government of Cuba."

The Platt Amendment continued in force until 1934. During those years the Cubans changed their old appeal for freedom from Spain into a new appeal for freedom from the United States. These appeals were always accompanied by a long list of grievances. In 1920 the United States marines returned to Cuba. It was not until 1925 that Cuba acquired control of the Isle of Pines, which had been under the American flag. The history of Cuba's relations with the United States written by Portell Vilá fills four large volumes. The episodes to which this relationship gave rise have generated an antipathy toward Yankee imperialism and a belligerent poetry such as that of the well-known Negro, Nicolás Guillén.

But the history of Cuba could also be written, and often has been written, around the figure of José Martí. The other Spanish colonies had for their liberators soldiers, men on horseback. Cuba's liberator was a great poet and one of the most significant writers his America ever produced. At the end of the nineteenth century Martí still glowed with the fire of Romanticism. His great battles were fought and won in speeches in Madrid, New York, Mexico, Guatemala, Caracas. On the military field his first and only action was suicide. From then on he won his battles from the grave, a feat in keeping with the tradition of Spain, whose great hero, Ruy Díaz, the Cid, won victories after his death. The people of Cuba cultivate and love oratory. They are loquacious, vehement. The students have been the motor force of its revolutions. In the first revolt against Spain the man who took the city of Bayamo was a musician. The city's fall was foretold days before it happened by a military march he had composed, which everyone began to whistle in the streets. The music swelled and the city capitulated. The musician entered the city at the head of the troops, with his daughter riding beside him as ensign. As he rode, using the pommel of his saddle as desk, he wrote the words of his march, and thus the Cuban national anthem came into being. The musician was shot by the Spaniards, but his song lived on and permeated the island. The words of the anthem contain the phrase: "To die for the fatherland is to live." This was Martí's motto. A strange one, perhaps, but one shared by many Cubans.

Visitors to Cuba are always struck by the fact that where freedom of the press is concerned no holds are barred. During the last presidential campaign hundreds of articles were written whose general tone can be judged by the following lines selected at random from one by Eduardo R. Chibás, then the most violent opponent of the party in power. The title of the article was "Jail the thieves!" and it was published in the magazine *Bohemia*, the best in Havana:

"The party bigwigs . . . who sympathize with the swindlers never give a thought to the old people, women, and children who during the last ten years have died in the hospitals because the thieves of the Batista and Grau administrations stole the money for their medicines, and this continues under the government of Prío. These are the real victims, these are the truly unfortunate. It is they whom the Pueblo Cubano party defends, not the barefaced, shameless thieves, who have become multimillionaires and bought themselves mansions and estates with the money stolen from the nation . . ."

Those under attack by the press have no choice but to answer. When it seemed to Chibás that his accusations demanded a more dramatic presentation he had recourse to a traditional procedure: he shot himself at the end of a radio broadcast, hoping that the shot would be heard by his listeners. He would win his battle in death. And he was right. At his funeral, the largest ever witnessed in Cuba, all Havana followed his coffin to the cemetery.

The Cuban wants to talk and he wants others to have the same right. The present government has ventured to close down only one newspaper, a Communist organ. This action called forth a sympathetic suspension of publication by the other papers. The struggle for freedom of speech is still a very living memory in Cuba. Opinion might be said to fall into two groups, one that says: "Let even the Communists speak," the other that says: "Let them talk, beginning with the Communists." The muzzling of the press by a dictatorship is followed by attack, revolt, anarchy. Where liberty exists, an incident leaves as its wake only two or three romantic heroes. Under a despotism order rests on many corpses.

Havana is one of the most beautiful cities of Latin America, and one of the largest. Its population today is approaching one million. It is an ideal city for international gatherings. It has free speech. Symbolically the two most impressive buildings the visitor finds in Havana are the Congress and the University.

In 1925 General Gerardo Machado, former manager of the Electric Power Company of Cuba, became President. The Liberal party elected him because of his administrative gifts. He announced that his would be a progressive government. He was favored by the last years of high sugar prices and large sales. But the bottom dropped out of the sugar market, and Machado's stock fell. He was a man of despotic temperament, and though he had been elected for a four-year term he extended his tenure and remained in power until he was overthrown in 1933. In 1930 the press had lost its freedom, the University had been seized by the army, and hundreds of students had been taken from the class room to jail and some to the cemetery. Gangster methods had been intro-

duced. Students, labor leaders, and men in public life began
to disappear mysteriously. Julio Antonio Mella, one of the
most brilliant figures in the opposition to Machado, had to
flee to Mexico City, where he was found murdered one day in
1927.

Corruption in office was widespread. Public works cost ex-
orbitant amounts. The Capitol, begun on an estimate of
$3,000,000, cost $20,000,000. Highways were constructed at
a figure twice that in the United States. The part taken
by the Chase National Bank in this chapter of Machado's
administration has been laid bare in an investigation conducted by the United States Senate on the operations of
banks in Latin America. At this same time there was a great
influx of American capital in Cuba: it has been estimated that
during this period it amounted to more than $100,000,000.
Cuba was to continue to be a sweet flower for the busy bees
of New York. The United States census of 1947 revealed the
fact that United States industrial investments alone in Cuba
were only slightly less than in Brazil: $65,000,000 in Brazil,
$64,000,000 in Cuba.

As pointed out above, Machado's rise and fall were closely
linked to the sugar market. He governed from 1925 to 1933.
Between 1921 and 1930 the duty on sugar entering the United
States went up from .0148—.016 cents in 1920 to .0176 in
1922 and .02 in 1930. "The result of these successive increases," writes Raúl Róa,[2] "was the decline in sugar exports
from 3,643,121 tons in 1929 to 1,396,119 in 1933. The price
of sugar dropped, at the same time, to less than one cent. In
1932 it reached .057, and in 1933 .053. During the same
period, as a result of North American protectionist policy, the
Philippines' exportation of sugar to the United States, duty
free, rose from 324,000 tons in 1924 to 1,141,000 in 1938;

[2] Raúl Roa, *Quince Años Después*, La Habana, Editorial Selecta, p.
184.

and that of Hawaii from 608,000 in 1924 to 950,000 in 1935. The figure for Puerto Rico was doubled . . ."

When Machado was tottering, the Chase National Bank extended a helping hand, lending him $50,000,000. Machado put the public works program under the control of the bank. Adverse opinion grew more and more hostile, the repression more drastic. The jails were full of students, but many had fled to Miami, where they organized campaigns of opposition. Secret societies were formed for the purpose of terminating Machado's rule. Communism took on unexpected strength, and from then on was to play an important role in Cuba's political life. The younger army officers, particularly Fulgencio Batista, an opportunist with the keenest faculty for detecting which way the wind is blowing, joined the opposition. The students marched through the streets shouting: "Down with Machado! Down with Yankee imperialism!" The casualties mounted. Enrique José Varona, the noblest figure in Cuban education, was brutally handled by the police. In the United States hair-raising accounts of Machado's bloody regime were published, and President Roosevelt sent Sumner Welles to pour oil on the troubled waters and persuade Machado to leave office. Machado held out as long as he could, but he finally (August 1933) climbed aboard a plane that left him in Bermuda.

The compromise Welles proposed—the replacement of Machado by Carlos Manuel de Céspedes—did not satisfy the Cubans, who demanded a more radical solution. Céspedes assumed power on August 12, 1933, and was forced out on September 5. A coalition *junta* headed by Dr. Ramón Grau San Martín took over, and lasted five days. On September 10 it handed over the power to Dr. Grau San Martín. Grau managed to govern for four months. He introduced a number of social reforms, created the Ministry of Labor, returned its autonomy to the University, ordered the secondary schools re-opened, attacked racial discrimination, and established woman's suffrage. Washington did not recognize him. When he left Havana, after turning the government over to Colonel Carlos Mendieta, the people saw him off at the dock with the applause and honors reserved for a liberator.

Colonel Mendieta took power in January 1934 and left it in December 1935. He was recognized by Washington. The strong man in the government was the commander of the army, Fulgencio Batista. From that moment everything that happened paved the way for Batista's rise to power. Colonel Mendieta was unable to govern, and he was followed by Miguel Mariano Gómez and Federico Laredo Brú. Under the latter, Batista came forward with his three-year plan, and launched his slogan "Cuba for the Cubans." He gathered up in one basket Communist, Falangist, and Nazi eggs, and he won the elections of 1940. Batista is the good-fellow type, a self-made, clever, unscrupulous man who came out of office a millionaire. His government had many points of resemblance to Machado's dictatorship, and the elections of 1944 represented the widespread disapproval of his rule: Batista was not what Cuba wanted, and Grau San Martín was chosen president once more. Grau was not so lucky this time. His government was corruption-ridden. The myth he incarnated when he took office was dissipated in the later years of his occupancy. He was succeeded by Carlos Prío Socarrás, who took office on October 10, 1948.

Prío Socarrás can show on the credit side of the ledger certain accomplishments: the National Bank, the Agricultural and Industrial Development Bureau, the University of Oriente, the work of the Secretariat of Culture in the Ministry of Education. But he is winding up, as is inevitable in Cuba, in the hurricane of electoral campaigning. Eduardo Chibás stirred up the masses with his impassioned speeches. With Chibás's death the Pueblo Cubano party lost its most forceful leader. Paradoxically, the possibility of the return of a figure of the old days, Fulgencio Batista, does not seem too far-fetched. Another force to be reckoned with is Communism. For some time now Cuban Communism has been the strongest in Latin America. Among its leaders are men of intellectual stature. It has been estimated that the party in Cuba has between fifteen and twenty thousand members. In the days of Machado it had already put forward the idea of a government of labor and agricultural soviets, and under Batista it won legal recognition. Prío Socorrás has been very outspoken in condemning and combatting it. "Here in Cuba," he said when the Second Conference of the CIT met in Havana in September 1949, "we are Cubans first, then Americans, and then world citizens . . . We can have no understanding with organizations that put other interests above those of Cuba; and for this reason we leave the Communists to the error of their ways. We allow them to shout to their heart's content, for we have faith that their rope of lies will hang them . . . But to us they are not Cubans, but the hirelings of a foreign power . . . Our attitude toward the Communists is not prejudiced . . . If the American Federation of Labor, for example, should attempt to carry on international efforts on behalf of the United States, placing the interests of that nation above those of Cuba, it would get the same treatment from us as the Communist Party."

One problem always hangs heavy over Cuba's economy, and it has made itself felt very forcibly on Prío Socarrás's government during its last months: the problem of sugar. The final episode to date has been the law passed by the United States Senate in 1951, reducing Cuba's sugar quota in favor of those of the Dominican Republic, Peru, and Puerto Rico. This law, which threatens the island's economic stability, has aroused deep resentment.

IV HAITI, LAND OF BONFIRES, DRUMS, AND VOODOO

I ONCE heard George S. Schuyler of the *Pittsburgh Courier* say in Brussels: "They ask us Negroes why we are not Communists. The answer is very simple, and the white people will never be able to feel it as we do. The memory of slavery is still very fresh in the mind of the Negro. He has experienced it in his own flesh. We are well informed about what goes on within the Russian frontiers. We don't want to be slaves again . . ."

Nowhere has the struggle for freedom been more hard-fought than in Haiti. It is the only instance of a nation of enslaved Negroes that challenged a great European power—the France of Napoleon Bonaparte—defeated it, and established itself as a republic. To bring the Haitians to heel, Napoleon sent to the island one of his best generals and a large, well-equipped army. The Negroes made them chew the bitter dust of defeat. The Haitians wanted to guard against the remotest possibility of ever again falling into the hands of their former masters, and King Henri-Cristophe erected on the summit of a mountain of Cap Haitien the Citadel, a fortress capable of housing, for months or for years, the whole population of the country. It might well be called the eighth man-made wonder of the world. No one can understand how the Haitians were able to haul to the mountaintop the heavy building materials and the huge cannon, which can still be seen there today. It was a feat comparable to the building of the Egyptian Pyramids. The machinery the Negro King used is not diagramed in the textbooks on engineering: it was the flame of liberty kept burning in each Negro by the magic throb of the voodoo drums that reverberated through the Haitian hills.

The labor pains of free Haiti's birth were excruciating. France finally withdrew, leaving the infant republic to starve. and to pay an indemnity of 60,000,000 francs. For France it was a bitter pill to have to give up a slave colony that yielded it several times England's return from its thirteen North American colonies put together.[3] An international vacuum surrounded the new republic.

A state of anarchy engulfed the island. Of the twenty-nine heads of state in Haiti from 1804 to 1922 only one completed his term of office and stepped down voluntarily, observing the law. Of the others, four retained power until they died of natural causes, eighteen were overthrown by revolution, one committed suicide, another was torn to shreds by a mob, and six were assassinated in other ways.

In 1915 the United States marines landed. Their mission was, in part, to carry out the self-imposed vigilance of the United States over the political life of the Caribbean, and in part to help the banks carry on their operations without risk. The Report of the United States Senate Select Committee on Haiti and Santo Domingo (June 26, 1922) summed up the situation as follows:

"The disorders of which Haiti has been subject since the achievement of its independence attained such destructive frequency during the last decade before the American intervention in 1915, that in the space of 10 years no less than eight presidents assumed office (it would be a mistake to say that they were elected) for the nominal constitutional term of 7 years each. Three of the eight fled the country; one was blown up in the presidential palace; another died mysteriously, and according to popular belief by poison, while two were murdered. The last Haitian President who held office before

[3] Raymond E. Crist: "Resources of the Caribbean" (in *The Caribbean at Mid-Century*, University of Florida Press, 1951).

the landing of the American forces was [Vilbrun Guillaume] Sam, who had caused several scores of political prisoners to be massacred as they huddled in their cells. He himself was dragged from the French Legation by a mob, his head and limbs were torn from his body to be carried aloft on sticks and bayonets, while his bleeding trunk was dragged through the streets of the capital city."

The American intervention lasted nineteen years. The Haitians hated the marines, and the marines felt as though they were living a foretaste of Hell's darkness and flames. The National City Bank made a good deal in 1922, making Haiti a loan of $40,000,000, receiving every possible guarantee. Between 1918 and 1920 the Haitians revolted because they did not want to work like slaves on a road-building project. They were killed off pitilessly. The marines finally were withdrawn by Franklin D. Roosevelt in 1934. The National City Bank sold its Port-au-Prince branch to Haiti for $1,000,000.

The overpopulation of the island—the Negroes multiply with extreme rapidity in Haiti, which is the most densely populated region of Latin America—drove many of them to seek work in the Dominican Republic. One day General Trujillo decided to kill them off. It was one of the most atrocious carnages the world has ever seen. It was so appalling that Trujillo agreed to pay Haiti an indemnity for the dead. He reckoned the coverage at $750,000, and paid the first installment punctually.

Haiti was governed until 1946 by Élie Lescot, who had been on Trujillo's payroll. He had come to power in 1941. The Haitians decided to get rid of him. The army removed him, and Dumarsais Estimé was elected president. As Estimé is a mulatto, and the people wanted a Negro, mourning, tears and clashes ensued. But Estimé moved tactfully and managed to stay in power until 1950. During the last years of his government he had to be on guard against plots hatched against him by Trujillo. The matter was brought before the Organization of American States, and it was proved that Trujillo had gone so far as to give money, through the secretary of his Embassy in Port-au-Prince, to those who were to overthrow Estimé. The Organization of American States had to speak severely to Trujillo.

In 1950 Estimé fell from power, and was succeeded by a governing *junta*. The Negroes ousted the mulattoes from office because in their eyes the mulattoes constituted an oppressive oligarchy.

V PUERTO RICO, COFFEE AND SUGAR

PUERTO RICO is an island of coffee and sugar hanging suspended between the world that was Spanish and the English world. When it was first governed by the United States, English was made the official language in the schools. But the Puerto Rican is born and bred in Spanish, and the experiment failed. This is Puerto Rico's drama. The language means to the Puerto Ricans many aspects of life, of history, of the point of view from which they judge the passing moment. Now Spanish is again taught in the schools. One of the great men of Spanish America, of the entire Spanish-speaking world, was born in Puerto Rico and belongs to its history: Eugenio María de Hostos (1839–1903). Today the University at Río Piedras—one of the better universities of America—is raising the cultural level of the island. The review *Asomante*, published in Río Piedras, is considered one of the best periodicals in the Spanish-speaking world. The tiny island is literally unable to hold its population, which proliferates without check, pause, or repose. In 1900 it had 953,243 inhabitants; in 1920, over one million, and in 1940 1,869,255; it had passed the two million mark in 1950. Today Puerto Rico has two major cities, San Juan and New York. In San Juan, with its 237,623 inhabitants, many of the people live, poor though most of them are, with a measure of stability and do not set out to seek their fortune elsewhere. The Puerto Ricans in New York, where they number half a million, are those whom economic necessity has forced to emigrate. At first just the men emigrated; now whole families go to New York.

Puerto Rico's economy has oscillated between coffee and sugar. Coffee was cultivated there, as in Colombia, Guatemala, and Costa Rica, on the inland hillsides in the shade of protecting trees, and those who lived by it gathered in gay comradeship at the picking season and then went back to their mountain shacks. But a hurricane, one of the Caribbean scourges, destroyed the sheltering trees and up-rooted the plantations, and the people had to move in mass to the cane fields, where a poverty-stricken, dissatisfied pro-letariat sprang up.

The Puerto Ricans in Puerto Rico have done much to re-claim the land, and the results have been good. Vocational schools have been more active there than anywhere else in Latin America. Under way is a huge project that includes ir-rigation, reforestation, diversification of crops, the founding of government loan banks, the opening of new markets, and a better organization of the rural communities. "Puerto Rico," says Ramón Colón Torres,[4] "is, despite its limited area, a land of contrasts. In a space of 3500 square miles there are 128 varieties of soil representing 327 different types and phases of geological development. There are seven different areas of rainfall, which vary from an average of 200 inches of pre-cipitation annually in the mountains of the north to 30 in the southwestern plains."

On a political platform whose motto was "Bread, Land, and Liberty" Luis Muñoz Marín conducted a campaign that put

---

[4] *The Caribbean at Mid-Century*, p. 112.

him in as Governor in 1948. His program, now in the process of realization, encompasses a vast effort to transform the land and give the Puerto Ricans decent living conditions.

The life of the Puerto Ricans in New York is in marked contrast to this. The problems involved in the struggle for existence too often blacken their name on the police blotters. Rabble-rousing politicians after their votes make them extravagant promises. They live in Harlem alongside the Negroes, in dirty, run-down tenement houses abounding in filth and rats. They have gone back to a kind of primitive magic, trying to find in the realm of the irrational the defenses their own efforts cannot provide them. This explains the brisk trade carried on in Harlem in colored candles, dreambooks, potions, philtres, charms, and prayers combining African, Spanish, and gypsy formulas.

While it formed a part of Spain's colonial empire, Puerto Rico suffered the same ups and downs as the other colonies. It was settled by Ponce de León, the indefatigable seeker after the magic fountain of eternal youth. In the seventeenth century it discovered a fountain of progress and good business —occasionally interrupted by plundering raids—in its dealings with corsairs, pirates, and filibusters. In the eighteenth century it benefited from the progressive ideas of Economic Societies animated by the ideas of the Enlightenment. It had a foretaste of parliamentary life at the time of the Cortés of Cádiz, and though it failed to achieve independence at the beginning of the nineteenth century, in 1897 it was granted autonomy within the Spanish empire. But the next year came the sinking of the *Maine* in Havana harbor and the Spanish-American War. In consequence, two weeks after Puerto Rico had inaugurated the legislative bodies provided for by the terms of its autonomy, a United States government was set up there. By the terms of the peace treaty between Spain and the United States, Puerto Rico became a possession of the United States.

"The North American occupation of the island," says Arturo Morales Carrión,[5] "did not ostensibly pursue a policy of intervening, as it did in the case of Cuba, to insure victory for the insurgents and set up an independent nation under United States protection. Puerto Rico was in the nature of a marginal operation for strategic ends. It was animated by the expansionist drive of the younger generation of the Republican Party, which looked to establishing North American supremacy in the Caribbean and controlling the approaches to the projected canal across the Isthmus. Captain A. T. Mahan, apostle of the naval power of the United States, wrote on the heels of the occupation of the island: 'Puerto Rico, from the military point of view, is with relation to Cuba, to the future Isthmian canal and our Pacific coast, what Malta is, or can be, to Egypt; and it is just as necessary for us to hold and fortify the first, in its entirety and in its immediate environs, as it is for Great Britain to hold the second to insure its position in Egypt, its use of the Suez Canal, and its protection of the route to India.' "

Puerto Rico was drawn into the economic orbit of the United States, but remained outside its way of life. It was governed by a Washington appointee, without its people having a share in governing themselves. The United States Senate passed a law forbidding landholdings in excess of 500 acres. "But, since the resolution fixed no penalties for those who violated it, it was not respected," writes Raymond E. Crist. "By 1930, violators of the 500-acre law—367 out of a total of 58,371 landholders—controlled almost one-third of all farmland, whereas farms of less than 20 acres, comprising 72 per cent of existing farms, occupied only 12.4 of all farmland." The large sugar companies had, naturally, been busy extending their *latifundios*, thus steering Puerto Rican economy into dangerous channels.

With regard to its incorporation into the United States, there have been very different trends of thought in Puerto

[5] *Ojeada al Proceso Histórico de Puerto Rico.* Puerto Rico, 1950.

Rico. At an earlier date, José Celso Barbosa, chief of the ortho-
dox autonomists, was in favor of Puerto Rico's demanding ad-
mission as the 49th state of the union, while Luis Muñoz
Rivera, founder of the Liberal party, favored autonomy. The
poet José de Diego insisted on a separate status for the island
and exalted its Hispanic culture. Eugenio María de Hostos
founded the Patriotic League whose ideal was a great Antillean
confederation.

In 1947 President Truman signed the bill giving Puerto
Rico the right to elect its own governor. On November 2,
1948, Luis Muñoz Marín was elected to the post.

The two figures about whom Puerto Rican politics crystal-
lize are Muñoz Marín and Pedro Albizu Campos. Muñoz
Marín favors autonomy. "The proponents of nationalism," he
says, "prefer the despotic government of their own to the
democratic rule of those removed from them." Albizu Campos
demands absolute independence.

Albizu Campos is a product of Harvard, where he studied
law, and of his condition as a mulatto, which has left him
with resentful memories of the North American university.
He has read widely and has distinct personal charm. With a
touch of the mystic and the magician, he combines qualities
of a patriot and a demagogue. "He is anti-imperialist, anti-
Yankee, and vehemently pro-Hispanic. He attacks Masonry
and staunchly defends the Catholic Church, more as a
weapon of combat than out of religious conviction. He at-
tired his handful of followers in black shirts, and inculcated
them with a military discipline, not without its Fascistoid
touches." [6] More than this, Albizu's followers are fanatics willing to risk their lives. In 1932, they put up candidates for election and polled only 10,000 votes. Smarting under this defeat,
they began a campaign of terrorism. Two of Albizu's followers
assassinated the chief of police of San Juan and were immediately shot down. On October 30, 1950, five of his men assaulted

[6] Morales Carrión, *op. cit.*

La Fortaleza, the residence of Governor Muñoz Marín, and attempted to assassinate him. On November 1 of the same year two members of the party tried to break through the guards of Blair House to kill President Truman. Albizu was put in prison in Puerto Rico, not the first time this had happened to him as a result of his fight against the United States.

Muñoz Marín, too, received part of his education in the United States. He did not attend so illustrious an institution as Harvard, but lived in New York's Bohemian center, Greenwich Village. At that time he had Socialist leanings. The Russian and Mexican revolutions attracted him. His first inclination was toward independence for Puerto Rico. Originally a member of the old Liberal party, he later worked out a new program and founded the Party of the People. He was elected governor by an overwhelming majority in 1948. His party slogan is that of the mountaineers as they ascend the hills: "*Jalda arriba*" (Up and On!).

The election of Muñoz Marín marks a new era in the life of Puerto Rico. Whatever party takes the lead in his administration, it will be impossible to overlook the fact that the Governor freely chosen by the island's people has formed an administration much superior to the governments of those who formerly represented the authority of Washington.

VI CARIBBEAN MEANS ARCHIPELAGO

To sum up, the Caribbean is a setting against which some of the most exciting performances in the human comedy are being played. It is the theater of America. The United States and Mexico to the North and Colombia and Venezuela to the South, are the spectators of a play in unnumbered acts between republics and empires. "In the great arch of colonial territories," says Paul Blanshard, "that stretches from the

Bahamas on the north to French Guiana on the south, more than 2,000 miles, there are almost 6,000,000 people living under the flags of four great powers, about 3,000,000 under the rule of Great Britain, 3,000,000 under the United States, 600,000 under France, and 300,000 under the Netherlands." [7]

In the Panama Canal the United States has one of the most important bases of its military power and the artery through which world trade circulates. Only a step away is Venezuela with its oil wells. In the green fields of the sugar islands and in the "banana" republics, United States stockholders have invested fabulous sums, and they keep their eyes glued on the moving ball of the political roulette wheel. The ambitions of international interests and of the native caudillos are as violent as the hurricanes that sweep the region; they prevent the Antillean world from uniting and that of Central America from federating. There is something symbolic in the fact that the chain of islands stretching from Trinidad to Cuba and the Bahamas is the peaks of a submerged mountain range. It seems as though the unity of the West Indies had been swallowed up by the sea in a similar cosmic cataclysm. The people of the islands and of the Caribbean coast compensate for their political drama with an outpouring of song, dance, and rum. Each of the islands has a name of its own on the liquor map. Anyone who goes to the Caribbean catches the contagion of these things. Despotism is not a native disease. There is a dreary monotony about all the regimes that have ruled there: French, English, North American, German, Dutch, Spanish, African. The Danes, whose fairy tales related by Hans Christian Andersen delighted our childhood days—and delight us now—issued a law in the Virgin Islands at the end of the eighteenth century which runs as follows: "The leader of runaway slaves shall be pinched three times with a red-hot iron, then hung. Each other runaway slave shall lose one leg, or if the owner pardons him,

[7] *Democracy and Empire in the Caribbean,* Macmillan, 1947.

shall lose one ear and receive one hundred and fifty stripes . . ."
It is worth noting that there are places in this continent of
freedom where similar procedures are still employed.

There lives in Puerto Rico a distinguished scientist, Carlos
E. Chardón, whose work in the field of agronomy and plant
pathology has blazed a trail for his followers. Dr. Chardón
says:[8]

"We must consider first that the Caribbean is a *geographical region*; and second, that we are dealing also with a series
of *political entities*. For more than three centuries the political patterns have prevailed over the geographical reality,
which has brought about a disarticulated economy among the
islands forming part of an archipelago. In considering separately the political units and their problems, by far the majority of students have neglected the fact that in a sound
economy the political units (without interference with their
sovereignties or those of the metropolitan governments) may
in many cases play an important economic role with reference to the economy of the others. So far, efforts have been
isolated and fragmentary; the perspective of the whole has
been ignored, and each country or each colony or group of
colonies, has fought its own battle, trying to solve its problems independently. This reminds us of the man who failed to
see the forest for the trees."

These words of Dr. Chardón must be set against the reflections of the Cuban writer Herminio Portell Vilá:

"The insular world which Franklin used to call the 'Sugar
Islands' is potentially very rich and has a larger combined
foreign trade than all the countries in South America put together, Argentina and Brazil excepted. The Greater Antilles,
that is Cuba, Haiti, the Dominican Republic, Puerto Rico,
and Jamaica have a combined total population of more than
fifteen million people or almost the population of Argentina,

[8] *Scientific Monthly*, September, 1949 (quoted by Raymond F. Crist
in *Resources of the Caribbean*).

though the four islands do not cover the territorial extension
of the province of Buenos Aires. Helped by Cuba's whop-
ping foreign trade of more than twelve hundred million dollars a year, the people of the Greater Antilles account for
nearly two billion dollars in imports and exports . . .

"For years the only universities were to be found in Cuba,
the Dominican Republic, and Puerto Rico, but Haiti has
lately added hers. The old Institute of Jamaica has just become a University of Jamaica, and across the strait separat-
ing her from Cuba, the new University of Oriente is offering
its third course. The Dutch give the last touches to their University of Surinam, thus doing in the New World what they
never did in the East Indies for the Indonesians. The French
are conspicuously absent in the general trend toward the creation of more universities in the Caribbean . . ." [9]

To bring the islands together in one political system is difficult. It would be like asking the submerged mountain range
to rise and turn the archipelago into mainland. What may
reasonably be hoped for is the growing strength of general
cultural movements and a better economic understanding, and
that certain universal laws, such as the rights of man, which
recognize human dignity, will be accepted by the local authorities. Unless respresentative democratic systems can be
made to grow in the Caribbean, the people will put their
trust in magic or gunpowder. Because deep in the heart of
the people is an altar before which they secretly pray that a
hurricane will come along with its voodoo drums and carry
off the Trujillos.

In Central America a new hope has arisen. In October
1951 the foreign ministers of El Salvador, Guatemala, Costa
Rica, Nicaragua, and Honduras met in San Salvador for a preliminary discussion of the bases for a new union of Central
America. It is regrettable that the foreign minister of Panama
was not invited. The document that was signed has received the

[9] "The Caribbean Today" (*The Pan American*, November, 1949).

name of the Salvador Charter. It was officially stated that the purpose of this charter was to bring about joint action to strengthen the ties of brotherhood among the five states of Central America and to create instruments for the study and solution of their common problems. The statutes of the new organization will be submitted by the foreign ministers to their respective congresses for approval. But even before this takes place, a *de facto* secretariat will begin to function in San Salvador. Special committees will be named to study the special problems of each country. The economic committee will work toward a customs union, the committee for education on a unification of the programs of study and the establishment of a Central University of Central America. This is an outgrowth of Resolution 23 of the Conference of Bogotá, in which the foreign ministers agreed "to combine the forces of the five republics of Central America to endeavor to find a solution to the problem of Belize [British Honduras] within the framework of the just and traditional aspirations of the Americas."

XVI

MEXICO, OR THE EAGLE AND
THE SERPENT

*I was born in Mexico, capital of northern America, in New
Spain.*
FERNÁNDEZ DE LIZARDI

> *Raise, proud America,*
> *Your crownéd head;*
> *Spread wing, American eagle,*
> *In imperial flight.*
> SOR JUANA INÉS DE LA CRUZ

MEXICO'S HISTORY differs from that of the rest of America.
When the Spaniards came to Mexico they found there not the
Aztec empire alone, but many other kingdoms with their own
cultures, their own languages, with cities and huge temples
serving other gods. Mexico was not one nation, but a continent. The colony established there after the conquest assumed
a grandeur unknown elsewhere. The emancipation was not
the work of generals like Bolívar and San Martín, nor were
the architects of the republic men like Juan Bautista Alberdi
of Argentina, Francisco de Paula Santander of Colombia, or
Andrés Bello of Venezuela. "The independence and the reform," says Justo Sierra, the great Mexican historian, "are
wholly the work of the boundless energy of the mongrel race
of Mexico." In order to survive as a nation Mexico has had
to combat foreign powers who attacked only Mexico.

The empire of the Aztecs was so lordly that the Spaniards
with all their power were unable to blot out its traces. Its

heroes still weigh heavily in the scales of history, and there is not a Mexican who accepts Cortés's superiority over Cuauhtémoc. Works in praise of Cortés have been written outside Mexico since the time of López de Gómara (1552), and the list of their titles is imposing, yet one would look in vain to find a single monument honoring him in Mexico. But in the center of the city, in a circle of the Paseo de la Reforma stand a statue of Cuauhtémoc as the national hero of the sixteenth century. The Mexican, Leopoldo Zea, could not get over his astonishment when he visited Peru at seeing in the main square of Lima a monument to Francisco Pizarro, but none to Atahuallpa.

There are still millions of Indians in Mexico, but these are Indians who were once civilized. Their rise today is a return to what they once were, is in the nature of a renaissance. The descriptions left us by the conquistadors of the city of Mexico as they found it reveal that there was nothing finer in sixteenth-century Spain. To Bernal Díaz del Castillo it seemed like something out of the enchanted pages of *Amadis de Gaula*. Others compared it with the cities of Italy. In order to capture it, Cortés had to ally himself with great Indian armies hostile to the Aztecs. From the lake on which it was built emerged its white pyramids with their colored friezes. From all parts of the empire Indians came along the highways or by boat on the canals to a market richer than any Spain could boast and hardly equaled by the best in Europe. Tens of thousands of merchants, nobles, slaves, priests, and warriors filled its immense squares, its temples, the gardens and palaces of Moctezuma. These Indians did not know the wheel, or gunpowder, or iron or horses, but they did have paper, books, architecture, gods, refinement in their table manners, in their cooking, in their dress, and in their habits of cleanliness, to all of which the accounts of the Spanish historians bear abundant witness.

The Cathedral of Mexico City is still the greatest temple

on this continent and one of the largest in the world. The Cathedral of Puebla is not far behind. Why did the Spaniards build these mammoth monuments in Mexico? So that their religion would not seem less impressive than that of the conquered Indians. The Cathedral in Mexico City was built on the very site where the Indians had built their sacred pyramid. Excavations carried on in the streets adjoining the Cathedral have laid bare the foundations of the Aztec temple with its monsters carved in stone; it was no less admirable than is the Spanish church that took its place. From the pyramid came the stones to build churches, palaces, sidewalks. It was impossible for the Spaniards to efface all the sacred images, the symbols of the ancient faith, and so they buried them. The Aztec Calendar Stone was not found until sewers were being laid during the last century. Today we see great Catholic churches scattered about the Mexican countryside far from any city. They are there because the Spaniards were obliged to erect impressive testimony of the civilization they had brought if they hoped to blur the memory of past grandeur.

But the memory endured. Four centuries have passed, and the shadows of the past still project their images. At times they become luminous. The 25,000,000 inhabitants of Mexico today are for the most part *mestizos*, part Indian, part Spanish. And the *mestizo* is alert of spirit, ready to awake. Toynbee has acutely observed a phenomenon that he sums up in these words:

"The Russians have taken up a Western secular social philosophy, Marxism; you might equally well call Marxism a Christian heresy, a leaf torn out of the book of Christianity and treated as if it were the whole gospel. The Russians have taken up this Western heretical religion, transformed it into something of their own, and are now shooting it back at us. This is the first shot in the anti-Western counteroffensive; but this Russian counter-discharge in the form of Communism may come to seem a small affair when the probably far more potent civilizations of India and China respond in their turn to our Western challenge. In the long run China and India seem likely to produce much deeper effects in our Western life than Russia can ever hope to produce with her Communism. But even the comparatively feeble native civilization of Mexico is beginning to react. The revolution through which Mexico has been passing since A. D. 1910 may be interpreted as the first move to shake off the top-dressing of Western civilization which we imposed on Mexico in the sixteenth century . . ." [1]

The court of Moctezuma was a dazzling one. The Spaniards replaced it with a viceroyalty that reproduced the court of Spain. Mexico was called New Spain. During the three centuries of the viceroyalty the capital was beautified, adorned, refined, until of the lake on which it had been built there remained only the memory and a few canals. Temples and palaces sprang up. Through the huge central square there now moved nobles and magistrates, friars of many orders, inquisitors, captains—*gachupines*, the opprobious name the Mexicans applied to the Spaniards—in picturesque clothes of velvet and lace, with buckles of silver, their horses caparisoned like those on playing cards, or in sombre ecclesiastic habits. There were litters of red and gold or inlaid with silver. On Sundays the Paseo de la Alameda was as animated as a Paris boulevard, and there were medieval processions and bullfights. There was jousting in the square, and crimson damask hangings glowed in the windows . . . Until the day the liberty bell of Dolores rang out in 1810.

It was Father Manuel Hidalgo who sounded the tocsin of the revolution. In Mexico it did not happen as in Caracas or Santa Fe de Bogotá or Buenos Aires, where the Creoles, practically Spaniards, presided over a people's assembly and

[1] Arnold J. Toynbee, *Civilization on Trial*. Oxford University Press, 1948.

assumed the generalships. Here it was the village priest who rose with the Indians and restive *mestizos* against the aristocracy of the *gachupines* and the monarchical, inquisitorial Church. A few months later Father Hidalgo faced a firing squad. His place was taken by another priest, José María Morelos, who threw his cassock over his shoulder, mounted his horse, and rode off to war. He, too, was captured by the Spaniards, tried by the Inquisition, excommunicated by the Church, and shot. But the Independence had been accomplished. Hidalgo and Morelos carried as their banner the image of the dark Lady of Guadalupe, the Spaniards that of the blonde Virgin of los Remedios. When a flag fell into enemy hands, the rebels shot the Virgin of los Remedios, the Spaniards Our Lady of Guadalupe. Hidalgo and Morelos declared slavery abolished, promised the Indians the return of their lands, and ended class privileges. The revolution began in 1810. Or perhaps before.

Finally a general appeared on the scene, Agustín Iturbide, who had all the deviousness that characterized the viceregal court. He fought under the flag of the revolution, entered Mexico City in triumph, and shortly afterward (1822) had a few soldiers acclaim him emperor. He was crowned in the Cathedral, but his empire was short-lived. He had to flee, but then he returned and was shot.

The military, the monarchical clergy, the conservatives would not resign themselves to having the pompous occupants of the golden thrones overthrown. In 1864 they imported an Emperor and Empress from Europe, Maximilian and Carlota. The Castle of Chapultepec on the crest of a hill in a wooded park gives Mexico City something of the charm of Edinburgh. From the imperial residence there the Emperor and Empress observed that there was no more respect for crowned heads in Mexico than in Scotland. And while Carlota, in despair, went knocking at every royal door in Europe in the hope of securing aid and support, Maximilian was taken before a firing squad at Querétaro: a volley of bullets ended his imperial career. The *mestizos* killed him. To them, says Justo Sierra, "Maximilian was not a divinity, but an enemy."

In 1884 Porfirio Díaz made himself dictator, bringing in an enlightened despotism of festivities, political prisoners, and railroads. He was like an emperor, too, but as he was home-grown and foxy he remained in power until 1911. In 1911 the clock ran out for him. With Francisco Madero began the cycle of revolutions, the wide hats and crossed cartridge belts, the bristling mustaches that reeked of powder. Pancho Villa's troops advanced to the music of "*La Cucaracha*" and "*Adelita.*"

Mexico's fight has been to break up empires and reduce them to the simple, common terms of a republic. In the rest of America there had not been this mortmain of empire— Tizoc, Axayacatl, Moctezuma, Cuauhtémoc, Iturbide, Maximilian. For this reason the Mexican Revolution is closer akin to that of France or Russia than to other Latin American revolutions. There are streets in the history of Mexico that are like those of Paris or St. Petersburg. The people watched the mighty fall and the lowly rise, and sang:

> *Crash! went the tree*
> *Where the peacock used to roost;*
> *Now let him sleep on the ground*
> *As the rest of the animals do . . .*

The Church was always involved in these upheavals. Its economic power was very great. It had vast holdings of land, and much of the urban property was in its hands. There were revolutionary priests and monarchical priests. Benito Juárez— the Well-Deserving of America, as the Radicals of Colombia called him—expropriated the holdings of the Church and gave his government the name the Protestants had employed in their struggle in Europe, the Reform. The most beautiful street in Mexico bears this name in honor of Juárez: Paseo de la Reforma. In 1950, when the *sinarquistas*, the clerical and Falangist party, held a demonstration in Mexico, they marched to Juárez's statue and bedaubed it with verbal and other filth, and scrawled on the walls of the government palace by night: "Juárez is in Hell." The average Mexican has a much greater awareness of his history than other Americans. The fact that his national hero, Morelos, was condemned by the Inquisition; that the dictator Antonio López de Santa Ana rose to power on the shoulders of the clericals, the military, and the conservatives; that Maximilian went to receive the papal benediction before setting out to occupy a throne that did not belong to him; that Alvaro Obregón was assassinated by fanatical Catholics—these are all factors which keep alive the state of conflict between the Church and the Revolution. This clash was less acute in the rest of America. The Church elsewhere did not take such a stubborn stand in the political struggle, nor was the State so uncompromising. In Mexico there was a moment when the conflict between Church and state reached unbelievable intensity. In 1926 the Archbishop of Mexico ordered the Catholics not to obey certain constitutional decrees that he considered prejudicial to the Church. President Plutarco Elías Calles's answer was to expel all non-native priests, nationalize all Church property, and forbid religious teaching in the schools. This war without quarter lasted for years. In 1932 the Pope issued an encyclical condemning the legal persecution of the Church. The Papal Legate was deported by congressional order. The Mexican states passed laws limiting the number of priests. In Chiapas the clergy was reduced to four to attend to the spiritual needs of a population of 500,000. In Tabasco, Catholic priests were forbidden to officiate unless they first married. The Church closed its places of worship. The government closed the religious schools.

Only now are there signs of understanding. In 1936 President Lázaro Cárdenas did much to smooth out the state of affairs. In 1951 the Mexican episcopate published a joint pastoral letter in honor of the fortieth anniversary of the "*Rerum Novarum*" encyclical. Detaching themselves from all political affiliations "and speaking in the name of a people that by the grace of God and the special guardianship of Santa María of Guadalupe is still in its great majority Catholic," the bishops employed terms approaching those of the revolution. Among other things the letter says:

"We regard the proletariat of our native land not as an individual or racial phenomenon, but as a collective social phenomenon; like the proletariat created in other countries by capitalist industrialism, great masses of our people live like the excommunicated, shut off from the temporal benefits of society, and outside the human community as a result of their bitter poverty.

"Under these subhuman conditions, where every vice finds a breeding-place, these masses are almost unable to receive the advantages of spiritual, divine teaching. As always, for the Church to make its message heard, and above all, for the people to accept it, there has to be at least a minimum of well-being (*Rerum Novarum*). This minimum is not present among the proletariat . . .

"We have no hesitation in affirming with the Pope 'that it is your obligation to fight for a more equitable distribution of wealth.' This is and continues to be the heart of the Catholic social doctrine. The natural development of things unquestionably carries with it certain limitations and an unequal distribution of the world's goods. The Church is opposed to the accumulation of these goods in the hands of relatively small groups while the great masses are doomed to hunger and to an economic status unworthy of human beings."

Mexico is the most anti-Yankee of all the Latin American countries, notwithstanding the fact that nowhere else in Indo-America are so many visitors from the North enchanted with the country and the proofs of good neighborliness they receive. A Mexico City cartoonist good-humoredly pointed up the anti-Mexican attitude of Texas, drawing two restaurants facing each other across the border. The one on the United States side had a sign reading: "No Mexicans allowed." That on the Mexican side read: "Even Yankees allowed."

But the Mexican has an almost morbid awareness of his nationality, and its roots go deep. Mexico is the only country of the continent that has had to fight its war of independence several times. In the rest of America the Spaniards, the English, the French, the Portuguese received their *congé*, and that was that. There was no attempt to reconquer the emancipated colonies, and each republic went its own way. In Mexico in 1846 there was an American invasion, and General Winfield Scott marched into the capital. The Mexicans still commemorate the sacrifice of the "boy heroes," the cadets of Chapultepec. By the terms of the Treaty of Guadalupe Hidalgo (1848) Mexico was stripped of half its territory. The largest states in the United States—Texas, California, New Mexico—are of Mexican origin. In 1836 the French dispatched a fleet that took Vera Cruz, and Mexico had to pay $600,000 to get rid of Louis-Philippe's sailors. In 1862 the English, French, and Spaniards formed a league against Mexico, French troops disembarked in Vera Cruz, invaded the country, and set Maximilian on his brief throne. In 1916 General Pershing led a punitive expedition against Pancho Villa.

These experiences have left the Mexican with a belligerency, a defensive attitude against the powers that have reduced his territory, killed his countrymen, and imposed foreign governments upon him. To the Mexican the date May 5, commemorating the defeat of the French in Puebla, is as important as September 16, when Father Hidalgo raised the standard of freedom against the Spaniards. And he sings with wicked delight the ballad telling how Pancho Villa and his guerrillas outwitted General Pershing's army:

In Chihuahua and Ciudad Juárez
People stared and were amazed
To see all the gringos and carrancistas
Whose ears Pancho Villa had shaved.

So you thought, spay-footed "bolillos,"
Your cannon would make us quake!
So you've got your squads of airplanes!
We've got what it really takes.

But Mexico's attitude is not merely a negative one. It both denies and affirms. Over the ashes of the revolution Emiliano Zapata—a machine gun of flesh and blood—advanced under a flag that had for its motto these two words: "Land and Schools." The Revolution had promised two thousand new schools a year. Cárdenas came to power and exceeded the promise. In five years the attendance at the schools rose from 1,400,000 children to 1,800,000, and since 1920 illiteracy has gone down from 75% to 45%. The Revolution expropriated the lands of the wealthy which were not under cultivation. 17,980 acres in Chihuahua that belonged to William Randolph Hearst were confiscated in 1938. By 1945 the number of farmers who had become owners of a plot of land under the agrarian laws rose to 1,812,936.

In 1938 the oil wells were expropriated. Perón, with all his demagoguery about nationalization in Argentina, has never taken such a determined stand. Cárdenas was carrying out not an administrative decision, but a national affirmation. He interpreted the wishes of the Mexicans, who wanted the wells to be theirs whether they were worked or not. Frank Tannenbaum, who was in Mexico at the time, writes:[2]

"The oil expropriation in 1938 over a labor dispute that was on the verge of compromise was politically motivated. When the oil companies declared that they would not obey

[2] *Mexico: The Struggle for Peace and Bread*, Alfred A. Knopf, 1950.

the decisions of the Mexican Supreme Court, they impugned the dignity of the President and assumed a position that amounted to rebellion. When they did this by announcing in public advertisements that from then on they were not responsible for what might happen to the country, they precipitated a political crisis that, morally speaking, could be met in only one way. Cárdenas acted in defense of what seemed to him the essentials of national dignity, and the response from the people was such as to unify the country as it had never been unified before. Cárdenas became a national idol, even to his opponents. At last a President had come upon the scene who was not afraid to bridle the foreign interests and to assert that the national estate and dignity had to be protected at all hazards.

"The flood of popular enthusiasm was so great as to be almost pathetic. Men felt as if a new day had dawned. Simple Indians in their bare feet brought their pennies, or even a chicken or a pig, and offered them to the President toward the payment of the expropriated industries. Even the Church permitted collections in front of its doors for the payment of this debt. Cárdenas remarked that this was the first time in many generations that the Church had publicly supported the government. He was pleased with having finally broken the impasse between the Church and the State. Two years earlier he had used his influence to bring the persecution of the Church to an end."

Around 1921 José Vasconcelos held the post of Secretary of Education, and he strongly fostered arts and letters in their expression of the principles of the Revolution. From that time Diego Rivera, José Clemente Orozco, and David Alfaro Siqueiros launched a wave of mural paintings which stands as one of the most vigorous achievements of art in our time. The Russian revolution has not produced a single painter who bears comparison with these Mexicans. The Mexicans have drenched with color the schools, the libraries, the stairway of

329

the Presidential Palace, the Palace of Cortés, the Supreme Court. If all the books written in this era should disappear, these murals would suffice to reconstruct the history of these fervent years of Mexican endeavor in all its extremes.

In the early murals it is not unusual to find flags inscribed with the words of the *corridos* (ballads) of the Revolution intermingled with the hammer and sickle. Even today every now and then Diego Rivera informs the world that he is a Communist. The Mexicans saw in the revolution that overthrew the czar a movement similar to that of Mexico—that is to say, the redemption of the oppressed through a union of peasants and workers, who would substitute republics of workers for the capitalist or military governments. The mural Diego Rivera painted in the Palace of Cortés in Cuernavaca shows the tyrannical conquistadors flogging the Indians, branding the slaves, and building their colony on the blood, sweat, and tears of the vanquished. In the National Palace the villains are the Yankees and the clergy. Orozco held justice up to scorn in the Supreme Court building. For the museum in Chapultepec Castle he painted a gigantic head of the Indian Juárez, after the manner of the paintings of Lenin in Russia, against a red flag. Beneath the flag, scurrying like cockroaches, go Goyesque images of death wearing the Jesuit biretta pushing the catafalque carrying the remains of Emperor Maximilian into the fires of Hell. The Mexican atheists cannot do without Hell: it has to exist so that they can cast the enemies of their cause into its flames. But Rivera has done other frescos in which he evokes the ancient marketplaces of Tenochtitlán or paints the Indians coming from the floating gardens of Xochimilco with their baskets of flowers; and there are those of Orozco's which exalt universal, enduring love.

Some critics have thought that the Mexican painters went to Italy for inspiration for these monumental works and found it in the Sistine Chapel, in the churches of Florence, in

Giotto's murals. This is a mistake. Their painting was in the
tradition of Mexico. In Teotihuacán, as well as in the far-off
empire of the Maya, there are paintings of this sort done
centuries ago. Today in Bonampak we can see the dances,
the wars, the ceremonies, the crafts, the dress, the musical
instruments of the Indians in frescoes painted twelve hundred years ago. And everything is there, with its color, its
movement, its meaning. There was nothing of the sort in the
European painting of the same period.

A characteristic of the Mexican Revolution is that everything had to be set down in color on walls. It was not a revolution of black ink on newsprint. Orozco claimed to have
painted twenty square kilometers. The last thing on which he
worked before his death was a religious fresco for the Church
of Jesus.

How did the Mexican Revolution begin? What were its
dates? Is the Mexico of today still in the process of revolution, or is it the creation of the Revolution?

The revolution was set afoot by Francisco I. Madero, on a
two-plank platform: effective suffrage and no re-election; distribution of the land. The first was to put an end to Porfirio
Díaz's regime and avoid future self-perpetuating dictatorships.
Díaz had first been elected President in 1877, and from then
on he had dominated the Mexican scene without let or hindrance. He was re-elected in 1884, 1888, 1892, 1900, 1904 . . .
Enough was enough! In 1910 all Mexico swung into action
behind Madero. The Revolution brought to an end an epoch
that had signified both progress and enslavement.

Díaz's name is associated with every advance in Mexico
over a period of thirty years. But this was not so much his
accomplishment as the general trend of the times. The same
thing was happening all over the world. If, during the time
he held power, there had been six presidents, the credit
would have been divided among the six of them. One would
have established telegraph communication; another would

have built this or that railroad; another would have beautified the capital, another would have put through a road-building program. But as there was only one instead of six, everything that was done in Mexico for a third of a century was chalked up to Porfirio Díaz's eredit.

What Mexico lost during those years was training in representative government, the effective use of its franchise. In this sense Porfirio Díaz was more harmful than Iturbide or Maximilian or Santa Ana. In 1911 Díaz had to flee the country and Madero was elected President.

Madero was a civilian. He had studied at the University of California and polished off his education in France. His chief weapon against Díaz was his book, *La Sucesión Presidencial de 1910.* The fervor and sincerity with which he addressed the illiterate masses won him the name of "Apostle." The circumstances of the situation made him the leader of an army that could more properly be called a mob. But Madero lacked the invulnerable authority backed by lead and steel, and the path he had chosen lead to martyrdom. He was assassinated by the forces of General Victoriano Huerta in 1913.

Like the coldblooded monster he was, Huerta endeavored to set himself up by stamping out the live embers of Madero's work. To overthrow him, to raise the banner of revolution once more and carry out the program of social justice which was its other aim, it was necessary for the generals to step into the breach. And generals were to succeed one another in the presidency. The last to hold office was General Manuel Ávila Camacho (1940–46). Not until 1946 did the Revolution feel itself secure or accomplished. Then, for the first time since Madero, a civilian was elected, Miguel Alemán.

From Madero to Cárdenas every Mexican, whether president or unknown peasant, was a bullfighter moving within reach of the horns of death. President Venustiano Carranza and President Alvaro Obregón were assassinated, as Madero had been. Emiliano Zapata, the guerrilla leader of the South, whose figure appears on so many of Mexico's great frescoes, was assassinated while riding his white horse. From ranch to village to roadside a chain-call spread: Let's join Pancho Villa. Among Villa's followers were some of Mexico's greatest writers, men like Martín Luis Guzmán and José Vasconcelos. (Villa had put thousands to death, and he made his exit from this world in a Ford whose riddled remains are still on view in his widow's home.) At this time the land of the eagle and the serpent bristled with cactus chill in the moonlight—bayonets. Frank Tannenbaum tells how, when he asked people about husbands, sons, or fathers, the answer was: He's been killed. No dramatic effect was intended; it was a routine explanation.

Out of all this violence finally emerged the Constitution of 1917. The new order rested on a three-point basis: Article 27, which states that Mexico's land and water are the property of the Mexican people and that the Church cannot acquire, hold, or manage lands; Article 23, which authorizes the president of the republic to expel without legal formalities any undesirable foreigner; and Article 123, which sets forth the right of workers to share in the profits of industry and to strike. These articles represent the achievement of ideals of long standing. In the capital there is a street called "Artículo 123." Whatever may be said of the Revolution, it had one distinct merit; it was Mexican. It copied no other country. It preceded the Russian revolution. It broke out while the Tsar was still a powerful, living reality and Lenin was spinning his theories in some cafe or beerhouse in Germany. The Mexican Revolution, says Daniel Cosío Villegas, "was the first frontal attack on the fortress of Liberalism, at least on Liberalism's doctrine of *laissez-faire, laissez-passer.*"

For ten years the strong man of Mexico was General Plutarco Elías Calles. He ruled as President from 1924 to 1928, then from the wings until 1934. General Cárdenas made an end to this state of affairs by putting him into a plane and sending him out of the country. From then on Cárdenas, who was President from 1934 to 1940, gave the orders. After his term of office his prestige, which was based on the others' fear of his disapproval, grew like a myth. He was still the man who had the confidence of the people, who never side-stepped a responsibility, who turned the distribution of land from theory to fact, who built more and more schools.

The Revolution came to an end with Cárdenas. The Revolutionary Party has inherited a name, commemorates a historic event. The republic of Mexico is the child of the Revolution. No longer do people feel their cautious way down the narrow street that runs between life and death. Of the slogan "Effective suffrage, no re-election," the second part has remained a reality. Cárdenas by his own example barred the way to re-election. But what has grown up is a government party. For the opposition to win, violence would be required, the forcible overthrow of the present order. This would demand the power Madero commanded when he threw out Díaz. There is a story about the Mexican who found very amusing the boast that the results of a United States election could be announced within six hours. "Here we know the results a year beforehand . . ." Government in Mexico is more for the people than by the people.

In November 1946 Daniel Cosío Villegas analyzed the impasse Mexico had reached; the original objectives, he said, had been superseded to the point where the very term "revolution" had lost its meaning:

". . . all the revolutionaries proved inferior to the work the revolution needed to do. Madero destroyed 'porfirismo,' but failed to create democracy in Mexico. Calles and Cárdenas did away with the 'latifundio,' but failed to create a new Mexican agriculture . . . The men who carried out the Revolution can now be judged without fear of error: they were magnificent destroyers, but nothing they have created in substitution of what they destroyed has proved indisputably better. Naturally, this does not imply that the Revolution has created nothing, absolutely nothing; it has given rise to new institutions, an important network of highways, impressive irrigation projects, thousands of schools, a goodly number of public services, solid industries and agricultural developments; but none of these things, despite their importance, has brought about a tangible change in the country in the sense of making it happier . . .

"The achievements of the Mexican Revolution in accomplishing its three main objectives: political freedom, agrarian reform, and labor organization, have been neither scant nor meager; they would have sufficed to uphold the moral authority of the revolutionary governments for a long time if in the eyes of the nation the efforts to bring them about had been accompanied by unquestionable integrity . . . Widespread administrative corruption, unabashed and insulting, behind a cloak of impunity . . . has undone the program of the Revolution . . ." [3]

Cosío Villegas's criticism proves two things: that there is freedom of speech in Mexico and that the meaning of the struggle has not been lost.

In 1946 Miguel Alemán was elected president. In 1949 Jesús Silva Herzog, editor of Mexico's most important review, *Cuadernos Americanos*, emphasized that the Mexican Revolution was no longer a thing of the present, but one of the past. Referring to Alemán's government, he said:

"Say what you will, the government of President Alemán no longer is, nor can it be, the continuation of previous governments. It may be better or it may be worse; the moment has not yet come to argue this point; but it is different; it marks a new phase in the history of Mexico . . . It is not of the right because it is impossible to break with tradition; it is a middle-of-the-road government, which veers right or left according to international developments and the internal

[3] *Extremos de América.* Tezontle, Mexico, 1949.

335

pressure of the more active political parties and social organizations, such as labor unions and farmers' leagues on the one hand, and chambers of commerce and industry, management groups, etc., on the other. Possibly in the long run the external pressure carries more weight than that which can be exerted within our frontiers because of the magnitude of the world struggle between powerful economic and political interests that lie behind the diplomatic controversies." [4]

Alemán is to the democratic Mexico that was born of the Revolution what Porfirio Díaz was to the Mexico of personal absolutism. He is imbued with the idea of progress. His government has built roads, dams, schools, and a great university development and has beautified Mexico City. It has also worked toward another goal, industrialization. It has endeavored to strike a balance between the country and the city. "To make the land more productive and step up the pace of industrialization."

Mexico is primarily an agricultural country, and as such it is poor. It needs water, fertilizers, machinery, and improved farming methods.

"Alemán has not by any means de-emphasized the importance of Mexico's agrarian problem. He is cognizant of the fact that the overwhelming majority of Mexicans live on the soil, that only 12 per cent of the country's area is arable, and that most of this is deficient in production. For example, the average corn yield per acre in Mexico is ten bushels, as compared with sixty bushels in Iowa. This is due to a number of reasons, including poor land, lack of fertilization, and inefficient utilization of farm labor. It takes 126 man-hours to produce an acre of corn in Mexico; in the United States, with improved methods, it takes but 17 man-hours." [5]

[4] "The Mexican Revolution is a Historic Fact." *Cuadernos Americanos*, Mexico, September-October, 1949.

[5] J. Lloyd Mecham: "An Appraisal of the Revolution in Mexico" (in *The Caribbean at Mid-Century*, University of Florida Press, 1951).

Irrigation development began under Calles in 1925. During the last years there has been a great increase in dams, irrigation ditches, and acreage benefited thereby. In twenty years, from 1926 to 1946, thirty-five major and sixty-one minor irrigation projects were carried out affecting 800,000 hectares (nearly 2,000,000 acres). In three years, from 1947 to 1950, thirty-seven major and one hundred sixty-two minor developments, benefiting 426,000 hectares (more than 1,000,000 acres) were carried to completion. The Papaloápan and Tepalcatepec projects, among the largest in Latin America, follow along the lines of the T.V.A. A joint plan is being worked out by Mexico and the United States for the Rio Grande. Half the Falcón Dam, one of the largest in North America, has already been built. It will form a lake fifty miles long, with a surface of 80,000 acres. Its cost will be $48,000,000, to be shared by the United States and Mexico on a 58.6, 41.4 per cent basis respectively, in proportion to the benefits derived by each.

Of the loan made to Mexico in 1948 by the Import-Export Bank, $5,000,000 was earmarked for agricultural machinery. The rise in yield of the crops listed in the table below shows that agriculture has not declined in Mexico as a result of the division of land:

PRODUCTION IN KILOGRAMS
(a kilogram equaling about 2.204 pounds)

Corn		Wheat	
1935	1,674,565,617	1935	346,630,000
1947	2,517,593,400	1947	421,859,000

Rice		Potatoes	
1935	70,549,640	1935	59,760,000
1947	137,821,000	1947	128,823,000

Similar increases have been registered in the production of chile, beans, sesame seed, cotton, hemp, tobacco, and coffee.

Mexico's output of oil is not as great as in 1921, the peak year under foreign management. The wells at that time were yielding 550,000 barrels per day. In February 1938, the month before the expropriation, production had fallen to 143,000 barrels. In 1950 it was up to 210,000. The production curve under national management, beginning in 1938, was as follows: 1938, 39 million barrels annually; 1940, 44 million; 1941, 43 million; 1942, 35 million; 1944, 38 million; 1945, 44 million; 1946, 50 million; 1947, 56 million; 1948, 59 million; 1949, 63 million.

The rise of Mexican industry has been spectacular in many aspects. Its rate of steel production is even higher than that of Brazil. In 1937 Mexico produced 15,000 tons; in 1947, 321,000. Electrification, too, has made great strides. The plants built by the Federal Commission, which in 1939 generated only 50,000 kilowatts, in 1949 were generating 554,700. The city of Mexico is today probably the largest of Latin America, having passed both Buenos Aires and Rio de Janeiro in number of inhabitants. Great modern buildings have been erected, challenging the soft nature of its swampy subsoil, which, beneath a cement surface, is still the mud of the old lake-bottom.

In 1936 and 1937, when the joint efforts of the Spanish Falange, German Nazism, and Italian Fascism dealt the Spanish Republic its death blow amid the general indifference of the democracies, Mexico, under Cárdenas, remained loyal to the Republic and refused to establish relations with Franco. In its subsequent conduct it has followed the lines laid down at the San Francisco Conference. Thousands of Spanish Republicans sought and found a generous refuge in Mexico. There they became incorporated into the universities, industry, and labor. The Nazi-Falangists, in turn, formed in opposition to them a tiny but aggressive party, to which elements opposed to the Mexican Revolution attached themselves. From this union came the *sinarquista* party, which applied to the government for land in Lower California to found a state within the Mexican State. Naturally, the petition was turned down. This reactionary group was joined by persons like José Vasconcelos, who at that moment saw in the Jews, the Masons, the Yankees, and the Protestants the reincarnation of Satan and his host.

The Mexican State, its writers, and the nation as a whole turned their backs on the international forces represented by the Nazis, the Fascists, and the Falangists, and have never wavered in attachment to all that Spain stands for in human warmth, love of liberty, and even such details as bullfights. In 1950 President Alemán sponsored a plan to hold a meeting in Mexico of all the Spanish language academies, that is to say, that of Spain and those of the Hispanic American republics. Three members of the Mexican Academy went to Madrid to tender the invitation, and the Spaniards enthusiastically accepted. They got ready for the trip, and Mexico had made reservations for them at the de luxe Hotel del Prado. In April 1951 all the delegates had gathered in Mexico City except those from Spain. At the last moment General Franco forbade them to attend. The newspaper *Arriba* of Madrid gave this explanation:

"It is deplorable that an assembly of the academies of the Spanish language should be held without the presence there of the only one that has authority in the field . . . But did not inviting the Spanish members, under existing circumstances, mean subjecting them to disagreeable contact with the emigré committee that Mexico chooses to recognize as the government of Spain?"

On inaugurating the Congress, President Alemán made no allusion to Spain. He said only:

"If any proof were necessary to confirm unequivocally the title of nobility of the Spanish we speak in America . . . it would suffice to recall that this was the language in which the seer of Yanga, during the first decade of the seventeenth century in what is now the Mexican state of Vera Cruz, proclaimed the freedom of all men . . . The Spanish language has been to the nations of America the language of liberty and human dignity. It was in this tongue that Hidalgo called upon his followers and Bolívar made his speeches; this was the language Morelos employed to abolish slavery and to give the people land; Martí to write his impassioned articles; and the poet Plácido for his last verses the night before he was executed for having fought for freedom . . . Voice of liberty, our language is also an instrument of democracy . . ."

On second thought, the Spanish delegation did well not to attend the Congress.

It is often wondered how much the Mexicans are drawn to Russia. In the murals painted when Vasconcelos was Secretary of Public Education, the Mexican rebels are often shown under flags bearing the hammer and the sickle. Recently, one of the peace congresses encouraged by the Russian military was held in Mexico. Thousands of Mexicans signed the Stockholm Peace Petition calling upon the United States to disarm. A profusion of anti-Yankee literature is published in Mexico. But the Russian under the orders of Stalin, who has insulated him from the rest of the world with a soundproof curtain, and the Mexican, set free by the Revolution, are like oil and water. For the Mexican, to be the master of his tongue, of his freedoms, is as vital a need as to be the owner of his land, his oil, or captain of his destiny. On the banners of the Revolution the first word was freedom, the second justice. The first act of justice was to make men free. A man as far to the left as Jesús Silva Herzog, who has been uncompromising in his condemnation of the capitalism of the United States, says:

"All dictatorships are despotic, unyielding, and on occasion cruel. All dictatorship carries with it the curtailment of freedom and admits of no divergence of opinion; everyone must

340

think and act as the dictators do or as they wish others to do. The Russian people alone, until not long ago serfs and slaves, never knew the sweetness of freedom even in a limited form. Therefore they cannot now miss a blessing they never knew and have as yet to know . . . The conclusion we come to is that the Soviet system is good, or may be good, for the inhabitants of the old Russian empire; but . . . we do not believe that the Soviet man is the measure of man, nor that the Soviet way of life represents the aspiration of the peoples of the world. The goals of Soviet Russia are not and cannot be the ideal of the other inhabitants of this tiny planet of ours, who were born in other climates under a brighter and bluer sky. May they achieve their constructive aims within their own world. We of Hispanic America have our world, too, and the ability to chart our own routes . . ." [6]

Mexico is a democracy, with all the shortcomings, defects, problems, anxieties, virtues, and hopes of the democracies. It made itself the champion of the lowly and the Indians well before this had become prescribed political procedure. It is now beginning to steer its course without the need of a general as a figurehead. Citizen Miguel Alemán will turn over the presidency to citizen Adolfo Ruíz Cortines, and the two will leave and enter office without decorations and without top hats. Alemán will have governed for six years; his successor will govern for six years. This holds out a great hope, for Mexico occupies a large space on the map of Latin America.

In October 1951, when he accepted the nomination for the presidency, Ruíz Cortines said:

"We shall unswervingly uphold the line established by the Revolution defending the freedoms guaranteed by our Constitution and our laws: freedom of thought, of the press, of employment, of public opinion, of religion; freedom to criti-

[6] "The United States or the Soviet Union?" *Cuadernos Americanos,* Mexico, May-June, 1950.

cize the government, spiritual and economic freedom. To our way of being, to our Mexican sensibility, human existence is unthinkable without full enjoyment of freedom, which we will never give up. Under the protection of our laws and the watchful care of our officials, every citizen feels and knows that he is assured the enjoyment of all his freedoms, without other limitations than those implicit in the law and the respect for the rights of others. This right presupposes corresponding obligations. I am convinced that less harm is done the republic by the abuse of civic liberties than by the most moderate form of dictatorship . . ."

These words, which might well be the text of a message to all the nations that make up the Latin American world, only reinforce those of Benito Juárez, who brought a gleam of undying light to Mexico in the nineteenth century when he said: "Peace is respect for the rights of others."

XVII

THE ARMY AND THE ARMIES
OF LATIN AMERICA

*Blessed those happy ages which knew not the dread fury of
these fiendish engines of war, whose inventor, it is my belief,
is receiving in Hell the reward for his diabolical invention ...*

CERVANTES

WE ARE LIVING in a world conditioned by past wars and the
threat of wars to come. The United States, which with every
passing day becomes more deeply involved in its inevitable
destiny, is obliged to take stock of its hemispheric neighbors
and calculate the military potential of Latin America. At
times this country's judgment has been extremely clear, at
times muddled.

If it is to the interest of the United States to seek military
pacts with the Atlantic nations or with Franco Spain, or to
hold bases in the Pacific, it is evident that it is no less vital to
evaluate the military aid the Western hemisphere can furnish. This co-operation has been postulated on an ideal assumption: the democracy of America. We were all to unite in
common action to affirm the rights of man and to make common cause against all forms of totalitarianism. Now, what is
the extent of the credit that can be assigned the existing governments in America, and can they be entrusted with the
armies intended for this purpose? To some this seems beside
the point. The people who like simple solutions are carried
away by the idea of an army recruited from 150,000,000
Latin Americans. As a man-power reserve, this puts Latin

America in a class with Russia, China, and the United States.

But there is a basic error in this estimate. Latin America is not a political unity. It is twenty nations with twenty armies and twenty chiefs of staff. It is twenty nations that might fight a guerrilla war to defend their territory against an invasion, Red or anti-Red. But any connection with events in Europe or Asia would be practically non-existent for the peasant, worker, manufacturer, or business man of the Latin American countries, which have been living on the fringe of world history—at any rate, of world history as represented by war.

Each of these twenty nations has its own flag and its own national awareness. If tomorrow the United States were to consider spending one hundred million or one billion dollars in building up a Latin American army, it could not hand the sum over to a single general staff or a single commander-in-chief, but would have to allocate the money among twenty countries. And when each country's share had been converted into its national currency, it would automatically pass into the hands of the party in power, the ruler of the moment, who might very well be one of the army officers who had led a *coup d'état*. In this way funds raised to serve the ends of democracy would become an instrument for its destruction. There is no greater unknown quantity in the sale of munitions today than machine guns consigned to what may prove to be the wrong address.

In keeping with agreements approved by the United Nations, there was a certain obligation on the part of Latin America to furnish soldiers in the event of an emergency such as that of Korea. And what happened? Of the 150,000,000 Latin Americans only 1,000 Colombian peasants were sent to Korea.

In April 1951 a meeting was called in Washington of the

foreign ministers of all the Latin American nations to discuss with the Secretary of State of the United States plans for hemispheric co-operation. One of the chief topics on the agenda was the military question. The conclusions reached dealt with three topics: a routine declaration of the spiritual union of the Americas and their respect for the rights and liberties of man; specific agreements concerning economic aid; and agreements regarding military co-operation.

With regard to Korea, the meeting approved an agreement by which the conference of foreign ministers:

". . . Considering that International peace and security have been breached by the acts of aggression in Korea, and the United Nations, despite its efforts to find a peaceful solution, was obliged, pursuant to resolutions of the Security Council and the General Assembly, to take action to restore peace in that area . . . [the Conference] declares: that the present world situation requires positive support by the American Republics for: 1) achievement of the collective defense of the Continent through the Organization of American States, and 2) co-operation, within the United Nations Organization, to prevent and suppress aggression in other parts of the world; and RECOMMENDS: 1) that each of the American Republics should immediately examine its resources and determine what steps it can take to contribute to the defense of the Hemisphere and to United Nations collective security efforts, in order to accomplish the aims and purposes of the 'Uniting for Peace' resolution of the General Assembly; 2) that each of the American Republics, without prejudice to attending to national self-defense, should give particular attention to the development and maintenance of elements within its national armed forces so trained, organized, and equipped that they could, in accordance with its constitutional norms, and to the full extent that, in its judgment, its capabilities permit, promptly be made available, 1) for the defense of the Hemisphere, and 2) for service as United Nations unit or units, in accordance with the 'Uniting for Peace' resolution."

What force did these recommendations have in each country? Mexico, Argentina, and Guatemala took a stand very close to isolationism from the point of view of sending troops to armed conflicts outside the continent. Rather than a point of view, these countries were registering a fact. But it is important to see the form in which each of them expressed itself, both in the conference room and afterwards.

Manuel González Ramírez, who summarized the work of the conference for *Cuadernos Americanos,* defined the Mexican attitude in the following terms:

"To the excited demand for troops to be sent immediately to any part of the planet, Mexico replied with arguments of a juridical nature which can be summed up in these words, easily grasped by the public opinion of the world: Mexico is not prepared to trade the lives of its citizens for dollars."

In Guatemala, President Jacobo Arbenz declared on April 6, 1951, one day after the Meeting signed its final Act:

"Guatemala cannot deprive itself of a single one of its men, nor does the slender budget of the nation, embarked on a broad six year program of production, permit this. From this it is manifest that the peaceful co-existence of nations is absolutely essential for Guatemala, and for this reason we have adopted the position of avoiding, by all means within our power, the possibility of the extension of existing conflicts. As yet we have no concrete information with regard to the outcome of the discussions of the Meeting in the plenary sessions, but Guatemala will maintain this position to the end, absolutely faithful to the foregoing considerations, and instructions to this effect have been sent to the delegation headed by Minister Galich. Nevertheless, if the opposition of Guatemala should lead to the invalidation of the right of the other American nations to determine the course that best suits their interest, Guatemala will vote affirmatively, but with the express, definitive, and categorical reservation that Guatemalan troops shall not be sent outside the continent."

The Argentine opinion is the most important from the military point of view, inasmuch as Argentina has the largest army in Latin America, a force equipped with modern weapons and a strong air arm, and is even hopeful of manufacturing the atomic bomb, a project on which it is spending large sums of money. It has some 300,000 trained reserves and quantities of jet planes. The lion's share of the national budget goes to the army. The military might of Argentina is a natural cause of concern to its neighbors because it has no justification merely for internal needs. Following is the reservation put on record by the Argentine delegate when the Final Act was approved in Washington:

"In voting affirmatively, in compliance with instructions from his Government, and though the clause on constitutional norms in the text of the Resolution makes provision therefor, the Representative of Argentina makes reservation to the effect that any use of its national armed forces, whether on a world-wide or a Hemisphere scale, is conditioned by the National Constitution, which reserves the said authority, exclusively and unassignably, to the National Congress. And moreover, he goes on record specifically that his Government will take no decision, except after express consultation with and upon the decision of the Argentine people, because it concerns a proper exercise of their sovereignty and an inalienable right of the people."

The significance and scope of this reservation can be grasped by bearing in mind the fact that the Perón doctrine, in the international field, is based on what he calls the third position: neither Moscow nor Wall Street. Consultation with the people, which is carried on from the balcony of the Casa Rosada, really means consultation with the *peronistas*. No sooner was the meeting over and there was talk in Buenos

Aires of possible obligations that had been assumed in Washington, than Perón addressed his people on May 1, reassuring them with these words:

"No decision in the field of international policy which involves any military action outside our boundaries will be taken without previous consultation with the people . . . Let us remember that the defense of *justicialismo* is the mainspring of our struggle: in foreign relations, against imperialism and reaction; in the domestic field, against politico-oligarchic treachery."

All these questions must be evaluated against the background of what took place during the Second World War. Then, too, the question of the military contribution of Latin America arose. Only Brazil sent regular troops, which fought in Italy. The value of this contribution was assessed by the *New York Times* correspondent, Milton Bracker, in the following terms: "Its record was honorable, but its over-all contribution was unquestionably more political than tactical."

Yet it would be grossly unfair to say that Latin America was indifferent to the struggle against the Axis. In no sense was this true. A survey of the situation from another point of vantage will bear this out. Let us suppose that the people of Latin America had been sympathetic toward Fascism or Nazism, that they had allowed the Germans to establish air and naval bases in this hemisphere, that instead of immediately nationalizing the German airlines in South America they had given Hitler the opportunity to bomb the United States from bases in neighboring countries. Then the United States would have been obliged to open another front, with all the complications involved in military action in far-flung regions well adapted to guerrilla or camouflaged warfare. Let us suppose that it had been necessary to double the watch over the Panama Canal, or that a sneak attack similar to that of Pearl Harbor had been carried out there. There is no question but that the power of the United States would have been dealt a severe blow and that the war might have taken a different course.

Why did nothing of the sort occur? Because of governmental decisions? No. It was the people of Latin America who uttered the "They shall not pass" to the Nazi-Fascists. It was public opinion that defended the continent. And there was no vacillation or doubt in this opinion. There were small groups of Nazi sympathizers—just as there were in the United States —but the weight of public opinion was overwhelmingly against them. The more or less restricted play of public opinion determined the course of those in power—or supported them where the governments were democratic. In Argentina the government sympathized with the Axis powers, but it was held in check by the press, by the man in the street, the university, and the factory. Farrell and Perón saw that their natural inclinations faced an insurmountable barrier. Vargas, then dictator of Brazil, who could hardly be called a champion of liberty, and whose *Estado Novo* had dispensed with the forms of liberal democracy, was shrewd enough to keep his ear to the ground, and in the end sent troops to Italy. In Colombia the group of Axis sympathizers headed by Laureano Gómez took the line that it was better that the Panama Canal should pass under the control of England, Germany, or Japan than that it continue in the possession of the United States. They opposed the breaking-off of relations with Germany, but they represented an insignificant minority that was drowned out in the freely expressed opinion of the whole country. The anti-Nazi policy of President Eduardo Santos rested on the broad base of national opinion.

Because of the will of its people, Latin America contributed to the Second World War with natural resources; with measures of internal policy, such as dissolving the Nazi centers clandestinely maintained by the Germans; with loyally observed pacts for the formation of a united front for hemispheric defense, accepting the natural leadership of

Franklin D. Roosevelt, who found the warmest, most enthusiastic support below the Rio Grande. In many countries Roosevelt enjoyed greater prestige than the local authorities, and in others he was as highly esteemed as their own greatest statesmen. This prestige of Roosevelt's was not the result of the economic aid extended to Latin America at that time. It was based mainly on the fact that the people saw in him an outstanding personality, a moral authority who openly placed himself at the head of the fight for the defense of freedom. It put one in a shameful position not to align himself with the ideas of respect for human rights upheld in the continental family by that cordial, persuasive voice. His example made itself felt on each of the rulers of the twenty republics.

In the case of Latin America the moral forces represented an asset as valuable as, or more valuable than, arms. These forces are the only ones that have counted in the decisive moments of history. Those who carried out the French Revolution of 1789, the struggles for the independence of the English and the Spanish colonies in America, or the more recent wars of Indonesia had only this arm at the beginning of their struggle, and their adversaries were great military powers. The first weapon in the fight, and that which in the long run has proved decisive, is public opinion.

In an hour of universal disruption, in the event of a Third World War, it is evident that the intimate, peculiar manner in which each country thinks will be of maximum importance. In Latin America there can be no great troop concentrations, no common general staff, nor any commander-in-chief whom twenty nations, each jealous of its sovereignty, will docilely obey. Latin America's principal contribution will be its economic reserves, its raw materials, and its permeability or impermeability to determined political ideologies. In all this it is not a matter of indifference to give assurance and faith to public opinion. And it may be a dangerous game, having explosive repercussions, to undermine this opinion by giving aid and comfort to the dictatorships. This will demoralize faith in democratic principles. It represents a perhaps fatal underestimation of the devotion of peoples to human rights and liberties.

Discounting the direct military participation of Latin America in a Third World War, what is the object of armies there? Is there any justification for building up an offensive and defensive force in each country on the same scale as has been necessary in Europe? In keeping with the terms of the regional organization that links the members of the old Pan American Union, there is not the slightest possibility of international wars between them. There is no other example in the world of a code that so completely guarantees peace among a group of nations as that which these countries have adopted. It is, moreover, a code having at its command the instruments necessary for its enforcement. Following are the fundamental points of the Inter-American Treaty of Reciprocal Assistance signed in Rio de Janeiro in 1947, the agreement that has already been invoked in the cases of Costa Rica vs. Nicaragua and the Dominican Republic vs. Haiti, which were settled by this international body:

"Art. 6. If the inviolability or the integrity of the territory or the sovereignty or political independence of any American State should be affected by an aggression which is not an armed attack or by an extra-continental or intra-continental conflict, or by any other fact or situation that may endanger the peace of America, the Organ of Consultation shall meet immediately in order to agree on the measures which must be taken in case of aggression or, in any case, the measures which should be taken for the common defense and for the maintenance of the peace and security of the Continent.

"Art. 7. In the case of a conflict between two or more American States, without prejudice to the right of self-defense in conformity with the article 51 of the Charter of the United Nations, the High Contracting Parties, meeting in consultation, shall call upon the contending States to suspend hostilities and restore matters to the *statu quo ante bellum*, and shall take in addition all other necessary measures to re-establish or maintain inter-American peace and security and for the solution of the conflict by peaceful means. The rejection of the pacifying action will be considered in the determination of the aggressor and in the application of the measures which the consultative meeting may agree upon.

"Art. 8. For the purposes of this Treaty, the measures on which the Organ of Consultation may agree will comprise one or more of the following: recall of chief of diplomatic missions; breaking of diplomatic relations; breaking of consular relations; partial or complete interruption of economic relations or of rail, sea, air, postal, telegraphic, telephonic and radiotelephonic communications; and use of armed force."

The treaty of Rio de Janeiro was only a first step in the establishment of the Organization of American States in keeping with the Charter of Bogotá, which was approved at the Ninth Pan American Conference (1948). The treaty and the charter are not innovations in Latin American relations. They are based on previous experiences and stem from a long international tradition.

In contrast to what took place in Europe, the armies of Spanish America did not come into being as offensive forces to threaten, conquer, or dominate neighboring countries. Their appearance had a clear and definite purpose: the fight for freedom. Bolívar led the troops he had recruited in Colombia and Venezuela to the very boundaries of Argentina, fighting and winning a war involving territory twice the size of Napoleon's empire, without seeking any change of frontiers, without shifting a single boundary line one inch in favor of any country. San Martín crossed the Andes and was victorious at the Battle of Chacabuco in Chile, but it occurred to nobody to ask for a foot of Chilean territory in compensation for this service. When the War of the Triple Alliance

(Brazil, Argentina, and Uruguay) was fought against Paraguay, someone suggested to the Argentine government headed by Sarmiento that a part of the territory of the defeated country should become the spoils of war. The minister to whom the suggestion was made replied with a phrase that has become famous: "Victory gives no rights." Compare the map of the wars of the Roman Empire with that of the wars of Spanish American independence. It will be seen that the area of conflict in this hemisphere was incomparably larger. But the soldiers of Rome marched to subjugate peoples; the soldiers of Spanish America marched to free them. When modern armies made their appearance in Europe they followed the Roman ideal. France's army won its spurs by invading Italy; Spain's by invading first Italy, then, Flanders; Prussia's by invading France . . . and thus down to our own days.

In Spanish America during its century and a half of independence, there have been only three international wars worth the name. The War of the Pacific between Chile and Peru, that of the Triple Alliance against Paraguay, and the Chaco War between Bolivia and Paraguay are such exceptional incidents in the normal life of the continent that they hardly affect its history. In general, the only kind of war that can be considered typical of nineteenth-century Latin America is civil war, internal revolution. The only war that really brought about a serious change of frontier, an important territorial loss, was that between Mexico and the United States, fought on the boundary between the Indo-Spanish and the English worlds.

The Latin American tradition is to settle boundary disputes by arbitration. Nowhere else in the world has arbitration had so constant, so decisive, and so repeated an application as among the twenty republics. They definitely prefer the juridical solution to that of force. Perhaps in this lies one of the characteristics of their historic development. If today the

Dominican Republic or Argentina, Colombia or Peru, Venezuela or Nicaragua, Paraguay or Bolivia is building up a large army, an army out of all proportion to its national income, it is for home consumption. The troops are not being armed or trained to oppress or kill the inhabitants of neighboring countries, but to repress or kill the citizens of their own countries. The only country that has acted logically is Costa Rica. There the head of the governing *junta*, José Figueres, disbanded the army the day after the revolution. The former Bella Vista Barracks has been turned into a Museum of Fine Arts. This act in itself defined the position of Figueres's government.

XVIII

LATIN AMERICA'S HOPES AND FEARS

Arms have given you independence; laws will give you freedom.

SANTANDER

LATIN AMERICA is synonymous with instability. Paraguay has had twenty-two presidents in thirty-two years; Ecuador had thirteen constitutions between 1830 and 1950 and twenty-seven revolutions in twenty-five years; between 1931 and 1932 Chile had five presidents and two military *juntas;* in 1930 the presidents of Brazil, Bolivia, Peru, and Argentina were thrown out of office; in 1931, in addition to the president of Chile, the presidents of Panama, Salvador, and Ecuador were overthrown; in 1932 there was a revolution against Getulio Vargas in Brazil, a war between Bolivia and Paraguay, and war between Peru and Colombia, and in Mexico ex-President Calles forced the resignation of President Pascual Ortiz Rubio; between 1913 and 1928 three presidents of Mexico were assassinated: Madero, Carranza and Obregón. And so the story goes. This instability has lasted for more than a century. Speaking of the situation of the president of Bolivia in 1826, the Bolivian historian, Enrique Finot, says: "He was sitting on a volcano." We could say the same thing today of Bolivia's present incumbent. There in 1827 the first president, Marshal Antonio José de Sucre, during his first year had to put down the first barracks coup, and was wounded in the affray. He said to the loyal troops who frustrated the rebellion: "You have conquered the conquerors of the conquerors who were victorious for fourteen years." The following year

355

Bolívar escaped death at the hands of the conspirators of Bogotá by slipping out of a window of his bedroom under cover of night. Like variations on a theme, similar episodes have taken place one hundred years later.

At times something worse than this instability occurs: stability. Dr. Francia was the absolute master of Paraguay for twenty-seven years; Juan Vicente Gómez of Venezuela for twenty-six; Porfirio Díaz of Mexico for twenty-four; Rosas of Argentina for twenty-three; Leguía of Peru for twenty-two; to date Trujillo has been the "savior" of the Dominican Republic for twenty-two years. Guatemala had three presidents who among them ruled the country for sixty-two years. The dictatorships came in with the republics. Dr. Francia's got under way in Paraguay in 1813; Juan Manuel Rosas took over in Argentina in 1829. If one hundred and seventeen years after Rosas, Perón can make himself dictator, it is no wonder that people ask if there has been any change.

It seems to me that nowhere in the world does one find such sharp contrasts. To foreign eyes it seems that the reasons for this state of affairs today are the same as those which led to the anarchy or despotism of the nineteenth century. The business, they say, of governing a potpourri of *mestizos*, Indians, Negroes, mulattoes, and Spaniards is next to impossible, and Latin America is faced with a Hobson's choice of Porfirio Díaz or Pancho Villa, Rosas or the breaking-up of Argentina. The assumption is that Perón is as inescapable or as necessary today as was Rosas in his time. The blame for the difference between the institutional development of the United States and that of Latin America lies in the race, in the Latin American's inability to abide by the normal processes of civil, representative democracy. How much truth is there in this hypothesis?

The uprisings and anarchy in Haiti have been a matter of Negroes. Or of Negroes vs. whites, or Negroes against Negroes, or Negroes against mulattoes. The Mexican revolution

356

was carried out by *mestizos* and Indians against whites or *mestizos*. Juan Vicente Gómez's dictatorship was that of a *mestizo* in a nation of *mestizos*. That of Rosas was of a white man in Buenos Aires, where the population was white and black. That of Perón is that of a white man in a land that may be said to be all white, of a first generation descendant of immigrants in a land that teems with immigrants. That of Getulio Vargas is the work of a gaucho in a nation whose overall hue is cinnamon.

The Peruvian Indian, who makes up the rural population of his country, is the descendant of the most peaceful, law-abiding civilization the world has ever seen; it could serve as the model for a republic as peaceable as that of Switzerland. The Mexican Indian, on the other hand, was of a warrior race that overran the territory of its neighbors in search of slaves and sacrificial victims for its gods. Paraguay, which has been the scene of the bloodiest wars in South America, is composed of descendants of the Guaraní Indians whom the Jesuits turned into a colony probably as close to Utopia as anything that has existed. The Chileans, whose republic has suffered fewer interludes of anarchy than any other, descend on the one hand from the most bellicose Indians of all South America, the Araucanians, and on the other from superior European groups—Basques, Scots—and they have always had the best army, trained by Prussian instructors.

This diversity of circumstances, these antecedents so often completely at odds with the results that might have been expected from them, lead one to think that the despotism and anarchy that have blotted the pages of Latin America's history have a historical rather than a racial explanation. They are the result of the mold in which these twenty republics were originally cast, of the circumstances that have attended their development. And the question of whether the events of the twentieth century are owing to the same causes as those of the nineteenth demands closer scrutiny.

The Spanish American republics are the progeny of a colonial system under which the practice of representative government was nonexistent. They developed in a climate of absolutism foreign to the English colonies, notwithstanding the strong popular current that characterized Spain and the strongly monarchic trend of England. The contrast is important.

From their founding, the English colonies of North America had charters that they guarded jealously, and which were democratic constitutions. The Puritans who came to America really issued their proclamation of independence as they took ship, and the power of the royal governors was limited by the local assemblies. In many of the colonies the religion that was practiced was not the official religion of England, and a variety of faiths sprang up which had to work out a way of living together. Possibly the declaration of independence and the revolutionary spirit of the first settlers in the new country was of greater consequence than that which inspired the troops under Washington's command one hundred and fifty years later. The Constitution of Philadelphia was the logical culmination of a process that had been going on for a long time. Its framers did not so much overthrow an existing order as reaffirm and clarify that which existed in the mind, the heart and the habits of the colony. It was a step in evolution, not revolution. The war of 1776 was fought for the purpose of establishing political rights rather than to overthrow institutions.

The situation in Spanish America was the complete opposite. Spain had extended its empire to its colonies. The viceroy fully represented the king, who was an absolute monarch, and the Spanish Catholic Church, which was guided by the Inquisition. The powers of the municipalities were very limited; the city councils had jurisdiction only in matters of slight importance; the weight of the monarchy was felt even in the outlying regions of the empire. There was no provision for or training in autonomy or representative government. The laws were drawn up to their last detail in Spain, and if the viceroys or governors had tongue in cheek as they swore to uphold them, what they did with this was to create in the colonials a capacity for legal hairsplitting and connivance which has had disastrous consequences. It would have been far better if they had willed us a sense of respect for law.

Once the colonies had made themselves independent of Spain, they had to begin by turning their inherited institutions inside out. The war of independence was only the military phase; it was concluded in less than fifteen years. When all foreign authority had disappeared from Spanish America, the overhauling of the colonial machinery began. Popular suffrage had to be invented and established, as did the three branches of the government. Provision had to be made for popularly elected executives with a limited term of office, for separation of Church and State, for education—and there were no schools designed for this—for preparing the people for a radically different way of life. There were, to be sure, old and established universities, but their purpose was to train a "fundamentalist" clergy, divorced from the physical world, hostile to mathematics and science. In many places the conflict with the Church endured for one hundred years. The native sons had to be broken like broncos to make them reasonable and tractable, for their first idea was to assume the privileges the Spaniards had enjoyed. Even today, after the lapse of more than a century, there are still small conservative groups who regard themselves as the legal heirs of the privilege of governing the people by divine right, holding the masses to be of different and inferior clay. It is hard for them to accept the fact that the *mestizo*, the Indian, the Negro, or anyone of the lower classes has the same civil rights as they. It is more a matter of social standing than of race. The mulattoes or Indians who become rich achieve white status, and if they come to form a part of the so-called oligarchy, they too join those anointed with the right to power, which is one of the deepest-rooted of human instincts. The people and those who represent the spirit of independence have been obliged to face this reality and combat it from some forty years before the war of independence up to the present day. They have fought in guerrilla bands, with machetes, with speeches, with books, in romantic battalions, in lodges, openly or in secret, to penetrate the closed world left by the colony. In this endeavor every arm was utilized, from the Encyclopedia and the French Revolution to the Constitution of Philadelphia, the economists of the Manchester School, French socialism of 1848 and that of the twentieth century to the Charter of Human Rights of the United Nations . . .

The struggle, carried on with such disparate human elements in the mountains or on the barren pampa brought to the surface apostles and caudillos. The clearest, most carefully thought-out program of independence was that of Bolívar, and from it emerged the most sinister dictatorships. With each setback the successive combatants in this long revolution must begin afresh. When enough time has elapsed, and this process can be seen in better perspective, it may be that the nineteenth century in Latin America will be known as the Hundred Years' War.

Is Perón (1946) Rosas (1829)? Do the events of the first fifty years of the twentieth century stem from the causes that gave rise to the anarchy and despotism of the nineteenth?

During the nineteenth century in Argentina, as in Colombia, Peru, or Venezuela, the situation was of a purely local nature. There were no international forces at work. There may have been a touch, or even a substantial lacing, of French romanticism, but the terms of the conflict were native, and not a few of the caudillos were completely illiterate like Juan Vicente Gómez or Mariano Melgarejo of Bolivia. The heart of the matter was an endeavor to adjust social differences among people who overnight found themselves on an equal plane. In 1950 these problems no longer have the same significance. Today Latin America has become an apple of international covetousness. Hitler in his day had his eye fixed on America, and for years Russia has realized its usefulness. Latin America is an ideal base from which to strike at the United States. Hitler's master plan, which was set forth in the American Blue Book, and which we South Americans were aware of long before, has been taken over by Russia. A thousand proofs bear this out, and it has been clearly described by Eudocio Rabínez, the former Peruvian Communist who was for a time *persona grata* at the court of Moscow. Even Franco grasped the idea, and there is a connection between this and his active share in the establishment of the dictatorship in Colombia. He has seen in the restoration of Hispanidad the opportunity to acquire international strength, and Latin American votes have been of invaluable aid to him in his horse-trading deals with the United Nations.

Perón received his training in the local branch of Nazism set up by the military of Argentina, completed his studies in Italy, and seized power with the support of a lodge modeled on classic Hitlerian lines. Villarroel's operations in Bolivia had the same origin. Odría of Peru was one of Perón's disciples, and Pérez Jiménez of Venezuela learned his trade from Odría. The Colombian officers who seized President López in 1944 were members of a lodge that was a counterpart of Perón's, as were the Chilean officers who plotted against González Videla. Perón, too, has an international plan. His fine Italian hand could be seen in the uprisings in Paraguay and Bolivia and in the Brazilian election. His main points of support were originally in Peru and Venezuela, and he has been in close touch with the Colombian dictatorship. *El Siglo*, Laureano Gómez's Bogotá newspaper, is perhaps the only one in all South America that defended Perón when he closed down *La Prensa*. In 1951 the *peronista* journalists, with the help of their Paraguayan stooges, tried to disrupt the Inter-American Press Association at the meeting in Montevideo in order to set up an organization of their own. Perón has been hard at work to bring the Latin American labor movement under his control. The labor attachés of the Argentine embassies are doing everything in their power to woo the union leaders of other countries, inviting them to come to Argentina to establish the contacts needed to set the *peronista* international in motion. The situation boils down to a tug of war for the Latin American unions between the labor organizations of the United States and those whose center is in Moscow or Buenos Aires. There is still a fourth contestant, Vicente Lombardo Toledano, the head of a Mexican labor movement. The path followed by this intellectual leader has been so involved and devious that it is impossible to evaluate either his importance or his orientation. All one can say is that as between the United States and Russia he favors Russia.

In the matter of constitutional reform, which has always been high on the agenda of Latin American conflicts, Getulio Vargas came forward in 1937 with his charter for the *Estado Novo*, which has been described as one of the most totalitarian in the entire continent. That of the Movimiento Nacional Revolucionario of Bolivia is a carbon copy of that of the German Nazi party. The dictatorship of Colombia has designated a committee headed by Father Restrepo, S. J., to draw up plans for a new constitution. Father Restrepo, an ardent admirer of Franco, has announced that this constitution will be of a corporative nature. In Panama, Arias incorporated Hitler's racial doctrines into the constitution.

Everybody in Latin America is in agreement that Latin Americans are not, strictly speaking, Nazis or Fascists, Communists or Falangists. Those who really subscribe to these ideas have always formed meager minorities—small military lodges, little intellectual groups, left or right extremists. But they are all aggressive, belligerent, and well-disciplined. For this reason the Communists have managed to acquire important positions in the labor unions and the Nazis have provided presidents of certain republics.

For good or for bad, the United States has played an important role in Latin American affairs. Nobody has yet properly assessed the influence of the founding fathers of this country, and of Jefferson and Lincoln, on the beginnings of South America's republican era. Sarmiento's faith in the power of the school was reaffirmed by his stay in the United States as ambassador of his country, and on these foundations he created a new Argentina. Roosevelt activated the exportation of democratic ideas with his Good Neighbor Policy, and brought about a renewal of faith in the civilian way of life in the South. On the other hand, the swinging of the big stick during the epoch of Manifest Destiny left many a bruise, in the Caribbean area particularly, and this was followed by the offensive of four or five companies interested in bananas, transportation, oil, copper, or loans which found it helpful to throw a little sand in the gearbox by buying governments. By and large, the seeds of progress sowed by these companies were watered with tears, and the investors favored colonial tactics. The companies often found support in Washington; rarely were they rapped over the knuckles, and almost always they had the backing of the United States ambassadors in the countries where they operated. As a result, two extremist attitudes have developed: that of collaborationist presidents and that of the enemies of Yankee imperialism.

The North American health missions, their technical guidance, the Point Four program, the loans of the Import-Export Bank, the establishment of fellowships in North American universities, the generous aid of the Rockefeller, Carnegie, and Guggenheim foundations, and the moral support the democrats of Latin America have received from the outstanding newspapers of the United States have been most effective in assisting the progress of these countries and in putting them out of the reach of European imperialist greed, and have greatly helped to assuage old, deep wounds. But on the other hand the sale of arms to the Latin American countries, whatever the original intention, has had as a result the assassination of democracy and the elevation of colonels to power. This topic is under constant discussion in Latin America, but in Washington it is discussed only with the representatives of the dictators who have a vital interest in getting tanks and machine guns by any possible means. A typical instance of the reaction across the border is to be found in a resolution passed by the first assembly of the workers and farmers of Panama, in which they register a protest against the fact that of the $62,000,000 grant to Latin America by the United States under the Point Four program, $40,000,000 was for military supplies and $22,000,000 for technical aid. The assembly resolved:

"To protest to the United States against the assignment of the better part of the funds allotted under President Truman's Point Four Program to the acquisition of armaments by the dictators of Latin America in order to strengthen their position and continue their oppression of the people . . ."

The resolution of the workers of Panama coincides, moreover, with repeated warnings by United States citizens in a position to know what they are talking about. Spruille Braden, for example, has said:

"One thing was that, at the instance of the Pentagon, a bill has been sent to the Congress calling for the arming of Latin America. This was a program I had long opposed because it would tend to promote an arms race, and I felt that new supplies of arms would be used by some governments of Latin America against their own people. Further, I felt that if we were to provide any aid it should be for the economic betterment the countries of Latin America badly needed." [1]

[1] "Let's Stop Buying Dictators," *Look*, September 25, 1951.

Washington's policy has been a wavering one, and therefore demoralizing. It veered from Braden's attitude toward Perón, which was frankly hostile, to that of Ambassador Bruce, which is one of brotherly love. At the Inter-American Press Conference held in New York in October 1950, Assistant Secretary of State Edward G. Miller made a perfect analysis of the role of the newspaper in a democracy, showed how these principles had informed the life of the United States for two hundred years, and recalled the determination taken at the Fourth Inter-American Press Conference, held in Bogotá.

About this same time the United States Ambassador in Bogotá, Mr. Willard Beaulac, was showing esteem beyond that displayed by any other diplomatic representative except Franco's toward the heads of the Colombian dictatorship, Ospina Pérez and Laureano Gómez. In Mr. Beaulac's judgment "Ospina Pérez was the savior of democracy."

The sometime Ambassador of the United States in Buenos Aires, Spruille Braden, in his 1951 *Look* article, "Let's Stop Buying Dictators," reviewed the policy of the United States. In addition to his post in Argentina, Braden had been Ambassador to Colombia and Cuba and Assistant Secretary of State for American Republic Affairs. "We have traded," he says, "principle for expediency, and lost both unity and the respect of our neighbors . . . If principle came first, we would not do what we have done since World War II. We spent the lives and blood of our youth to erase Nazism from the face of the earth. We hated all Fascists and everything for which they stood. Yet today we court fascist-type dictators and sign treaties with them which solemnly pledge the defense of those human rights, civil liberties and democratic principles that those same dictators at this very moment are notoriously flouting. Such a standard of behavior in international relations, as with Latin America, can mean only one thing: that nobody will trust us. For if we operate according to expediency and not principle, every time something happens we will have to adopt a new line . . ."

One factor affects the political life of Latin America by its mere existence: the nearness of the United States. The question is not one of a good neighbor or a bad neighbor, but just a neighbor. The comparison is inevitable and constant between the have and the have-not neighbors, the one whose lines have been laid in a medium of lush prosperity and the one who must struggle against heavy odds. The phenomenon is a general one, but it is sharpened by the fact that the prosperous neighbor lives next door or, as has sometimes been said, in another wing of the same house. The screen, the pages of *Life* or *The Ladies' Home Journal*, and the advertisements of automobiles or electric refrigerators are constantly bringing before the Latin Americans' eyes the visual image of a civilization that holds certain truths to be self-evident. Everybody there knows that in the United States the traditional political parties have complete freedom, that the governing bodies are elected by the people, that everyone is free to express his opinion, that the president can be criticized and opposed.

The unquenchable aspiration of the Latin American masses to achieve a higher level of freedom and prosperity finds in the life of the United States a stimulus that may become explosive at any moment. Hate is a much more powerful reagent than love or ideals. Those who in one way or another represent the forces of injustice, the vested interests that recognize no rights on the part of the poor, are the objects of hatred. No one has expressed this underlying resentment in clearer terms than Eva Perón in the opening pages of her book *La Razón de Mi Vida* (*What Gives My Life Meaning*). Speaking of her childhood memories, she says: "I can clearly recall that it saddened me for many days when I learned that there were rich people and poor people in the world; and the strange thing is that I was not so distressed by the existence of the poor as by knowing that at the same time there

366

were those who were rich." Further along she observes: "One day I heard for the first time from the lips of a worker that there were poor because the rich were too rich; that revelation made a powerful impression on me."

The struggle in Latin America underwent a radical change in the twentieth century because of a demographic transformation. In the nineteenth century Latin America was almost exclusively rural. It was a world of landowners and peons, and its means of communication were dirt roads. The provincial capitals were villages, and the national capital was a larger village. The cities began to develop as such about 1910. Until then everything was conditioned by the wilderness, the swamps, the desert, the jungle, malaria, and anemia. A large proportion of the population was closer to the stone age than to the electrical age. The worship of the he-man, which paved many caudillos' way to the presidency, was a projection of this ranch life. It is impossible for a cowhand to conceive of a president who is not a rider capable of breaking a bronco. In Buenos Aires all the statues of presidents, with the single exception of Sarmiento, are equestrian. South American political cant is full of phrases like "the man on horseback," "holding the reins of power," and the fable on good government is often quoted:

> Bit and spur
> Had an argument
> About which was the better
> In government.

Argentina under Rosas was a gaucho festival, with sound effects provided by the crack of the foreman's quirt.

When one says "Latin America" the term includes the Andean mountains, the Amazon jungle, the Argentine pampa, the steppes of Bolivia, the green Hell of the Chaco, the mountain fastnesses where Pancho Villa's and Sandino's guerrillas had their hideouts, and where even today the peasants of

Colombia find refuge from the government's punitive planes. This untamed natural setting predominated in all the republics fifty years ago; today it represents only a partial aspect of their political and economic life. Every country is crisscrossed by highways and linked by a network of airlines. The donkey-trot is a thing of the past; even the peasant now moves on wheels. Today he can reach the capital in no time. He listens to the political leaders on the radio and hears the news over the air. The growth of the cities has been sudden, almost monstrous. Fifty years ago the largest of the capitals had 100,000 inhabitants. Today many cities have a population of one million and some have two and three million. Even the diseases have taken to their heels. Panama used to be the stronghold of yellow fever; today it is a health resort and playground.

Politics is no longer an affair of surprise attacks and guerrillas. Perón, Odría, the military of Venezuela, the Conservatives of Colombia, Trujillo, Somoza, organize parades of tanks through their capitals and aerial maneuvers at their military bases. San Salvador was almost wiped out by aerial bombardment. The Radicals of Argentina, the *apristas* of Peru, the members of Acción Democrática in Venezuela, the Liberals of Colombia, all of whom were and are the majority parties in their respective countries, have suddenly been obliged to organize an underground to communicate among themselves and evade government surveillance. If it were possible today to study the clandestine functioning of these parties in Latin America, one would encounter innumerable surprises. Hundreds of newspapers, radio stations, and labor cells operate God only knows how. Without intending to, the dictators are driving the opposition into organizing along lines that recall the Communists or the resistance movement in France. To destroy them the native Gestapos have been organized. It is a twofold threat against the normal workings of democracy. As long as Latin America was pastures, herds, and range, and war was encounters between opponents armed with machetes, the modus operandi was primitive, improvised. But with the large cities, the military machinery, and the totalitarian organization of the State the picture has changed completely.

Speaking in general terms, the objective of Latin Americans in their hundred years' war was representative democracy. An attempt to hold back a groundswell of this sort can only result in a tidal wave that may break any day.

Whenever a Latin American country has had an opportunity to vote freely during the last twenty years, the elections have resulted in an overwhelming democratic majority. This is what took place in Venezuela when Rómulo Gallegos ran for president, in Peru when the *apristas* were allowed to vote, in Colombia during the twenty years when there were free elections. In 1946 Perón had the support of the great mass of Argentine voters, but the outcome might have been a very different story if the Radicals had been able to campaign. But, at any rate, Perón polled a great vote. He stood for principles of social revision which satisfied the aspirations of the people. In 1951, however, Perón made it clear that what the people of Argentina wanted was not included in his program. They were demanding prosperity and justice, but with freedom. As this was not what he had to offer, he had to crush a strong opposition. If he had had the support of the country, he would have allowed free elections and freedom of speech, would have let the opposition have its newspapers, presses, radios, and transportation to bring its members to meetings. All this was denied it. It is obvious that even with the control of the electoral machine he was afraid of a free contest.

Even today in many republics the struggle is between the persecuted democratic majorities and the totalitarian minorities that have seized power. The worker aspires to a better life, to his right to join labor unions, to the use of those means provided for in the Declaration of Human Rights: "everyone has the right to form and to join trade unions for the protection of his interests." The farmer aspires to free himself from the serfdom that is still the order of the day in many Latin American rural areas. And all aspire to the right to voice their opinions freely. Nowhere in the world does a more imperious need for freedom of speech exist than in Latin America. The Latin Americans have been muzzled for centuries, and this suppression must find an escape valve.

Evita Perón has a double personality. For internal consumption she is "Evita of the shirtless ones." For export purposes she is Señora Eva Perón. She says this herself, and her theory, which is as old as the hills, throws much light on the Latin American situation. The dictators have a front establishment where tourists can see freedom and democracy on display and a back room where the real political business is carried on. In Europe no one has described the functioning of the double personality better than the German scientist, Klaus Fuchs, who worked for the English on the atom bomb project in their laboratories, and for the Russians, handing over secret information to them. With complete candor he explained this to the judge at his trial, saying: "I made use of my Marxist philosophy to keep my thoughts in two separate compartments. In one I was the man I wanted to be. I could live among other people in freedom, frankness and happiness, without fear of betraying myself, because I knew that the other compartment would seal itself off in time of danger. It seemed to me that I had made myself a free man because I managed to keep my real self in a separate compartment independent of the forces of society by which I was surrounded."

The double personality of the Peróns, their double truth, has made it possible for them to employ one half in their dealings with the international world, and the other half with their party. In her book Eva Perón says:

"I was not merely the wife of the president of the republic, I was also the wife of the leader of the Argentine people. I had to have a double personality to match that of Perón: on the one hand, Eva Perón, the wife of the president, whose duties were simple and agreeable, gala days, social festivities, receiving honors; and on the other, Evita, the wife of the leader of a nation that has reposed all its faith, hope, and love in him. On a few days of the year I played the role of Eva Perón; and it seems to me that I handle this with increasing skill, for I find it neither difficult nor disagreeable. The majority of the days I am Evita, the first *peronista* of Argentina, a bridge that stretches between the hopes of the people and the hands of Perón, who turns these hopes into reality, and this is a difficult role and one in which I never quite satisfy myself. It is of little interest to talk of Eva Perón. Her activities are all too fully described in the newspapers and magazines everywhere. But, on the contrary, it is of interest to talk of Evita, not because I feel any vanity in the matter, but because anyone who understands Evita will find it easy to understand her 'shirtless ones,' the people, and the one who does this will never feel himself to be more than he is . . . he will never turn into an oligarch, which is the worst thing that can happen to a *peronista*!"

The double personality of the Latin American holders of power has made it possible for them to put their signature to the greatest number of declarations in favor of human rights and liberties on record. Every one of the basic rights that disappear under a dictatorship is recognized in triplicate: in the constitution of the country, in the Pan American agreement, and in the United Nations Charter. Each has been approved with signature, speech, and photograph.

In 1951 the fourth meeting of the ministers of foreign affairs of all the American states was held in Washington. Personal representatives of General Perón, General Trujillo, General Odría, General Somoza, the military *junta* of Venezuela, and the Conservatives of Colombia were present. President Truman inaugurated the sessions with a speech from which the following words are taken:

"The American republics all owe their national beginnings to the same set of ideals, the same concepts of human and international freedom. We have all followed and we will continue to follow two basic principles. First, we believe that international affairs should be based upon cooperation among free and independent nations, and not upon coercion and force. Second, we believe that the aim and purpose of government is to promote the welfare of all the people—not just the privileged few . . ."

He was followed by Secretary of State Acheson, who said:

"What binds the nations of the free world together into a partnership is that they have a powerful interest in common: their concern for freedom. Freedom is the key. This is what free nations have, and other nations do not. This is the heart of the matter, for without freedom neither real peace, nor real security, nor any real progress is possible. To the nation, freedom means national independence, freedom to work out its destinies in its own ways. To the people, freedom is not only the very breath of life itself, but it is also the gateway of opportunity. Free men have the opportunity to better their lives, to abolish poverty, and to live in human dignity."

The Foreign Minister of Brazil, João Neves de Fontoura, answered, saying:

"With democracy and freedom again in danger, the free nations of the world will have to get together and strengthen themselves for the common defense or they will perish under the terror of a sinister imperialism . . . The nations of our hemisphere must not fail in this assembly to demonstrate their attachment to the love of nation, as well as to the idea of freedom for the human person and respect for spiritual liberties and the Christian way of life . . ."

All the foreign ministers greeted these words with strong

applause. They all set to work and eagerly approved the "Declaration of Washington," which said, among other things:

"Whereas . . . in any action for the defense of the Hemisphere and its institutions, the essential rights of man, solemnly proclaimed by the American Republics should not be lost sight of . . . The Fourth Meeting of Consultation of Ministers of Foreign Affairs Declares: . . . A reaffirmation of the faith of the American Republics in the efficacy of the principles set forth in the Charter of the Organization of American States and other inter-American agreements to maintain peace and security in the Hemisphere . . . and ensure respect for the fundamental freedoms of man and the principles of social justice as the bases of their democratic system . . ."

This was followed by the recommendation concerning the strengthening and effective exercise of democracy:

"Whereas . . . In order to achieve such identification of the people with their government, it is imperative that each country have an effective system of representative democracy that will put into practice both the rights and duties of man and social justice; and

"The American Republics and their origin and reason for being is the desire to attain liberty and democracy, and their harmonious association is based primarily on these concepts, the effectiveness of which it is desirable to strengthen in the international field, without prejudice to the principle of nonintervention . . . Resolves . . . To suggest that the Tenth Inter-American Conference consider . . . the provisions necessary in order for the purposes stated in Resolutions XXX and XXXII of the Ninth International Conference of American States to acquire full effectiveness in all the countries of America . . ."

These resolutions were unanimously passed. Resolutions XXX and XXXII of the Bogotá Conference referred to are the American Declaration of the Rights and Duties of Man, contained in Appendix C of this book, and The Preservation and Defense of Democracy in America. This recommendation covers respect for human life, for the profession of any religious faith, for freedom of expression by any means, for honor, reputation, for the family, for the inviolability of the home, for the right to write letters without their being opened by government censorship, to have a nation, to vote, to hold office. In other words, for all that is denied a vast group of the inhabitants of Latin America. All these principles were heartily acclaimed by the delegates of Argentina, where the most important newspaper of Latin America had been closed down during those selfsame days and taken over by the government; by the representatives of Colombia, where one year and a half earlier Congress had been closed by the army; by the delegates of Venezuela, where the members of Acción Democrática had been stripped of their political rights; by the delegates of Peru, where the *aprista* party had been declared illegal; by the delegates of General Trujillo, General Somoza . . .

In the pages of this book a few instances of the regard—or disregard—in which human rights are held in Latin America have been set forth, a few of the thousands that could be adduced. Comparing the text of the resolutions with the reality, one comes to the inescapable conclusion that rarely has history afforded an instance of more blatant cynicism. As a result there has been a loss of faith in international accords, in official pronouncements. And when authority loses its moral authority, violence steps in to take its place. Fear plays the leading role in the drama of Latin America.

Latin America was born and grew up in the Catholic faith. In a moment of revolt a Latin American may become an atheist or agnostic, but rarely, if ever, a Protestant. Either he is a Catholic or he has no religion. The liberalism of the nineteenth century brought forth generations of anticlericals, just as in Spain. But no one thought of founding a sect. The Radical families of Colombia, during the bitterest days of the struggle against the Church, never failed to gather for the rosary at night. One of the stock phrases was "The Conservatives are the ones who pray in public and get drunk in private; the Radicals are the ones who get drunk in public and pray in private."

But, again as in Spain, pressure was exerted on the Church to take a hand in the political struggle. At the time of the independence there were two Catholic churches: one that supported the republic, one that linked its fate to the monarchy. In his will Bolívar made a complete profession of his Catholic faith, and shortly before, in 1827, in a gesture of friendship—or reconciliation—with the Church, he raised his glass at a banquet in a toast to the archbishops of Caracas and Bogotá, saying: "The greatest cause brings us together today: the good of the Church and the good of Colombia. A chain more brilliant and more enduring than the stars of the firmament links us once more to the Church of Rome, which is the source of our hopes of Heaven." But in 1812, when he began his campaign of independence, this same Bolívar had said: "The influence of ecclesiastics was largely responsible, after the earthquake, for the disaffection in outlying cities and villages, and for the introduction of the enemy into the land, sacrilegiously taking advantage of the holiness of their calling to encourage the spreaders of dissension and civil war. Yet we must candidly confess that these traitors of the cloth were encouraged to commit the execrable crimes of which they were justly accused because they enjoyed complete immunity for such crimes, a state of affairs that found outrageous support in the Congress. This injustice went so far that in the insurrection of the city of Valencia, which was subdued only at the cost of nearly one thousand lives, not a single rebel suffered the penalty provided by law; all of them escaped with their lives, and most of them with their property . . ."

If Bolívar favored shooting such priests as opposed independence, the drastic measures later employed in all America by the anticlerical parties endeavoring to establish the republics and set them on the paths of progress which the church so often opposed are not to be wondered at. Maximilian in Mexico supported by the Church and García Moreno in Ecuador setting up a Jesuit despotism were instrumental in paving the way for the anticlerical reaction. For reasons that are readily apparent, the dictators have always put themselves forward as special emissaries of God. They create the impression that for years the lands lay in outer darkness, forgotten by Divine Providence, which remembers them only to hand them over to despots. The political history of Latin America abounds in testimony to this effect. In his memoirs General Perón goes this idea even one better, for he presents himself as lending Divine Providence a helping hand. He says:

"It is plain that my election did not happen by chance. Providence, undoubtedly, had a share in it, and for this I always give thanks to God. But the people and I helped Him. The key to the future lies in our taking care to see that this never fails to occur among us . . ."

The Church has never been the unconditional instrument of the dictatorships, but it has been divided. There are village priests, and even some in the cities, who make a machine gun of their pulpit. There are also priests who condemn violence, who stand up for liberty and place Christian charity above party lines. In many parts of America, and perhaps most of all in Colombia, what is happening today is often almost in the nature of a schism. The Bishop of Manizales in Colombia, for example, condemns the violence of the village priests and makes an appeal for peace—and the censorship of the clerical government forbids his letter to be published. In the state of Antioquia the priest of Ríonegro appeared at his window to upbraid the government supporters for setting fire to the city to the cry of "Long live Christ the King." The Mayor of Medellín, a stooge of the government that set up the reign of fire and sword, has made confession obligatory and has had confession boxes installed in the public offices. In many places Protestant chapels have been burned down. In the College of St. Simon, one of the oldest in Colombia, the administrative council has gone on record as follows: "Whereas, the Catholic Church has condemned the Masonic Lodge as an enemy of the Church, and the fact that the present legal member of the council is a member of said lodge violates the Provisions of the Concordat . . . it is Resolved to nullify the appointment of Luis Ayram Quijano as legal member of the council . . ."

The son of a provincial family of peasants, who had studied at the University in Bogotá and made a brilliant name for himself in science, whose activities lay completely outside the area of politics, received a telegram to the effect that his father was gravely ill. He flew to the capital of the province, and was soon in his village. His father had already died. The old man had been a member of a church sodality. The family never missed Mass on Sunday and had dutifully paid its tithes to the Church. But they were Liberals. Not belligerent Liberals—simply, at election time, they voted the Liberal ticket as their forefathers had done, more out of tradition than by active conviction. But because of this, the priest and the mayor refused to let the old man be buried with Church rites, or laid to rest in consecrated ground. The women were weeping, the men of the household at their wit's end. The priest and the mayor were adamant. The Church and the cemetery were for the Conservatives; the Liberals were the spawn of Satan. And these good Christians were faced with the prospect of burying their father out in the field like an animal, they who had the Sacred Heart of Jesus in the parlor, the Virgin of Perpetual Help above the bed, who had never omitted evening prayers or crossing themselves when they heard the *Ave Maria*. The Church in which their father had been baptized, had made his first communion, had been married, and had heard Mass on Sunday was barred to him. The scientist from Bogotá went to see everyone he knew who had any influence, begged and implored old friends who might be able to help him. Finally the priest and the mayor yielded to the point where they agreed that the corpse might be buried in the cemetery at three o'clock in the morning without the rites of the Church and without anyone seeing the funeral . . .

These little tragedies nobody hears about form the daily existence of thousands of peasants of the Colombian countryside. The simple application of Christian teachings, the utilization of Latin America's supposedly fortunate circumstance of professing a single religion could go a long way to smoothing out many conflicts. But the fanatical members of the clergy, encouraged by a truly diabolical reactionary government, are sowing God only knows what seeds of wrath in the hearts of the humble.

In 1951 Perón closed down *La Prensa*. In spite of the handwriting on the wall, this act produced the shock of a bomb. On the continent dedicated to liberty, in the paradise of the immigrant, in a nation that stood in the front rank of civilized countries, a soldier in the presidential chair was able to destroy one of the finest newspapers in the world. It was a warning. Five years earlier *La Prensa* was as much an institution in the Argentina as *The New York Times* is in the United States. But before closing down *La Prensa* Perón had already attacked many other newspapers, old, distinguished journals of the provinces and papers of noble tradition in Buenos Aires itself, which meant a great deal to the Argentines in the field of political and cultural ideas and which signified, above all, freedom.

Does this mark the end of an epoch in Latin America? The matter of freedom of the press was a question of major importance at the time of the independence. Journalists militated actively in the ranks against Spain. Journalists could rightly be called the midwives of independence in Argentina, as in Mexico or Colombia. Francisco de Miranda organized his first expedition of liberation in 1805 in New York. At the same time that he purchased arms, he bought a printing press. The *Leandro*, the first ship to fly the first flag of freedom in America on Caribbean waters, was a floating press, and Miranda's first shots were leaflets he addressed to his countrymen of Venezuela. When Bolívar invaded Venezuela and set up his headquarters on the banks of the Orinoco, the first thing he did was to found a newspaper. José Joaquín Fernández de Lizardi, who in 1816 wrote the first American novel, made the defense of the freedom of the press in Mexico his reason for existence. Francisco Javier Espejo, the forerunner of independence in Ecuador, like his counterpart Antonio Nariño in Colombia, fought for this same cause. When in 1820 Rafael del Riego y Núñez briefly triumphed over the despotism of Ferdinand VII in Spain, Puerto Rico took courage and proclaimed the freedom of the press. The same thing happened in every country. Now, as one by one the papers are closed down or censored, the victory won a hundred years ago is being engulfed by a landslide. The Inter-American Press Conference (New York, 1950) proclaimed: "America, by its tradition and by its destiny, must be a continent of public opinion."

Argentina came into being on the copysheets of a journalist, Mariano Moreno. The communication between Buenos Aires and the rest of America began in the pages of *La Gaceta*. The masterpiece of Argentine literature, Sarmiento's *Facundo*, was first published in Chile as a newspaper supplement. The same thing happened with the outstanding example of romanticism in the Plate region, the novel *Amalia*. Without a free press, the history of Argentina becomes meaningless. The formula Perón proposes for the present and the future is a complete inversion of terms. Instead of freedom of the press, his object is to free himself from the press. The press is to cease to exist except as an organ of his party.

The case of *La Prensa* marks the culmination of a policy. In 1950, before its seizure, a report covering the whole continent was made at the Inter-American Press Conference in New York. It was said that in Argentina in a single day fifty newspapers had been closed down, that the government had expropriated the paper stocks of the newspapers, that a number of journalists had been sent to jail, that a law had been passed making the penalty for criticizing the government or its members imprisonment up to four years, that a law had been put on the statute books making liable to a four-year imprisonment anyone "who without due authorization hands over, publishes, or gives out economic, political, military, or financial information which, without being secret or withheld, is not meant for publication." In addition, "anyone who in any way causes public alarm or contributes to depressing the spirits of the public, occasioning harm to the nation, will be subject to a prison term of from one to eight years." At the same meeting a report was made on the restrictions imposed on the press in Peru, Venezuela, Colombia, the Dominican Republic, Nicaragua . . .

C. Rizzo Baratta, one of the staff members of the *peronista* newspaper *Ahora*, assumed the defense of the dictatorship in a long letter addressed to the Conference. The following is taken from it:

"The [Argentine] people, through Congress and Congress as the expression of the people, appointed a committee representing both chambers to investigate the anti-Argentine activities and the violations of the law. This . . . proceeded to close down sixty-three newspapers . . . for failing to observe Article 2 of Law 13,661, which made it mandatory for all of them, as a tribute to San Martín, to denominate the year 1950 the Year of the Liberator . . . thirteen other newspapers were also closed down for sedition or for printing on their presses sheets, proclamations, fliers, etc., which incited to riot and rebellion, or which irresponsibly, because of their occasional appearance or the anonymity behind which they took refuge, contributed to public unrest or exhorted to violence . . . This same parliamentary commission examined the accounts of certain enterprises because of irregularities they had committed or were committing, which involved thirty-four newspapers, among them *La Prensa, La Nación, Democracia* of Junín, *El Insurgente* of Salta, *Semana Financiera* and *Veritas* . . . In our country beyond doubt we aspire to having more than a free press; what we want is a freed press. It is already free by the terms of the Constitution; it will be freed in the degree in which neither the government nor trusts nor monopolies nor public utilities corporations nor the privileged groups among the oligarchy nor subversive groups nor governments that attempt to thwart our sovereignty nor the exploiters of wealth and of the labor which makes such wealth possible and effective can deform it or limit its action and convert it into an instrument of their schemes of oppression, social inequality, and degradation . . ."

These last words of the commentator of the Perón doctrine coincide with those of General Perón himself, who, in September 1951, after the expropriation of *La Prensa*, expounded his ideas at the final session of his national press conference:

"Freedom of the press can be explained only in relation to the social function it fulfills. More than that, liberty can only be explained in relation to the service it renders to a social ideal politically activated . . ."

That is to say, the press can be free only in so far as it supports his party. The defender of this doctrine at the Press Conference went on to say that if there were journalists in prison they were there because of an offense punishable by law: the crime of "disrespect." The proper Argentine is expected to show even more submission to the person of General Perón than the Argentine of colonial times toward the king of Spain. There is not a European monarchy today, and perhaps there never was one, that demands of its subjects the homage expected by General Perón and his wife. Any reference to investigation of the personal fortune of the President of Argentina is sufficient grounds to expel a member from the Congress or put a journalist in jail. The Perón doctrine is now beginning to spread to other countries that gravitate in its moral orbit.

The information laid before the 1950 New York Conference was confirmed at that held in 1951 in Montevideo. At the latter, the commission assigned to study the problem reported that the freedom of the press had suffered "serious and tragic reverses" during the preceding twelve months and recommended that "in view of the growing tendency to restrict or destroy the freedom of the press in the hemisphere, the organization should take a more vigorous and determined stand in the fight to strengthen or restore this freedom." The *peronista* journalists, seconded by their satellites from Paraguay, attempted to disrupt the Montevideo conference by concerted action aimed at starting a riot. In this way a conflict has been posed between the Perón doctrine and the Charter of the Inter-American Press (*see* Appendix D of this book), approved by the Inter-American Press Conference, which is an extension of the Charter of Human Rights of the United Nations.

In August 1951 the Economic and Social Council of the United Nations, which had been working in Geneva on a convention governing freedom of information, was forced to abandon the project in order not to find itself obliged to approve a text implying official approval of censorship of the world press. What had happened was that a group of Russians, Arabs, and Latin Americans from the *peronista* zone of influence had formed a united front against freedom of information.

The thesis opposed to the Perón doctrine is fully set forth in a resolution adopted in Evanston in October 1951 by a group of newspaper editors and journalists of the United States and Latin America who met at the School of Journalism of Northwestern University. The resolution said in part:

". . . it is our urgent conviction that the liberties of men everywhere are dependent upon the independence and integrity of their sources of information. That the serious problems which disturb all peoples will be solved in honesty, justice and good morality only if the inhabitants of every nation are permitted to communicate with each other, and with the people of other nations, by freely speaking, writing and printing their thoughts. That the ways and means to attain and preserve the true dignity of mankind must come out of the people through their right to speak to their governments, so that public officers will be their servants and not their masters. That freedom of information is not and cannot be a matter for one nation or one people alone. That the right of freedom of information is a basic right of all the people of the 21 republics of the Western Hemisphere, not to be suppressed or put under duress by any government . . ."

XIX

VISIBLE AND INVISIBLE AMERICA

The freedom of America is the hope of the world.
BOLÍVAR

THE CAUDILLOS, the dictators, even the military coups in Latin America have started out with the backing of groups of the people, sometimes with a real majority of popular support. Invariably their programs have carried a glimmer of the democratic ideal: war on privilege, on electoral fraud and administrative corruption; representative government by the people and for the people. Never did they come to power on a platform of despotism or of doing away with freedom. One might even say that the caudillos had a democratic origin. When Perón went before the people and said: "We are fighting the oppression of gold and rank because they both mean suffering and tears for the people; we want the future generations of Argentines to be able to smile from the day they are born; for this some must divest themselves of their hatred and others of their selfishness," the people found in his words something that stirred them and gave them hope. They did not flinch from the revolutionary phrases that followed: "For those who refuse to divest themselves of their hatred or their selfishness, the more they resist, the tighter will the strait jacket have to be strapped to bring them under control . . . There may be suspicious and dissatisfied souls who object that free political interplay is still lacking; but I hasten to inform them that in all the historical crises of a country the general well-being cannot be accomplished without a strong

384

authority to bring those who coerce or exploit others under control . . ." [1]

Once in power, the caudillo goes on mouthing the defense of democratic principles unstintingly. Lincoln never uttered finer phrases in describing democracy than General Trujillo or Tacho Somoza uses in public statements. In his speech to congress in 1948 General Perón said:

"There is unquestionably one dangerous point in the reform law, that referring . . . to the possibility of the president's being re-elected without an intervening period. I am opposed to such a change . . . One only has to see what happens in those countries where such re-election to a second term is constitutional. There is no means that is not employed, licit or illicit; it is a school of fraud and an incentive to violence, as well as a temptation to political maneuvering on the part of the government or its officials . . ."

This is only one aspect. The caudillo has a powerful magic that upholds his prestige for a long time. The dictator everywhere is an advocate of progress. Caracas was made over by Antonio Guzmán Blanco. Porfirio Díaz gave Mexico railroads, and García Moreno built up Ecuador just as Mussolini made the trains run on time in Italy and constructed splendid stadiums and highways, and Huey Long built the great bridge at New Orleans. But does Latin America want only these material benefits, and has it lost its devotion to democracy? If Perón, in four years in power, had really been giving the Argentines what they wanted, he could have allowed the opposition complete freedom to carry on its campaign. There could have been freedom of the press, freedom of assembly, agreements among the opposition parties. But he clamped down on all this, even though he had control of the electoral machine. The Demócrata Nacional Party summed up the results of the election of November 1951 in these words: "If

[1] "The People Want to Know What It Is All About," *Colonel Juan Perón's Speeches* (Buenos Aires, 1946).

we wished to describe briefly the electoral process, we would say that it was made up of 364 days of fraud, and 1 day of simulated legality." We have it in General Perón's own words: ". . . re-election . . . is a school of fraud and an incentive to violence".

The long experience of generation after generation deceived by the very men in whom they had placed the most hope has given the majority of the Latin Americans a sharper judgment and a keener awareness than might have been supposed. They know that they must wait, that as yet they have no immediate means of defense. But a reserve of determination is building up which will surprise everyone when it can find expression. Bolívar knew how to make use of this reserve. One of the fundamental differences between the war of independence in North America and that in South America is that Washington had regular troops under his command whereas Bolívar's army was made up of the people, barehanded, with only their will, their determination to change things as weapons. The outbreak that followed the assassination of Gaitán in Bogotá at the time of the Pan American Conference is proof of the lengths to which the people will go once they burst through restraints.

There are two Americas: the visible and the invisible. The visible America, the America of presidents and embassies, expresses itself through official organs, through a controlled press. This America takes its seat at the conference table of the Pan American Union and has many votes in the United Nations. And there is the mute, repressed America, which is a vast reservoir of revolution. Both Americas are misleading in appearance.

Under its dictatorial regimes, visible America makes fervent protestations of its democratic faith, signs charters of liberties, manufacturing one line of goods for foreign and another for domestic consumption. This double personality has achieved a dexterity that is almost unbelievable. Even though everywhere and in all periods of history there has been something of this same split between what is said and what is done, the contrast has rarely been so brutal as that afforded today by the Latin American dictatorships. Laureano Gómez who had come to power on a wave of violence once said to a group of North American journalists: "This is a people of savage Communists; they have killed one hundred police officers. Is there a civilized nation anywhere that would tolerate the killing of one hundred police?" To understand this sophism we must analyze two words: "Communism" and "police." For the purposes of their practical dealings with the United States the dictators describe as Communists all those who do not support them. According to General Odría, the people of Peru are communists; according to the military *junta* of Venezuela, the people of Venezuela; according to the dictator of Bogotá, the people of Colombia; according to General Trujillo, the people of the Dominican Republic. The word "police" likewise requires definition. A policeman in the United States or London is a human being who helps an old lady across the street, a guardian angel for the children coming out of school, the protecting arm of the law. A policeman under a Latin American despot is a shady character not too far removed from the criminal, a man of dubious past who is handed a uniform and a revolver with orders to crush the opposition and maintain order by terror. The one hundred police officers over whom the North American journalists were asked to weep had been one hundred weapons turned on the peasants, members of a shock force that burned down homes, stole cattle, and attacked the wives and daughters of the peasants in scenes of barbarity that beggar description. When they got a chance the peasants fought back and killed. They were not Communists; the police officers were not police.

This arbitrary use of words has given rise to the greatest confusion. The despots use the word "democracy" to set up governments such as those described in the pages of this book. The common man asks himself if this can be democracy. The same thing holds true of the other words in the political lexicon: army, religion, freedom, Christianity, faith, republic, justice, judge, president, elections, congress, priest, university, peace, public opinion. By turning words inside out, dictators destroy the natural medium of communication among people. When one of the presidents of visible America speaks, his every word must be analyzed against the background of its accepted meaning and the application given to it by him inside his own country.

Although this theme may seem academic, its implications go very deep, because as a result of this deception moral principles are being undermined, good faith is being corrupted, and an atmosphere of cynicism and distrust is growing up. The story of the tower of Babel is not a fairy tale. At this very moment the greatest political campaign in the world is based on one word: peace. With special reference to Russia, her brand of peace is familiar to those Latin Americans who have suffered dictatorships. Paraguay enjoyed peace of this sort under Dr. Francia; this was the peace of Argentina under Rosas, of Venezuela under Juan Vicente Gómez. This peace is the objective of their legitimate successors. We call it a living cemetery. There are peace and order because no one can talk or criticize or object or join his fellows in assembly. It is the kind of peace guarded by the family servant who acts as a spy on the household.

Latin America, like other parts of the world, has fought against the peace of the colony, the peace of slavery, the peace of servility. At times with maximum passion and heroism. In his war against these kinds of peace, man has grown in dignity, intelligence has had a mission to fulfill, people have learned that they are entitled to an existence better than that of the beasts of the field, and a little decency has been brought into the world.

Theoretically it would seem that Latin America is a fertile

field for Communism. Yet it is amazing how few addicts this party has made. In fact, it may be said that in Latin America Communism is non-existent. France has many more Communists than all of Latin America despite the fact that the people of Latin America, badly fed, badly dressed, badly housed, and badly treated, are in much closer contact than any other with the capitalist world of their next-door neighbor. Why does Communism fail to take hold there? Because in Latin America the thirst for freedom is as great as the thirst for justice. Because there is a sense of national pride. The Mexican wants to be the master of his house, not the lackey of Moscow. What Schuyler said of the Negroes—that they cannot be Communists because they have emerged from slavery and are not buying a return ticket—holds true of the Latin Americans. They are through with being colonials.

By reasons of their historic formation the Latin American masses are well conditioned to absorb and spread ideas of representative government, the spirit of liberty, the doctrines of social justice. This is a world in which, from the beginning, different races have had to live together and have fused, where no old aristocracy exists, where privilege is not entrenched. But this potentiality which exists in the Latin American republics that enjoy free government must be assured to the others.

Like visible America, invisible America lies. The humble folk know that they cannot say what they think, and the upper classes have learned this, too. On one occasion, at the beginning of Perón's dictatorship, a group of ladies of the best families, gathered in the street and began to sing the Argentine national anthem:

> *Hark, mortals, the sacred cry:*
> *Liberty, liberty, liberty!*

The ladies spent the night in jail. In Barranquilla, Colombia, the director of one of the factories in that prosperous industrial city shouted in the lobby of the Hotel del Prado—the best in the city—"Long live the Liberal Party." A bullet from a policeman's revolver dropped him dead. If this can happen to persons who, by reason of their social position and wealth, generally receive preferential treatment from the authorities, what can the peasant expect? This book has touched only lightly on instances of the brutality that is of constant occurrence. The full account of the violence, the tortures, the concentration camps has not been told outside the frontiers. But if in one of the most cultured countries of Europe Nazism could unleash the dark forces it did, why wonder that similar things have taken place in backward lands? In invisible America, where a vast mass of the population lives with the cold breath of terror on its neck, the least word may bring reprisals. The part of prudence is to keep quiet, to wear a mask. Where machine guns have the floor a deep silence reigns. Life goes on under the cover of conventional phrases, lip-service, extorted votes. A Peruvian poet has described the attitude of the Indian in a famous poem in which each stanza ends with: "*¿Quien sabe, señor?*"

Nobody knows exactly what these 150,000,000 silent men and women think, feel, dream, or await in the depths of their being.

The attitude of the Indian is not the result of racial shortcoming; it has been developed by the life he has been forced to live. The same dissimulation is now found among white "Sons of the American Revolution," newly arrived immigrants—even in the third party, made up of business men, that is to be found in all the Latin American countries. Latin America's natural rate of growth is very rapid. The industrial world in the process of development there is creating great wealth. This is apparent in the cities, where the skyscrapers, shops, hotels, theaters, and apartment houses are among the best to be found anywhere in the world. Yet all this could be multiplied if only there were security, if the storm clouds could be rolled away from invisible America. Native capital flees from Latin America. Only in Montevideo and Mexico City have large fortunes found refuge. If the amount of Latin American funds on deposit today in the banks of New York and Switzerland were accurately known, one would conclude that Latin America possesses all the capital it needs. Even capital is invisible in America.

Europe had a brief span of security which reached its apex before the First World War. People there still preserve the habits of a safe world. Insecurity is Latin America's political tradition, and underlies the history of its economic crises. There was a day when its wealth was rubber; when rubber began to be produced in great quantity by the Far East, this wealth vanished. The same thing has happened for this or an analogous reason with quinine, cacao, nitrates, coffee, sugar, diamonds, Panama hats. At this very moment the vast development of colonial Africa holds a tremendous threat for Latin America. Carlos Dávila, who has studied these matters, says:

"Before World War II the United States was buying 94 per cent of its tropical imports, mostly strategic materials, from an undependable Orient ten thousand miles away, instead of from its neighbors in near-by Latin America, and was paying for this unsound course in mounting scarcities. In 1939 the United States' imports of essential and strategic commodities amounted to $400 million. Of this, six million, or 1½%, came from Latin America. When World War II broke out, it was freely stated this would 'never happen again'. But as events are shaping up now, it may very well happen again." [2]

What is the approach to Latin America? With two Americas, visible and invisible, each having a double personality, it is a region of complexities shot through with reserves, suspicion, resentment, wariness, and fears. There is one word that arouses an immeasurable reaction on the part of those who have emerged from a colonial world and

[2] *We of the Americas*. Ziff-Davis Publishing Company, 1949.

have heard about a semi-colonial one: "intervention." Intervention, too, has a double personality. It may take the form of landing marines, a diplomatic offensive, threats. It may also take the form of omission. For years Perón's best campaign slogan has been "Braden or Perón." Braden's speeches were looked upon in Argentina as American intervention. This intervention was violently denounced by Perón, who, however, was more than willing to accept another more effective intervention: a $125,000,000 loan and the honeyed words of Mr. Braden's successor.

Everything in Latin American politics depends on the approach. On analysis things turn out to be simpler than they look. The thing to do is to decide between two opposed methods and then adjust each action and the evaluation of each incident to the method decided upon. Either one accepts the position that the invisible America is a real factor that will sooner or later swing into action or one takes the position that it is negligible and that its people are a kind of still life that can be handled as seems most convenient. One of the dictators said not long ago at an intimate gathering: "What we have proved is that the people does not exist; nobody can frighten us any more with a ghost that has been laid." This is one opinion. If this is adopted, it should be carried to its ultimate conclusions. The dictatorships should be given arms, the police state strengthened, and the way paved for a silent, zombie continent where good business can be carried on and a new age of wizards established.

If, on the other hand, it is assumed that the love of liberty is still alive in the heart of Latin America, and that along with its material resources there is a human reserve that can produce more and better on a basis of dignity and justice, or that may kick over the traces any day, the approach to the problem must become radically different. In the light of this a Pan American Union of Public Opinion becomes a possibility. It will be conceded that the coming generations, the young people trained in the universities, are equipped to carry on a tradition of learning, scientific studies, and art, fields in which contributions of universal value already have been made. When Bernardo Houssay receives the Nobel Prize for his work as head of the Institute of Physiology of Buenos Aires, when the Nobel Prize for Literature is awarded to Gabriela Mistral for her poetry, when the work of the Mexican painters is accepted as one of the important artistic achievements of our century, there can be no quibbling about Latin America's cultural status.

During the first half of this century no other section of the world showed so high an index of material progress as Latin America. If this rate was formerly surpassed by that of the United States, the two are now on a level. In the briefest space of time—during the years from 1920 to 1950—six of the most beautiful cities in the world have grown up in Latin America. And, looking backwards, several of the most impressive civilizations history records once flourished in this same area. Is all this to end in a cemetery of living dead?

Using a little common sense, and with an eye to the future, it would seem far better to regard the Latin Americans as one of mankind's reserves that should be put to active use. Inside Latin America this is not accepted by those who favor a political system of servility. Nor is it accepted by those outside Latin America who share that idea. And yet, what today look like insurmountable difficulties may tomorrow be but the memory of a hideous nightmare. In America, where a handful of dictators struts and frets, there are great zones of light. And throughout the hemisphere, in the background, stands the people. The day they can make themselves heard they may be a consuming fire or a flood of light. In any case, they hold the light of that *mañana* which is omnipresent and enigmatic in the language of the Latin Americans.

APPENDIXES

APPENDIX A

Chronological Guide to Events in Latin America, 1930–51

1930

February 5 MEXICO. Pascual Ortiz Rubio assumes the presidency.

June 22 BOLIVIA. Military revolt against President Hernando Siles, who seeks asylum in the Brazilian Legation. Military *junta* formed, headed by General Carlos Blanco Galindo.

August 7 COLOMBIA. Doctor Enrique Olaya Herrera becomes Colombia's first Liberal president of this century.

August 16 DOMINICAN REPUBLIC. General Rafael Leonidas Trujillo becomes president for the first time.

August 22 PERU. Luis Sánchez Cerro, commander of the Arequipa garrison, starts a revolt against the government of Augusto Leguía and takes power.

September 3 DOMINICAN REPUBLIC. A hurricane all but destroys the city of Santo Domingo.

September 5 ARGENTINA. General José Francisco Uriburu, at the head of the military forces, advances on Buenos Aires and overthrows President Hipólito Irigoyen.

September 30 CUBA. The students of Havana organize riots against the dictatorship of Gerardo Machado.

October 24 BRAZIL. Getulio Vargas takes over leadership of the revolution, advances on Rio de Janeiro, and (November 3) assumes the presidency.

1931

January 2 PANAMA. Harmodio Arias directs a revolt that overthrows President Florencio Harmodio Arosemena. Rise of Doctor Ricardo J. Alfaro.

February 14 GUATEMALA. The presidency is taken over by Jorge Ubico Castañeda, who will remain dictator for thirteen years.

March 1 PERU. A military uprising forces General Sánchez Cerro to retire from the government, which he hands over to the Archbishop, who in turn delivers its powers to the Supreme Court of Justice.

March BOLIVIA. Doctor Daniel Salamanca inaugurates his regime.

July 24 CHILE. Revolt against General Carlos Ibáñez, who transfers the presidency to the president of the senate, who refuses it. Juan Esteban Montero remains at the head of the government.

397

August ECUADOR. Doctor Isidro Ayora resigns the presidency and is succeeded by Colonel Luis Larrea Alba.

August 15 PERU. Victor Raúl Haya de la Torre returns after eight years of exile. The people acclaim him as their candidate for president, but the old guard supports the candidacy of General Sánchez Cerro. At the elections (October) the government awards the victory to Sánchez Cerro.

October 26 PARAGUAY. Revolt in Asunción against President José Patricio Guggiari is suppressed.

December 3 EL SALVADOR. General Maximiliano Hernández Martínez overthrows President Arturo Araújo and takes over the presidency.

1932

May 5 PERU. The government of General Sánchez Cerro imprisons Haya de la Torre.

June 4 CHILE. Military revolution deposes President Juan Esteban Montero. A ruling *junta* is formed by General Puga, Eugenio Matte, and Carlos Dávila, the last exercising the powers of the presidency.

July 7 PERU. Popular uprising in Trujillo against President Sánchez Cerro is suppressed.

July 9 BRAZIL. Rebellion against Getulio Vargas, at the end of which he submits to the rebels.

July 15 BOLIVIA-PARAGUAY. The Chaco War breaks out.

September 3 MEXICO. Pascual Ortiz Rubio having been obliged to resign as president, Congress names as his successor General Abelardo L. Rodríguez.

October 2 CHILE. Carlos Dávila falls from the presidency as the result of a military action, and is succeeded by the President of the Court of Justice, Doctor Humberto Oyanedel. Shortly later, elections are held, and Arturo Alessandri is chosen president, assuming office on December 24.

1933

January 1 NICARAGUA. Doctor Juan Bautista Sacasa takes possession of the presidency; the United States marines leave shortly later.

January 1 HONDURAS. General Tiburcio Carías Andino inaugurates his first presidency; he will remain dictator until 1949.

April 30 PERU. President Sánchez Cerro assassinated in Lima. The Constituent Assembly elects as his successor Marshal Oscar Benavides. Shortly later, Haya de la Torre is removed from prison. His first public appearance in Lima occurs at an *aprista* meeting on December 18.

August 12 CUBA. In a popular revolution President Machado is over-thrown; he is succeeded by Carlos Manuel de Céspedes. Next there is a revolt against Céspedes, who resigns. On September 5 Doctor Ramón Grau San Martín assumes the presidency.

October 10 In Rio de Janeiro is signed the "Saavedra Lamas Pact," an agreement to fight against war, to abstain from aggression, and to employ conciliation; it is endorsed by Argentina, Brazil, Chile, Mexico, Paraguay, and Uruguay.

December 3–26 The Seventh Pan American Conference meets in Montevidio, Uruguay.

1934

January 15 CUBA. President Grau San Martín resigns and is succeeded by Carlos Hevia, who is deposed on January 18, when the power is taken over by Colonel Carlos Mendieta.

February 21 NICARAGUA. Assassination of the popular leader Augusto César Sandino by a guard commanded by Anastasio Somoza.

July 16 BRAZIL. Getulio Vargas becomes constitutional president. He produces a new constitution.

August 7 COLOMBIA. Alfonso López becomes constitutional president.

August 16 DOMINICAN REPUBLIC. General Trujillo inaugurates his second presidency.

September 9 GUATEMALA. As reprisal against a conspiracy discovered by Dictator Ubico, the government orders a large massacre.

November 27 BOLIVIA. At the *"cerco de Villamontes"* the military command deposes President Daniel Salamanca; the presidency is assumed by Vice-President José Luis Tejada Sorzano.

December 1 MEXICO. General Lázaro Cárdenas becomes constitutional president.

During 1934 the Italian Fascists publish the translation of the book by the Venezuelan writer Laureano Vallenilla Lanz.

1935

June 14 PARAGUAY-BOLIVIA. The Chaco War ends as far as hostilities are concerned; the official termination is October 28.

September ECUADOR. Colonel Luis Larrea Alba is deposed from the presidency; he is succeeded by Federico Páez.

November 27 BRAZIL. Communist uprising against Getulio Vargas.

December 17 VENEZUELA. Dictator Juan Vicente Gómez, who has ruled since 1908, dies of natural causes. The nation celebrates this occurrence with great demonstrations of joy. Congress elects as Gomez's successor General Eleázar López Contreras.

APPENDIX

1936

January 11 DOMINICAN REPUBLIC. Acting Vice-President Jacinto Peynado approves a law changing the name of the capital from Santo Domingo (the oldest city in America, given its name on its founding in 1496) to Ciudad Trujillo.

January CUBA. Doctor Miguel Mariano Gómez is elected president. In December, Congress, under the influence of Colonel Fulgencio Batista, expels Doctor Gómez from the presidency and installs in his place Vice-President Federico Laredo Brú.

February 17 PARAGUAY. Revolt against President Eusebio Ayala; the military overthrows him and replaces him with Colonel Rafael Franco.

April MEXICO. Ex-President Plutarco Elías Calles is expelled from Mexico.

May 17 BOLIVIA. Fall of President José Luis Tejada Sorzano; the presidency assumed by Colonel David Toro.

May 31 CUBA. The Senate of the United States approves the treaty that frees Cuba of the Platt Amendment.

September MEXICO. Confirmation of the law nationalizing churches and other Church-owned buildings.

December 1 In Buenos Aires, President Franklin D. Roosevelt inaugurates the Inter-American Conference for the Maintenance of Peace, which sits until December 23.

During 1936 the Nobel Peace Prize is awarded to the Argentine Carlos Saavedra Lamas. During 1936 the government of Colonel Toro in *Bolivia* declares inoperative the concessions granted to the Standard Oil Company of New Jersey eleven years before.

1937

January 1 NICARAGUA. Anastazio Somoza, inaugurating his presidency, begins his dictatorship.

August 13 PARAGUAY. Second Lieutenant Ramón Paredes begins a revolt. The cabinet of President Franco is forced to resign. On August 15 Franco resigns and is replaced by Doctor Félix Paiva. On September 7 there is a rebellion by the military against Doctor Paiva, but it is quashed.

November 9 BRAZIL. Sanctioning of the constitution of the *Estado Novo,* which incarnates the ideas of Getulio Vargas.

During 1937 in *Chile* there are riots against President Alessandri by Nazi groups. During 1937 President-Dictator Trujillo of the *Dominican Republic* orders the great slaughter of Haitians, the dead being calculated at 12,000. In 1937 in *Bolivia* President Toro is overthrown and Colonel Germán Busch takes power.

1938

February 20 ARGENTINA. Doctor Roberto M. Ortiz becomes constitutional president.

March 8 MEXICO nationalizes petroleum.

May DOMINICAN REPUBLIC. Jacinto Peynado becomes nominal president.

August 7 COLOMBIO. Doctor Eduardo Santos becomes constitutional president.

October 3 MEXICO. In the confiscation of lands in the possession of great holders, which are to be returned to the Mexican peasants, are included 17,980 acres in the State of Chihuahua belonging to William Randolph Hearst.

December 9–27 The Eighth Pan American Conference meets in Lima, Peru.

December 24 CHILE. Pedro Aguirre Cerda becomes constitutional president.

1939

August 15 PARAGUAY. General José Félix Estigarribia becomes president.

August 23 BOLIVIA. Colonel Germán Busch, dictator, commits suicide; he is succeeded by General Carlos Quintanilla.

September 23 The first Conference of the Foreign Ministers of the American Republics meets in Panamá, sitting until October 3.

1940

March BOLIVIA. General Enrique Peñaranda is elected president.

May COSTA RICA. Doctor Rafael Ángel Calderón Guardia becomes president.

July ARGENTINA. President Roberto M. Ortiz retires because of illness. He is succeeded by Vice-President Ramón S. Castillo.

July 21 The second Conference of the Foreign Ministers of the American Republics meets in Havana, sitting until July 30.

August 20 MEXICO. Attempt on Leon Trotsky's life; he dies the following day.

September 7 PARAGUAY. General José Félix Estigarribia, dictator, dies in an airplane accident; he is succeeded by his Minister of War, General Higinio Morínigo, who inaugurates a dictatorship.

October 10 CUBA. Colonel Fulgencio Batista becomes president.

December 1 MEXICO. General Manuel Ávila Camacho becomes constitutional president.

APPENDIX

1941

January 31 Inauguration of the Regional Economic Conference of the Río de la Plata, participated in by Argentina, Bolivia, Brazil, Paraguay, and Uruguay.

April VENEZUELA. General Isaías Medina Angarita is elected president by the Congress, succeeding General Eleázar López Contreras.

September. PANAMA. By a *coup d'état* the presidency of Arnulfo Arias is ended; he is succeeded by Ricardo Adolfo de la Guardia.

During 1941 these things happened in these countries: ARGENTINA—President Castillo maintained diplomatic relations with the Axis powers; BOLIVIA—the Nazi-inspired Movimiento Nacional Revolucionario party was founded and the government discovered a Berlin-directed conspiracy to impose a Nazi government on the country, whereupon the German Minister was handed his passport; CHILE—President Pedro Aguirre Cerda died and the police discovered the functioning of a Nazi party.

1942

January 15 The third Conference of the Foreign Ministers of the American Republics meets in Rio de Janeiro, sitting until January 28.

January 29 PERU and ECUADOR sign a treaty delimiting their common boundaries.

January 29 CHILE. Juan Antonio Ríos becomes constitutional president.

August 7 COLOMBIA. Alfonso López becomes constitutional president.

August 16 DOMINICAN REPUBLIC. General Trujillo begins his third presidency; the United States Ambassador, Avra M. Warren, transmits to him the honorary degree of *doctor honoris causa* bestowed on him by the University of Pittsburgh.

1943

June 3 ARGENTINA. During the night, troops march on Buenos Aires; on the following day occurs a *coup d'état* that overthrows President Castillo, and General Arturo Rawson becomes president.

June 7 ARGENTINA. President Rawson falls, and is succeeded by his Minister of War, General Pedro Ramírez.

October ARGENTINA. Professors in the Argentine universities address to the government a memorial asking for effective democracy and American solidarity; all of its signers, including future Nobel Prize-winner Bernardo Houssay, are deprived of their posts.

December 20 BOLIVIA. General Gualberto Villarroel organizes a military revolt against President Peñaranda, and wins the presidency.

December ARGENTINA. The government intervenes in the internal affairs of five universities and outlaws the Federation of Students.

1944

February 24 ARGENTINA. President Ramírez is forced to resign, and is succeeded by his Minister of War, General Edelmiro Farrell, while the vice-presidency is taken over by Farrell's Minister of War, General Juan Domingo Perón.

April 25 ARGENTINA. In Buenos Aires the newspaper *La Prensa* is closed for five days for having published an item concerning hospital funds.

May 8 EL SALVADOR. The dictatorship of Maximiliano Hernández Martínez having come to an end, he flees from the country; his Minister of War, General Andrés Ignacio Menéndez, takes over the presidency. On October 21, the military obliges General Menéndez to resign, and in his place impose the Director of Police, Osmín Aguirre.

May 29 ECUADOR. A revolutionary *junta* forces President Carlos Arroyo del Río to resign and substitutes for him Doctor José María Velasco Ibarra; the Constituent Assembly, meeting in August, confirms the presidency of Velasco Ibarra.

May 31 CUBA. Ramón Grau San Martín is elected constitutional president.

June 29 GUATEMALA. Dictator-President Jorge Ubico is forced to resign; he seeks asylum in the Spanish Embassy, and is succeeded by a military *junta* headed by General Federico Ponce; Ponce is overthrown on October 20 and replaced by a military *junta;* in December Doctor Juan José Arévalo, in a popular election, wins the presidency.

July 10 COLOMBIA. In Pasto, a military group captures President Alfonso López; a national movement forces the military to liberate him; the head of the Conservative party, Laureano Gómez, flees to Ecuador.

August 6 BOLIVIA. General Gualberto Villarroel becomes president.

November 19 BOLIVIA. In Oruro a revolt against President Villarroel breaks out; the government shoots its ringleaders.

1945

February 20 Inter-American Conference on Problems of War and Peace meets in Mexico City; on March 7 it approves the "Act of Chapultepec," and on March 8 it adjourns.

March 1 EL SALVADOR. General Salvador Castañeda Castro succeeds Osmín Aguirre in the presidency.

APPENDIX

March 15 GUATEMALA. Doctor Juan José Arévalo becomes constitutional president; during his term, a new constitution is approved.

June 10 PERU. Doctor José Luis Bustamante y Rivero, helped by *aprista* votes, is elected president.

July 6 ARGENTINA. Under Farrell's regime, Perón establishes censorship of the press: "Tonight freedom of the press terminates in Argentina. The government does not permit opposition from the Argentine press."

July 15 PANAMA. Enrique A. Jiménez is elected president; Arnulfo Arias tries to overthrow him, but is sent to jail.

July 26 ARGENTINA. The union of the Confederation of Commercial Employees of Buenos Aires attempts to storm *La Prensa*.

August COLOMBIA. Alfonso López resigns the presidency; Congress names as his successor Alberto Lleras Camargo.

September 28 ARGENTINA. Alberto Gainza Paz, director of *La Prensa*, is imprisoned for eighteen hours.

October 13 ARGENTINA. Under pressure from very widely expressed public opinion, President Farrell is obliged to imprison General Perón, his vice-president and minister of war; Perón is taken to the island of Martín García; on October 17 takes place the "march of the shirtless" on Buenos Aires; Perón is set free and acclaimed as the leader of the people.

October 19 VENEZUELA. President Isaías Medina Angarita is overthrown by a military *coup;* he is replaced by a revolutionary *junta* headed by Rómulo Betancourt.

October 29 BRAZIL. Getulio Vargas resigns under pressure from the opposition; on December 2 elections are held and Major General Enrico Gaspar Dutra is elected president.

During 1945 the Nobel Prize for Literature was awarded to the Chilean writer Gabriela Mistral (pseudonym of Lucila Godoy).

1946

February 24 ARGENTINA. General Juan Domingo Perón is elected president for the first time; he takes over the presidency on June 4; on June 11 he is visited by the Bolivian leader Doctor Victor Paz Estenssoro, and they declare the identity of principals of the Argentine and Bolivian revolutions.

May 2 ARGENTINA. The government intervenes in the internal affairs of all universities.

June 27 CHILE. President Juan Antonio Ríos dies; at the elections on September 4, Gabriel González Videla is elected.

July 7 MEXICO. Miguel Alemán, a civilian, is elected constitutional president.

July 17 BOLIVIA. The followers of Dictator-President Villarroel attack the University; on the following day student manifestations are suppressed by the army; on July 21 there is a popular uprising, during which the government palace is besieged and General

Villarroel is hanged from a lamppost in the main plaza of La Paz; the provisional government is headed by the President of the Supreme Court, Doctor Tomás Monje Gutiérrez.

August 7 COLOMBIA. Mariano Ospina Pérez, a Conservative, becomes constitutional president (the Liberals having lost the election because, though a majority, they had divided their votes between Jorge Eliécer Gaitán and Gabriel Turbay).

September 17 BRAZIL. The constitution that Vargas had given Brazil having been nullified, a new one is proclaimed.

October-November ARGENTINA. More than one thousand professors are dismissed from the universities by the dictatorship.

1947

January 5 BOLIVIA. Enrique Hertzog is elected president.

May 1 NICARAGUA. Leonardo Argüello succeeds Anastasio Somoza as president; Somoza remains as head of the National Guard; on May 26 Argüello is forced out and Somoza returns to the presidency; in August, Somoza installs Victor Román y Reyes as president and returns to his post with the National Guard.

June 5 Former President Alberto Lleras Camargo of Colombia is installed as Director General of the Pan American Union (Organization of American States).

August 2 URUGUAY. Luis Batlle Berres succeeds as president Tomás Berreta, who had been elected in 1946 (November 24), and who died in office.

August 5 ARGENTINA. Ernesto Sammartino is expelled from the Argentine Congress.

August 15 Inter-American Conference for the Maintenance of Continental Peace and Security is inaugurated at Quitandinha, Brazil, by President Harry S. Truman; it sits until September 2.

August 16 DOMINICAN REPUBLIC. General Trujillo begins his fourth administration.

August 23 ECUADOR. *Coup d'état* overthrows President Velasco Ibarra; he is succeeded by Colonel Carlos Mancheno; on August 31 the Conservatives rise against Mancheno in Guayaquil, march on Quito, and overthrow Mancheno (September 2); on September 16, Carlos Julio Arosemena is elected president.

December 14 VENEZUELA. Rómulo Gallegos is elected president in Venezuela's first truly popular election.

It was during 1947 that the Nobel Prize for Medicine was awarded to Doctor Bernardo Houssay, who had been expelled from his university chair by the Argentine dictatorship.

1948

February VENEZUELA. Rómulo Gallegos is inaugurated as president. On November 24 he is overthrown by a military *coup* and is succeeded by a military *junta* headed by his former Minister of War, Lieutenant Colonel Carlos Delgado Chalbaud.

February 8 COSTA RICA. Doctor Otilio Ulate is elected president; his election being disregarded, a popular revolution is organized, headed by José Figueres; the revolution triumphs on May 8 and Figueres heads a provisional government.

March 30 The Ninth Pan American Conference is inaugurated in Bogotá by General George C. Marshall; it is under the presidency of the Conservative Colombian Minister of Foreign Relations, Laureano Gómez.

April 9 COLOMBIA. The leader of the Liberal party, Doctor Jorge Eliécer Gaitán, is assassinated in Bogotá; the people rise and burn the business center of the city; to normalize the situation, Conservative President Ospina Pérez asks for and obtains Liberal cooperation in a government of national union, naming as first minister the liberal leader Dário Echandía; the Conservative leader Laureano Gómez, presiding over the Pan American Conference, flees to Spain.

May 2 The Ninth Pan American Conference closes in Bogotá having adopted the American Declaration of the Rights and Duties of Man (See Appendix C).

May 31 CUBA. Carlos Prío Socarrás is elected president.

June 3 PARAGUAY. *Coup d'état* against President Higinio Morínigo, who is succeeded by Juan Manuel Frutos; on August 15 Juan Natalicio González becomes constitutional president (having been elected on February 15); on October 25 a rebellion against Natalicio González breaks out in the military school and the navy, but is subdued.

June 9 ECUADOR. Galo Plaza Lasso is elected president.

October 28 PERU. Under the leadership of General Manuel A. Odría, a *coup d'état* overthrows constitutional President José Luis Bustamante y Rivero; on October 31 Odría takes over the presidency and begins to persecute the *apristas;* Haya de la Torre finally takes refuge in the Colombian Embassy; Odría claims him as a common criminal, but Colombia asks that the right of asylum be respected; the affair goes to the International Court of Justice at The Hague, which on November 19, 1950, gives an ambiguous decision; Haya remains in the Colombian Embassy in Lima.

November 2 PUERTO RICO. Luis Muñoz Marín is elected first locally chosen governor.

December 14 EL SALVADOR. General Salvador Castañeda is toppled from the presidency by a *coup d'état,* and is succeeded by the president of a military *junta,* Major Oscar Osorio.

During 1948 the Mexican writer and educator Jaime Torres Bodet was named Director General of UNESCO (United Nations Educational Scientific and Cultural Organization).

1949

January 1 HONDURAS. After sixteen years, Dictator-President Tiburcio Carías Andino relinquishes power; he is succeeded by Juan Manuel Gálvez.

January 29 PARAGUAY. Military *coup d'état;* President Natalicio González is overthrown; he is succeeded by General Rolón, who is turned out in February and replaced by Felipe Molas López, who in turn is replaced on September 11 by Federico Chaves.

June 9 ARGENTINA. Deputy Agustín Rodríguez Araya is expelled from Congress.

June 25 COLOMBIA. The leader of the Conservatives, Laureano Gómez, returns from Spain; the campaign of his party against Congress begins.

August 23 PANAMA. President Domingo Díaz Arosemena dies and is succeeded by Vice-President Daniel Chanis.

August 29 BOLIVIA. A section of the army and the Movimiento Nacional Revolucionario stir up a revolt; by September 15 the uprising has been quelled.

September ARGENTINA. Congress names bicameral commission that quickly closes sixty-three daily newspapers for omitting the formula of homage to San Martín and thirteen for sedition; the commission sends investigators to look at the books of thirty-four newspapers.

September 8 COLOMBIA. The Conservatives fire on Liberal members of the House of Representatives in Bogotá; they kill Representative Jiménez and gravely wound the Liberal leader of the House, Doctor Jorge Soto del Corral.

September 29 ARGENTINA. Doctor Ricardo Balbín, Radical leader and candidate for governor of Buenos Aires Province, is stripped of his parliamentary rights and put in jail.

October 22 BOLIVIA. President Enrique Hertzog resigns and is succeeded by Mamerto Urriolagoitia.

November 8 COSTA RICA. The revolutionary *junta* headed by José Figueres, having completed its work, turns over the mandate to the constitutional president, Otilio Ulate.

November 9 COLOMBIA. On receiving word that the Senate will study the possibility of summoning him to judgment, President Ospina Pérez closes Congress by force, suspends the state legislatures and municipal councils, establishes press censorship, declares martial law, and begins to govern by dictatorship.

November 24 PANAMA. Arnulfo Arias, by a *coup d'état,* takes possession of the presidency, ejecting Daniel Chanis.

November 25 COLOMBIA. In Bogotá police from ambush shoot at the Liberal party chief, Darío Echandía; his brother Vicente Echandía and four students fall, riddled by bullets; on November 27, on learning the electoral results, President Ospina Pérez congratulates the police.

November 27 COLOMBIA. With the Liberals refraining from going to the polls, Conservative Laureano Gómez is elected president.

December 12 ARGENTINA. Atilio Cattaneo is expelled from Congress.

1950

February 28 ARGENTINA. The government confiscates 2,598 tons of newsprint from *La Prensa* of Buenos Aires.

March 9 ARGENTINA. *La Prensa* is eliminated from the list of importers of paper.

April 11 BOLIVIA. The Communist Party is declared illegal.

May 12-14 The Conference for Democracy and Liberty meets in Havana.

May 20 BOLIVIA. A strike for pay increases ends in a revolt against the government, which is quashed; some one hundred workers die, and four hundred are arrested.

May 21 NICARAGUA. Anastasio Somoza again assumes the presidency.

July 2 PERU. With the *apristas* unable to vote, General Manuel A. Odría, chief of the military *junta* that has governed for two years, is elected president.

July 16 PARAGUAY. Federico Chaves, who has ruled as the result of a *coup d'état* since September 11, 1949, is elected president; his first act in office is to visit President Perón in Buenos Aires.

September 14 EL SALVADOR. Lieutenant Colonel Oscar Osorio becomes president.

October 3 COLOMBIA. By a decree of the dictatorship of Laureano Gómez, the vice-presidency of Liberal Eduardo Santos is declared void.

October 10 At the Sixth Inter-American Press Conference in New York, the "Charter of the Inter-American Press" (See Appendix D) is approved.

November 13 VENEZUELA. The president of the ruling military *junta*, Lieutenant Colonel Carlos Delgado Chalbaud, is assassinated in Caracas; the newly constituted *junta* of dictatorship is made up of Doctor Germán Suárez Flamerich, Lieutenant Colonel Marcos Pérez Jiménez, and Lieutenant Colonel Luis Felipe Llovera Páez.

November 16 ARGENTINA. The government reduces by one fifth the paper that *La Prensa* may use.

During 1950 a loan of $125,000,000 is made to Argentina by the United States.

1951

January 25 ARGENTINA. The newsvendors of Buenos Aires present an ultimatum to *La Prensa;* on January 26 the paper cannot be published; on February 17 employees wishing to return to work are driven off by shots, with one dead and fifteen wounded; on March 15 President Perón convokes a special session of Congress to decide the case of *La Prensa;* on March 19 Congress names a committee of nine to take over the paper; later, Perón places *La Prensa* in control of the General Confederation of Labor; on November 19 the newspaper begins publication under the direction of *peronistas.*

March 15 GUATEMALA. Lieutenant Colonel Jacobo Arbenz, constitutionally elected president, receives the office from Doctor Juan José Árévalo.

March 26 The fourth Conference of the Foreign Ministers of the American Nations meets in Washington, D. C., sitting until April 7.

April 20 VENEZUELA. Attempt, in Havana, on the life of ex-President Rómulo Betancourt.

May 6 BOLIVIA. The presidential election is won by Victor Paz Estenssoro, head of the Movimiento Nacional Revolucionario, in exile in Buenos Aires since the fall of President Gualberto Villarroel; to nullify this election, President Mamerto Urriolagoitia transfers the presidential power to a military *junta* headed by General Hugo Ballivían.

May 10 PANAMA. A popular rebellion overthrows the government of Arnulfo Arias; he is succeeded by the President of the Court, Alcibíades Arosemena.

June 21 ECUADOR. President Galo Plaza Lasso, visiting the United States, addresses a joint session of Congress in Washington.

September 30 In Evanston, Illinois, honoring the visit of the proprietor of *La Prensa* of Buenos Aires, Alberto Gainza Paz, the Forum of Newspaper Editors issues a declaration on freedom of information.

October 3 URUGUAY. Congress approves the constitutional reform replacing the presidential system with a federal council of nine members, similar to that of Switzerland.

October 11 Seventh Inter-American Press Conference held in Montevideo; the *peronistas* attempt to dissolve it.

October 14 In San Salvador the foreign ministers of the Central American republics (except Panama) sign a charter providing for many phases of international co-operation among them.

October 31 ARGENTINA. During the presidential elections, the Communist candidate, Rodolfo Ghioldi, is shot in Paraná.

November 5 COLOMBIA. Laureano Gómez leaves the presidency because of illness, and is succeeded by the vice-president, former Minister of War Roberto Urdaneta Arbeláez.

November 6 In Paris, the Mexican Luis Padilla Nervo is elected President of the Assembly of the United Nations.

November 11 ARGENTINA. Juan Domingo Perón is re-elected president.

APPENDIX B

The Nations of Latin America in 1951–52*

NATION	AREA IN SQUARE MILES	POPULATION	CAPITAL	POPULATION OF CAPITAL
Argentina	1,079,965	17,097,889	Buenos Aires	3,000,371
Bolivia	416,040	3,990,000	La Paz	319,600
Brazil	3,291,416	52,645,479	Rio de Janeiro	2,413,152
Chile	286,323	5,862,000	Santiago	975,000
Colombia	439,714	11,259,730	Bogotá	743,187
Costa Rica	19,238	795,044	San José	86,909
Cuba	44,217	5,415,000	Havana	659,883
Dominican Republic	19,327	2,121,083	Ciudad Trujillo	181,533
Ecuador	104,510	3,077,000	Quito	200,185
El Salvador	13,176	1,889,946	San Salvador	160,380
Guatemala	45,452	2,787,000	Guatemala	225,553
Haiti	10,748	3,111,000	Port-au-Prince	142,840
Honduras	59,145	1,533,625	Tegucigalpa	79,170
Mexico	760,290	25,564,218	Mexico	3,053,588
Nicaragua	57,143	1,503,189	Managua	146,819
Panama	28,575	801,982	Panamá	127,407
Paraguay	154,165	1,406,000	Asunción	130,067
Peru	482,133	8,406,000	Lima	800,460
Salvador, see El Salvador				
Uruguay	72,172	2,650,000	Montevideo	850,000
Venezuela	352,143	4,986,000	Caracas	342,921

*Obviously, many of these figures are estimates.

APPENDIX C

The American Declaration of the Rights and Duties of Man, adopted by the Ninth International Conference of American States, at Bogotá, March 30 to May 2, 1948

WHEREAS:

The American nations have acknowledged the dignity of the individual, and their national constitutions recognize that juridical and political institutions, which regulate life in human society, have as their principal aim the protection of the essential rights of man and the creation of circumstances that will permit him to achieve spiritual and material progress, and attain happiness;

The American states have on repeated occasions recognized that the essential rights of man are not derived from the fact of one's being a national of a certain state, but are fundamental attributes of the individual;

The international protection of the rights of man should be the supreme guide of an evolving American law;

Both the American affirmation of essential human rights and the guarantees given by the internal regimes of the respective states establish the initial system of protection considered by the American States as being suited to the present social and juridical conditions, not without recognizing that they should increasingly strengthen that system in the international field as these conditions become more favorable;

The Ninth International Conference of American States agrees to adopt the following

American Declaration of the Rights and Duties of Man

Preamble

All men are born free and equal, in dignity and in rights, and, being endowed by nature with reason and conscience, they should conduct themselves as brothers one to another.

The fulfillment of duty by each individual is a prerequisite to the rights of all. Rights and duties are interrelated in every social and political activity of man. While rights exalt individual liberty, duties express the dignity of that liberty.

Duties of a juridical nature presuppose others of a moral nature that support those duties in concept and are the basis therefor.

Inasmuch as the spirit is the supreme aim of human existence and the greatest expression thereof, it is the duty of man to serve that end with all his strength and resources.

Since culture is the maximum social and historical expression of that spirit, it is the duty of man to preserve, practice, and foster culture by every means within his power.

And, since morality and good manners constitute the noblest flowering of culture, it is the duty of every man always to hold them in high respect.

CHAPTER ONE: *Rights*

Article 1. (Right to Life, Liberty, and Personal Security)
Every human being has the right to life, liberty, and the security of his person.

Article 2. (Right to Equality before the Law)
All persons are equal before the law and have the rights and duties established in this Declaration, without distinction as to race, sex, language, creed, or any other factor.

Article 3. (Right to Religious Freedom and Worship)
Every person has the right freely to profess a religious faith, and to manifest and practice it both in public and in private.

Article 4. (Right to Freedom of Investigation, Opinion, Expression, and Dissemination)
Every person has the right to freedom of investigation, of opinion, and of the expression and dissemination of thought, by any medium whatsoever.

Article 5. (Right to Protection of Honor, Personal Reputation, and Private and Family Life)
Every person has the right to the protection of the law against abusive attacks upon his honor, his reputation, and his private and family life.

Article 6. (Right to a Family and to the Protection Thereof)
Every person has the right to establish a family, the basic element of society, and to receive protection therefor.

Article 7. (Right to Protection for Mothers and Children)
All women, during pregnancy and the nursing period, and all children have the right to special protection, care and aid.

Article 8. (Right to Residence and Movement)
Every person has the right to fix his residence within the territory of the state of which he is a national, to move about freely within such territory, and not to leave except by his own will.

Article 9. (Right to Inviolability of the Home)
Every person has the right to the inviolability of his home.

Article 10. (Right to Inviolability and Circulation of Correspondence)
Every person has the right to the inviolability and circulation of his correspondence.

Article 11. (Right to the Preservation of Health and to Well Being)
Every person has the right to the preservation of his health through sanitary and social measures relating to food, clothing, housing, and

medical care, to the extent permitted by public and community resources.

Article 12. (Right to Education)

Every person has the right to an education, which should be based on the principles of liberty, ethics, and human solidarity.

Furthermore, every person has the right to an education that will prepare him to lead a decent life, to raise his standard of living, and to be a useful member of society.

The right to an education includes the right to equality of opportunity in every case, in accordance with natural talents, merit, and the desire to utilize the resources that the state or the community is in a position to provide.

Every person has the right to receive, free, at least a primary education.

Article 13. (Right to the Benefits of Culture)

Every person has the right to take part in the cultural life of the community, to enjoy the arts, and to participate in the benefits that result from intellectual progress, especially scientific discoveries.

He likewise has the right to the protection of his moral and material interests as regards his inventions or any literary, scientific, or artistic works of which he is the author.

Article 14. (Right to Work and to Fair Remuneration)

Every person has the right to work, under proper conditions, and to follow his vocation freely, in so far as existing conditions of employment permit.

Every person who works has the right to receive such remuneration as will, in proportion to his capacity and skill, assure him a standard of living suitable for himself and for his family.

Article 15. (Right to Leisure Time and to the use thereof)

Every person has the right to leisure time, to wholesome recreation, and to the opportunity for advantageous use of his free time to his spiritual, cultural and physical benefit.

Article 16. (Right to Social Security)

Every person has the right to social security which will protect him from the consequences of unemployment, old age, and any disabilities arising from causes beyond his control that make it physically or mentally impossible for him to earn a living.

Article 17. (Right to recognition of Juridical Personality and of Civil Rights)

Every person has the right to be recognized everywhere as a person having rights and obligations, and to enjoy the basic civil rights.

Article 18. (Right to a Fair Trial)

Every person may resort to the courts to ensure respect for his legal rights. There should likewise be available to him a simple, brief procedure whereby justice will protect him from acts of authority that, to his prejudice, violate any fundamental constitutional rights.

Article 19. (Right to Nationality)

Every person has the right to the nationality to which he is entitled by law and to change it, if he so wishes, for the nationality of any other country that is willing to grant it to him.

Article 20. (Right to Vote and to Participate in Government)

Every person having legal capacity is entitled to participate in the government of his country, directly or through his representative, and to take part in popular elections, which shall be by secret ballot, and shall be genuine, periodic, and free.

Article 21. (Rights of Assembly)

Every person has the right to assemble peaceably with others in a formal public meeting or an informal gathering, in connection with matters of common interest of any nature.

Article 22. (Right of Association)

Every person has the right to associate with others to promote, exercise, and protect his legitimate interests of a political, economic, religious, social, cultural, professional, trade union, or other nature.

Article 23. (Right to Property)

Every person has a right to own such private property as meets the essential needs of decent living and helps to maintain the dignity of the individual and of the home.

Article 24. (Right of Petition)

Every person has the right to submit respectful petitions to any competent authority, for reasons of either general or private interest, and the right to obtain prompt action thereon.

Article 25. (Right to Protection)

No person may be deprived of his liberty except in the cases and according to the procedures established by pre-existing law.

No person may be deprived of liberty for non-fulfillment of obligations of a purely civil character.

Every individual who has been deprived of his liberty has the right to have the legality of the measure ascertained without delay by a court, and the right to be tried without undue delay or, otherwise, to be released. He also has the right to humane treatment during the time he is in custody.

Article 26. (Right to due Process of Law)

Every accused person is presumed to be innocent until proved guilty.

Every person accused of an offense has the right to be given an impartial and public hearing, and to be tried by courts previously established in accordance with pre-existing laws, and not to receive cruel, infamous, or unusual punishment.

Article 27. (Right of Asylum)

Every person has the right to seek and receive asylum in foreign territory, in case of pursuit not resulting from common law crimes, and in accordance with the laws of each country and with international agreements.

Article 28. (Scope of the Rights of Man)

The rights of man are limited by the rights of others, by the security of all, and by the just demands of the general welfare and the advancement of democracy.

CHAPTER TWO: *Duties*

Article 29. (Duties to Society)

It is the duty of the individual so to conduct himself in relation to others that each and every one may fully form and develop his personality.

Article 30. (Duties toward Children and Parents)

It is the duty of every person to aid, support, educate, and protect his minor children, and it is the duty of children to honor their parents always and to aid, support, and protect them when they need it.

Article 31. (Duty to Receive Instruction)

It is the duty of every person to acquire at least an elementary education.

Article 32. (Duty to Vote)

It is the duty of every person to vote in the popular elections of the country of which he is a national, when he is legally capable of doing so.

Article 33. (Duty to Obey the Law)

It is the duty of every person to obey the law and other legitimate commands of the authorities of his country and those of the country in which he may be.

Article 34. (Duty to Serve the Community and the Nation)

It is the duty of every able-bodied person to render whatever civil and military service his country may require for its defense and preservation, and in case of public disaster, to render such civil services as may be in his power.

It is likewise his duty to hold any popular elective office that devolves upon him in the state in which he is a national.

Article 35. (Duties with respect to Social Security and Welfare)

It is the duty of every person to cooperate with the state and the community with respect to social security and welfare, in accordance with his ability and with existing circumstances.

Article 36. (Duty to Pay Taxes)

It is the duty of every person to pay the taxes established by law for the support of public services.

Article 37. (Duty to Work)

It is the duty of every person to work, as far as his capacity and possibilities permit, in order to obtain the means of livelihood or to benefit his community.

Article 38. (Duty to Refrain from Political Activities in a Foreign Country)

It is the duty of every person to refrain from taking part in political activities that, according to law, are reserved exclusively to the citizens of the state in which he is an alien.

APPENDIX D

Charter of the Inter-American Press

(From the Constitution of the Inter-American Press Association approved by the VI Inter-American Press Conference at New York, October 10, 1950)

I

Honest, free and independent journalism is the best contribution toward peace in a world of free nations peopled by free men.

II

Without freedom of the press there is no democracy. Freedom of thought and its expression, spoken or written, are inseparable, essential rights. Together they constitute the guarantee and defense of the other liberties on which democracy is based.

III

Freedom of information is a right inherent in freedom of opinion. Information, whether national or international, should be received, transmitted and diffused without any restriction. Printed matter should circulate within a country or between countries with the same freedom. Any administrative measures that under any pretext restrain such freedom are anti-democratic.

IV

The exercise of journalism is free. Prohibitions, restrictions or permits to exercise it, whether they affect owners, editors, directors, collaborators or employees of a publication violate freedom of the press.

V

Political regimes that do not respect or cause to be respected fully freedom of the press are not democratic.

VI

Whatever may be expressed verbally may be expressed by means of the printed word. To close or make unusable any printing press is harmful to culture and to democracy.

VII

The free press is basic in forming and expressing public opinion. America, by reason of its tradition and its destiny, must be a continent of public opinion.

INDEX

i

A NOTE ON THE TYPE

This book was set on the Linotype in Janson, a recutting made direct from the type cast from matrices (now in possession of the Stempel foundry, Frankfurt am Main) made by Anton Janson some time between 1660 and 1687.

Of Janson's origin nothing is known. He may have been a relative of Justus Janson, a printer of Danish birth who practiced in Leipzig from 1614 to 1635. Some time between 1657 and 1668 Anton Janson, a punch-cutter and type-founder, bought from the Leipzig printer Johann Erich Hahn the type-foundry that had formerly been a part of the printing house of M. Friedrich Lankisch. Janson's types were first shown in a specimen sheet issued at Leipzig about 1675. Janson's successor, and perhaps his son-in-law, Johann Karl Edling, issued a specimen sheet of Janson types in 1689. His heirs sold the Janson matrices in Holland to Wolffgang Dietrich Erhardt of Leipzig.

Composed, printed, and bound by
H. WOLFF, NEW YORK.